SEVEN SEAS' GHOST SHIP PRESENTS

  VOL.14

story and a

TRANSLATION
Thomas Zimmerman

ADAPTATION
David Lumsdon

LETTERING AND RETOUCH
Phil Christie

COVER DESIGN
Nicky Lim, Hanase Qi (LOGO)

PROOFREADER
Dawn Davis, Kurestin Armada

EDITOR
Elise Kelsey

ASSISTANT EDITOR
Nick Mamatas

PREPRESS TECHNICIAN
Rhiannon Rasmussen-Silverstein

PRODUCTION MANAGER
George Panella

MANAGING EDITOR
Julie Davis

ASSOCIATE PUBLISHER
Adam Arnold

PUBLISHER
Jason DeAngelis

Seven Seas press and purchase enquiries can be sent to Marketing Manager
Lianne Sentar at press@gomanga.com. Information regarding the distribution
and purchase of digital editions is available from Digital Manager CK Russell
at digital@gomanga.com.

Seven Seas, Ghost Ship, and their accompanying logos are trademarks of
Seven Seas Entertainment. All rights reserved.

ISBN: 978-1-64827-488-6

Printed in Canada

First Printing: May 2021

10 9 8 7 6 5 4 3 2 1

FOLLOW US ONLINE: *www.ghostshipmanga.com*

READING DIRECTIONS

This book reads from *right to left*, Japanese style.
If this is your first time reading manga, you start
reading from the top right panel on each page and
take it from there. If you get lost, just follow the
numbered diagram here. It may seem backwards at
first, but you'll get the hang of it! Have fun!!

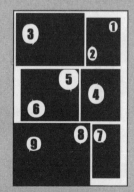

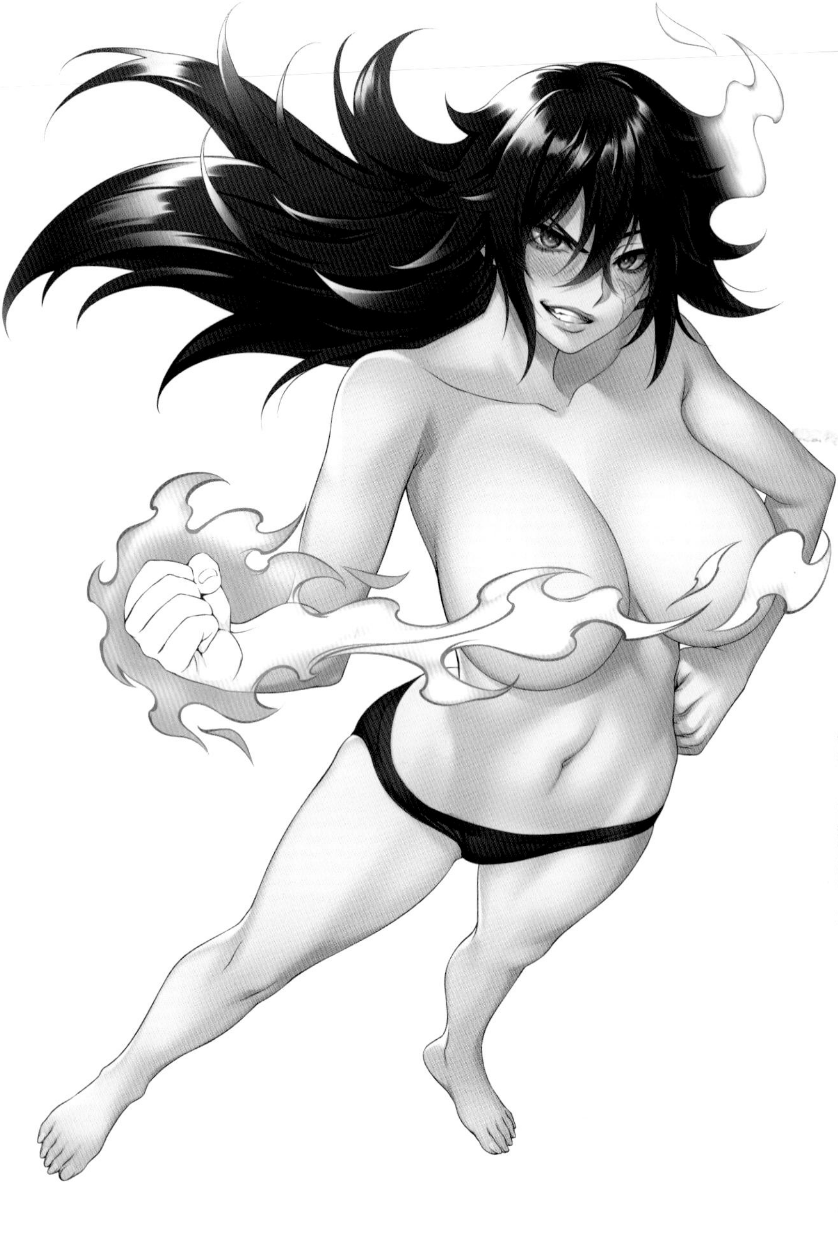

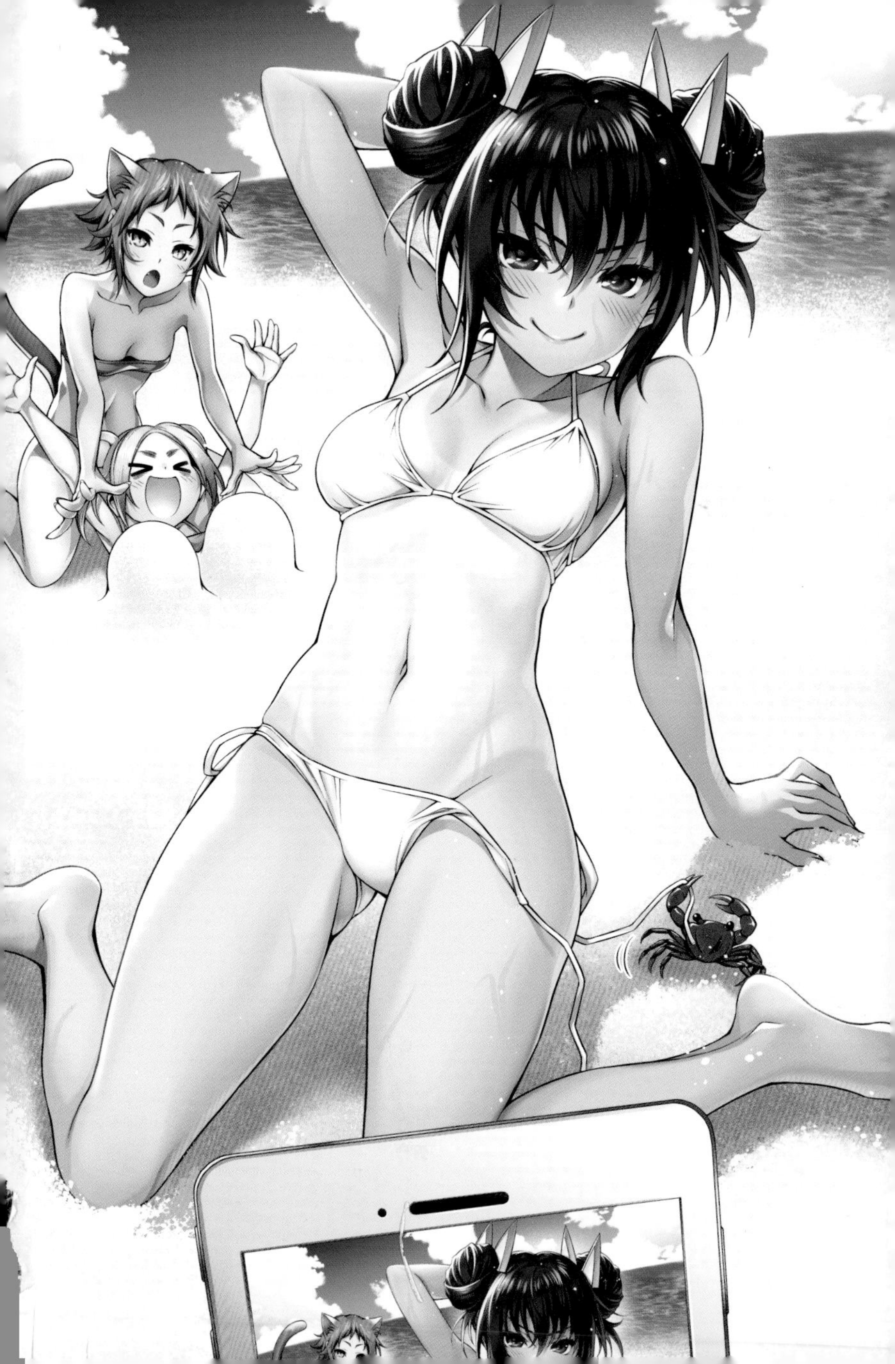

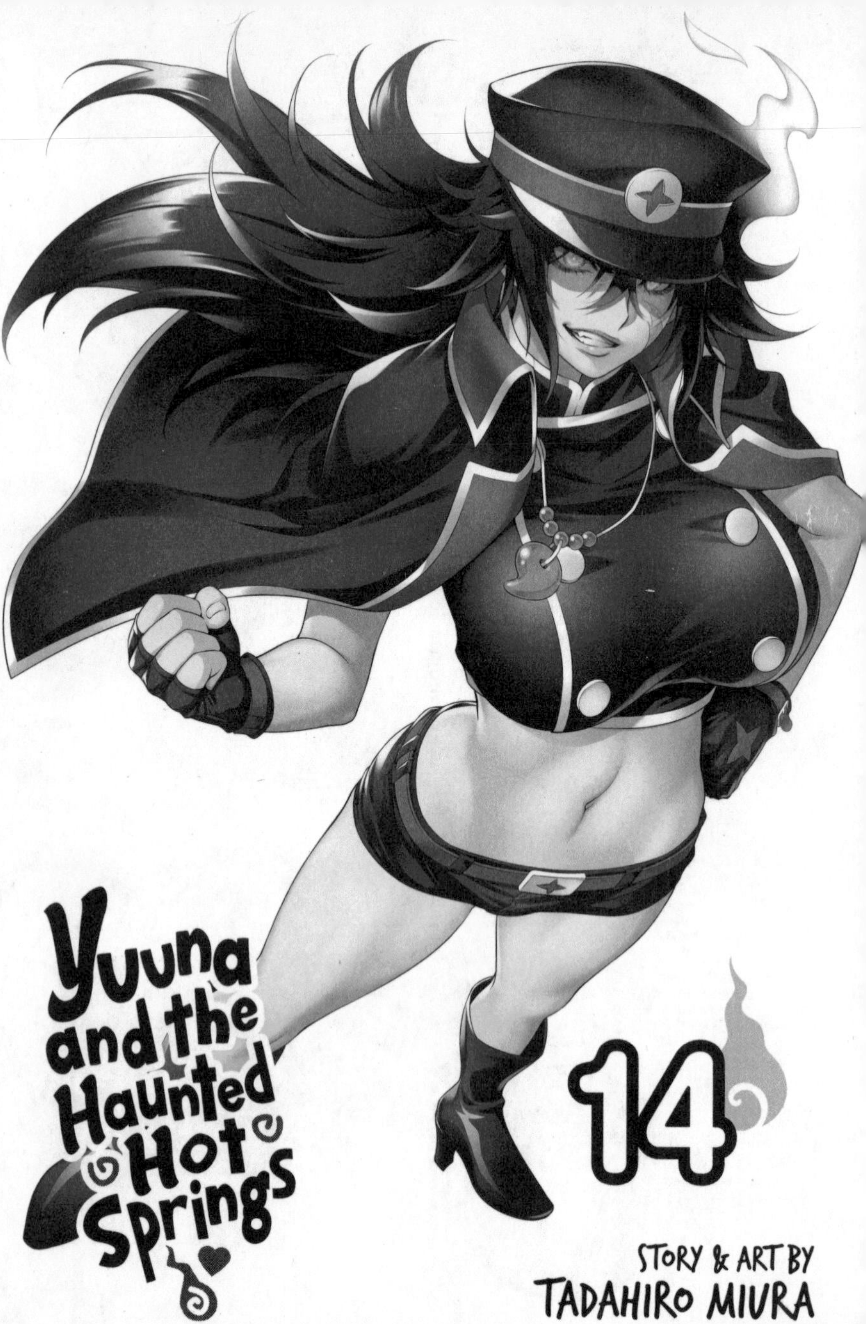

Yuuna and the Haunted Hot Springs

14

STORY & ART BY
TADAHIRO MIURA

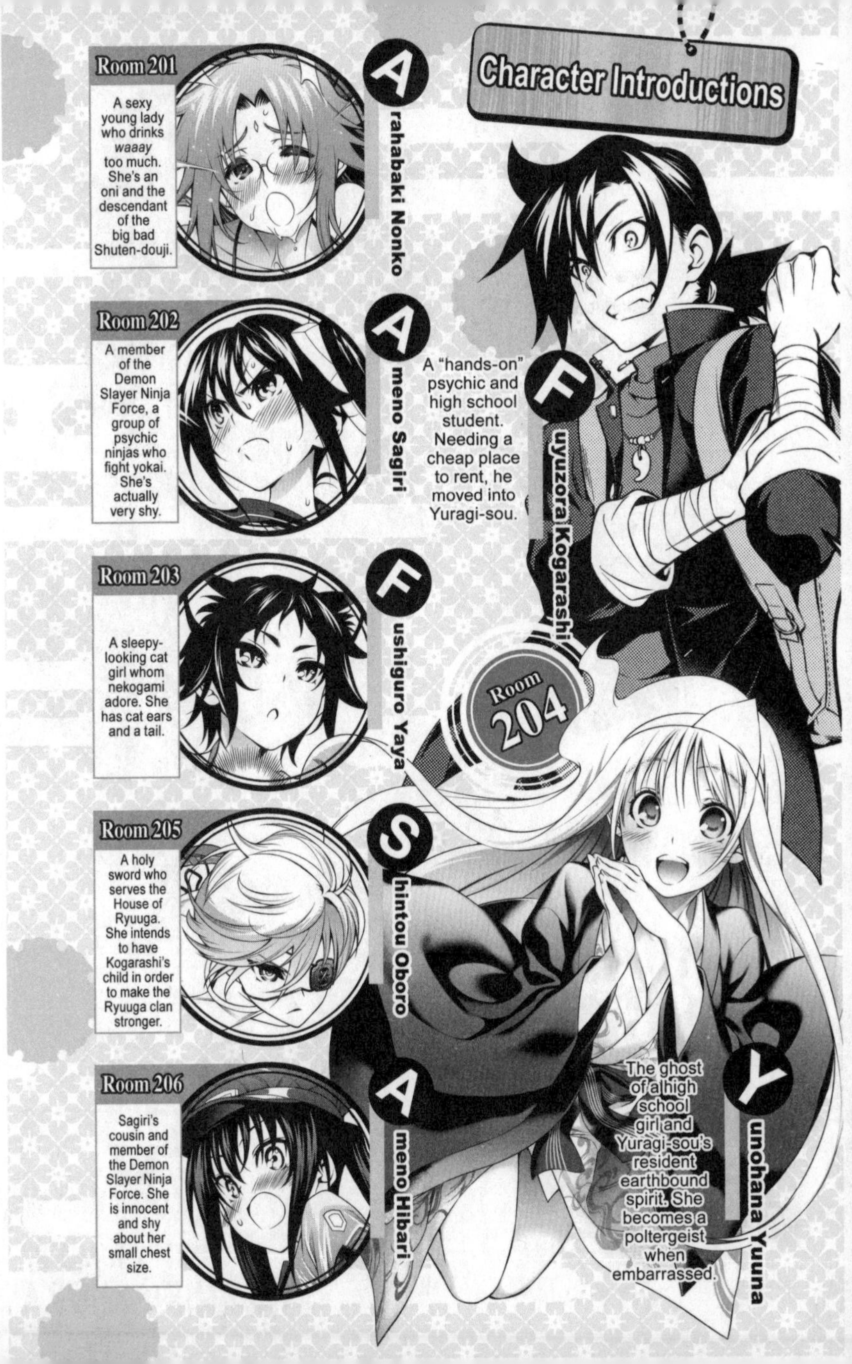
Character Introductions
Fuyuzora Kogarashi
A "hands-on" psychic and high school student. Needing a cheap place to rent, he moved into Yuragi-sou.
Room 204
Yunohana Yuuna
The ghost of a high school girl and Yuragi-sou's resident earthbound spirit. She becomes a poltergeist when embarrassed.
Room 201
Arahabaki Nonko
A sexy young lady who drinks *waaay* too much. She's an oni and the descendant of the big bad Shuten-douji.
Room 202
Ameno Sagiri
A member of the Demon Slayer Ninja Force, a group of psychic ninjas who fight yokai. She's actually very shy.
Room 203
Fushiguro Yaya
A sleepy-looking cat girl whom nekogami adore. She has cat ears and a tail.
Room 205
Shintou Oboro
A holy sword who serves the House of Ryuuga. She intends to have Kogarashi's child in order to make the Ryuuga clan stronger.
Room 206
Ameno Hibari
Sagiri's cousin and member of the Demon Slayer Ninja Force. She is innocent and shy about her small chest size.

Nakai Chitose

Caretaker's Room

Despite her youthful appearance, she's a zashiki-warashi and Yuragi-sou's oldest resident. She can manipulate people's luck.

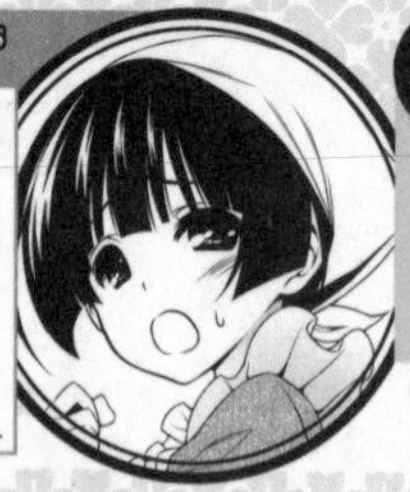

Hiougi Karura

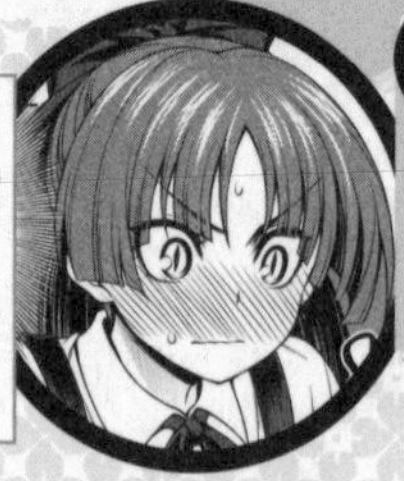

Daughter of the Dai-tengu, who governs Kyoto. Praised as a genius, she studies various techniques, reviving them in the modern era.

Shigaraki Koyuzu

Caretaker's Room

A young bake-danuki girl. She looks up to Chisaki and is studying her boobs.

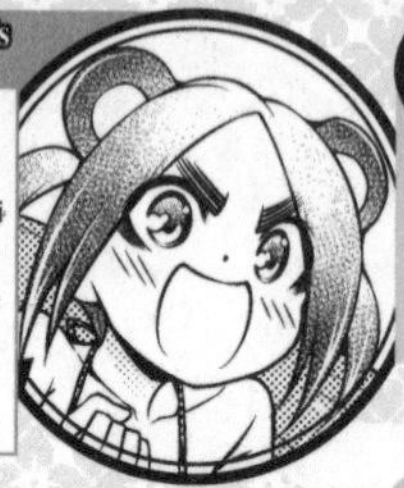

Mikogami Matora

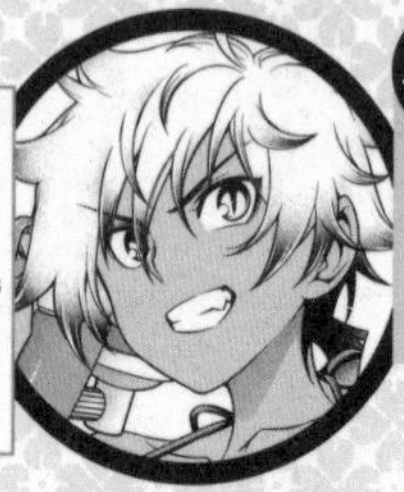

An extremely powerful yokai known as a Nue. Her hobby is fighting and is always seeking out stronger opponents.

Miyazaki Chisaki

The most beautiful and popular girl in Kogarashi's class. She has a naughty imagination.

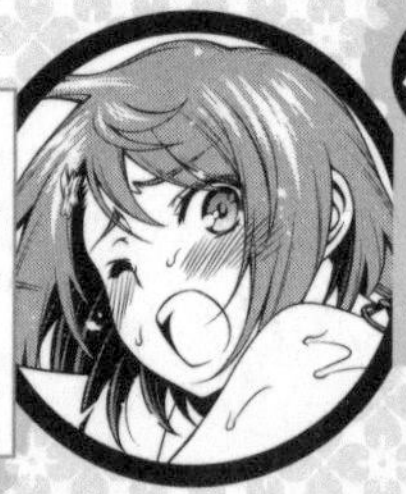

Yumesaki Harumu

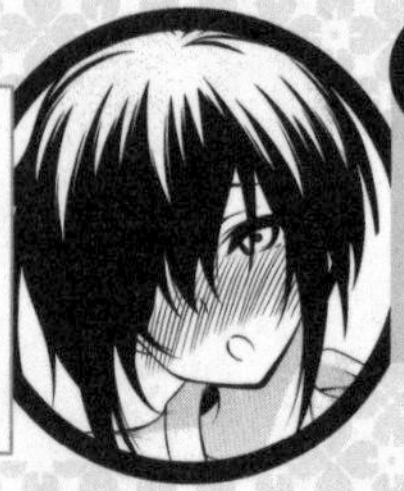

Kogarashi's new homeroom teacher. Being half succubus, her pupils are charged with charming magic.

Katsuragi Miria

A Youko Girl. A member of the Katsuragi family who desires to be among the top of the Tenko clan and must get close to Yuuna to accomplish it.

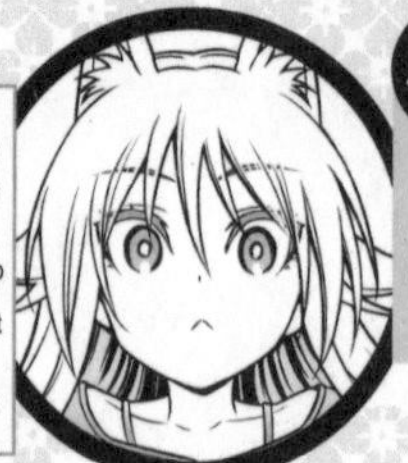

Todoroki Shion

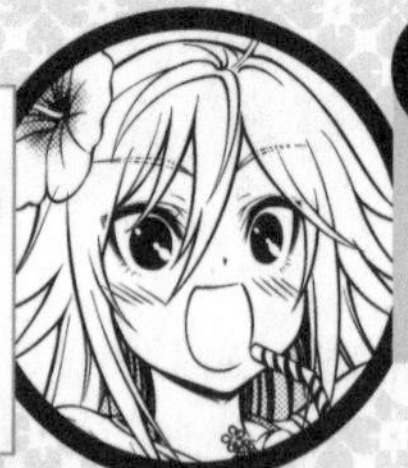

Seri's kouhai and former head delinquent in middle school. Her teddy bear panties are her favorite.

Summary

While living in Yuragi-sou, a hot-spring inn-turned-boardinghouse with an unusual history, "hands-on" psychic Fuyuzora Kogarashi promised Yuuna, the earthbound spirit of a high school girl, that he would make her happy and help her pass on. After being turned into a water gun during a survival game, being shrunk down by a talisman, and having his powers completely sealed away, Kogarashi finds that the only way to save his powers is to be in direct contact with Yuuna for one whole day. Now fully dizzy with both nervousness and embarrassment, whatever will happen to these two?!

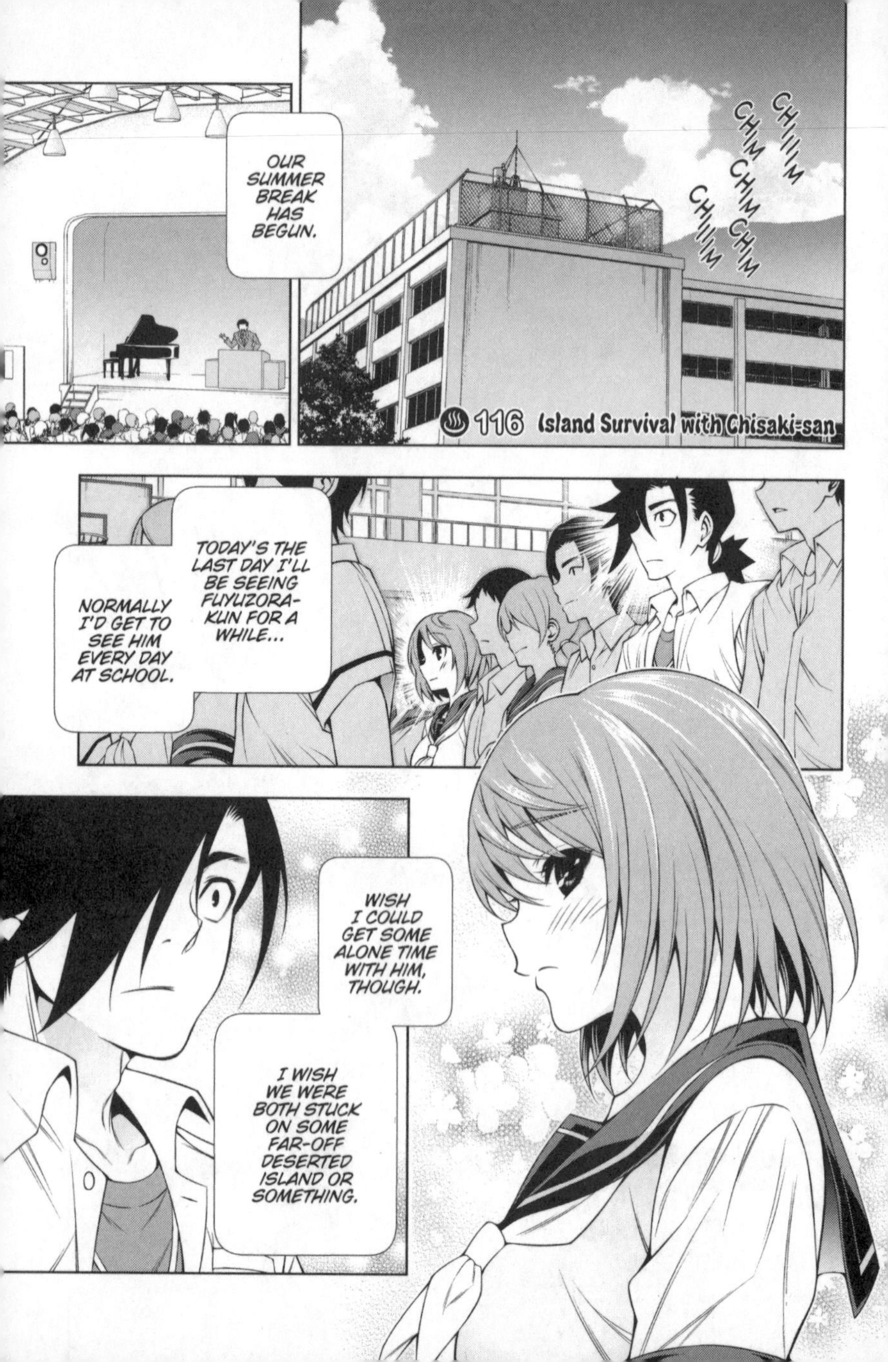
CHIIIIM
CHIM CHIM CHIM
CHIIIIM
116 Island Survival with Chisaki-san
OUR SUMMER BREAK HAS BEGUN.
TODAY'S THE LAST DAY I'LL BE SEEING FUYUZORA-KUN FOR A WHILE...
NORMALLY I'D GET TO SEE HIM EVERY DAY AT SCHOOL.
WISH I COULD GET SOME ALONE TIME WITH HIM, THOUGH.
I WISH WE WERE BOTH STUCK ON SOME FAR-OFF DESERTED ISLAND OR SOMETHING.

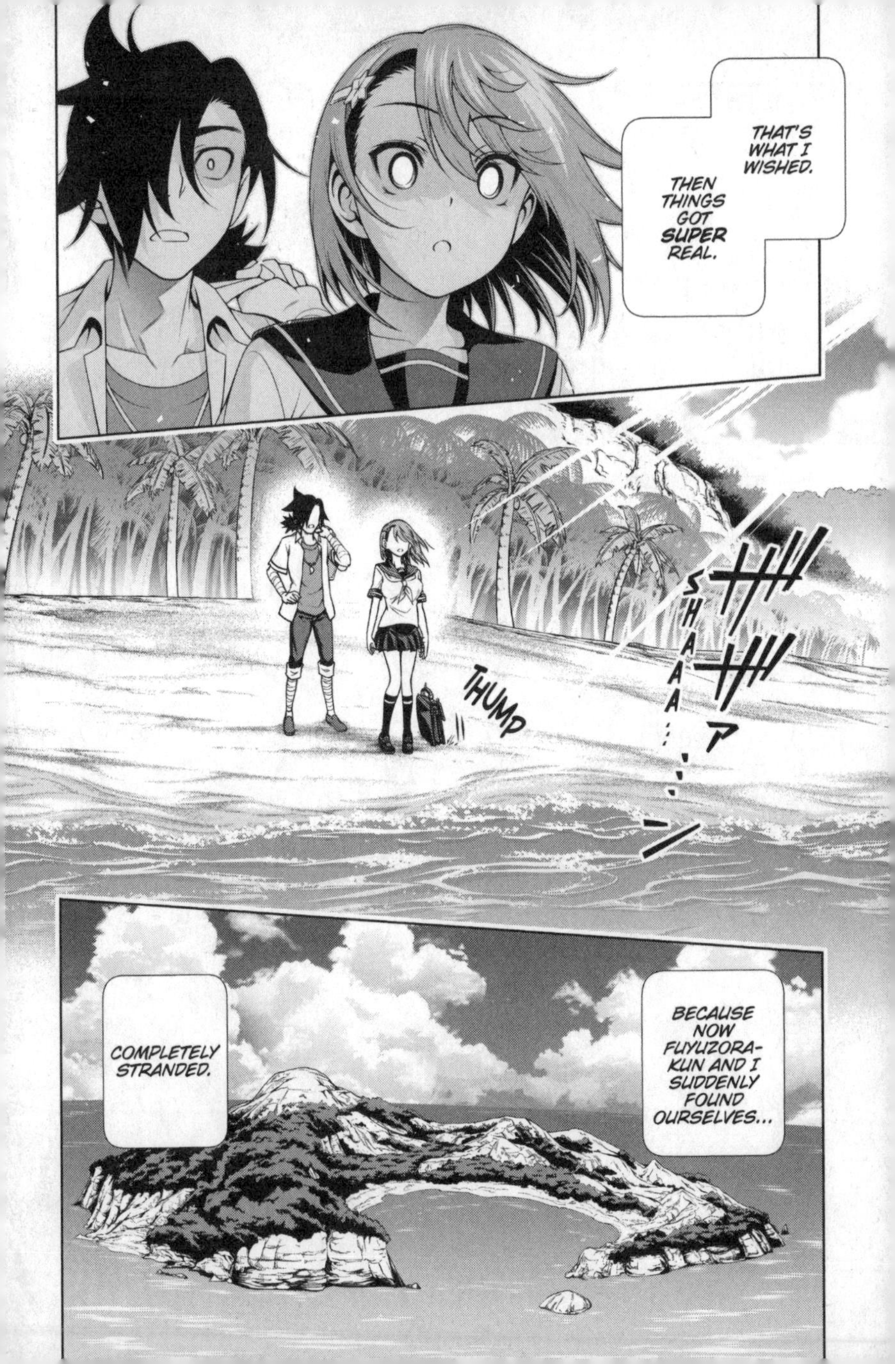
THAT'S WHAT I WISHED.
THEN THINGS GOT SUPER REAL.
SHAAAA...
THUMP
BECAUSE NOW FUYUZORA-KUN AND I SUDDENLY FOUND OURSELVES...
COMPLETELY STRANDED.

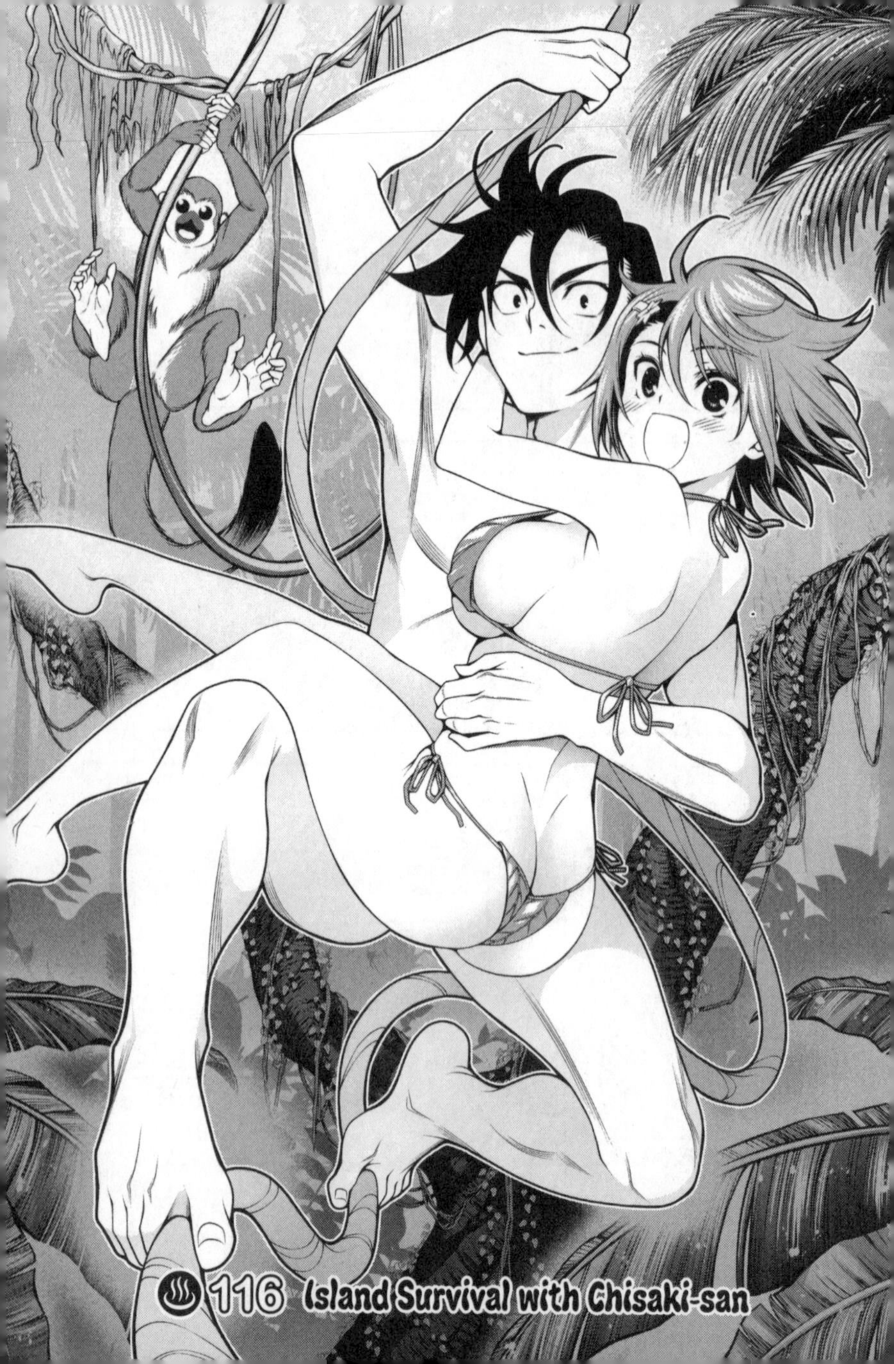

116 Island Survival with Chisaki-san

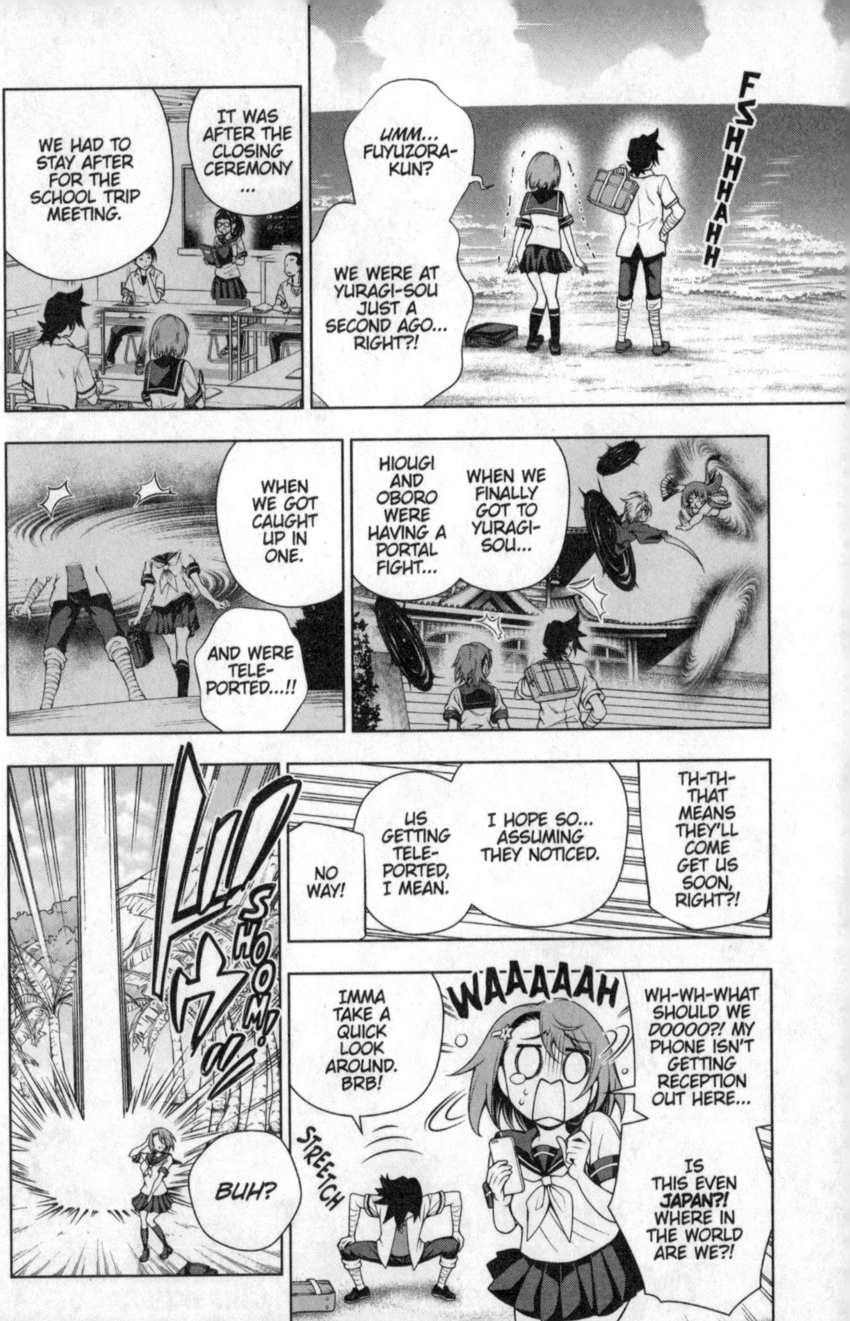

UMM... FUYUZORA-KUN?
WE WERE AT YURAGI-SOU JUST A SECOND AGO... RIGHT?!
FSHHHAHH
IT WAS AFTER THE CLOSING CEREMONY...
WE HAD TO STAY AFTER FOR THE SCHOOL TRIP MEETING.
WHEN WE FINALLY GOT TO YURAGI-SOU...
HIOUGI AND OBORO WERE HAVING A PORTAL FIGHT...
WHEN WE GOT CAUGHT UP IN ONE.
AND WERE TELE-PORTED...!!
TH-TH-THAT MEANS THEY'LL COME GET US SOON, RIGHT?!
I HOPE SO... ASSUMING THEY NOTICED.
US GETTING TELE-PORTED, I MEAN.
NO WAY!
WH-WH-WHAT SHOULD WE *DOOOO?!* MY PHONE ISN'T GETTING RECEPTION OUT HERE...
WAAAAAH
IS THIS EVEN **JAPAN?!** WHERE IN THE WORLD ARE WE?!
IMMA TAKE A QUICK LOOK AROUND. BRB!
STREETCH
SHOOM!
BUH?

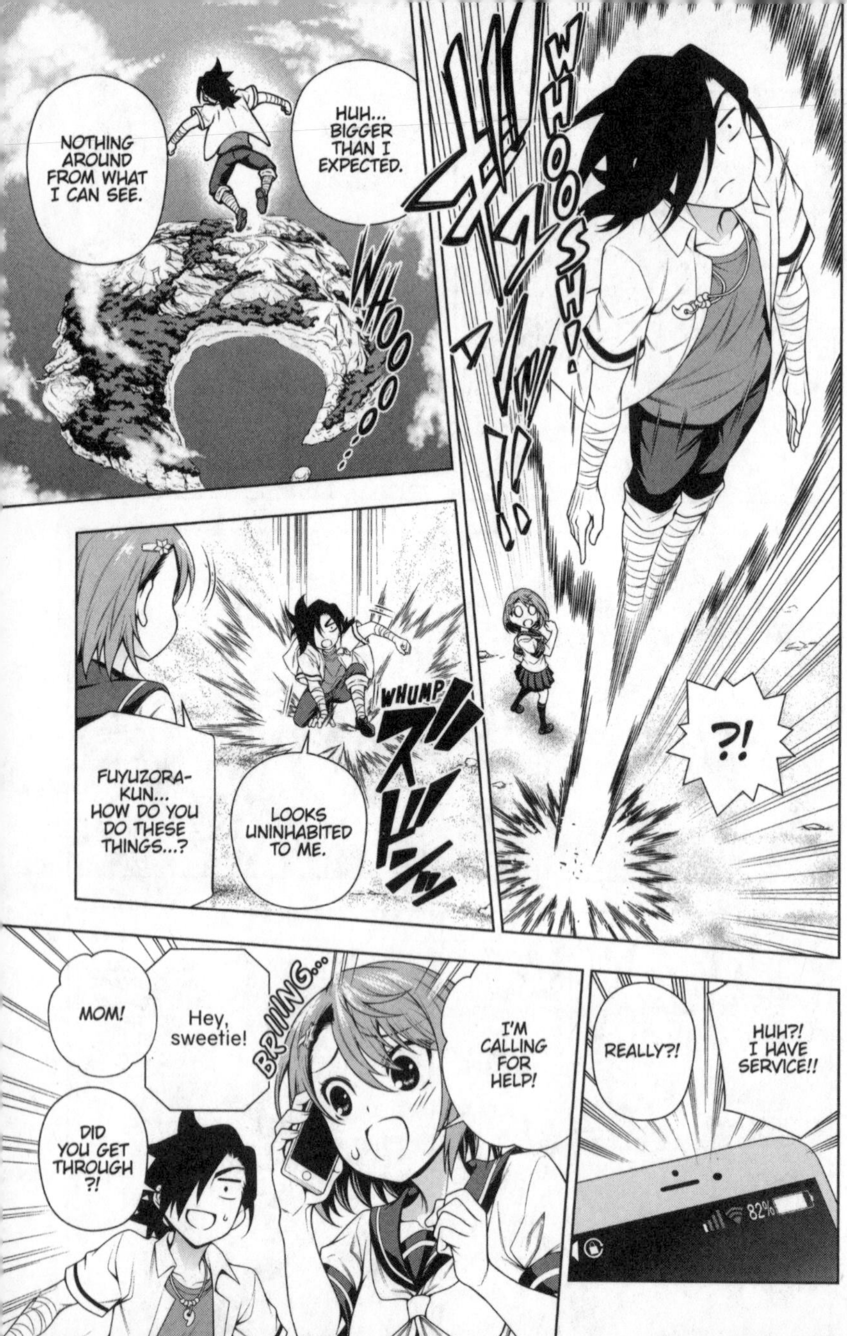
WHOOSH!
?!
HUH... BIGGER THAN I EXPECTED.
NOTHING AROUND FROM WHAT I CAN SEE.
WHOOOOO...
WHUMP
LOOKS UNINHABITED TO ME.
FUYUZORA-KUN... HOW DO YOU DO THESE THINGS...?
HUH?! I HAVE SERVICE!!
82%
REALLY?!
I'M CALLING FOR HELP!
BRIIING...
Hey, sweetie!
MOM!
DID YOU GET THROUGH?!

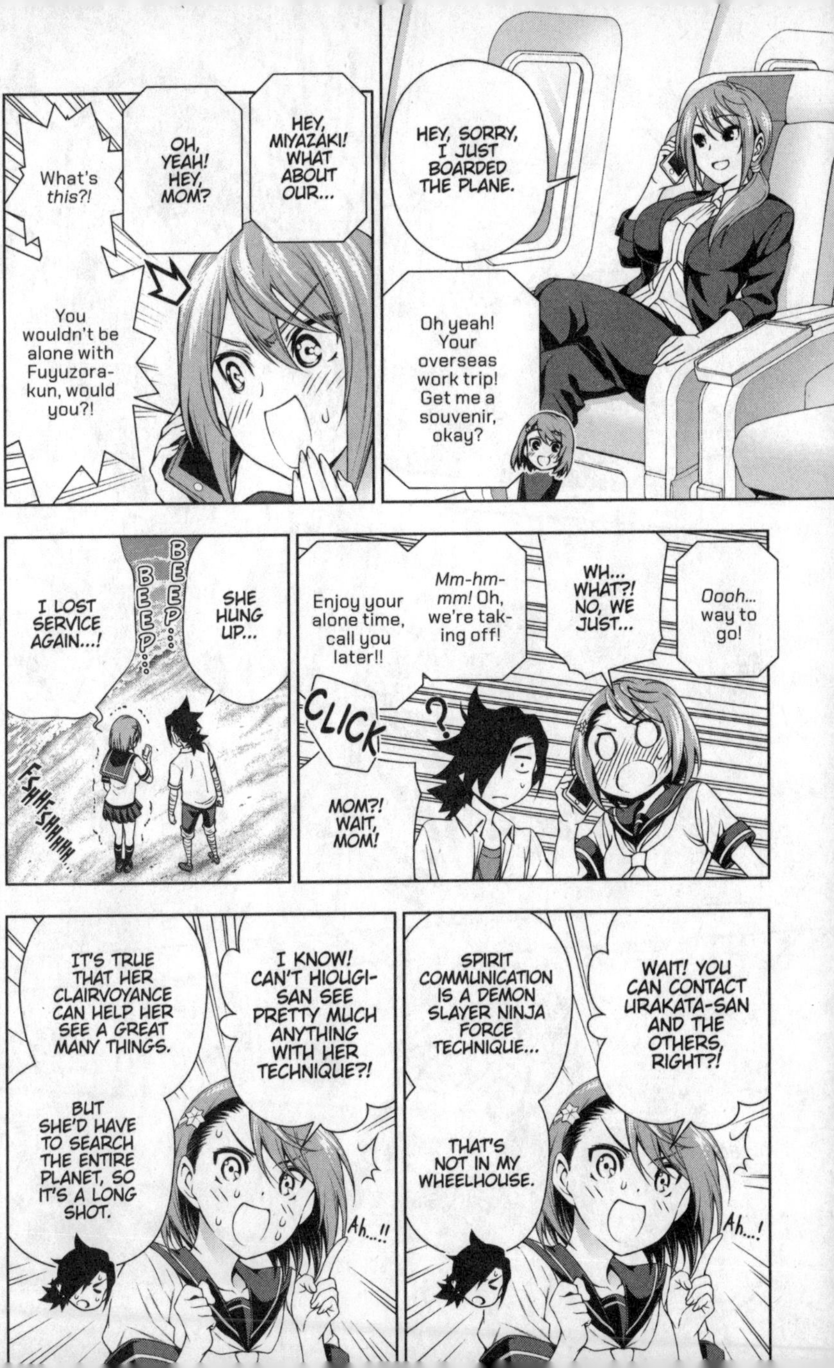
HEY, SORRY, I JUST BOARDED THE PLANE.
Oh yeah! Your overseas work trip! Get me a souvenir, okay?
HEY, MIYAZAKI! WHAT ABOUT OUR...
OH, YEAH! HEY, MOM?
What's this?!
You wouldn't be alone with Fuyuzora-kun, would you?!
Oooh... way to go!
WH... WHAT?! NO, WE JUST...
Mm-hm-mm! Oh, we're taking off!
Enjoy your alone time, call you later!!
CLICK
MOM?! WAIT, MOM!
SHE HUNG UP...
BEEP... BEEP...
I LOST SERVICE AGAIN...!
FSHHFSHHHH...
WAIT! YOU CAN CONTACT URAKATA-SAN AND THE OTHERS, RIGHT?!
Ah...!
SPIRIT COMMUNICATION IS A DEMON SLAYER NINJA FORCE TECHNIQUE...
THAT'S NOT IN MY WHEELHOUSE.
I KNOW! CAN'T HIOUGI-SAN SEE PRETTY MUCH ANYTHING WITH HER TECHNIQUE?!
Ah...!!
IT'S TRUE THAT HER CLAIRVOYANCE CAN HELP HER SEE A GREAT MANY THINGS.
BUT SHE'D HAVE TO SEARCH THE ENTIRE PLANET, SO IT'S A LONG SHOT.

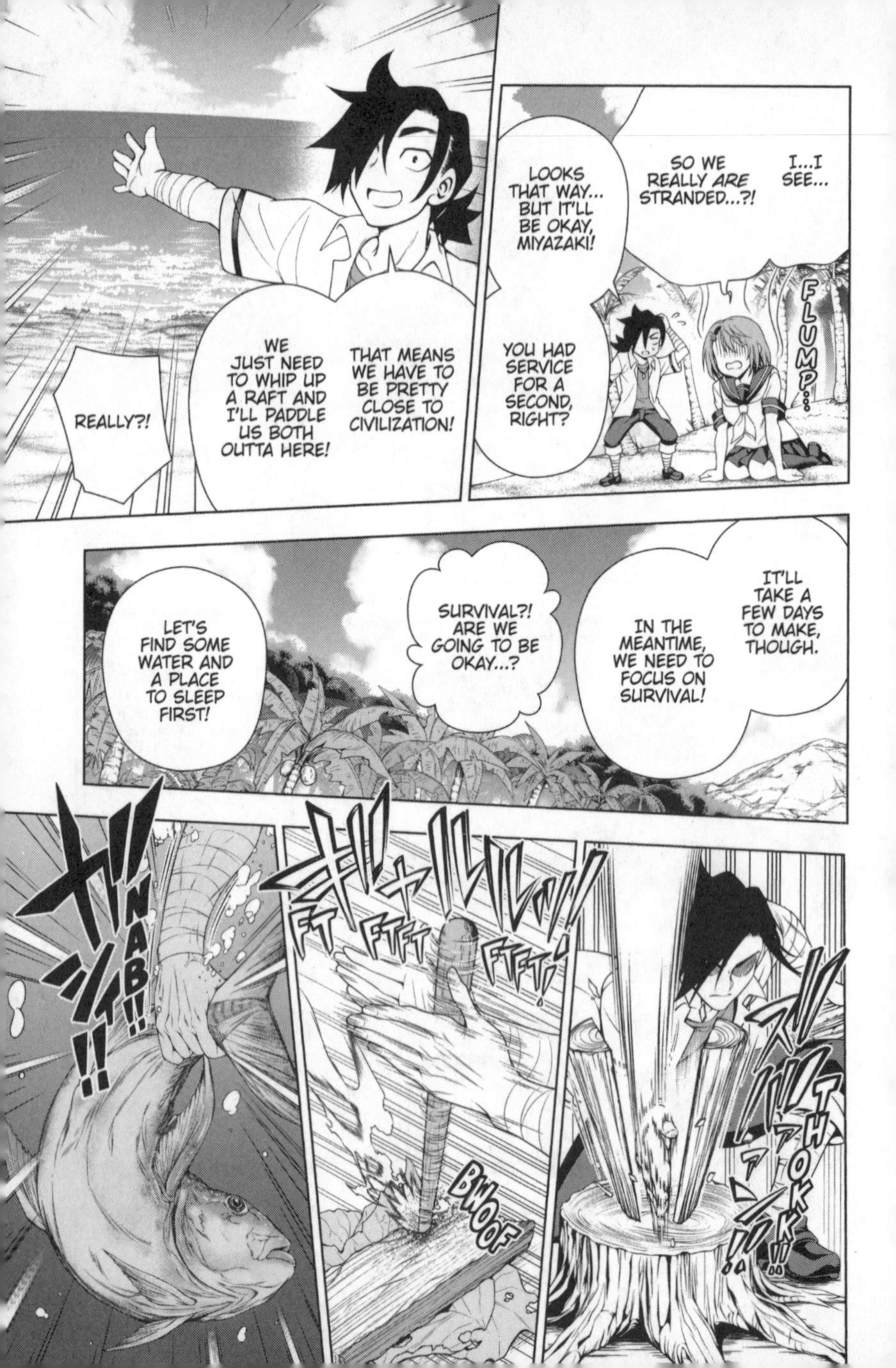

I...I SEE...
SO WE REALLY *ARE* STRANDED...?!
FLUMP...
LOOKS THAT WAY... BUT IT'LL BE OKAY, MIYAZAKI!
YOU HAD SERVICE FOR A SECOND, RIGHT?
THAT MEANS WE HAVE TO BE PRETTY CLOSE TO CIVILIZATION!
WE JUST NEED TO WHIP UP A RAFT AND I'LL PADDLE US BOTH OUTTA HERE!
REALLY?!
IT'LL TAKE A FEW DAYS TO MAKE, THOUGH.
IN THE MEANTIME, WE NEED TO FOCUS ON SURVIVAL!
SURVIVAL?! ARE WE GOING TO BE OKAY...?
LET'S FIND SOME WATER AND A PLACE TO SLEEP FIRST!
THOKK!!
FT FTFT FTFT!
BWOOF
NAB!!

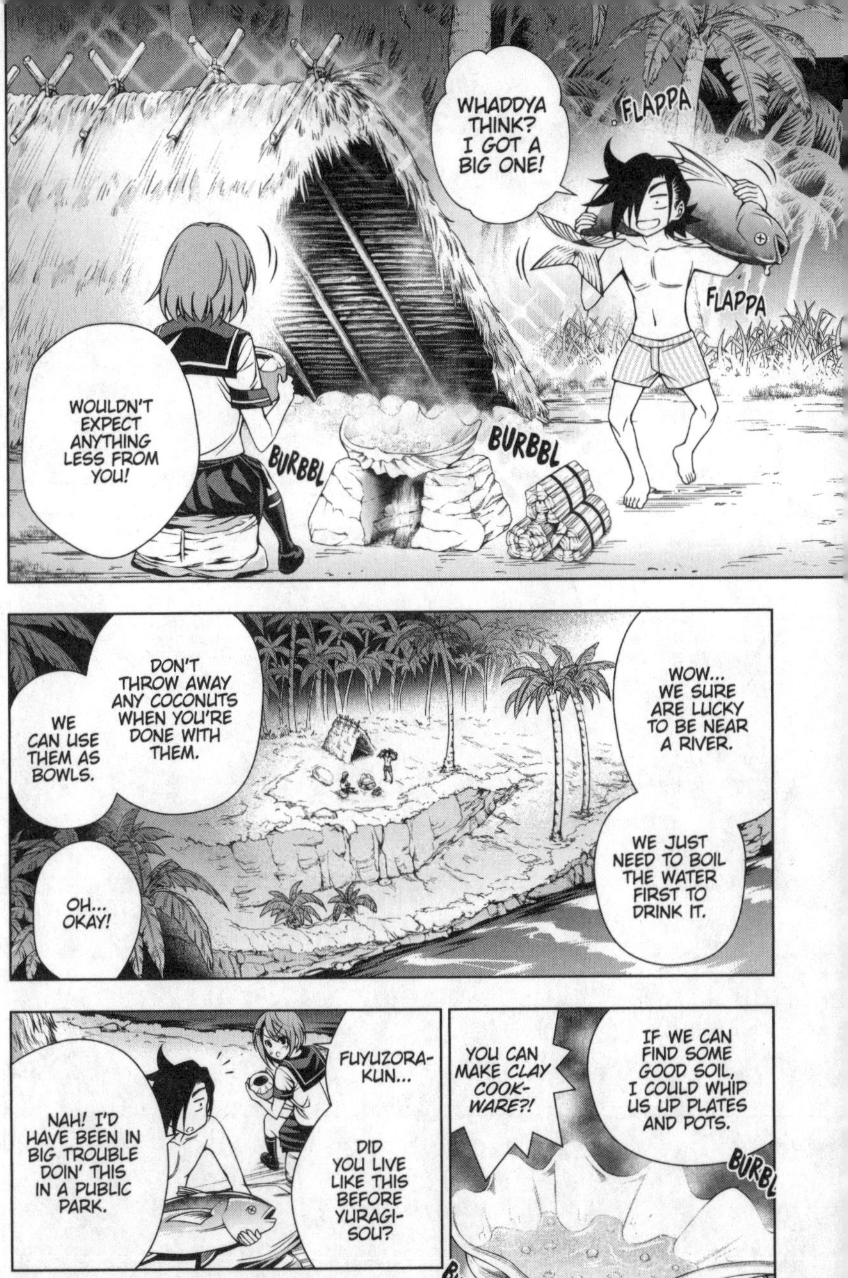
WHADDYA THINK? I GOT A BIG ONE!
FLAPPA
FLAPPA
BURBBL
WOULDN'T EXPECT ANYTHING LESS FROM YOU!
BURBBL
WOW... WE SURE ARE LUCKY TO BE NEAR A RIVER.
WE JUST NEED TO BOIL THE WATER FIRST TO DRINK IT.
DON'T THROW AWAY ANY COCONUTS WHEN YOU'RE DONE WITH THEM.
WE CAN USE THEM AS BOWLS.
OH... OKAY!
IF WE CAN FIND SOME GOOD SOIL, I COULD WHIP US UP PLATES AND POTS.
BURBL
YOU CAN MAKE CLAY COOK-WARE?!
BURBL
FUYUZORA-KUN...
DID YOU LIVE LIKE THIS BEFORE YURAGI-SOU?
NAH! I'D HAVE BEEN IN BIG TROUBLE DOIN' THIS IN A PUBLIC PARK.

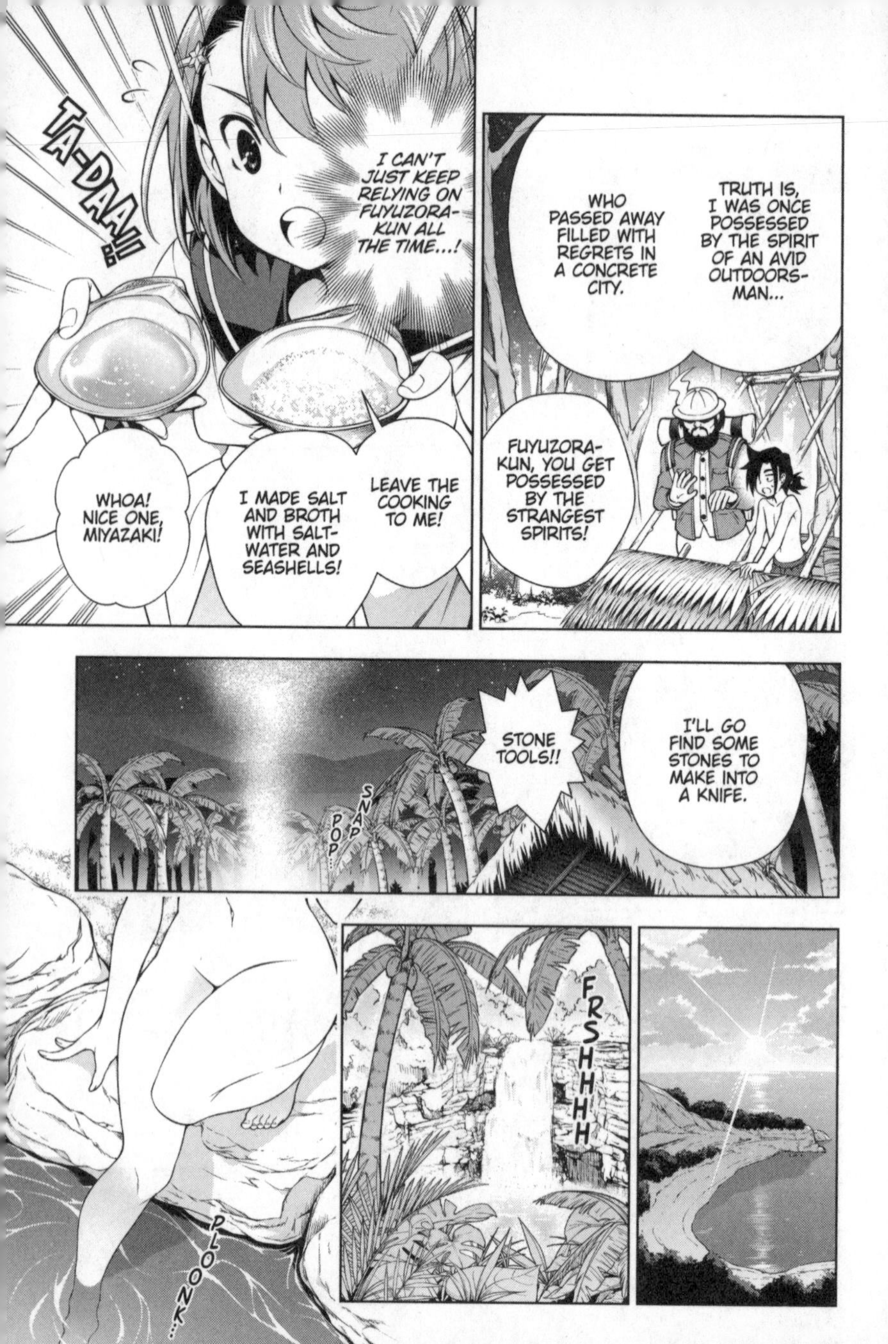
TRUTH IS, I WAS ONCE POSSESSED BY THE SPIRIT OF AN AVID OUTDOORS-MAN...
WHO PASSED AWAY FILLED WITH REGRETS IN A CONCRETE CITY.
FUYUZORA-KUN, YOU GET POSSESSED BY THE STRANGEST SPIRITS!
I CAN'T JUST KEEP RELYING ON FUYUZORA-KUN ALL THE TIME...!
TA-DAA!!
LEAVE THE COOKING TO ME!
I MADE SALT AND BROTH WITH SALT-WATER AND SEASHELLS!
WHOA! NICE ONE, MIYAZAKI!
I'LL GO FIND SOME STONES TO MAKE INTO A KNIFE.
STONE TOOLS!!
SNAP
POP...
FRSHHHH
PLOONK...

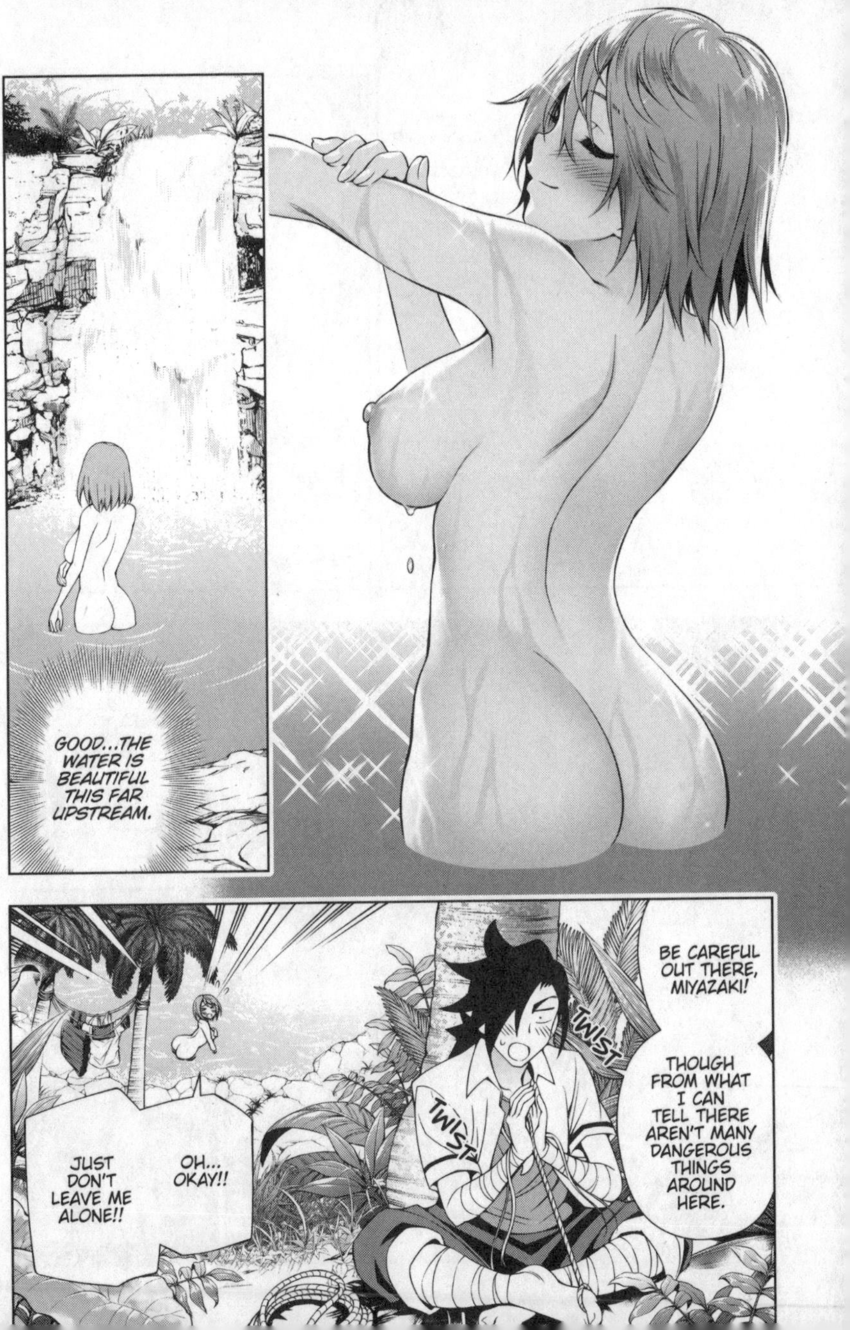
GOOD...THE WATER IS BEAUTIFUL THIS FAR UPSTREAM.
BE CAREFUL OUT THERE, MIYAZAKI!
TWIST
THOUGH FROM WHAT I CAN TELL THERE AREN'T MANY DANGEROUS THINGS AROUND HERE.
TWIST
OH... OKAY!!
JUST DON'T LEAVE ME ALONE!!

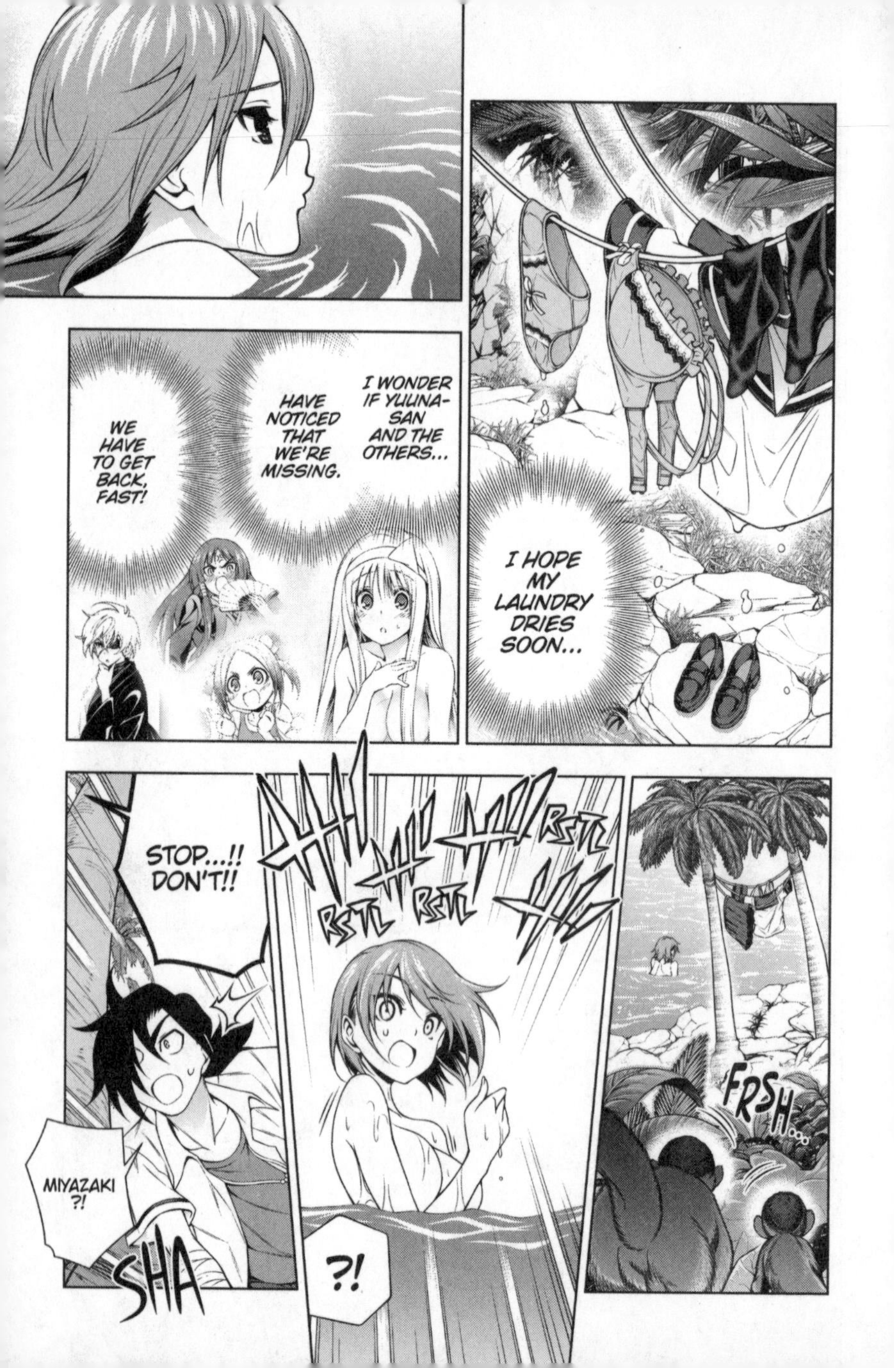

I HOPE MY LAUNDRY DRIES SOON...
I WONDER IF YUUNA-SAN AND THE OTHERS...
HAVE NOTICED THAT WE'RE MISSING.
WE HAVE TO GET BACK, FAST!
FRSH
RSTL
RSTL
RSTL
?!
STOP...!! DON'T!!
MIYAZAKI ?!
SHA

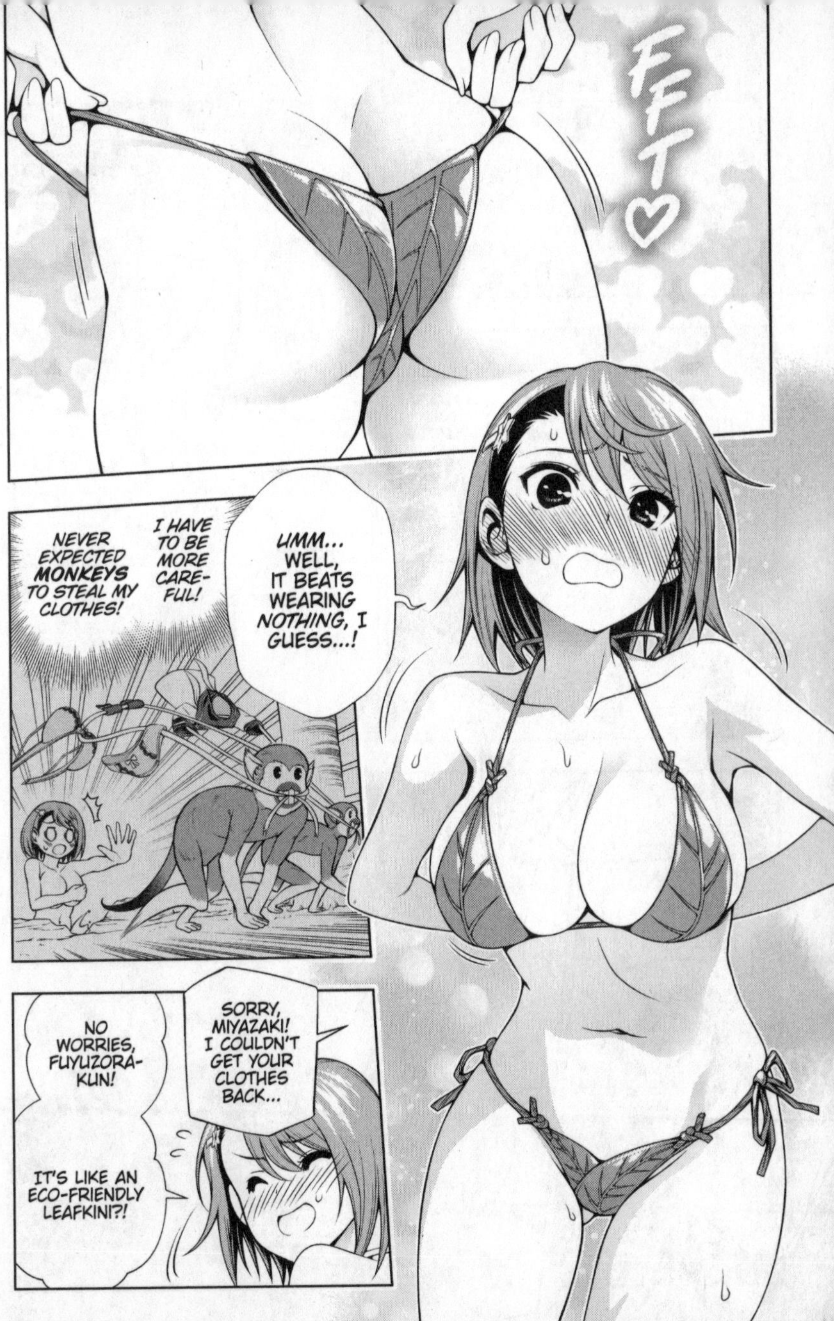
FFT♡
UMM... WELL, IT BEATS WEARING NOTHING, I GUESS...!
I HAVE TO BE MORE CAREFUL!
NEVER EXPECTED MONKEYS TO STEAL MY CLOTHES!
SORRY, MIYAZAKI! I COULDN'T GET YOUR CLOTHES BACK...
NO WORRIES, FUYUZORA-KUN!
IT'S LIKE AN ECO-FRIENDLY LEAFKINI?!

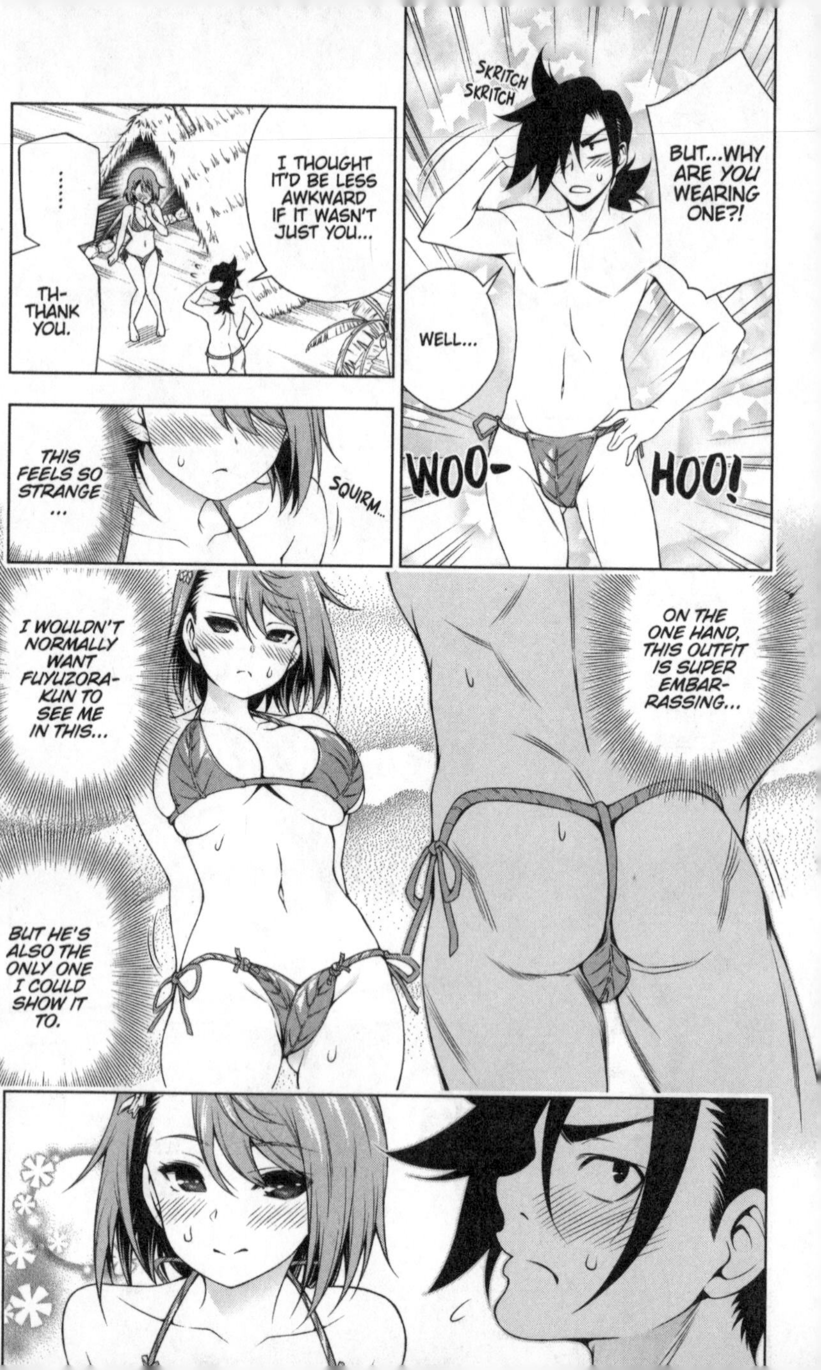
SKRITCH SKRITCH
BUT...WHY ARE YOU WEARING ONE?!
WELL...
WOO-HOO!
I THOUGHT IT'D BE LESS AWKWARD IF IT WASN'T JUST YOU...
......
TH-THANK YOU.
THIS FEELS SO STRANGE...
SQUIRM...
ON THE ONE HAND, THIS OUTFIT IS SUPER EMBARRASSING...
I WOULDN'T NORMALLY WANT FUYUZORA-KUN TO SEE ME IN THIS...
BUT HE'S ALSO THE ONLY ONE I COULD SHOW IT TO.

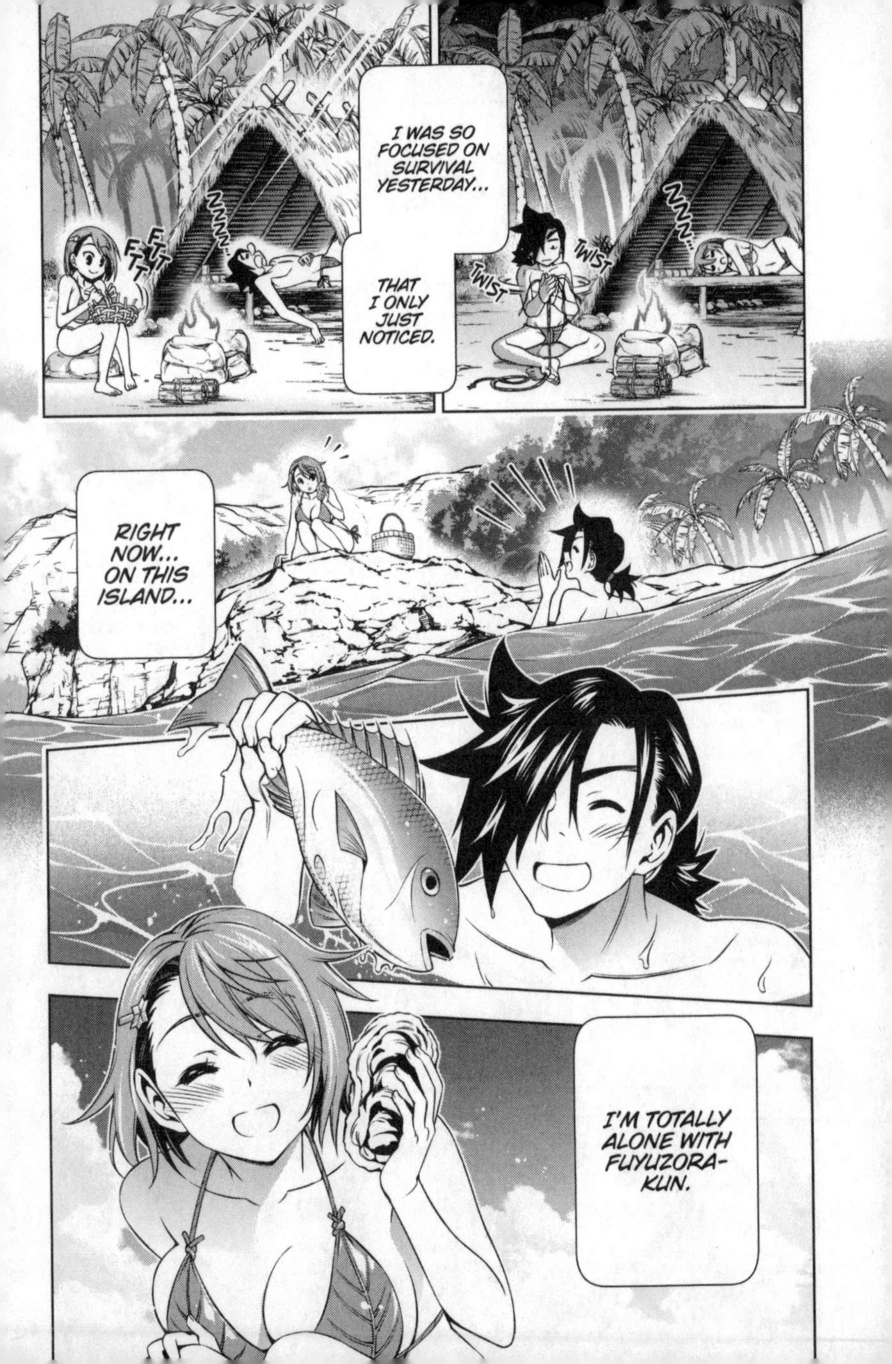
I WAS SO FOCUSED ON SURVIVAL YESTERDAY...
THAT I ONLY JUST NOTICED.
ZZZ...
TWIST
TWIST
ZZZ...
FTT
FTT
RIGHT NOW... ON THIS ISLAND...
I'M TOTALLY ALONE WITH FUYUZORA-KUN.

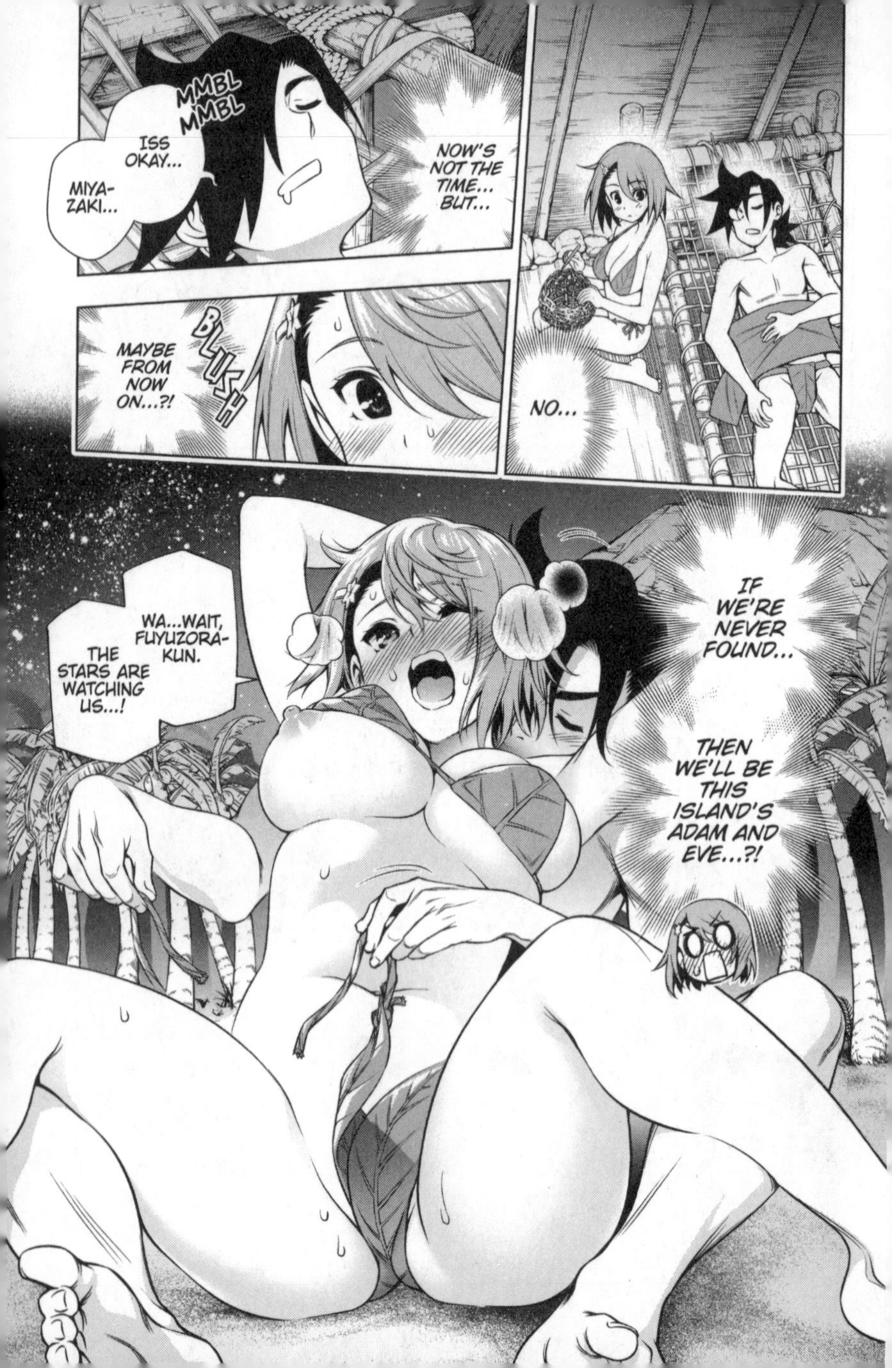
NO...
NOW'S NOT THE TIME... BUT...
MMBL MMBL
ISS OKAY...
MIYA-ZAKI...
BLUSH
MAYBE FROM NOW ON...?!
IF WE'RE NEVER FOUND...
THEN WE'LL BE THIS ISLAND'S ADAM AND EVE...?!
WA...WAIT, FUYUZORA-KUN.
THE STARS ARE WATCHING US...!

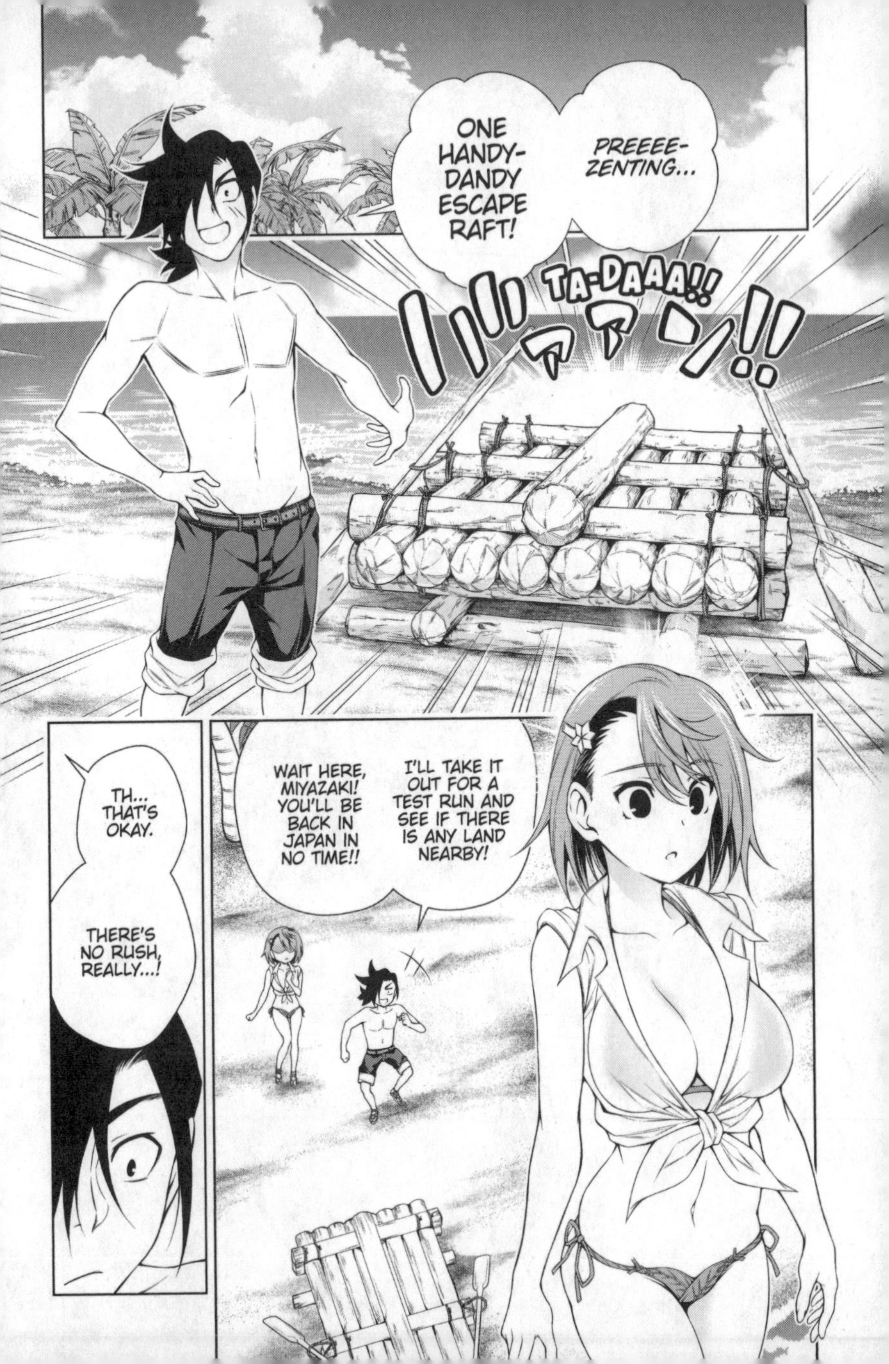
PREEEE-ZENTING...
ONE HANDY-DANDY ESCAPE RAFT!
TA-DAAA!!
I'LL TAKE IT OUT FOR A TEST RUN AND SEE IF THERE IS ANY LAND NEARBY!
WAIT HERE, MIYAZAKI! YOU'LL BE BACK IN JAPAN IN NO TIME!!
TH... THAT'S OKAY.
THERE'S NO RUSH, REALLY...!

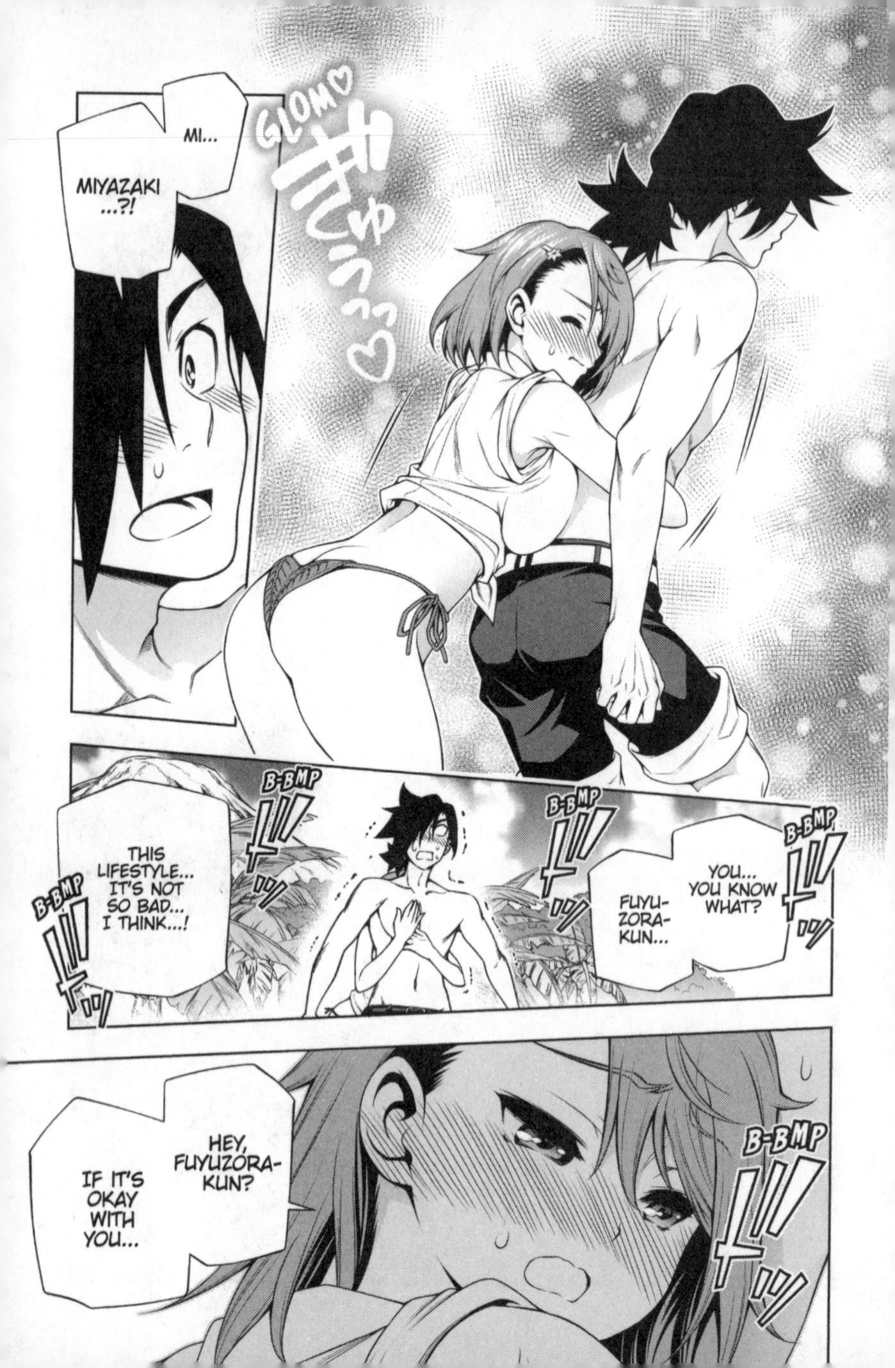
GLOM♡
MI...
MIYAZAKI...?!
B-BMP
B-BMP
YOU... YOU KNOW WHAT?
FUYUZORA-KUN...
B-BMP
B-BMP
THIS LIFESTYLE... IT'S NOT SO BAD... I THINK...!
B-BMP
HEY, FUYUZORA-KUN?
IF IT'S OKAY WITH YOU...

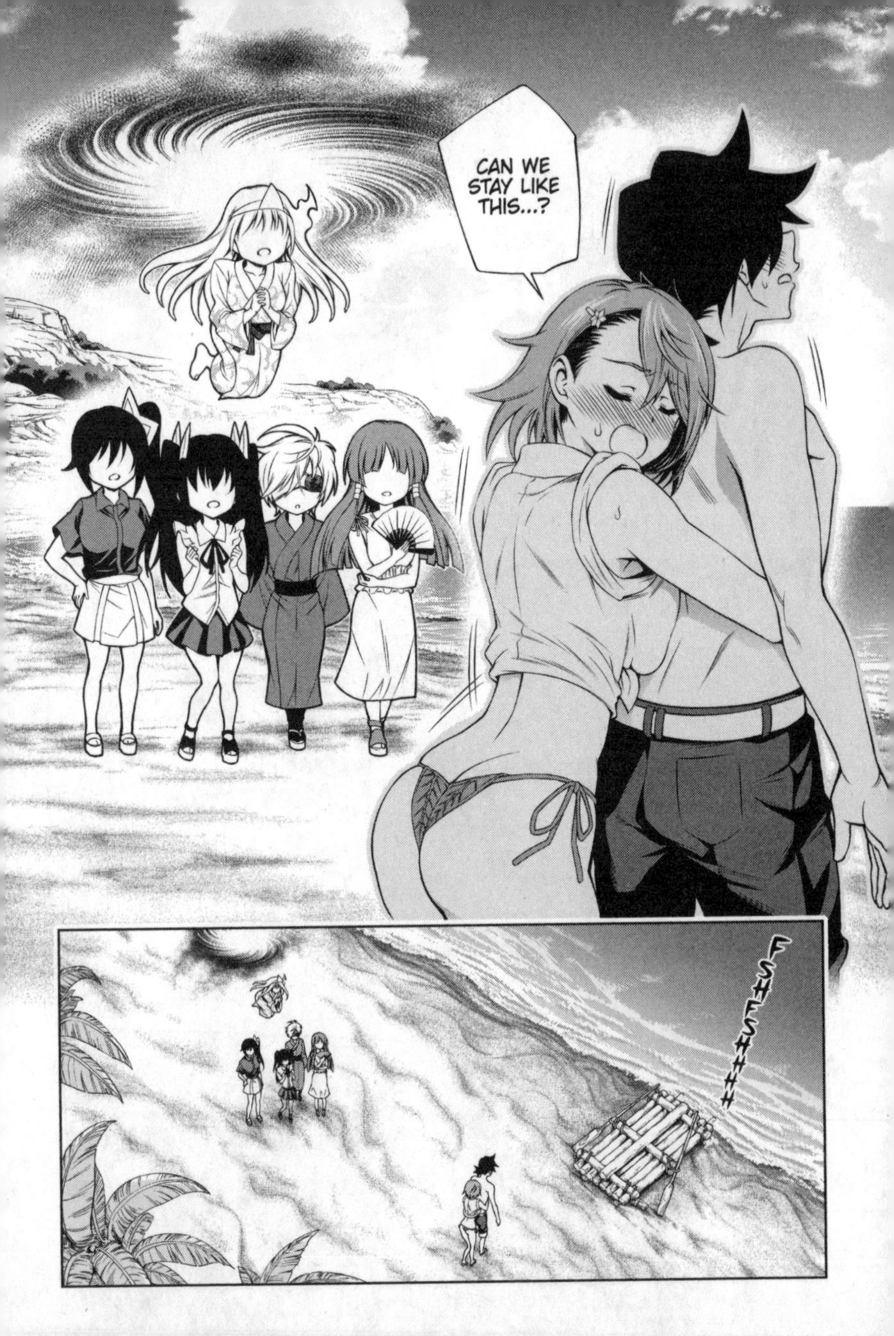
CAN WE STAY LIKE THIS...?
FSHFSHHHH

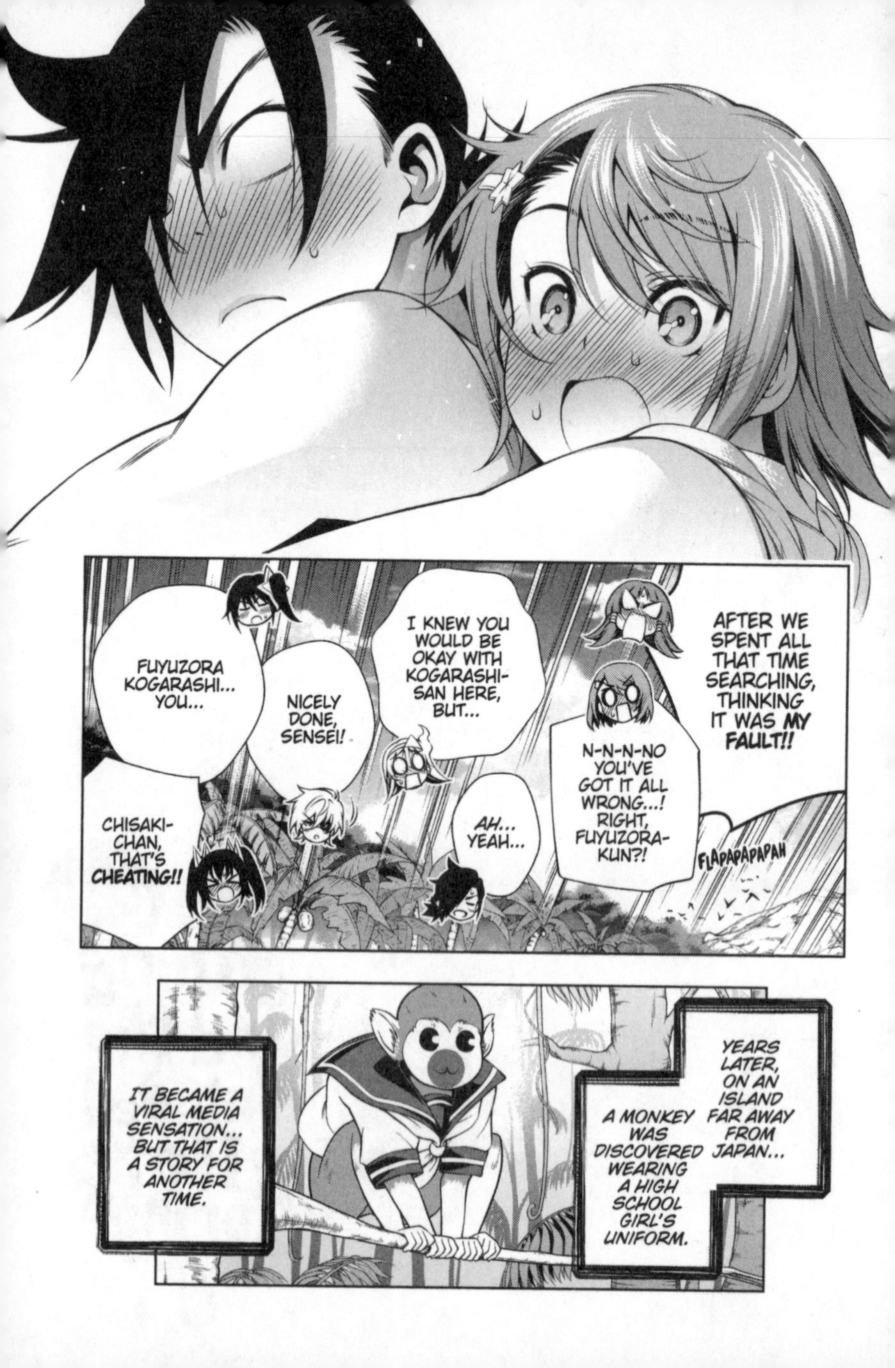
AFTER WE SPENT ALL THAT TIME SEARCHING, THINKING IT WAS MY FAULT!!
N-N-N-NO YOU'VE GOT IT ALL WRONG...! RIGHT, FUYUZORA-KUN?!
FLAPAPAPAPAH
I KNEW YOU WOULD BE OKAY WITH KOGARASHI-SAN HERE, BUT...
AH... YEAH...
NICELY DONE, SENSEI!
FUYUZORA KOGARASHI... YOU...
CHISAKI-CHAN, THAT'S CHEATING!!
YEARS LATER, ON AN ISLAND FAR AWAY FROM JAPAN...
A MONKEY WAS DISCOVERED WEARING A HIGH SCHOOL GIRL'S UNIFORM.
IT BECAME A VIRAL MEDIA SENSATION... BUT THAT IS A STORY FOR ANOTHER TIME.

Yuuna
and the
Haunted
Hot
Springs

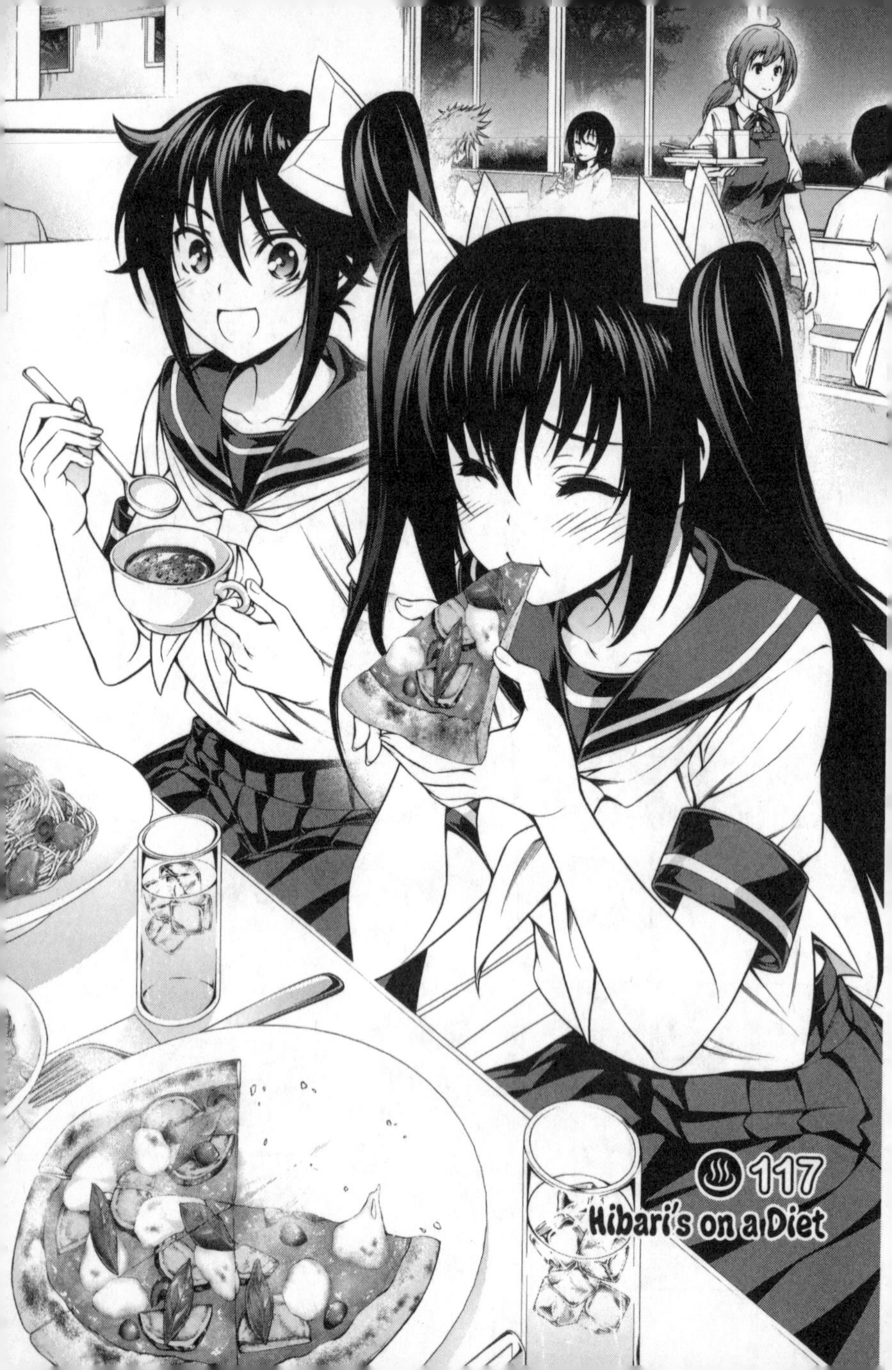
117
Hibari's on a Diet

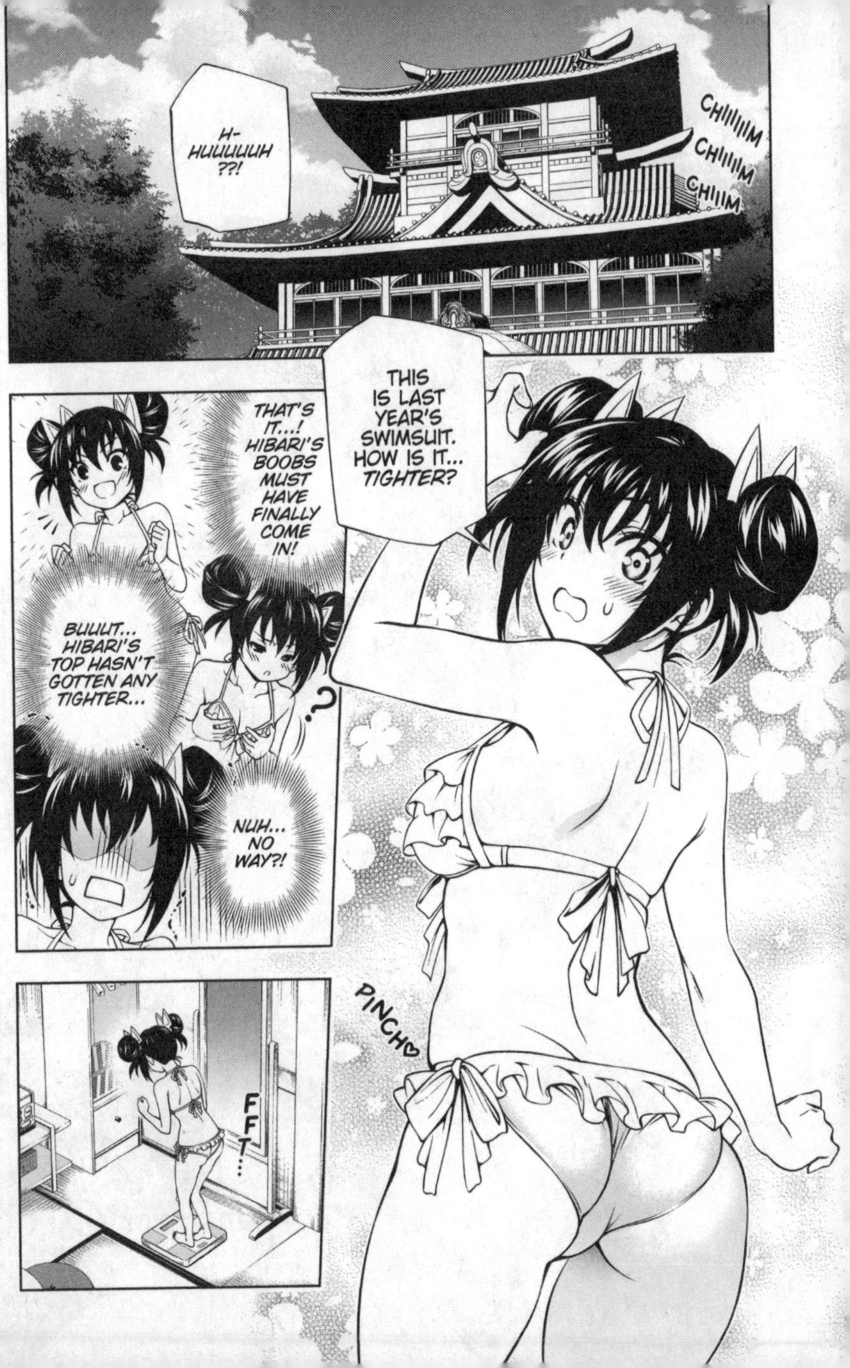
CHIIIIIM
CHIIIIM
CHIIIM
H- HUUUUUH ??!
THIS IS LAST YEAR'S SWIMSUIT. HOW IS IT... TIGHTER?
PINCH♡
THAT'S IT...! HIBARI'S BOOBS MUST HAVE FINALLY COME IN!
BUUUT... HIBARI'S TOP HASN'T GOTTEN ANY TIGHTER...
?
NUH... NO WAY?!
FFT...

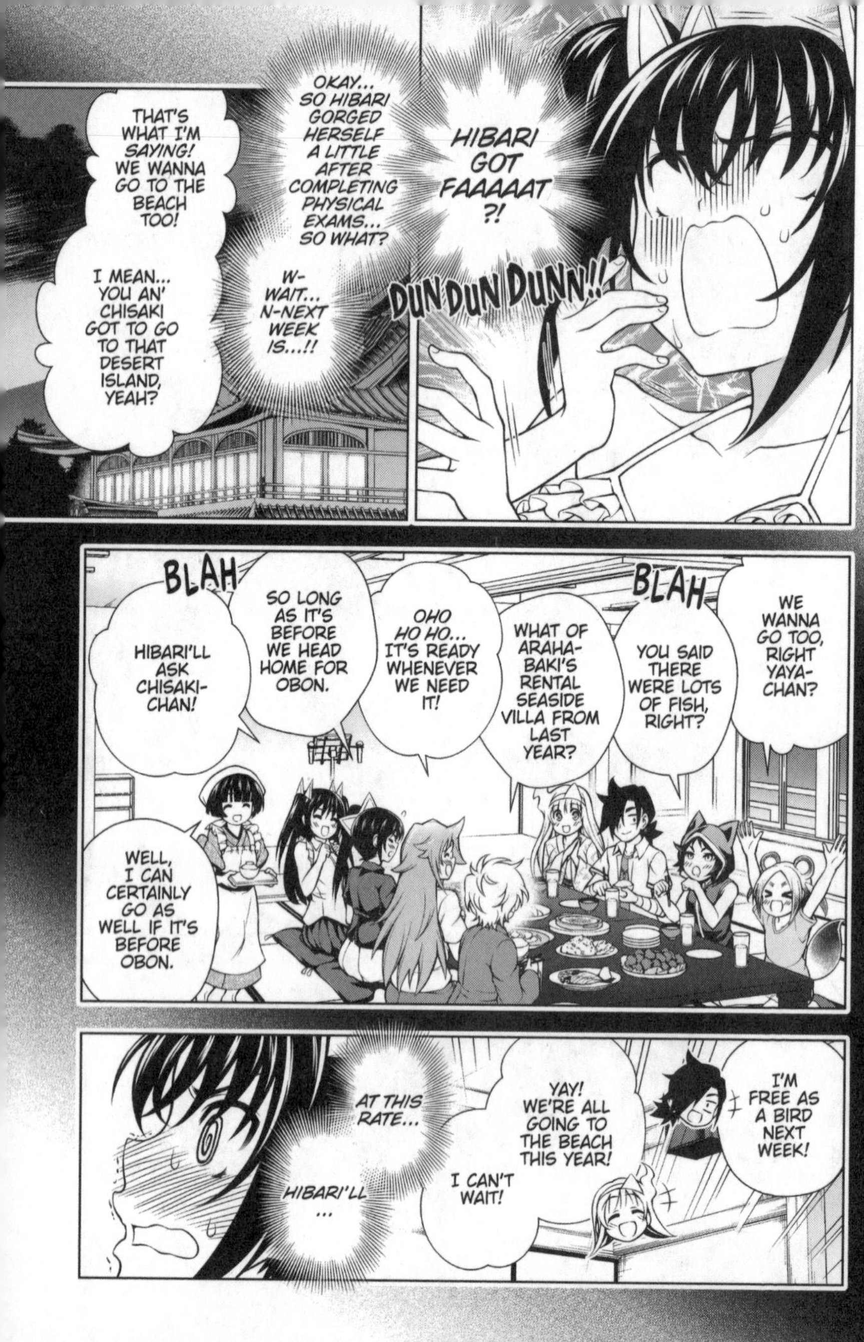
HIBARI GOT FAAAAAT?!
DUN DUN DUNN!!
OKAY... SO HIBARI GORGED HERSELF A LITTLE AFTER COMPLETING PHYSICAL EXAMS... SO WHAT?
W-WAIT... N-NEXT WEEK IS...!!
THAT'S WHAT I'M SAYING! WE WANNA GO TO THE BEACH TOO!
I MEAN... YOU AN' CHISAKI GOT TO GO TO THAT DESERT ISLAND, YEAH?
WE WANNA GO TOO, RIGHT YAYA-CHAN?
BLAH
YOU SAID THERE WERE LOTS OF FISH, RIGHT?
WHAT OF ARAHA-BAKI'S RENTAL SEASIDE VILLA FROM LAST YEAR?
OHO HO HO... IT'S READY WHENEVER WE NEED IT!
SO LONG AS IT'S BEFORE WE HEAD HOME FOR OBON.
BLAH
HIBARI'LL ASK CHISAKI-CHAN!
WELL, I CAN CERTAINLY GO AS WELL IF IT'S BEFORE OBON.
I'M FREE AS A BIRD NEXT WEEK!
YAY! WE'RE ALL GOING TO THE BEACH THIS YEAR!
I CAN'T WAIT!
AT THIS RATE...
HIBARI'LL ...

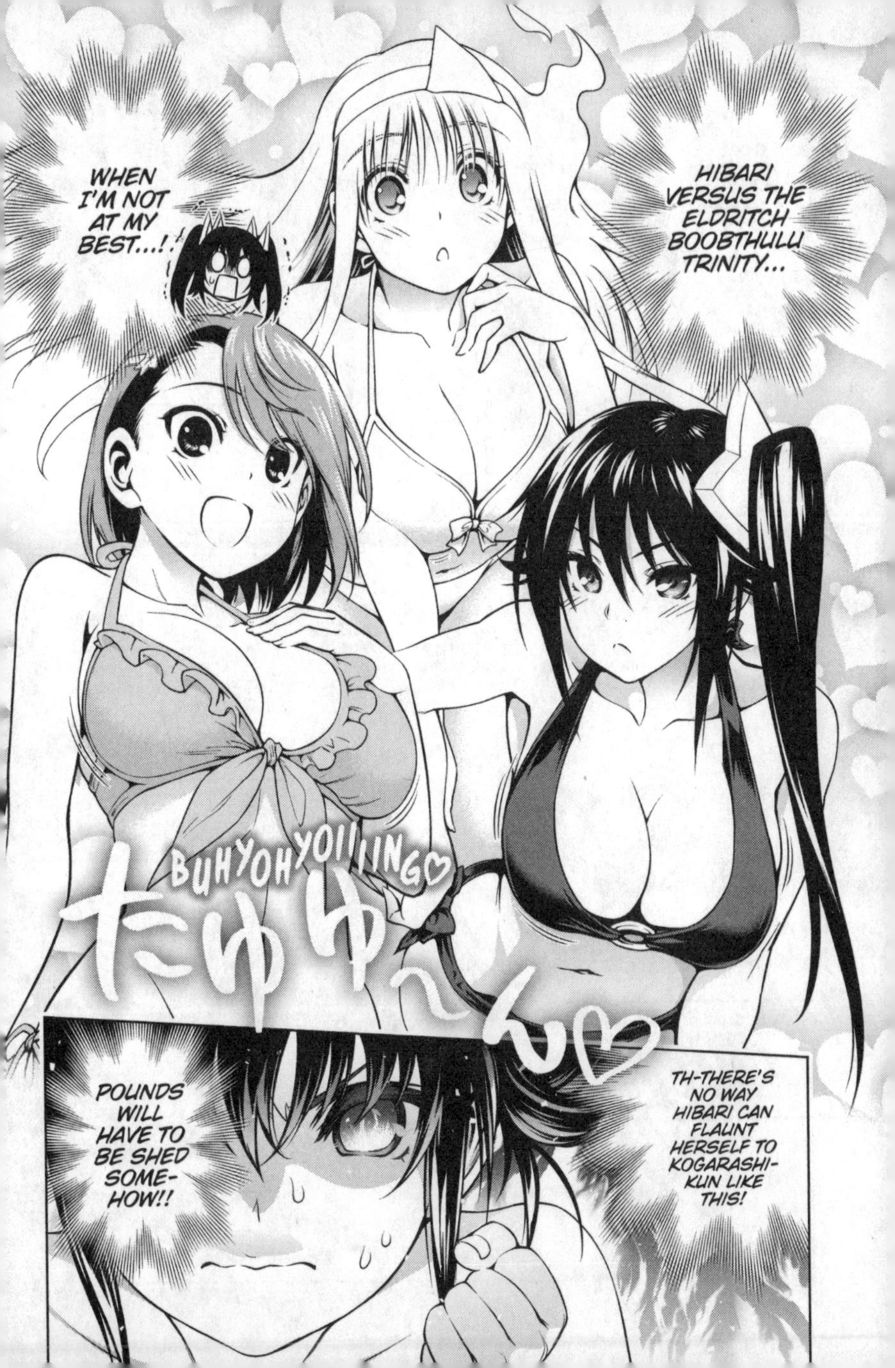
HIBARI VERSUS THE ELDRITCH BOOBTHULU TRINITY...
WHEN I'M NOT AT MY BEST...!
BUHYOHYOIIIING♡
たゆゆ〜ん♡
TH-THERE'S NO WAY HIBARI CAN FLAUNT HERSELF TO KOGARASHI-KUN LIKE THIS!
POUNDS WILL HAVE TO BE SHED SOME-HOW!!

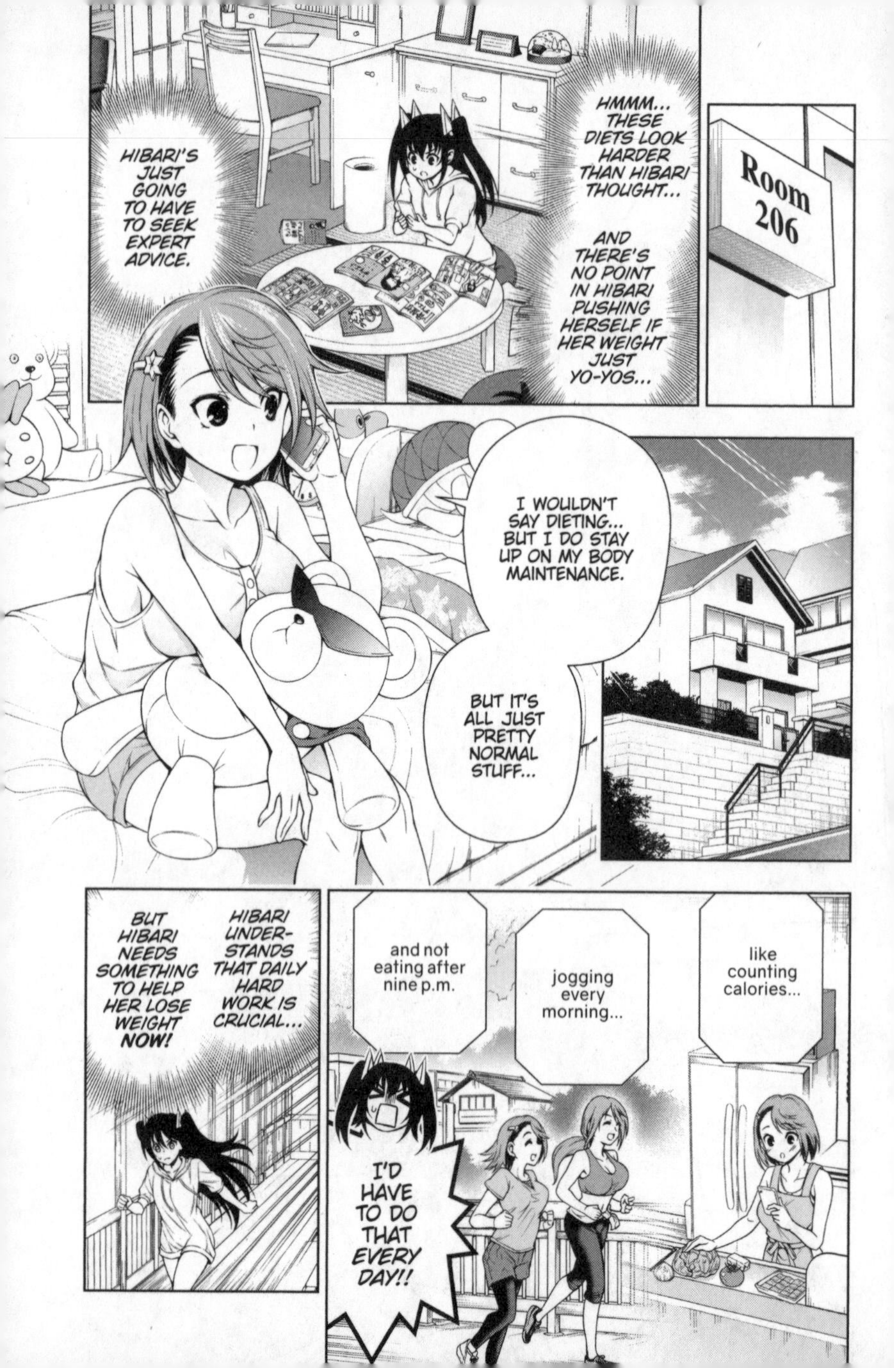
Room 206
HMMM... THESE DIETS LOOK HARDER THAN HIBARI THOUGHT...
AND THERE'S NO POINT IN HIBARI PUSHING HERSELF IF HER WEIGHT JUST YO-YOS...
HIBARI'S JUST GOING TO HAVE TO SEEK EXPERT ADVICE.
I WOULDN'T SAY DIETING... BUT I DO STAY UP ON MY BODY MAINTENANCE.
BUT IT'S ALL JUST PRETTY NORMAL STUFF...
like counting calories...
jogging every morning...
and not eating after nine p.m.
I'D HAVE TO DO THAT EVERY DAY!!
HIBARI UNDER-STANDS THAT DAILY HARD WORK IS CRUCIAL...
BUT HIBARI NEEDS SOMETHING TO HELP HER LOSE WEIGHT NOW!

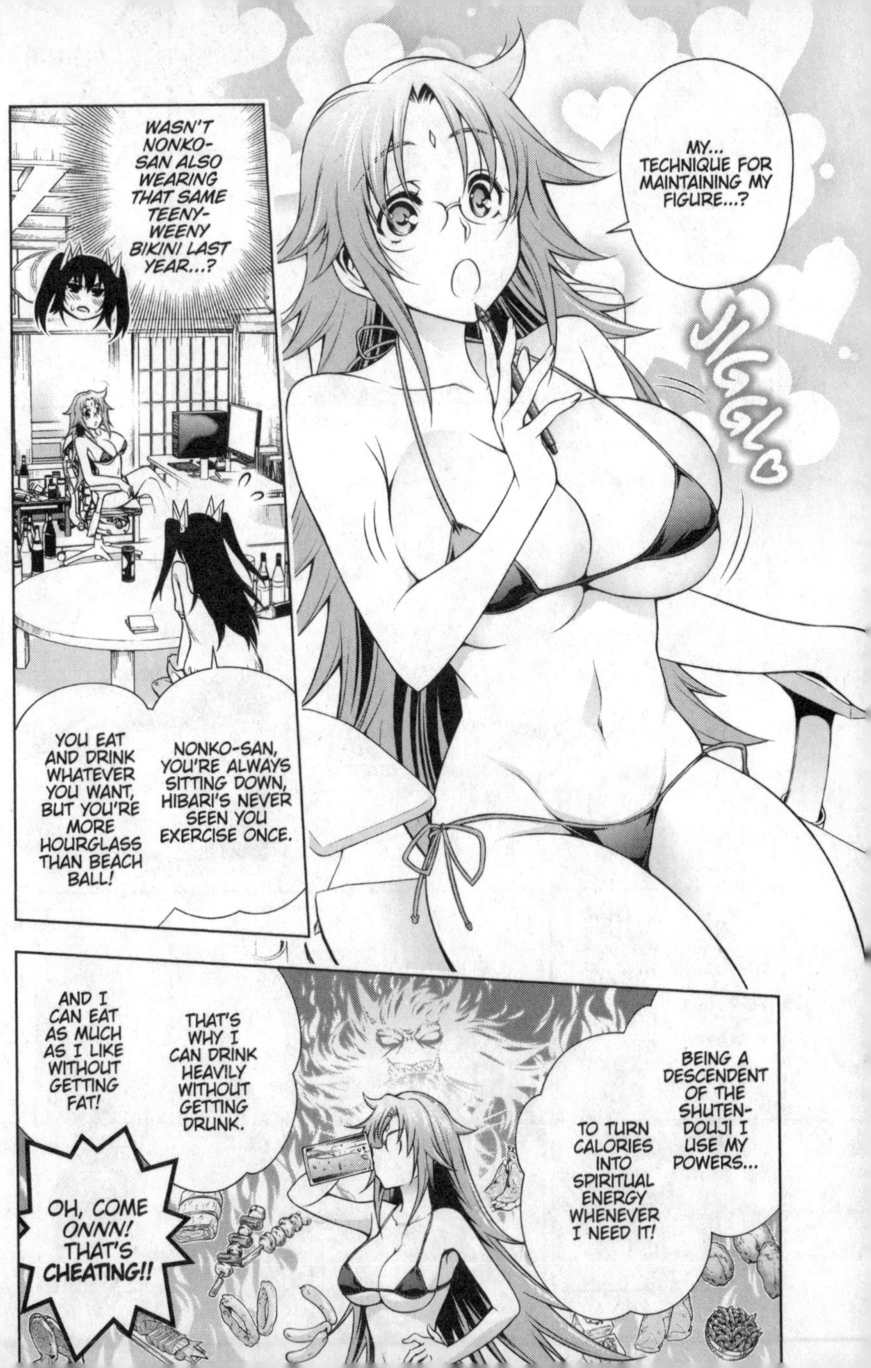

MY... TECHNIQUE FOR MAINTAINING MY FIGURE...?
JIGGLE
WASN'T NONKO-SAN ALSO WEARING THAT SAME TEENY-WEENY BIKINI LAST YEAR...?
NONKO-SAN, YOU'RE ALWAYS SITTING DOWN, HIBARI'S NEVER SEEN YOU EXERCISE ONCE.
YOU EAT AND DRINK WHATEVER YOU WANT, BUT YOU'RE MORE HOURGLASS THAN BEACH BALL!
BEING A DESCENDENT OF THE SHUTEN-DOUJI I USE MY POWERS...
TO TURN CALORIES INTO SPIRITUAL ENERGY WHENEVER I NEED IT!
THAT'S WHY I CAN DRINK HEAVILY WITHOUT GETTING DRUNK.
AND I CAN EAT AS MUCH AS I LIKE WITHOUT GETTING FAT!
OH, COME ONNN! THAT'S CHEATING!!

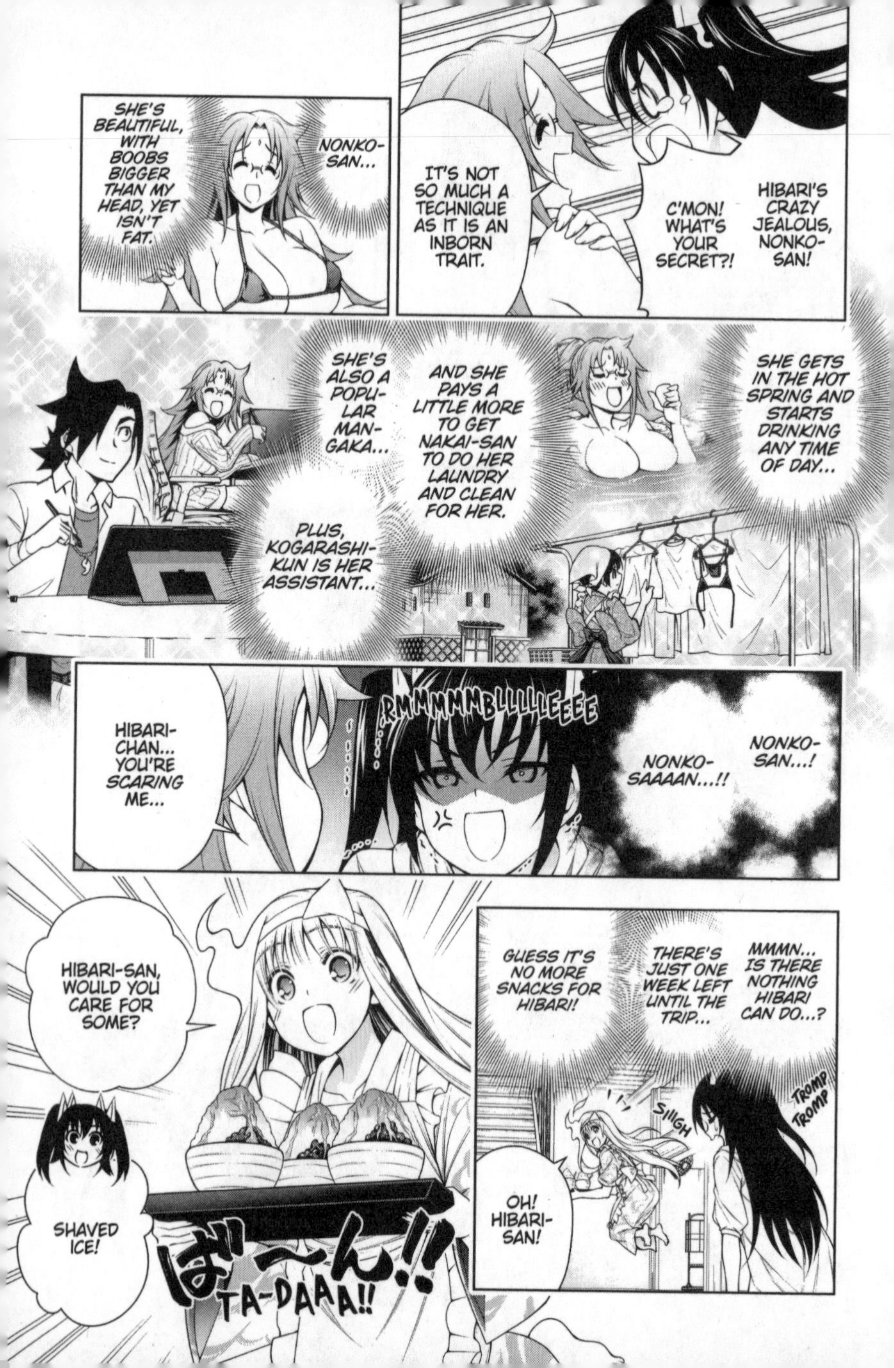
HIBARI'S CRAZY JEALOUS, NONKO-SAN!
C'MON! WHAT'S YOUR SECRET?!
IT'S NOT SO MUCH A TECHNIQUE AS IT IS AN INBORN TRAIT.
NONKO-SAN...
SHE'S BEAUTIFUL, WITH BOOBS BIGGER THAN MY HEAD, YET ISN'T FAT.
SHE GETS IN THE HOT SPRING AND STARTS DRINKING ANY TIME OF DAY...
AND SHE PAYS A LITTLE MORE TO GET NAKAI-SAN TO DO HER LAUNDRY AND CLEAN FOR HER.
SHE'S ALSO A POPULAR MANGAKA...
PLUS, KOGARASHI-KUN IS HER ASSISTANT...
NONKO-SAN...!
NONKO-SAAAAN...!!
RMMMMMBLLLLLEEEE
HIBARI-CHAN... YOU'RE SCARING ME...
MMMN... IS THERE NOTHING HIBARI CAN DO...?
THERE'S JUST ONE WEEK LEFT UNTIL THE TRIP...
GUESS IT'S NO MORE SNACKS FOR HIBARI!
TROMP TROMP
SIIIGH
OH! HIBARI-SAN!
HIBARI-SAN, WOULD YOU CARE FOR SOME?
SHAVED ICE!
ばーん!!
TA-DAAA!!

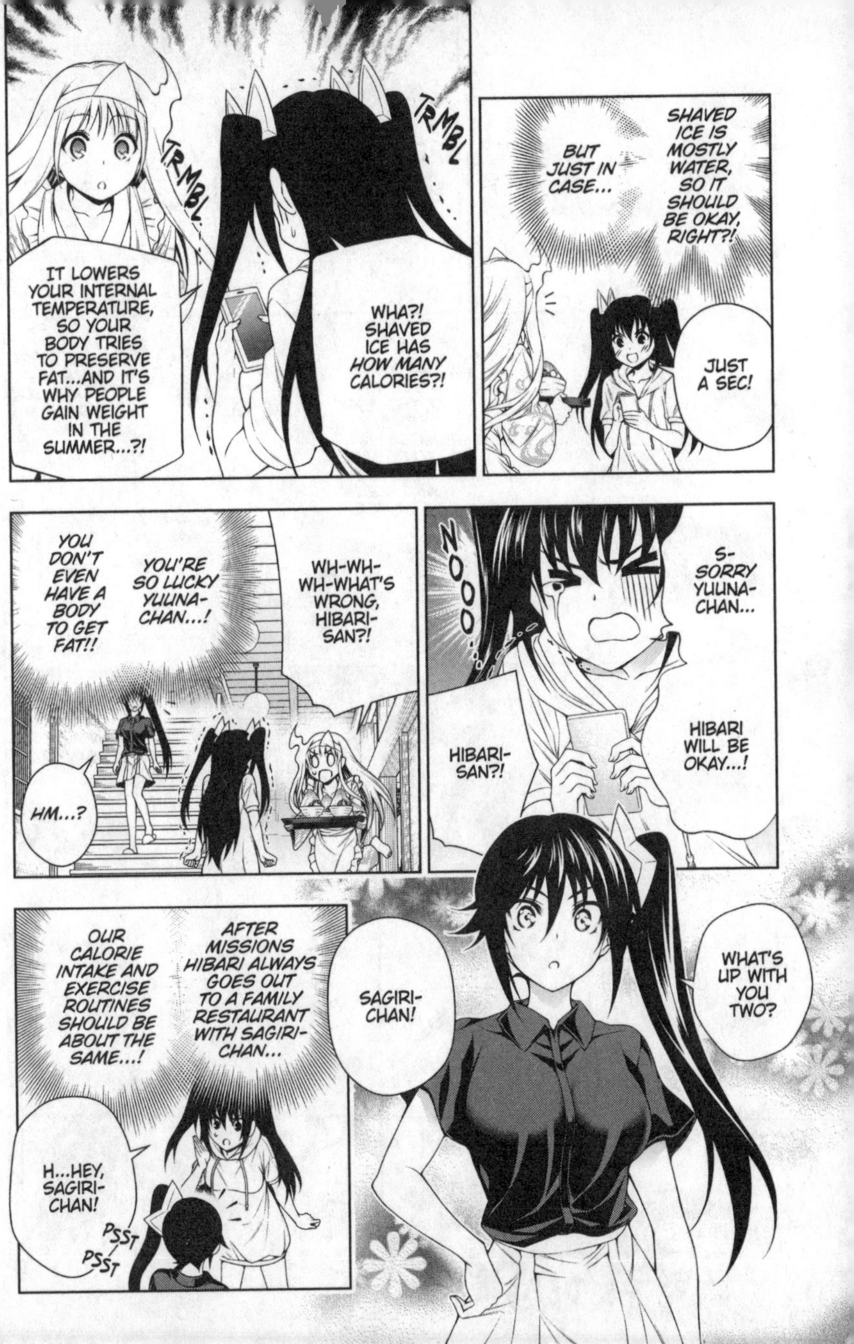
SHAVED ICE IS MOSTLY WATER, SO IT SHOULD BE OKAY, RIGHT?!
BUT JUST IN CASE...
JUST A SEC!
TRMBL
TRMBL
WHA?! SHAVED ICE HAS *HOW MANY* CALORIES?!
IT LOWERS YOUR INTERNAL TEMPERATURE, SO YOUR BODY TRIES TO PRESERVE FAT...AND IT'S WHY PEOPLE GAIN WEIGHT IN THE SUMMER...?!
NOOO
S-SORRY YUUNA-CHAN...
HIBARI WILL BE OKAY...!
HIBARI-SAN?!
WH-WH-WH-WHAT'S WRONG, HIBARI-SAN?!
YOU'RE SO LUCKY YUUNA-CHAN...!
YOU DON'T EVEN HAVE A BODY TO GET FAT!!
HM...?
WHAT'S UP WITH YOU TWO?
SAGIRI-CHAN!
AFTER MISSIONS HIBARI ALWAYS GOES OUT TO A FAMILY RESTAURANT WITH SAGIRI-CHAN...
OUR CALORIE INTAKE AND EXERCISE ROUTINES SHOULD BE ABOUT THE SAME...!
H...HEY, SAGIRI-CHAN!
PSST PSST

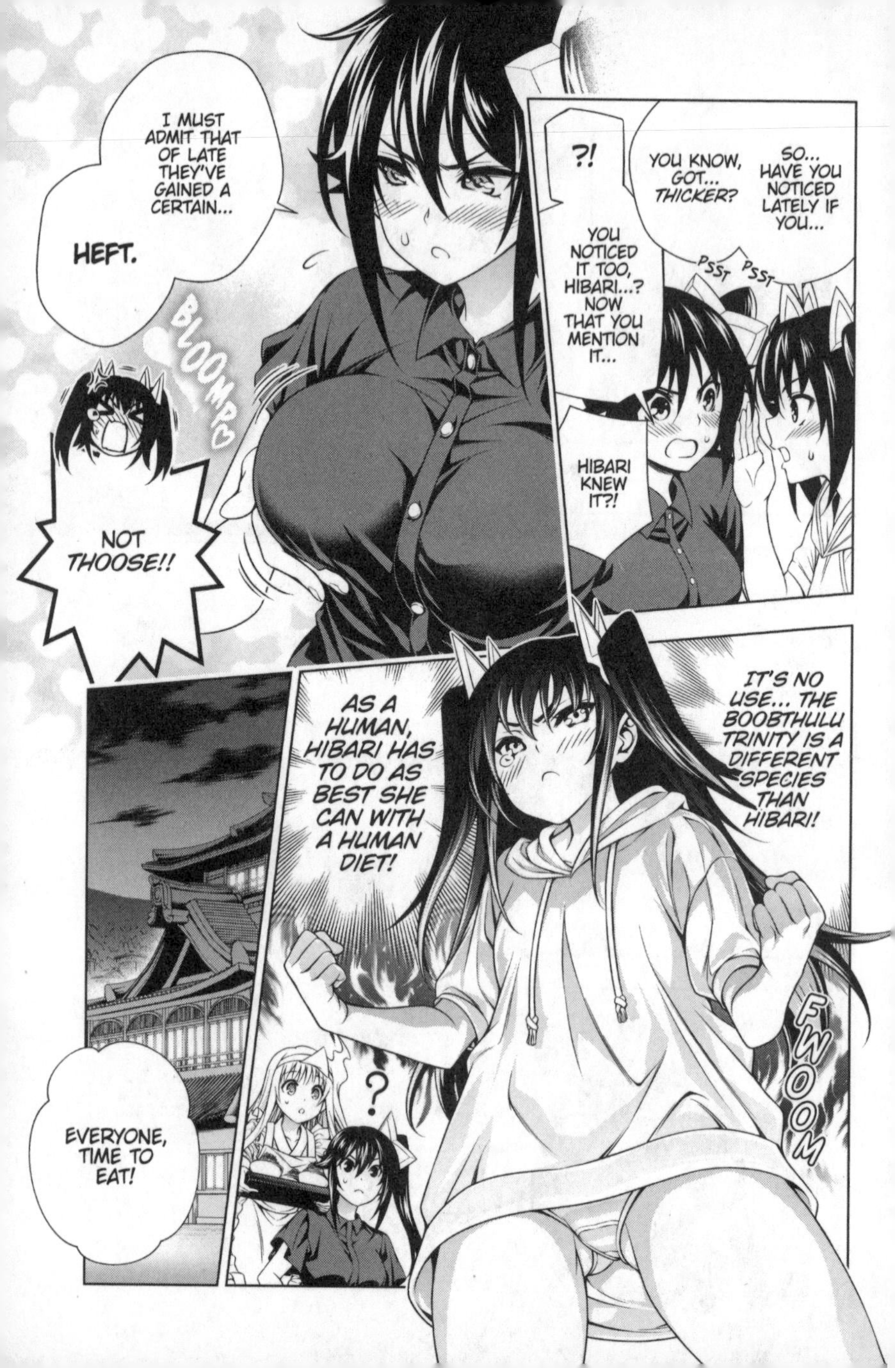
SO... HAVE YOU NOTICED LATELY IF YOU...
YOU KNOW, GOT... THICKER?
PSST PSST
?!
YOU NOTICED IT TOO, HIBARI...? NOW THAT YOU MENTION IT...
HIBARI KNEW IT?!
I MUST ADMIT THAT OF LATE THEY'VE GAINED A CERTAIN...
HEFT.
BLOOMP
NOT THOOSE!!
IT'S NO USE... THE BOOBTHULU TRINITY IS A DIFFERENT SPECIES THAN HIBARI!
AS A HUMAN, HIBARI HAS TO DO AS BEST SHE CAN WITH A HUMAN DIET!
FWOOM
?
EVERYONE, TIME TO EAT!

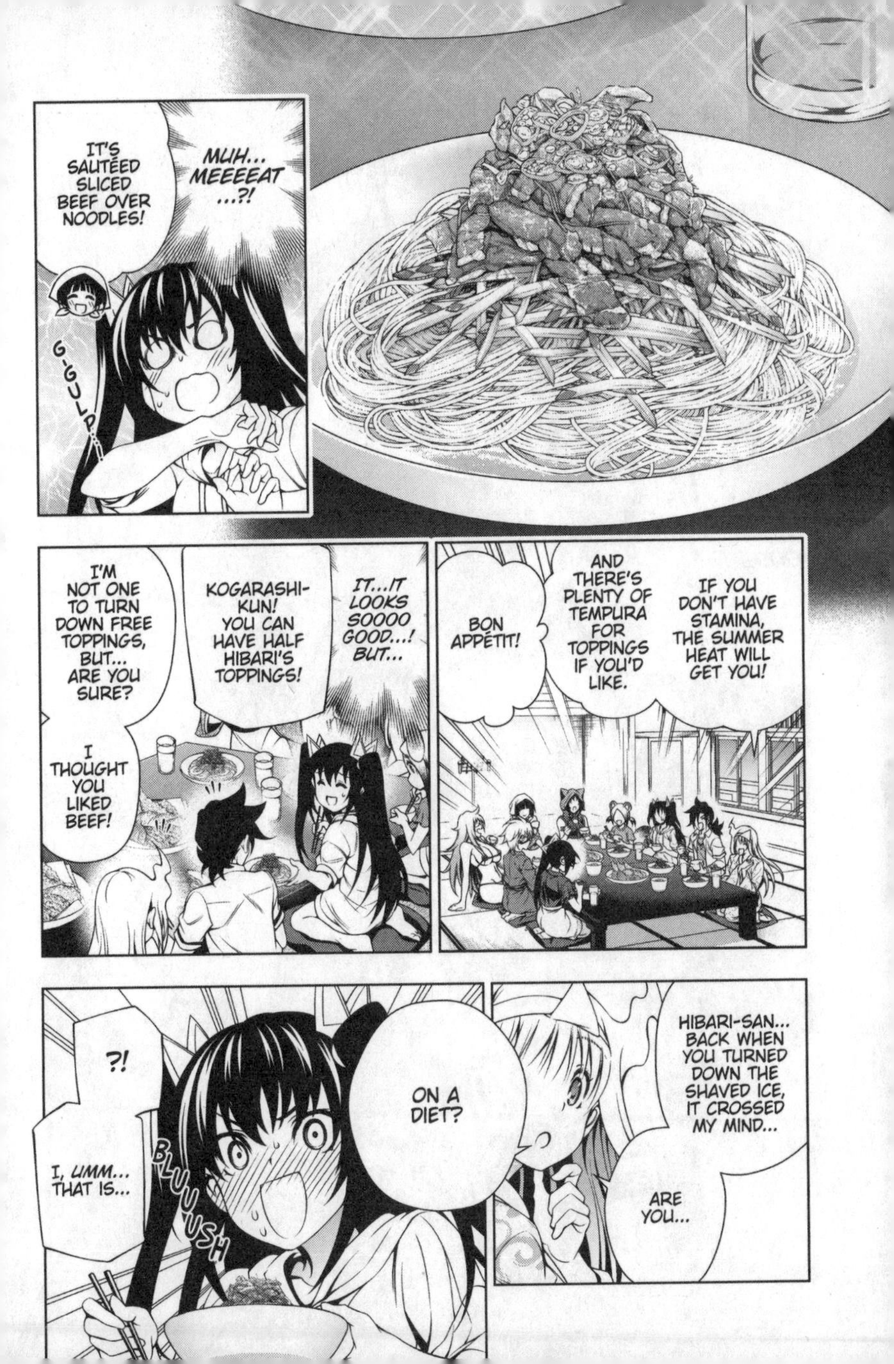

MUH... MEEEEAT ...?!
IT'S SAUTÉED SLICED BEEF OVER NOODLES!
G-GULP
IF YOU DON'T HAVE STAMINA, THE SUMMER HEAT WILL GET YOU!
AND THERE'S PLENTY OF TEMPURA FOR TOPPINGS IF YOU'D LIKE.
BON APPÉTIT!
IT...IT LOOKS SOOOO GOOD...! BUT...
KOGARASHI-KUN! YOU CAN HAVE HALF HIBARI'S TOPPINGS!
I'M NOT ONE TO TURN DOWN FREE TOPPINGS, BUT... ARE YOU SURE?
I THOUGHT YOU LIKED BEEF!
HIBARI-SAN... BACK WHEN YOU TURNED DOWN THE SHAVED ICE, IT CROSSED MY MIND...
ARE YOU...
ON A DIET?
?!
BLUUUSH
I, UMM... THAT IS...

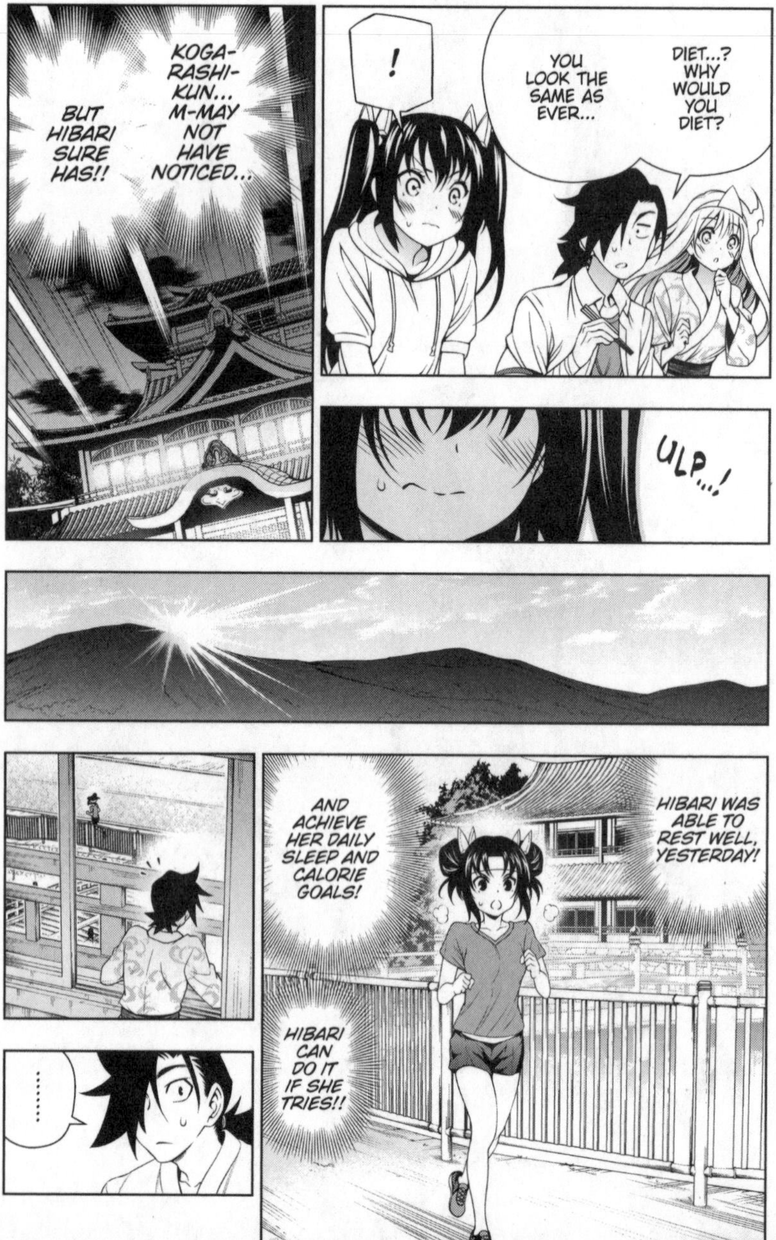
DIET...? WHY WOULD YOU DIET?
YOU LOOK THE SAME AS EVER...
!
ULP...!
KOGA-RASHI-KUN... M-MAY NOT HAVE NOTICED...
BUT HIBARI SURE HAS!!
HIBARI WAS ABLE TO REST WELL, YESTERDAY!
AND ACHIEVE HER DAILY SLEEP AND CALORIE GOALS!
HIBARI CAN DO IT IF SHE TRIES!!
......

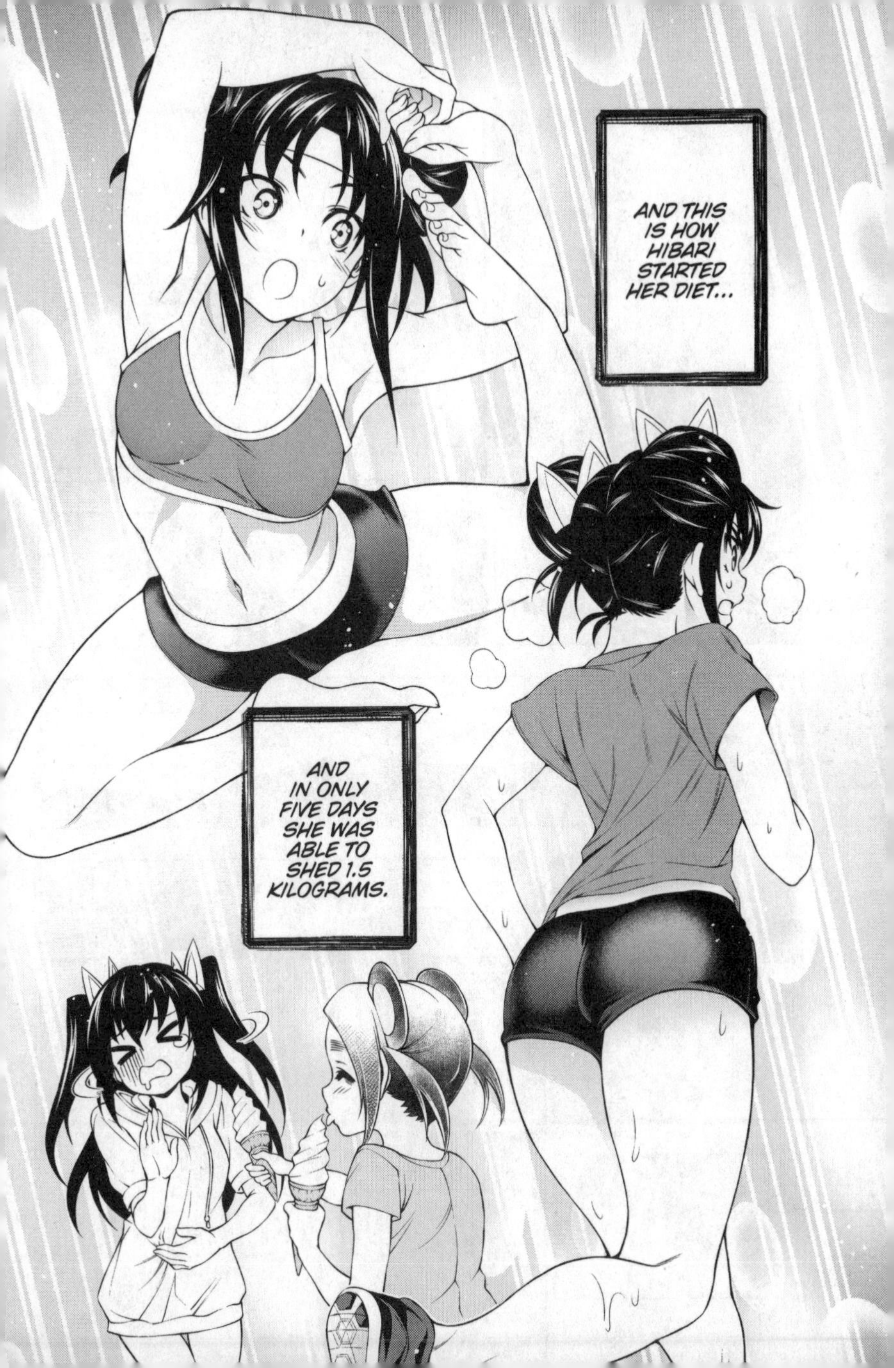
AND THIS IS HOW HIBARI STARTED HER DIET...
AND IN ONLY FIVE DAYS SHE WAS ABLE TO SHED 1.5 KILOGRAMS.

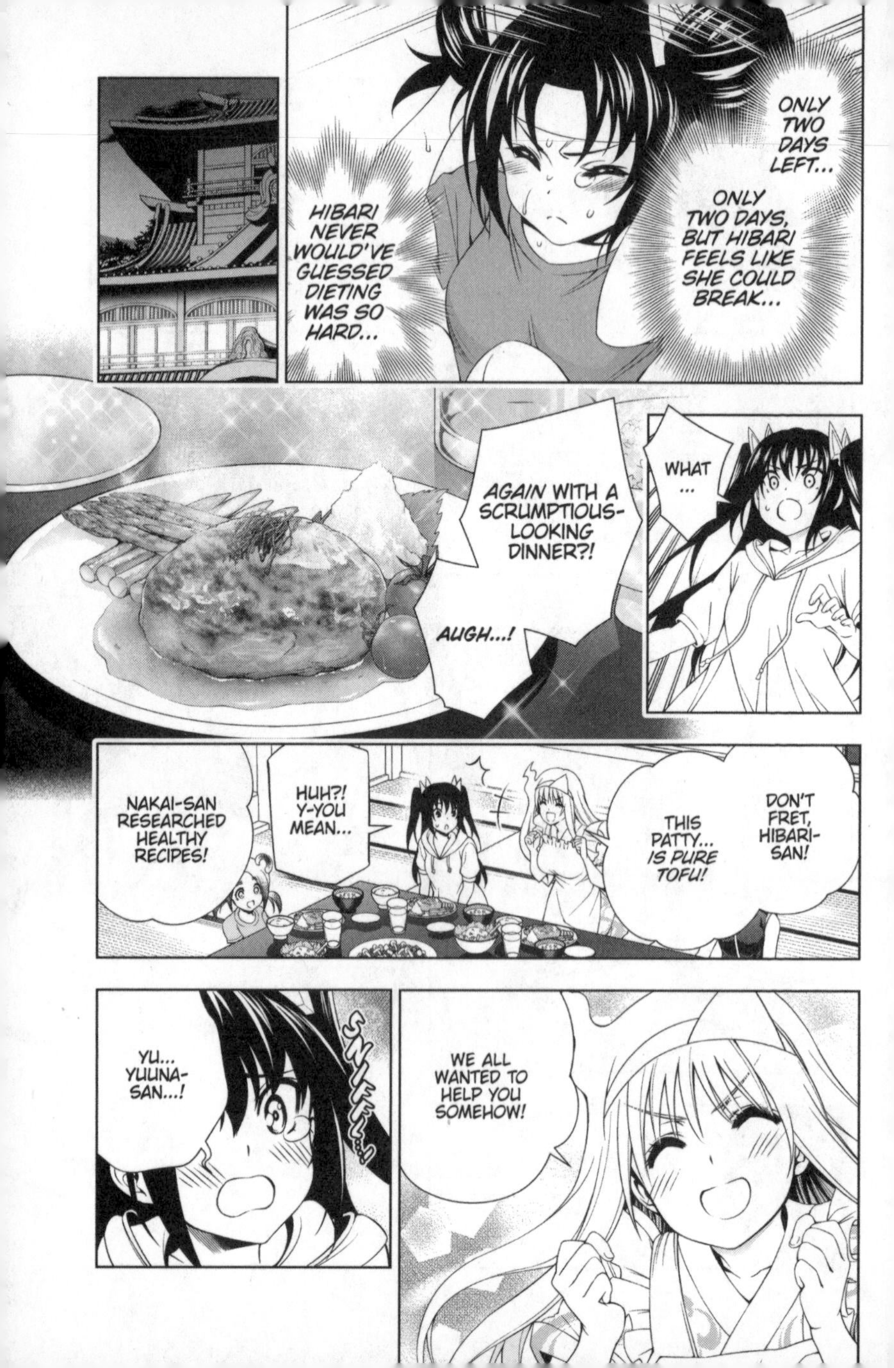
ONLY TWO DAYS LEFT...
ONLY TWO DAYS, BUT HIBARI FEELS LIKE SHE COULD BREAK...
HIBARI NEVER WOULD'VE GUESSED DIETING WAS SO HARD...
WHAT ...
AGAIN WITH A SCRUMPTIOUS-LOOKING DINNER?!
AUGH...!
DON'T FRET, HIBARI-SAN!
THIS PATTY... IS PURE TOFU!
HUH?! Y-YOU MEAN...
NAKAI-SAN RESEARCHED HEALTHY RECIPES!
WE ALL WANTED TO HELP YOU SOMEHOW!
YU... YUUNA-SAN...!
SNIFFL...!

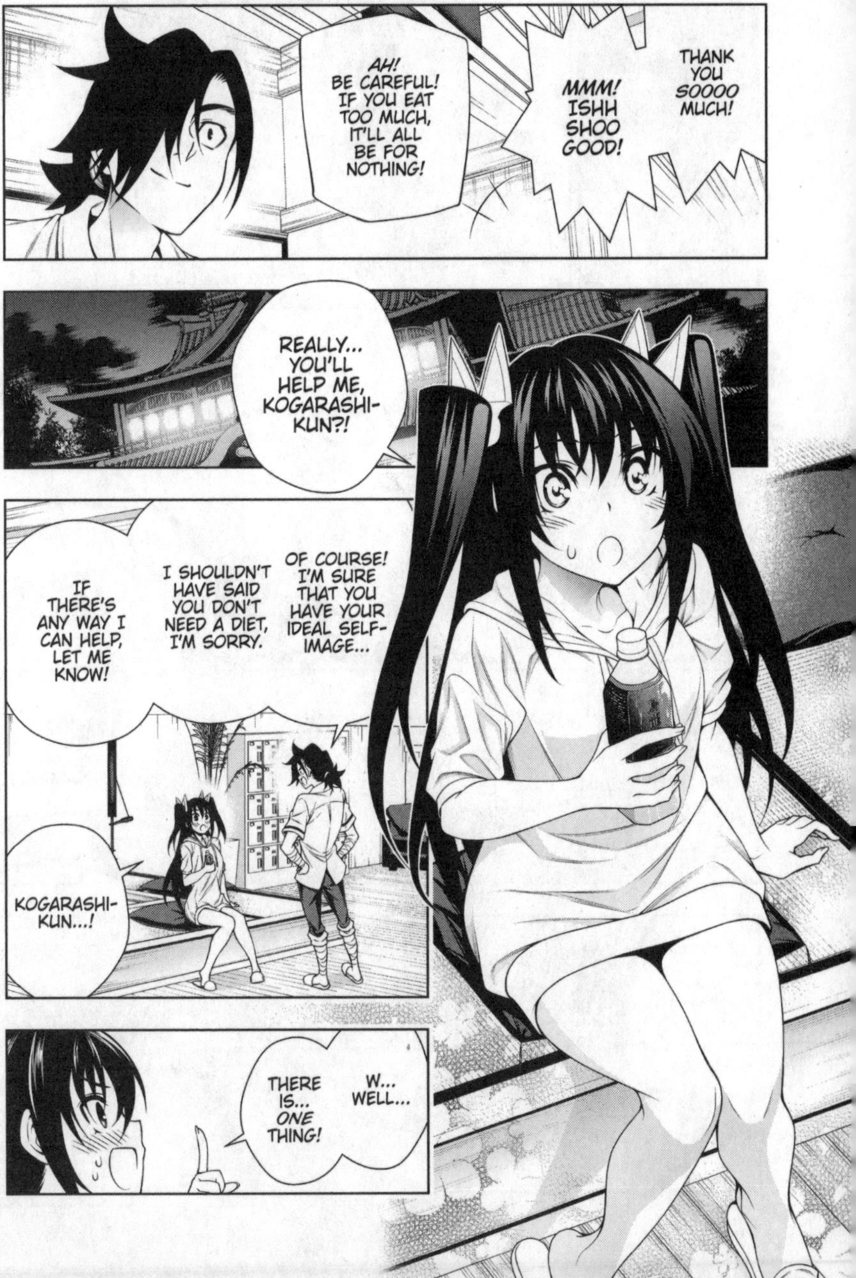
THANK YOU SOOOO MUCH!
MMM! ISHH SHOO GOOD!
AH! BE CAREFUL! IF YOU EAT TOO MUCH, IT'LL ALL BE FOR NOTHING!
REALLY... YOU'LL HELP ME, KOGARASHI-KUN?!
OF COURSE! I'M SURE THAT YOU HAVE YOUR IDEAL SELF-IMAGE...
I SHOULDN'T HAVE SAID YOU DON'T NEED A DIET, I'M SORRY.
IF THERE'S ANY WAY I CAN HELP, LET ME KNOW!
KOGARASHI-KUN...!
W... WELL...
THERE IS... ONE THING!

TUG

TUG

HAHH...

MMN...

Room 206

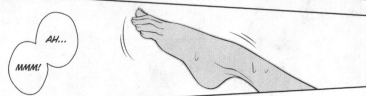

AH...

MMM!

IS THIS... REALLY PART OF YOUR... DIET?

HEY, HIBARI...?

HEY...

HAHH!

ARE... DOING IT.

HAHH!

NH...

OF COURSE...!

REAL... HARD...!

COUPLES... THE WORLD OVER...

HAHH!

HAHH!

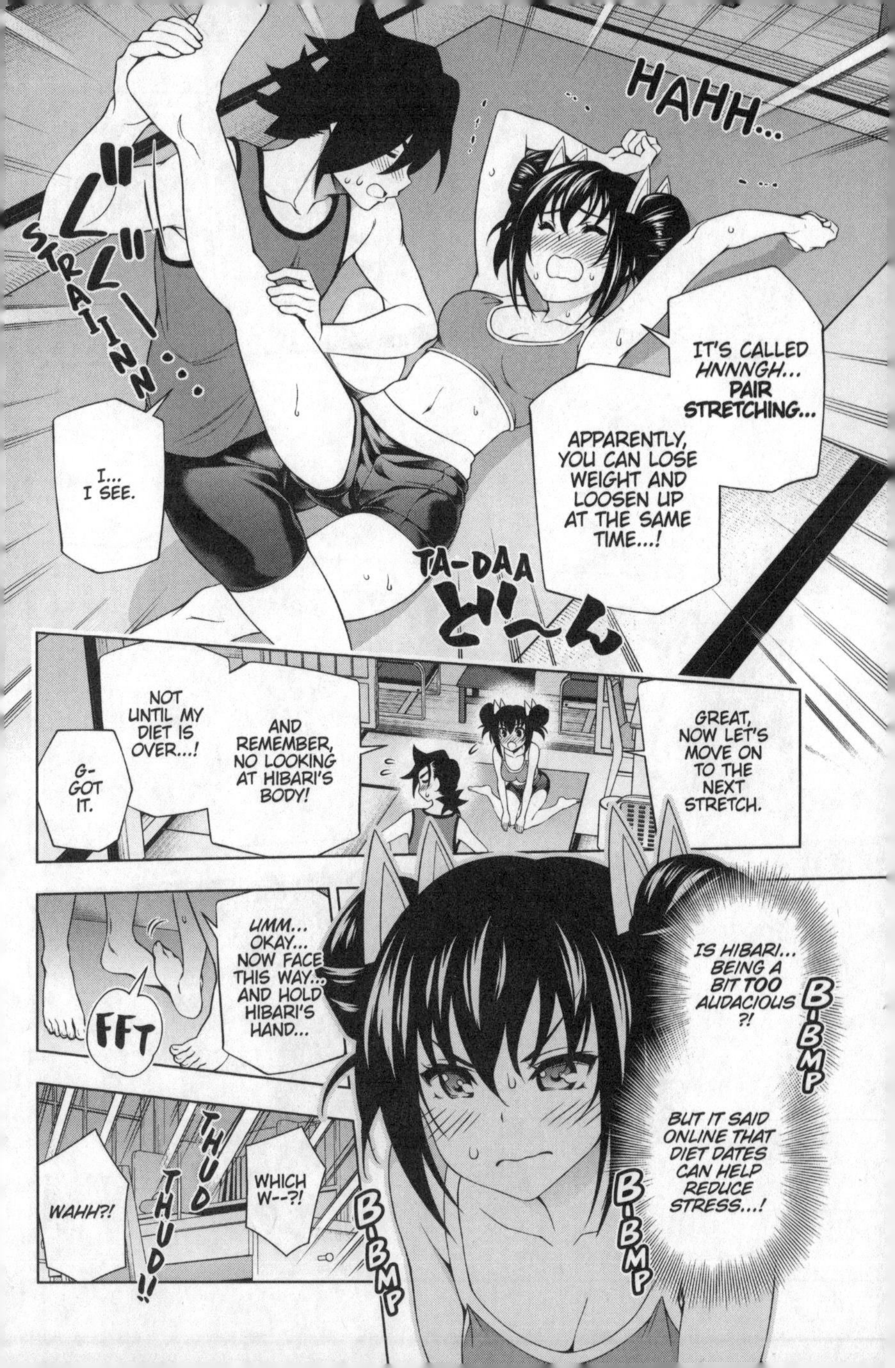
HAHH...
IT'S CALLED HNNNGH... PAIR STRETCHING...
APPARENTLY, YOU CAN LOSE WEIGHT AND LOOSEN UP AT THE SAME TIME...!
TA-DAA
どーん
STRAINN
I... I SEE.
GREAT, NOW LET'S MOVE ON TO THE NEXT STRETCH.
AND REMEMBER, NO LOOKING AT HIBARI'S BODY!
NOT UNTIL MY DIET IS OVER...!
G-GOT IT.
IS HIBARI... BEING A BIT TOO AUDACIOUS?!
B-BMP
BUT IT SAID ONLINE THAT DIET DATES CAN HELP REDUCE STRESS...!
B-BMP
UMM... OKAY... NOW FACE THIS WAY... AND HOLD HIBARI'S HAND...
FFT
THUD
THUD!!
WHICH W--?!
WAHH?!
B-BMP

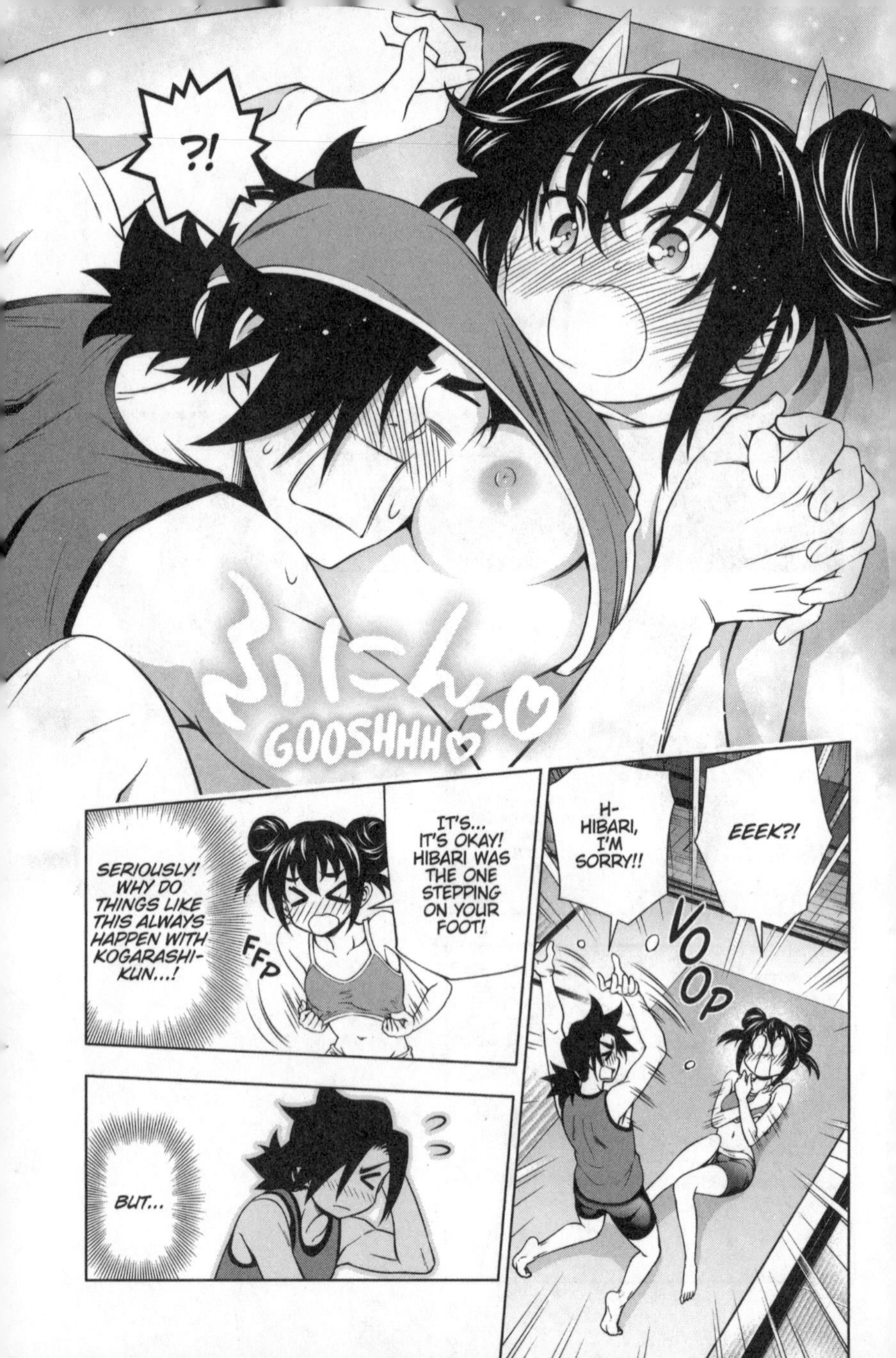
?!
ふにんっ♡
GOOSHHH♡
EEEK?!
H-HIBARI, I'M SORRY!!
VOOP
IT'S... IT'S OKAY! HIBARI WAS THE ONE STEPPING ON YOUR FOOT!
SERIOUSLY! WHY DO THINGS LIKE THIS ALWAYS HAPPEN WITH KOGARASHI-KUN...!
FFP
BUT...

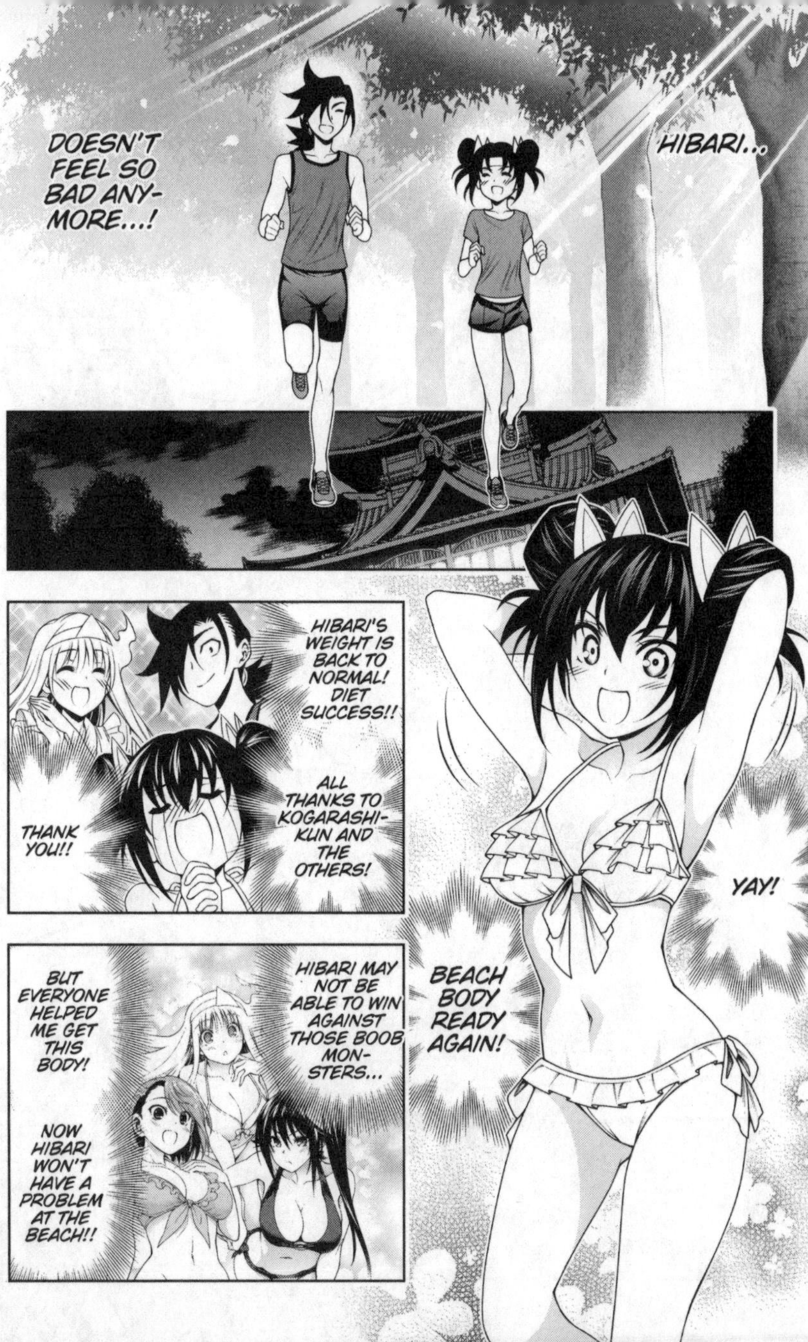
HIBARI...
DOESN'T FEEL SO BAD ANY-MORE...!
YAY!
BEACH BODY READY AGAIN!
HIBARI'S WEIGHT IS BACK TO NORMAL! DIET SUCCESS!!
ALL THANKS TO KOGARASHI-KUN AND THE OTHERS!
THANK YOU!!
HIBARI MAY NOT BE ABLE TO WIN AGAINST THOSE BOOB MON-STERS...
BUT EVERYONE HELPED ME GET THIS BODY!
NOW HIBARI WON'T HAVE A PROBLEM AT THE BEACH!!

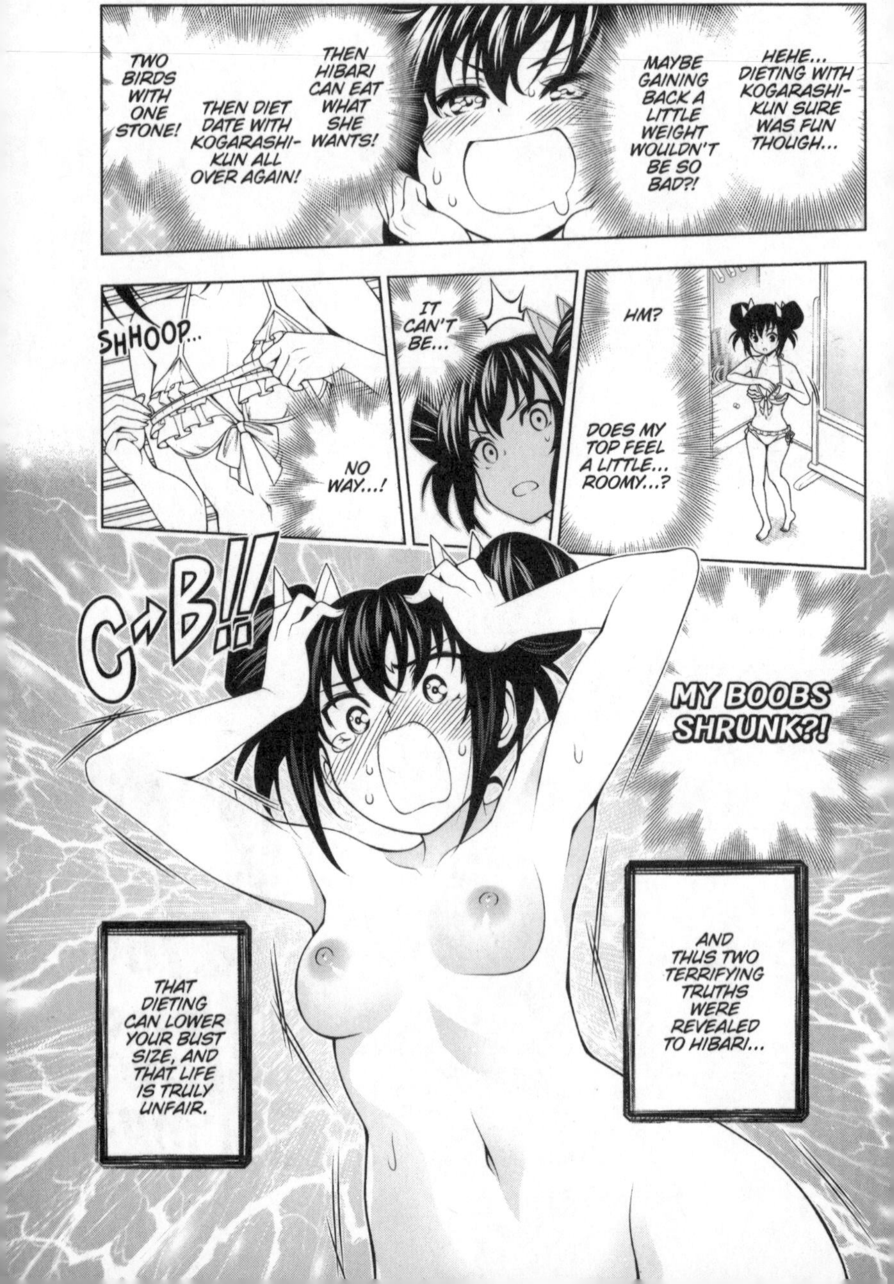
HEHE... DIETING WITH KOGARASHI-KUN SURE WAS FUN THOUGH...
MAYBE GAINING BACK A LITTLE WEIGHT WOULDN'T BE SO BAD?!
THEN HIBARI CAN EAT WHAT SHE WANTS!
THEN DIET DATE WITH KOGARASHI-KUN ALL OVER AGAIN!
TWO BIRDS WITH ONE STONE!
HM?
DOES MY TOP FEEL A LITTLE... ROOMY...?
IT CAN'T BE...
NO WAY...!
SHHOOP...
MY BOOBS SHRUNK?!
C→B!!
AND THUS TWO TERRIFYING TRUTHS WERE REVEALED TO HIBARI...
THAT DIETING CAN LOWER YOUR BUST SIZE, AND THAT LIFE IS TRULY UNFAIR.

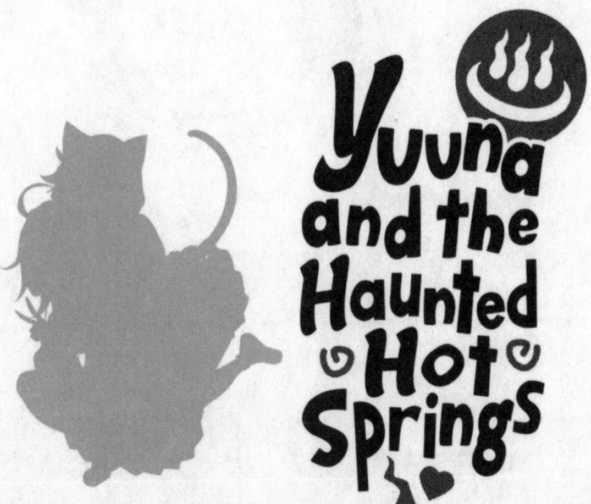

Yuuna and the Haunted Hot Springs

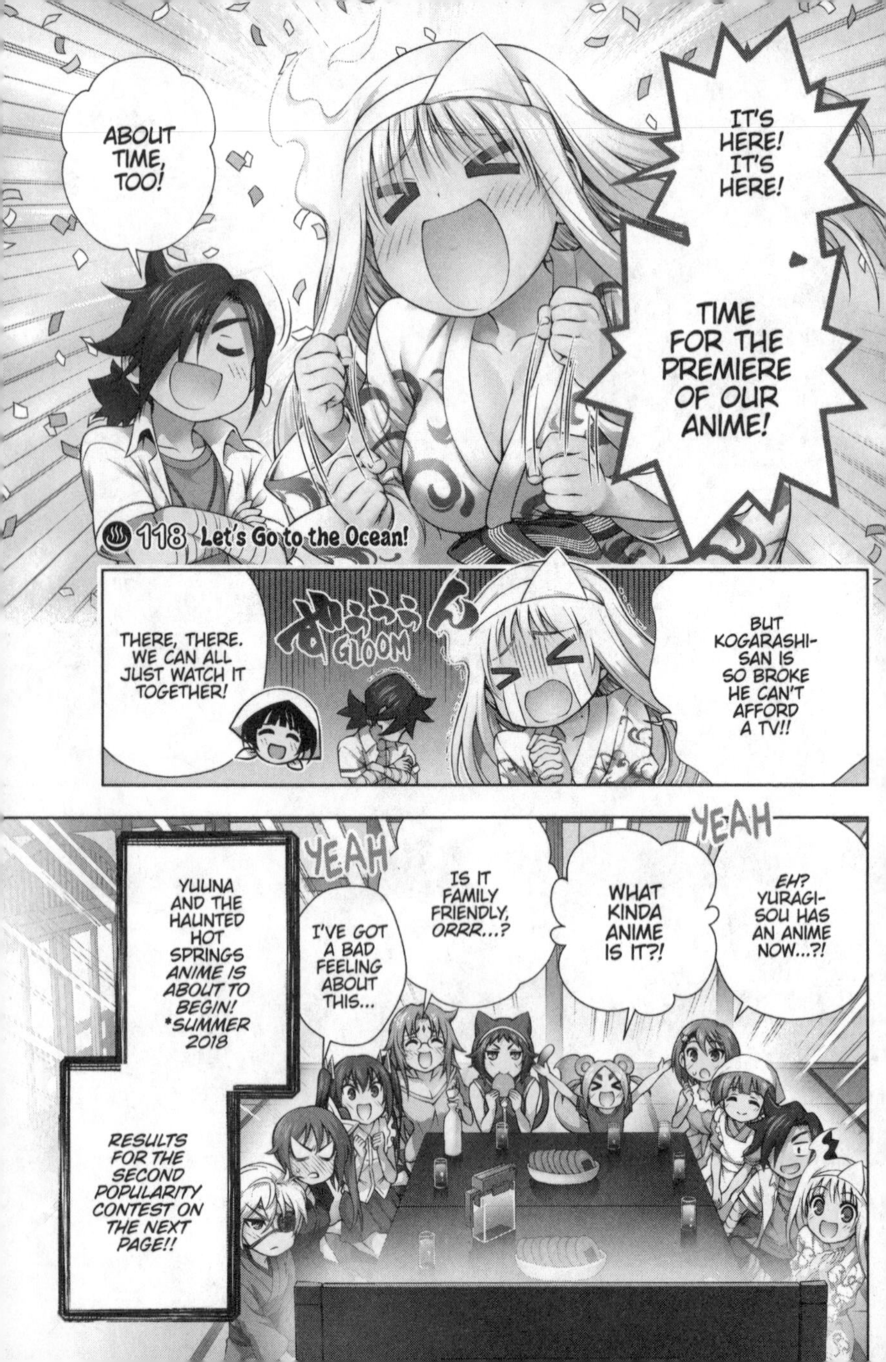
IT'S HERE! IT'S HERE!
TIME FOR THE PREMIERE OF OUR ANIME!
ABOUT TIME, TOO!
118 Let's Go to the Ocean!
BUT KOGARASHI-SAN IS SO BROKE HE CAN'T AFFORD A TV!!
GLOOM
THERE, THERE. WE CAN ALL JUST WATCH IT TOGETHER!
YEAH
EH? YURAGI-SOU HAS AN ANIME NOW...?!
WHAT KINDA ANIME IS IT?!
YEAH
IS IT FAMILY FRIENDLY, ORRR...?
I'VE GOT A BAD FEELING ABOUT THIS...
YUUNA AND THE HAUNTED HOT SPRINGS ANIME IS ABOUT TO BEGIN! *SUMMER 2018
RESULTS FOR THE SECOND POPULARITY CONTEST ON THE NEXT PAGE!!

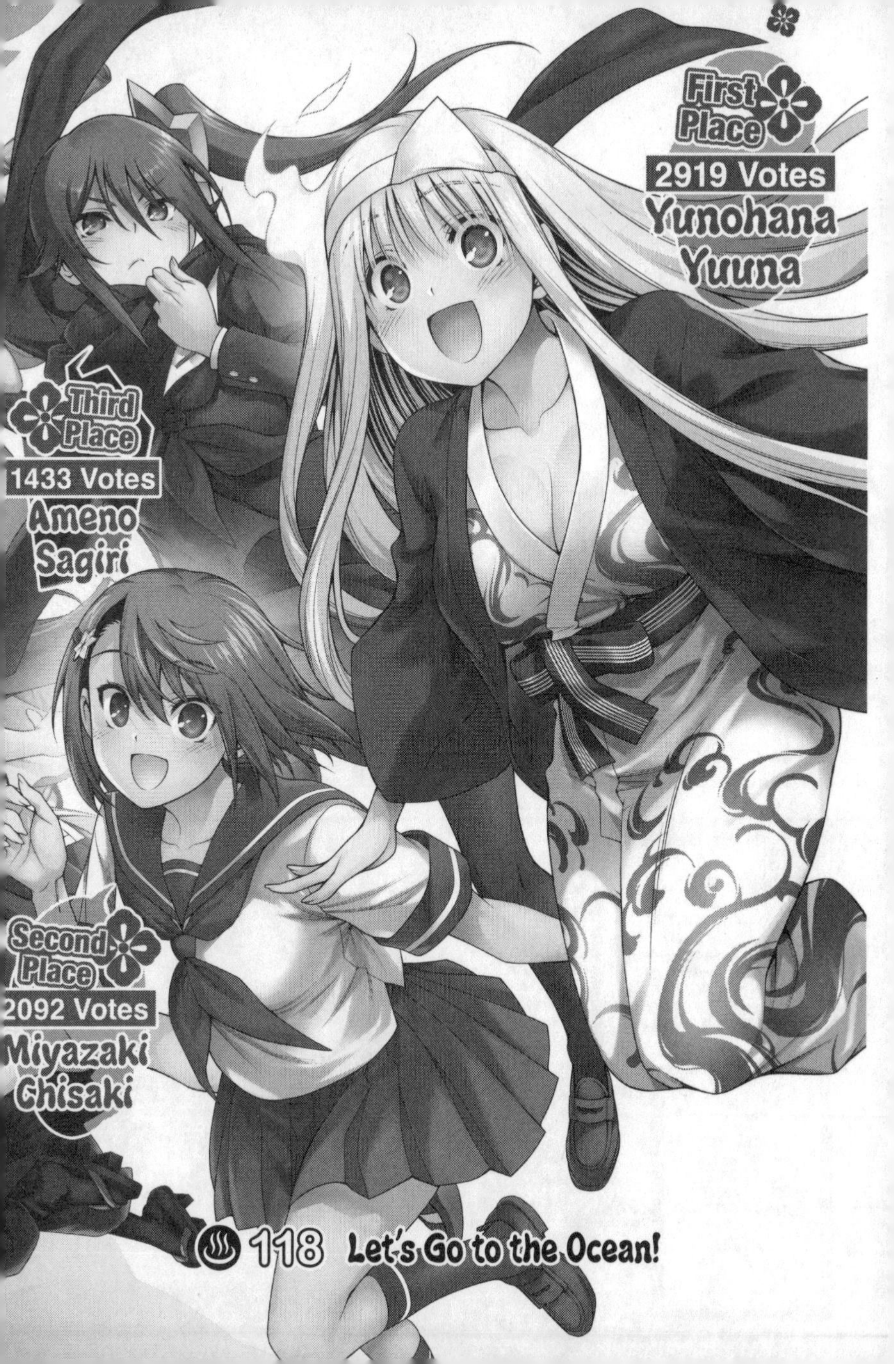
First Place
2919 Votes
Yunohana Yuuna
Third Place
1433 Votes
Ameno Sagiri
Second Place
2092 Votes
Miyazaki Chisaki
118 Let's Go to the Ocean!

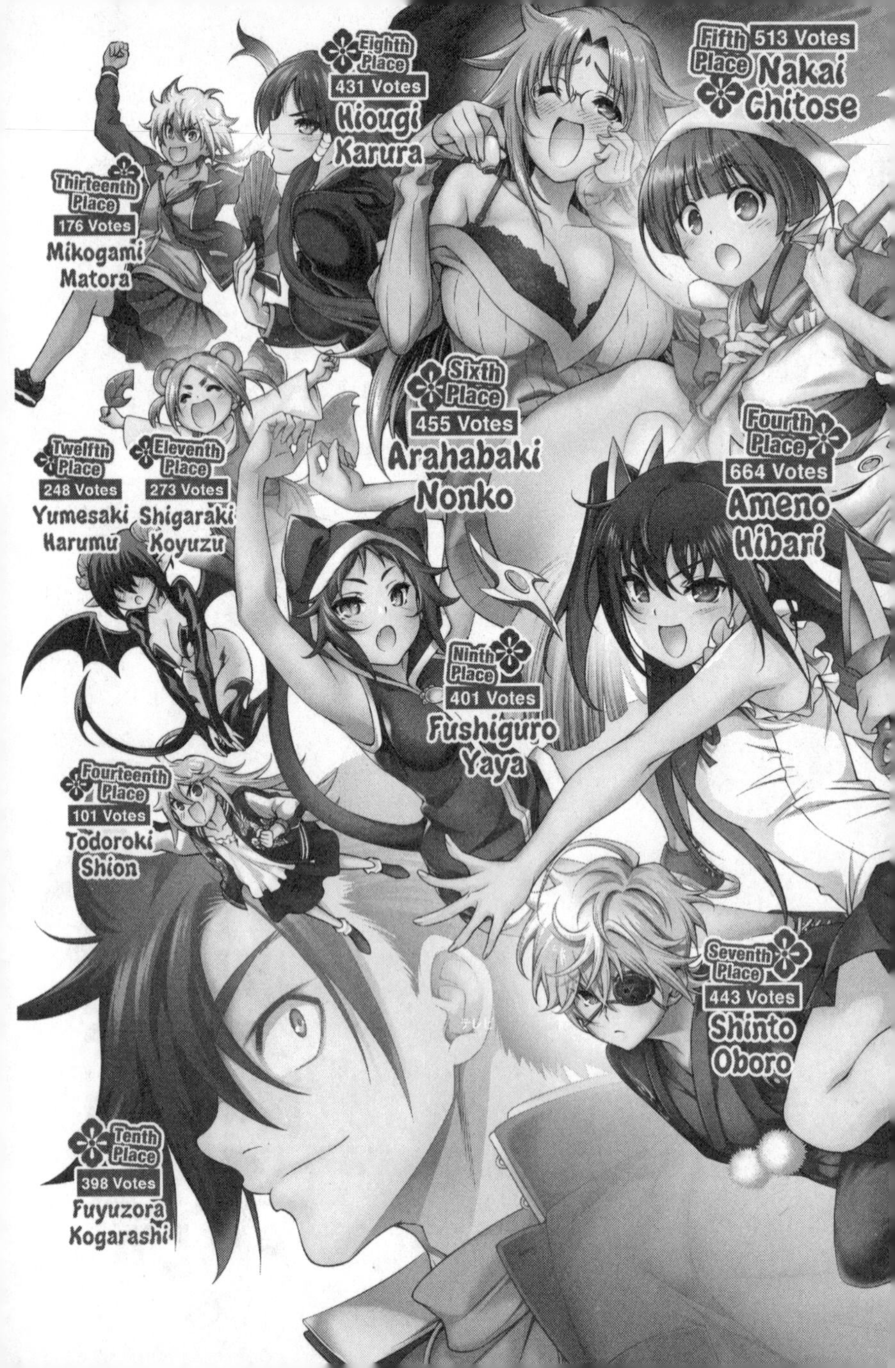
Fifth Place
513 Votes
Nakai Chitose
Eighth Place
431 Votes
Hiougi Karura
Thirteenth Place
176 Votes
Mikogami Matora
Fourth Place
664 Votes
Ameno Hibari
Sixth Place
455 Votes
Arahabaki Nonko
Eleventh Place
273 Votes
Shigaraki Koyuzu
Twelfth Place
248 Votes
Yumesaki Harumu
Ninth Place
401 Votes
Fushiguro Yaya
Fourteenth Place
101 Votes
Todoroki Shion
Seventh Place
443 Votes
Shinto Oboro
Tenth Place
398 Votes
Fuyuzora Kogarashi

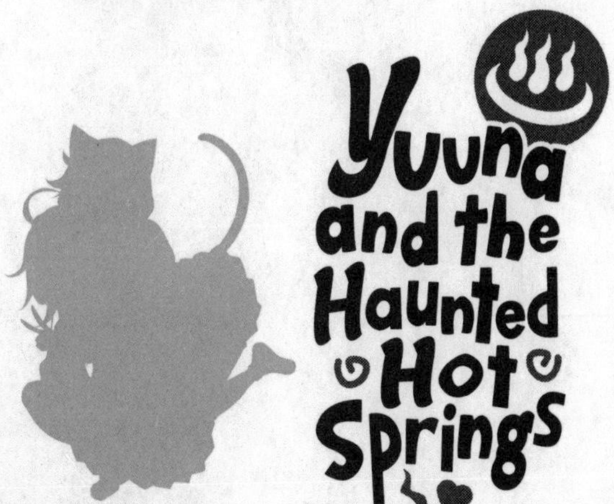

Yuuna and the Haunted Hot Springs

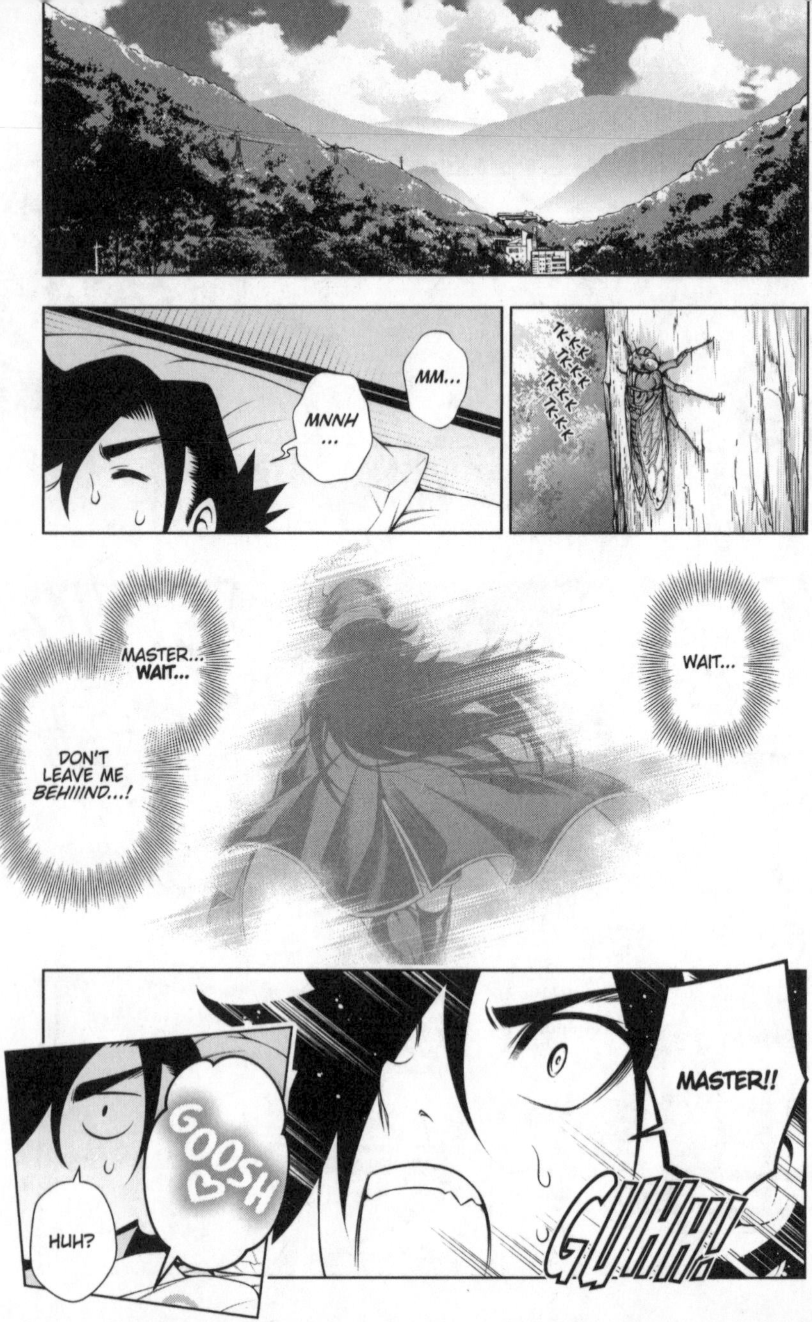
TK-K-K TK-K-K TK-K-K TK-K-K
MM...
MNNH ...
WAIT...
MASTER... WAIT...
DON'T LEAVE ME BEHIIIND...!
MASTER!!
GUHH!
GOOSH ♡
HUH?

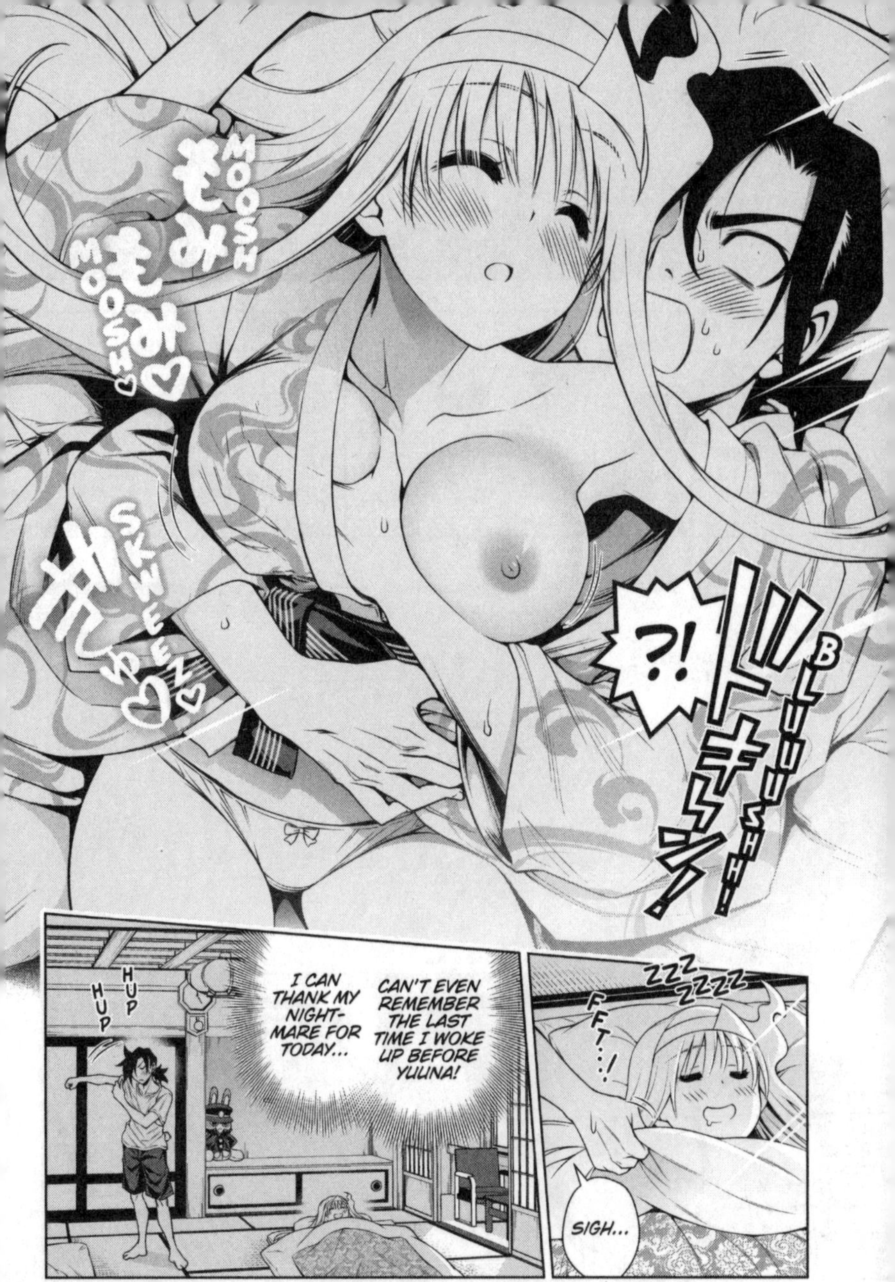
MOOSH MOOSH ♡
SKWEEZ ♡
?!
BLUUUSHH!
ZZZ ZZZZZ
FFT..!
SIGH...
I CAN THANK MY NIGHT-MARE FOR TODAY...
CAN'T EVEN REMEMBER THE LAST TIME I WOKE UP BEFORE YUUNA!
HUP HUP
HUP

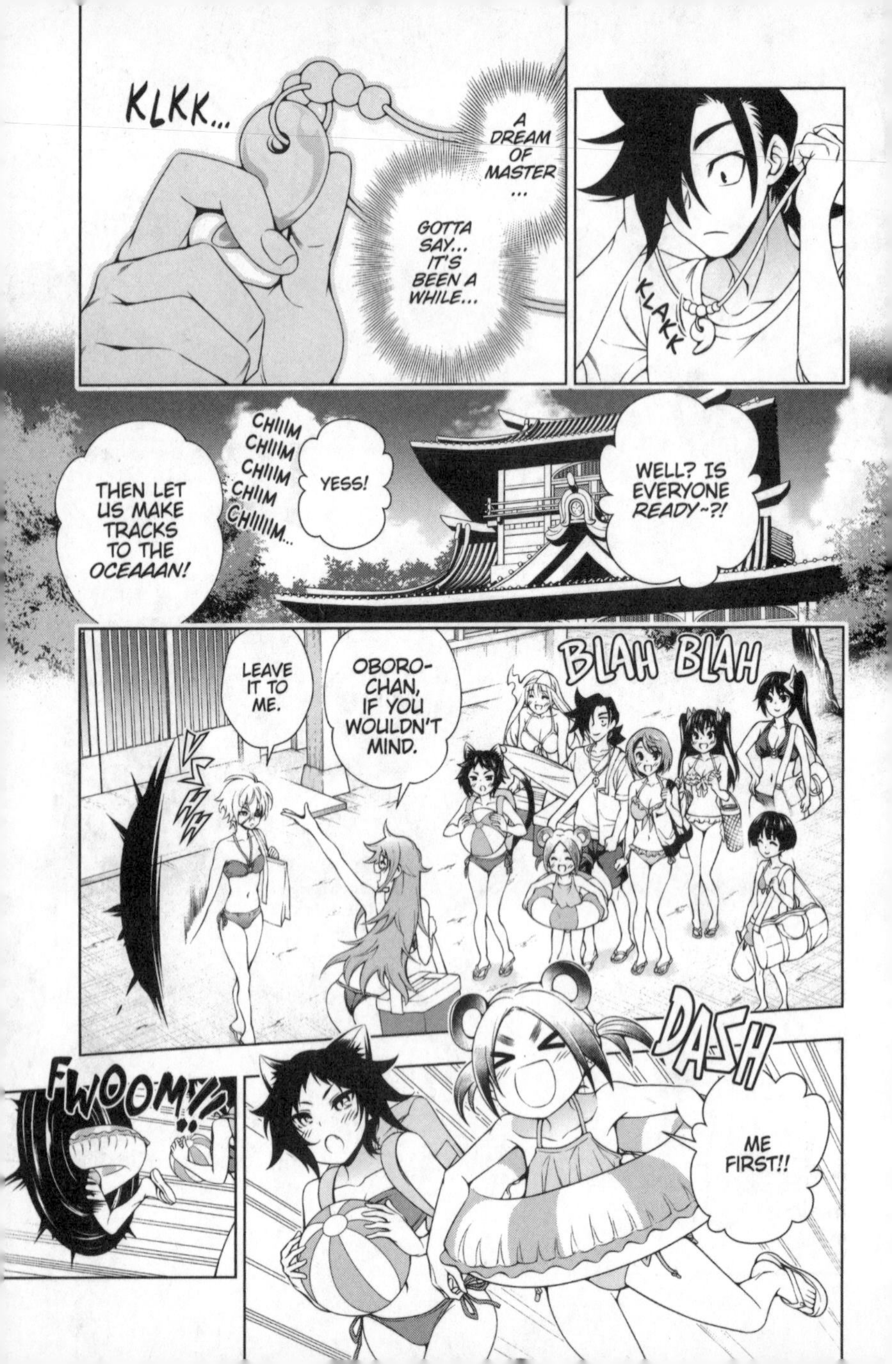
KLAKK
KLKK...
A DREAM OF MASTER...
GOTTA SAY... IT'S BEEN A WHILE...
WELL? IS EVERYONE READY~?!
YESS!
CHIIIM CHIIIM CHIIIM CHIIM CHIIIIM...
THEN LET US MAKE TRACKS TO THE OCEAAAN!
BLAH BLAH
OBORO-CHAN, IF YOU WOULDN'T MIND.
LEAVE IT TO ME.
DASH
ME FIRST!!
FWOOM!!

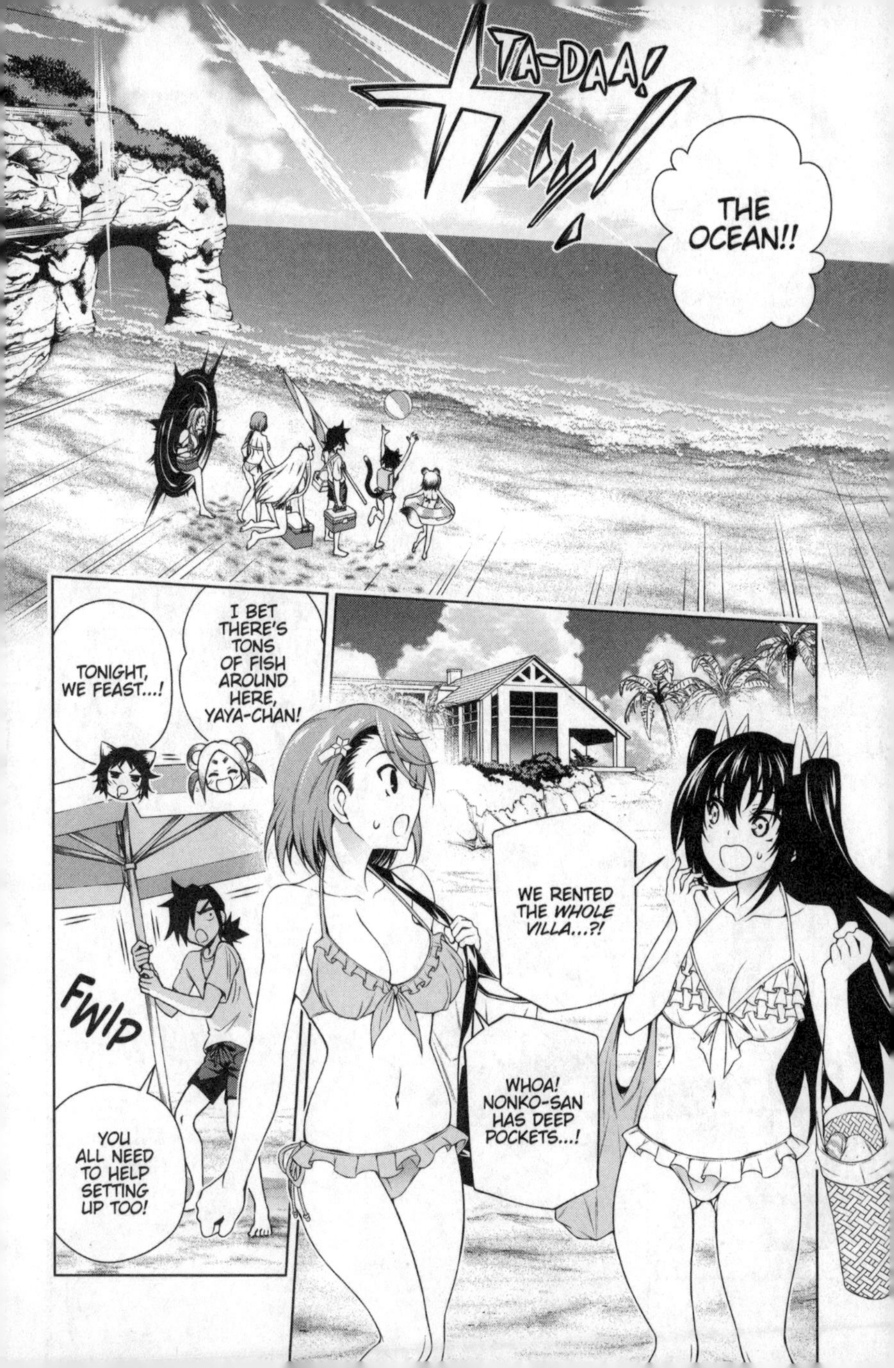
TA-DAA!
THE OCEAN!!
WE RENTED THE *WHOLE* VILLA...?!
WHOA! NONKO-SAN HAS DEEP POCKETS...!
I BET THERE'S TONS OF FISH AROUND HERE, YAYA-CHAN!
TONIGHT, WE FEAST...!
FWIP
YOU ALL NEED TO HELP SETTING UP TOO!

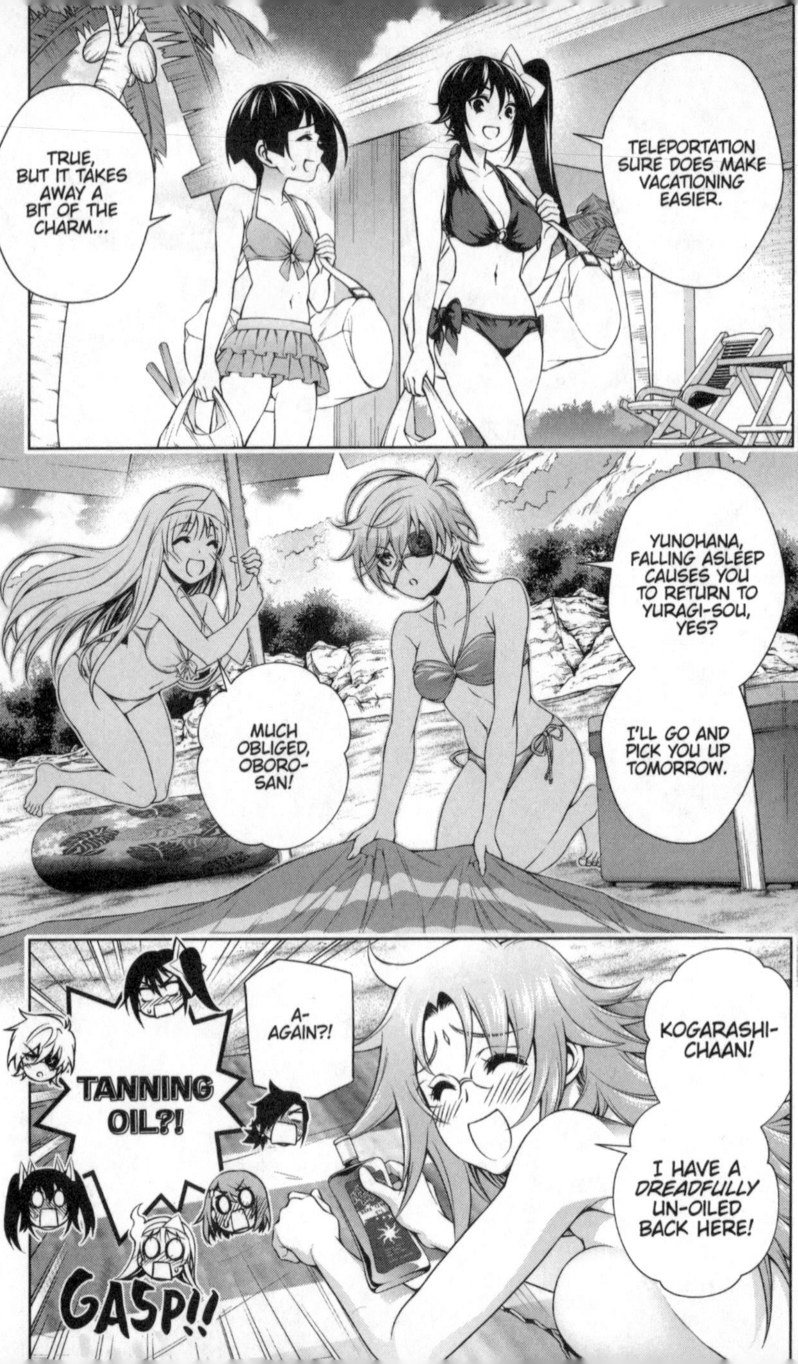
TELEPORTATION SURE DOES MAKE VACATIONING EASIER.
TRUE, BUT IT TAKES AWAY A BIT OF THE CHARM...
YUNOHANA, FALLING ASLEEP CAUSES YOU TO RETURN TO YURAGI-SOU, YES?
I'LL GO AND PICK YOU UP TOMORROW.
MUCH OBLIGED, OBORO-SAN!
KOGARASHI-CHAAN!
I HAVE A DREADFULLY UN-OILED BACK HERE!
A-AGAIN?!
TANNING OIL?!
GASP!!

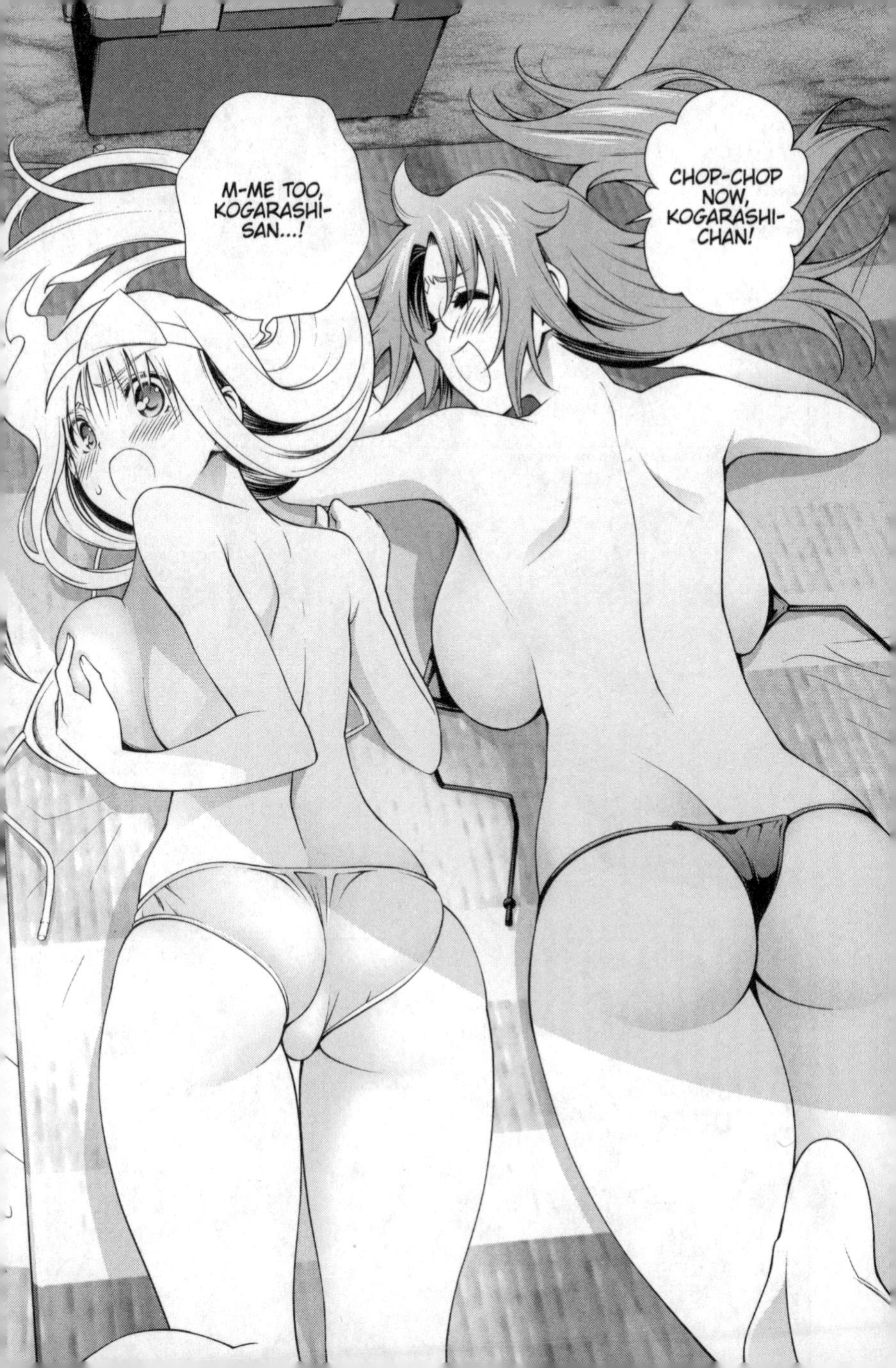
CHOP-CHOP NOW, KOGARASHI-CHAN!
M-ME TOO, KOGARASHI-SAN...!

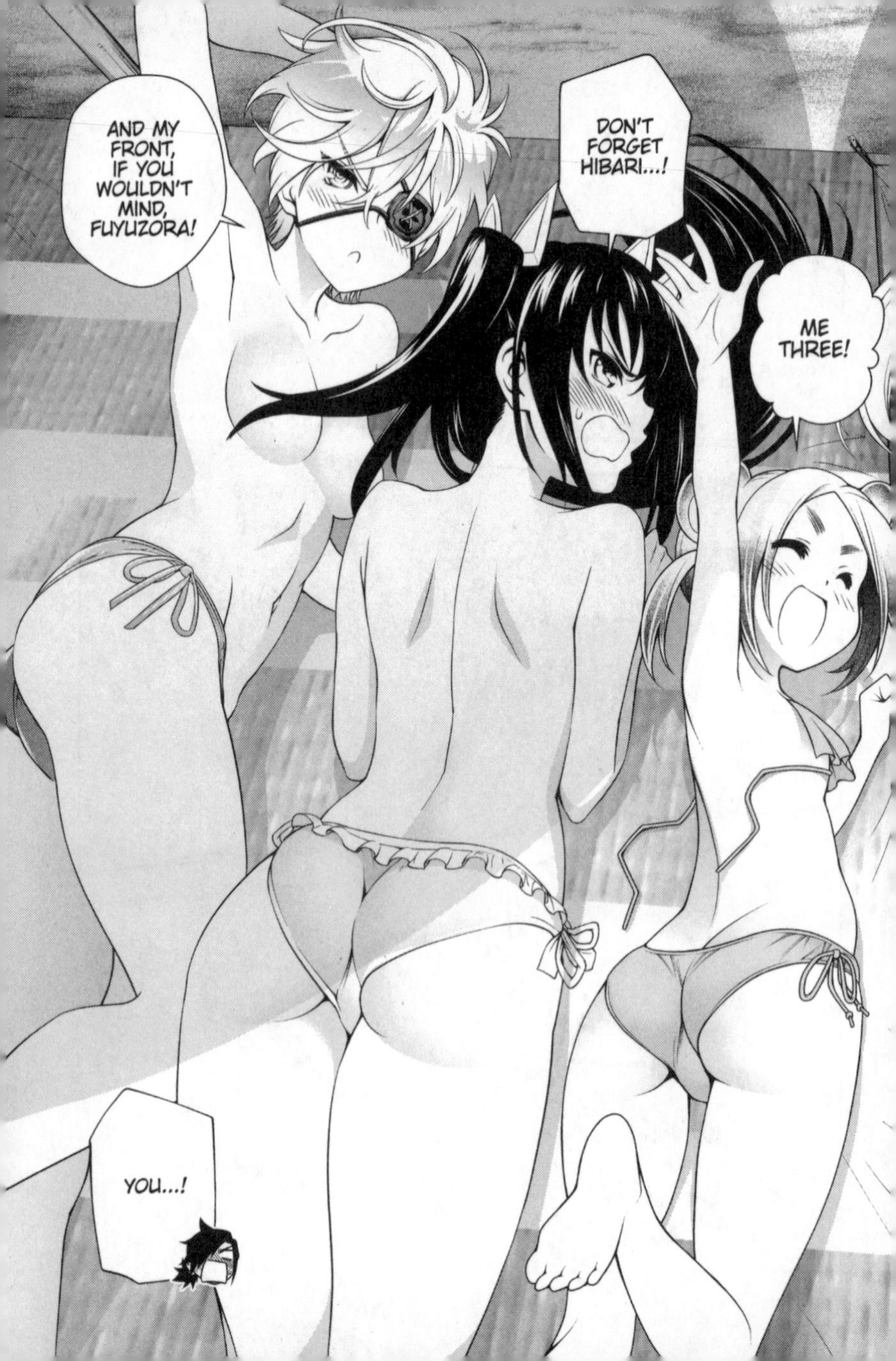
DON'T FORGET HIBARI...!
ME THREE!
AND MY FRONT, IF YOU WOULDN'T MIND, FUYUZORA!
YOU...!

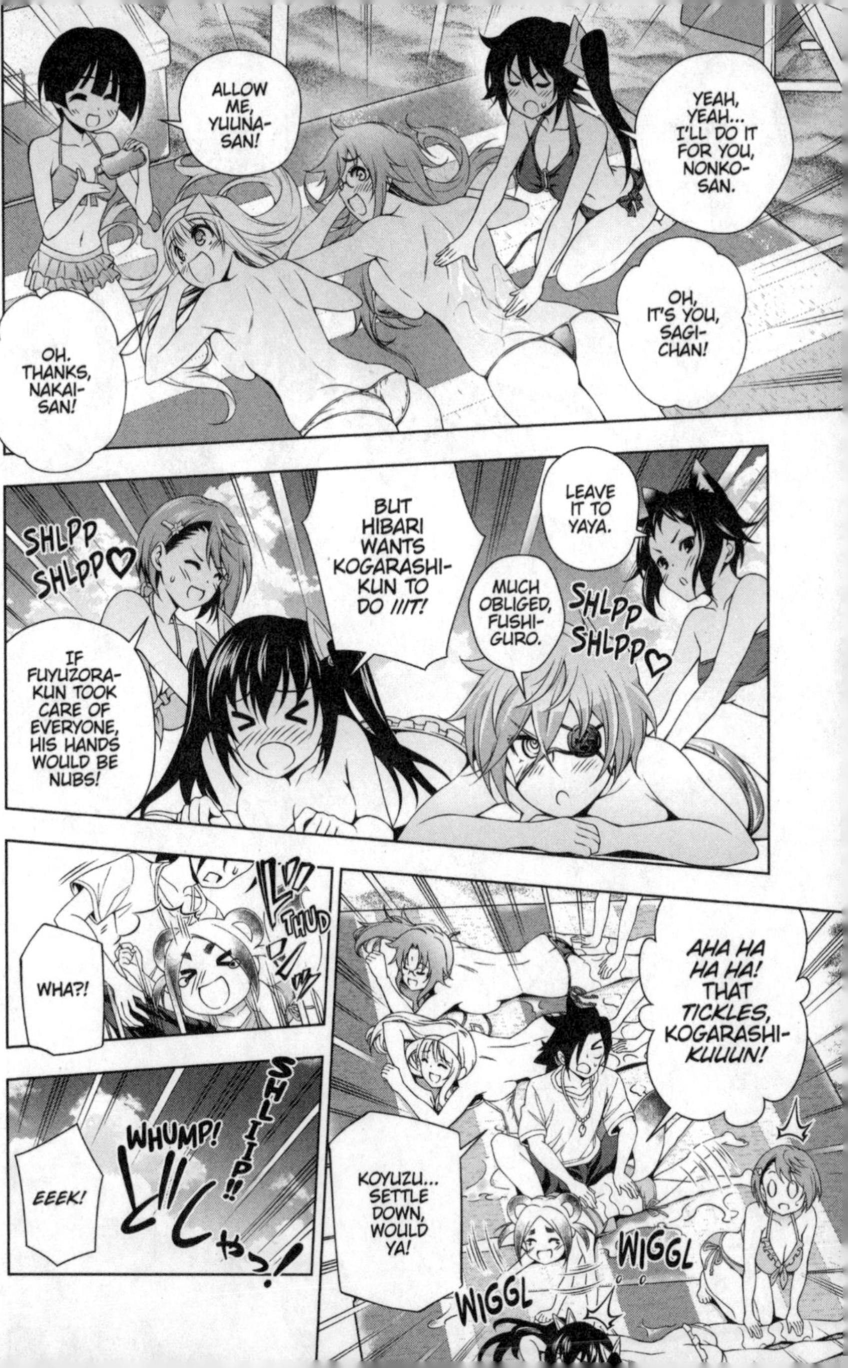
YEAH, YEAH... I'LL DO IT FOR YOU, NONKO-SAN.
ALLOW ME, YUUNA-SAN!
OH, IT'S YOU, SAGI-CHAN!
OH. THANKS, NAKAI-SAN!
LEAVE IT TO YAYA.
BUT HIBARI WANTS KOGARASHI-KUN TO DO IIIT!
SHLPP SHLPP♡
MUCH OBLIGED, FUSHI-GURO.
SHLPP SHLPP♡
IF FUYUZORA-KUN TOOK CARE OF EVERYONE, HIS HANDS WOULD BE NUBS!
AHA HA HA HA! THAT TICKLES, KOGARASHI-KUUUN!
KOYUZU... SETTLE DOWN, WOULD YA!
WIGGL
WIGGL
THUD
WHA?!
SHLIIIP!!
WHUMP!
どしゃっ!
EEEK!

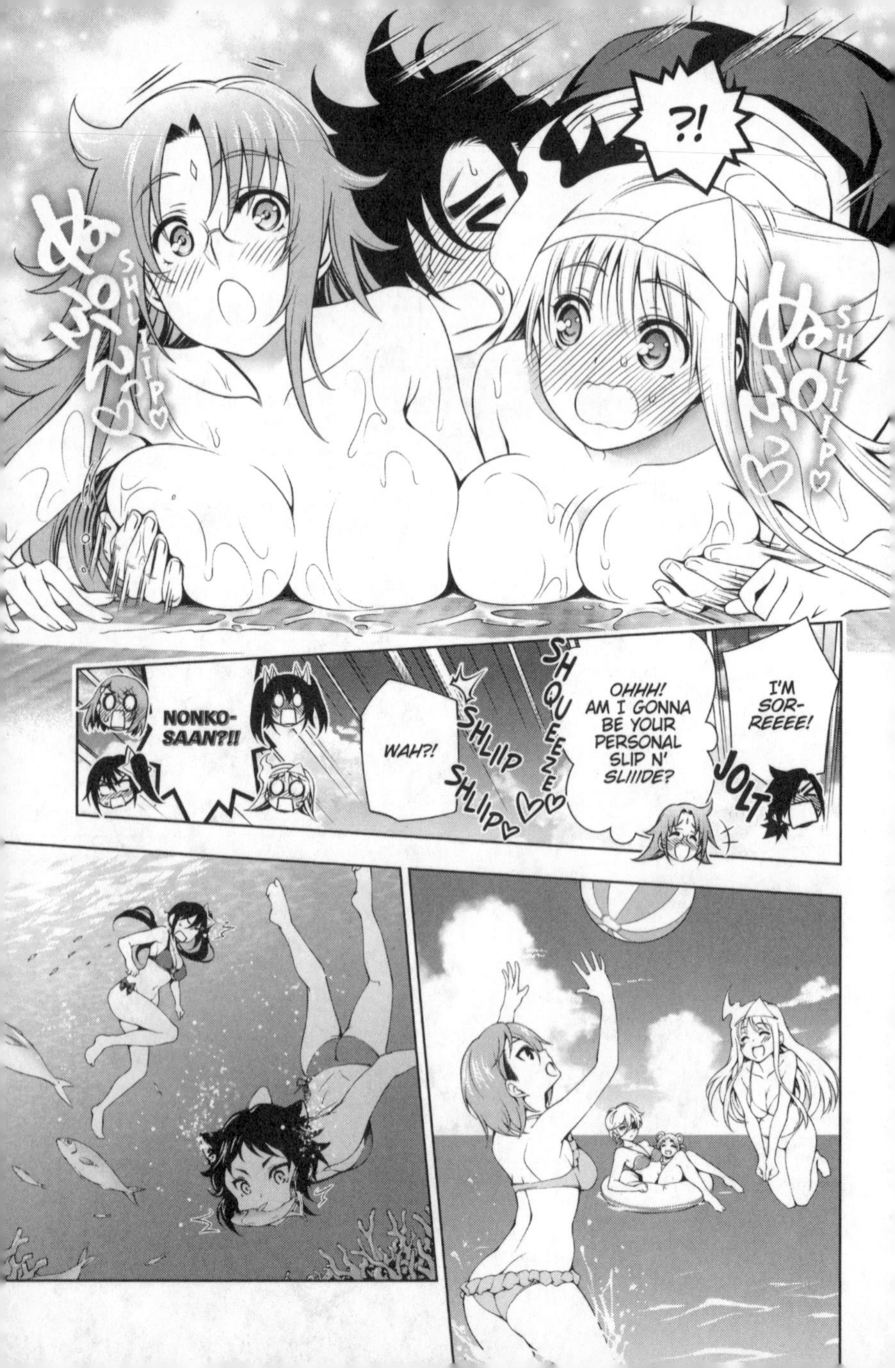
?!
ぬぷん
SHLIIP♡
ぬぷん
SHLIIP♡
I'M SOR-REEEE!
JOLT
OHHH! AM I GONNA BE YOUR PERSONAL SLIP N' SLIIIDE?
SHQUEEZE♡
SHLIIP
SHLIIP♡
WAH?!
NONKO-SAAN?!!

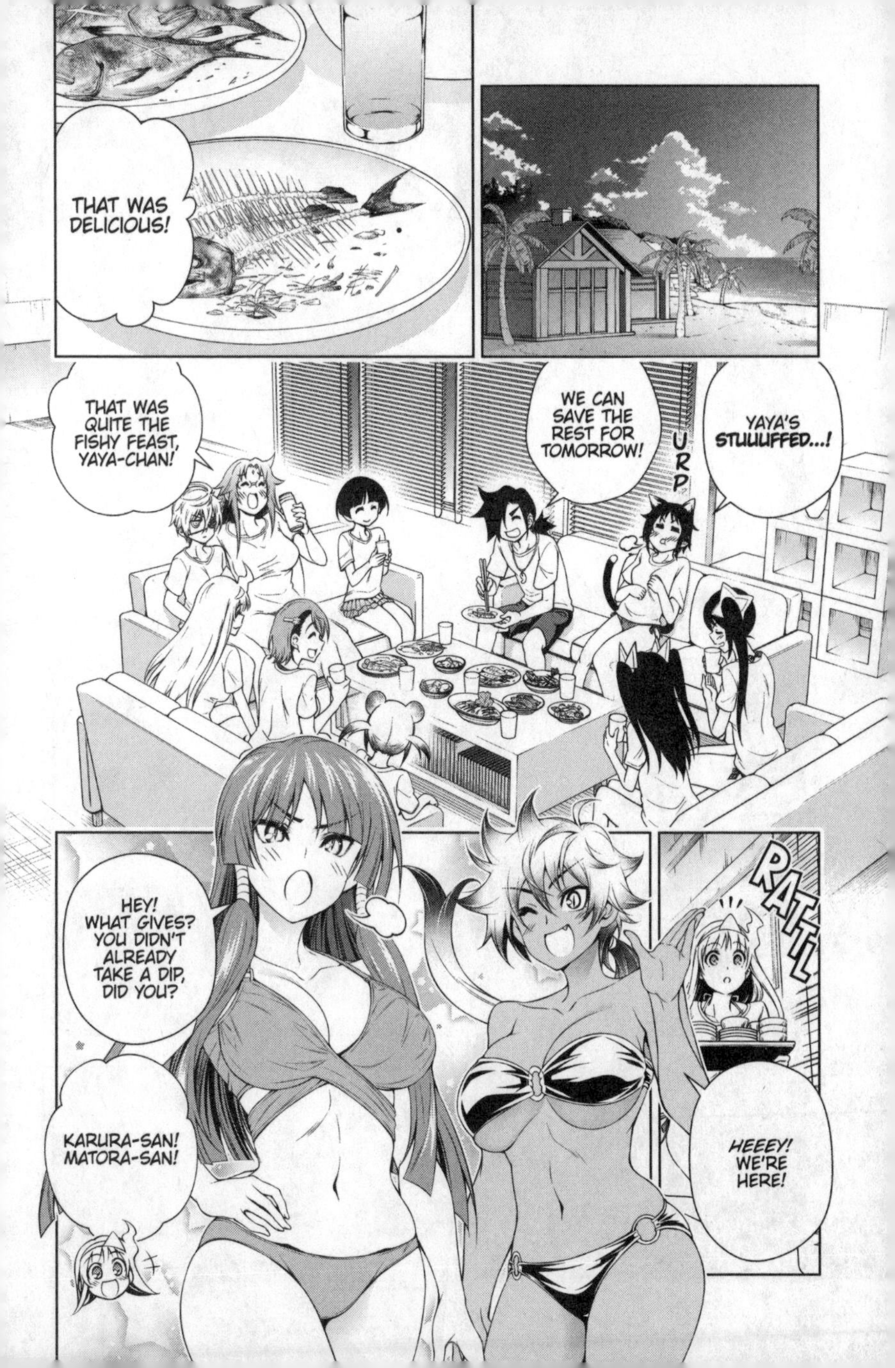
THAT WAS DELICIOUS!
YAYA'S STUUUFFED...!
URP
WE CAN SAVE THE REST FOR TOMORROW!
THAT WAS QUITE THE FISHY FEAST, YAYA-CHAN!
RATTL
HEEEY! WE'RE HERE!
HEY! WHAT GIVES? YOU DIDN'T ALREADY TAKE A DIP, DID YOU?
KARURA-SAN! MATORA-SAN!

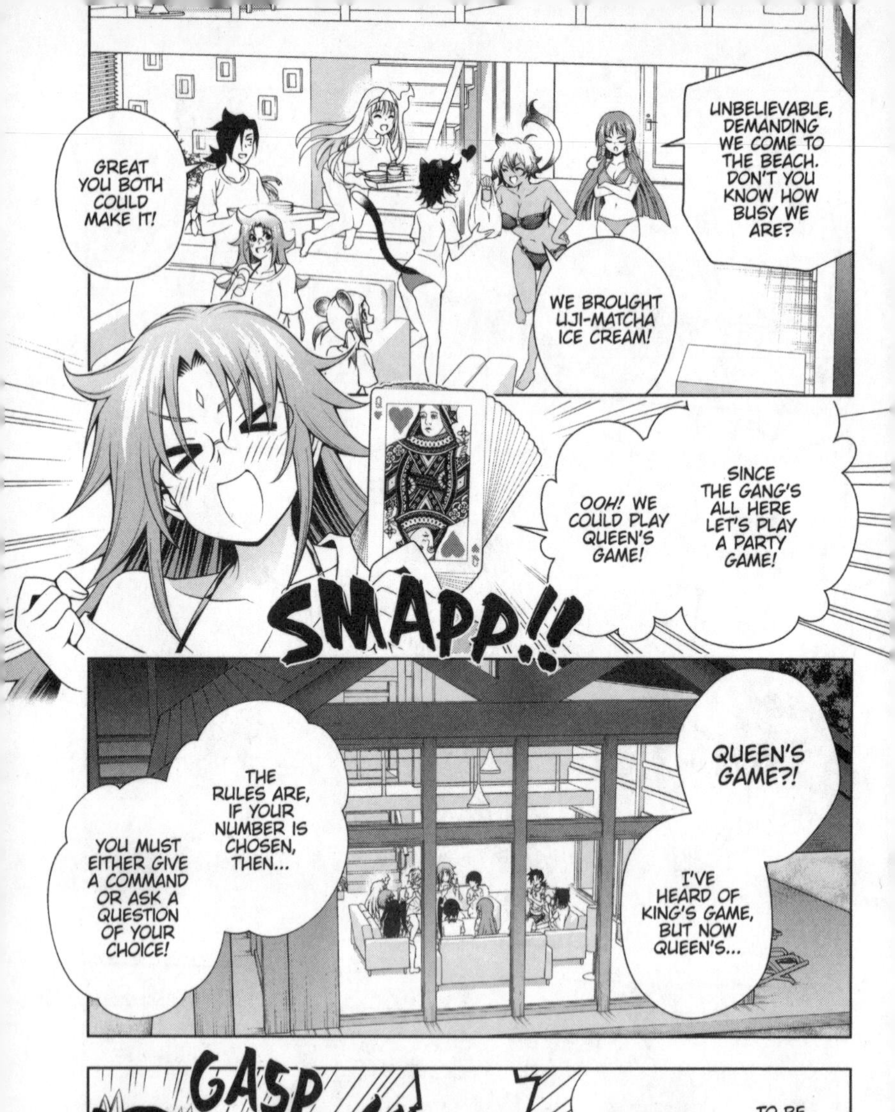
UNBELIEVABLE, DEMANDING WE COME TO THE BEACH. DON'T YOU KNOW HOW BUSY WE ARE?
WE BROUGHT UJI-MATCHA ICE CREAM!
GREAT YOU BOTH COULD MAKE IT!
SINCE THE GANG'S ALL HERE LET'S PLAY A PARTY GAME!
OOH! WE COULD PLAY QUEEN'S GAME!
SMAPP!!
QUEEN'S GAME?!
I'VE HEARD OF KING'S GAME, BUT NOW QUEEN'S...
THE RULES ARE, IF YOUR NUMBER IS CHOSEN, THEN...
YOU MUST EITHER GIVE A COMMAND OR ASK A QUESTION OF YOUR CHOICE!
TO BE HONEST, I DON'T REALLY KNOW THE RULES WELL.
BUT IF THE QUESTIONS ARE ABOUT LOVE THE GAME GETS EXCITING QUICK!
LUH... LOVE?!
GASP...!!!

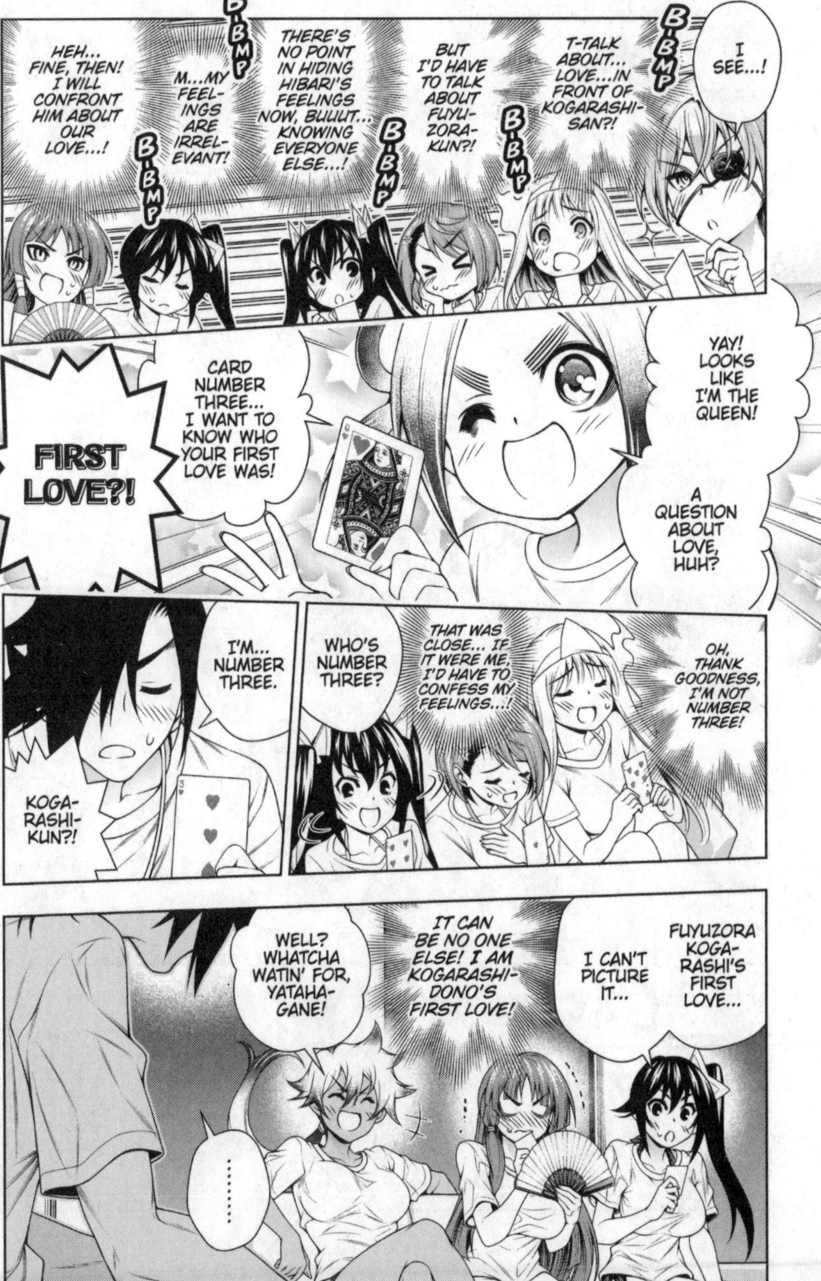
I SEE...!
B-BMP
T-TALK ABOUT... LOVE...IN FRONT OF KOGARASHI-SAN?!
B-BMP
BUT I'D HAVE TO TALK ABOUT FUYUZORA-KUN?!
B-BMP
THERE'S NO POINT IN HIDING HIBARI'S FEELINGS NOW, BUUUT... KNOWING EVERYONE ELSE...!
B-BMP
M...MY FEELINGS ARE IRRELEVANT!
B-BMP
HEH... FINE, THEN! I WILL CONFRONT HIM ABOUT OUR LOVE...!
YAY! LOOKS LIKE I'M THE QUEEN!
A QUESTION ABOUT LOVE, HUH?
CARD NUMBER THREE... I WANT TO KNOW WHO YOUR FIRST LOVE WAS!
FIRST LOVE?!
OH, THANK GOODNESS, I'M NOT NUMBER THREE!
THAT WAS CLOSE... IF IT WERE ME, I'D HAVE TO CONFESS MY FEELINGS...!
WHO'S NUMBER THREE?
I'M... NUMBER THREE.
KOGARASHI-KUN?!
FUYUZORA KOGARASHI'S FIRST LOVE...
I CAN'T PICTURE IT...
IT CAN BE NO ONE ELSE! I AM KOGARASHI-DONO'S FIRST LOVE!
WELL? WHATCHA WATIN' FOR, YATAHAGANE!
......

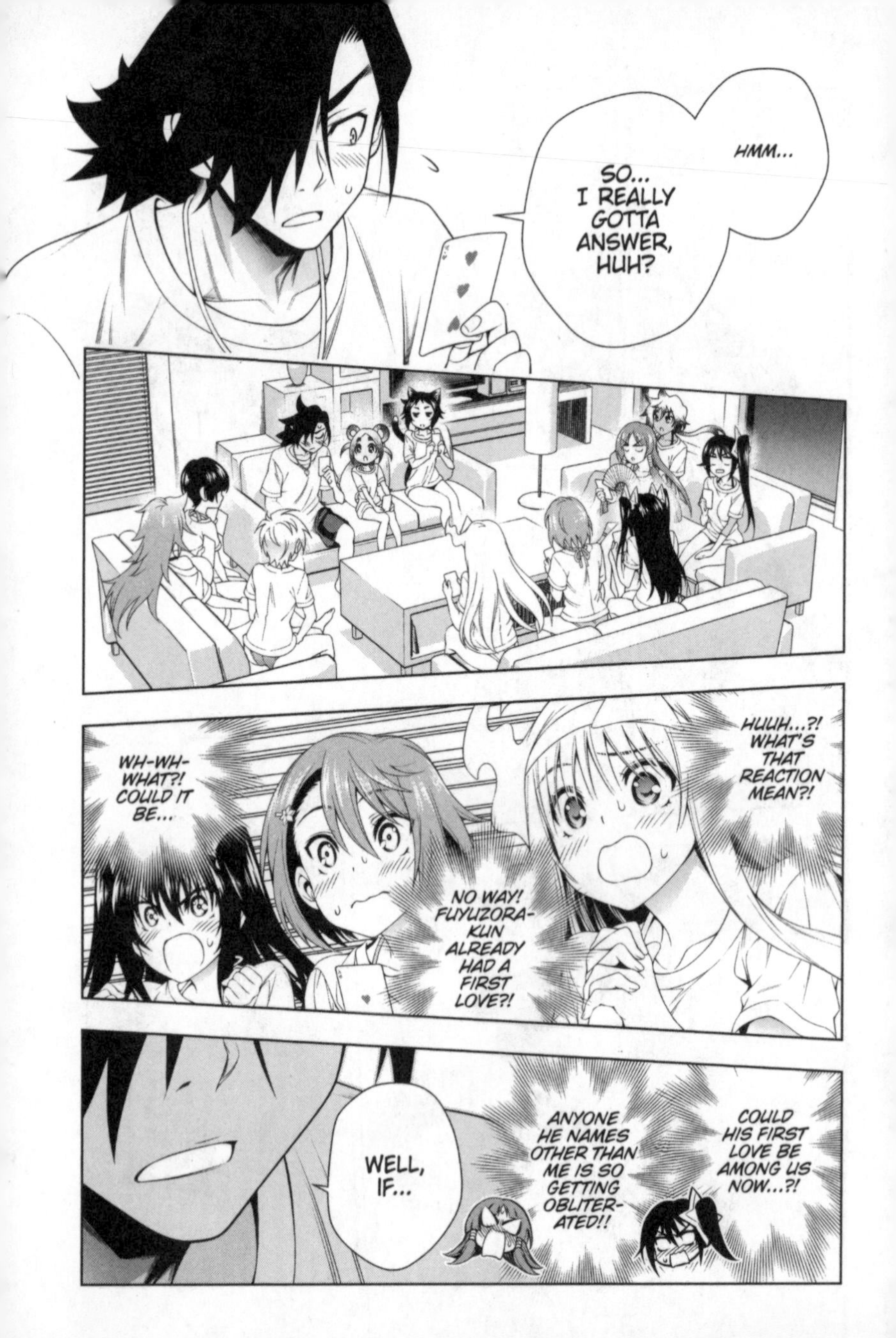
HMM...
SO... I REALLY GOTTA ANSWER, HUH?
HUUH...?! WHAT'S THAT REACTION MEAN?!
NO WAY! FUYUZORA-KUN ALREADY HAD A FIRST LOVE?!
WH-WH-WHAT?! COULD IT BE...
COULD HIS FIRST LOVE BE AMONG US NOW...?!
ANYONE HE NAMES OTHER THAN ME IS SO GETTING OBLITER-ATED!!
WELL, IF...

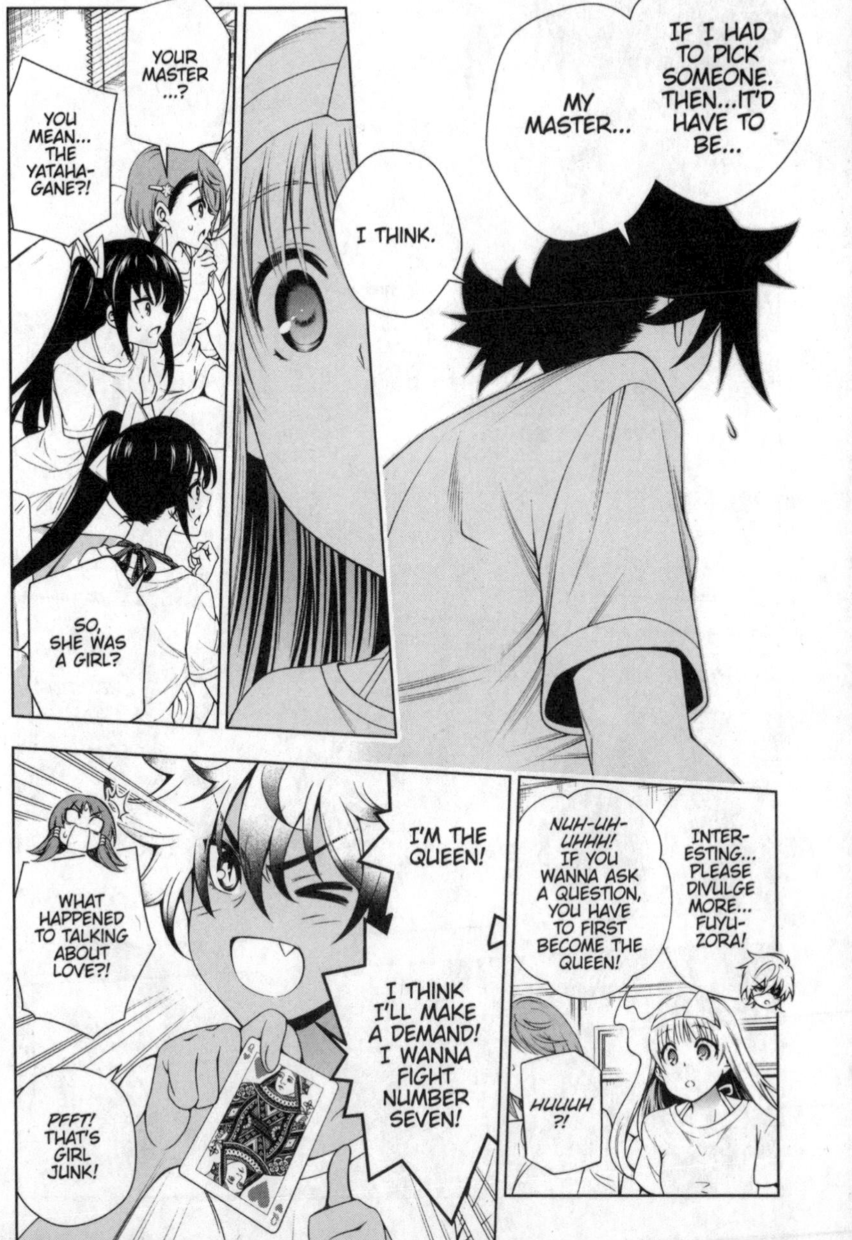
IF I HAD TO PICK SOMEONE. THEN...IT'D HAVE TO BE...
MY MASTER...
I THINK.
YOUR MASTER ...?
YOU MEAN... THE YATAHA-GANE?!
SO, SHE WAS A GIRL?
INTER-ESTING... PLEASE DIVULGE MORE... FUYU-ZORA!
NUH-UH-UHHH! IF YOU WANNA ASK A QUESTION, YOU HAVE TO FIRST BECOME THE QUEEN!
HUUUH ?!
I'M THE QUEEN!
I THINK I'LL MAKE A DEMAND! I WANNA FIGHT NUMBER SEVEN!
WHAT HAPPENED TO TALKING ABOUT LOVE?!
PFFT! THAT'S GIRL JUNK!

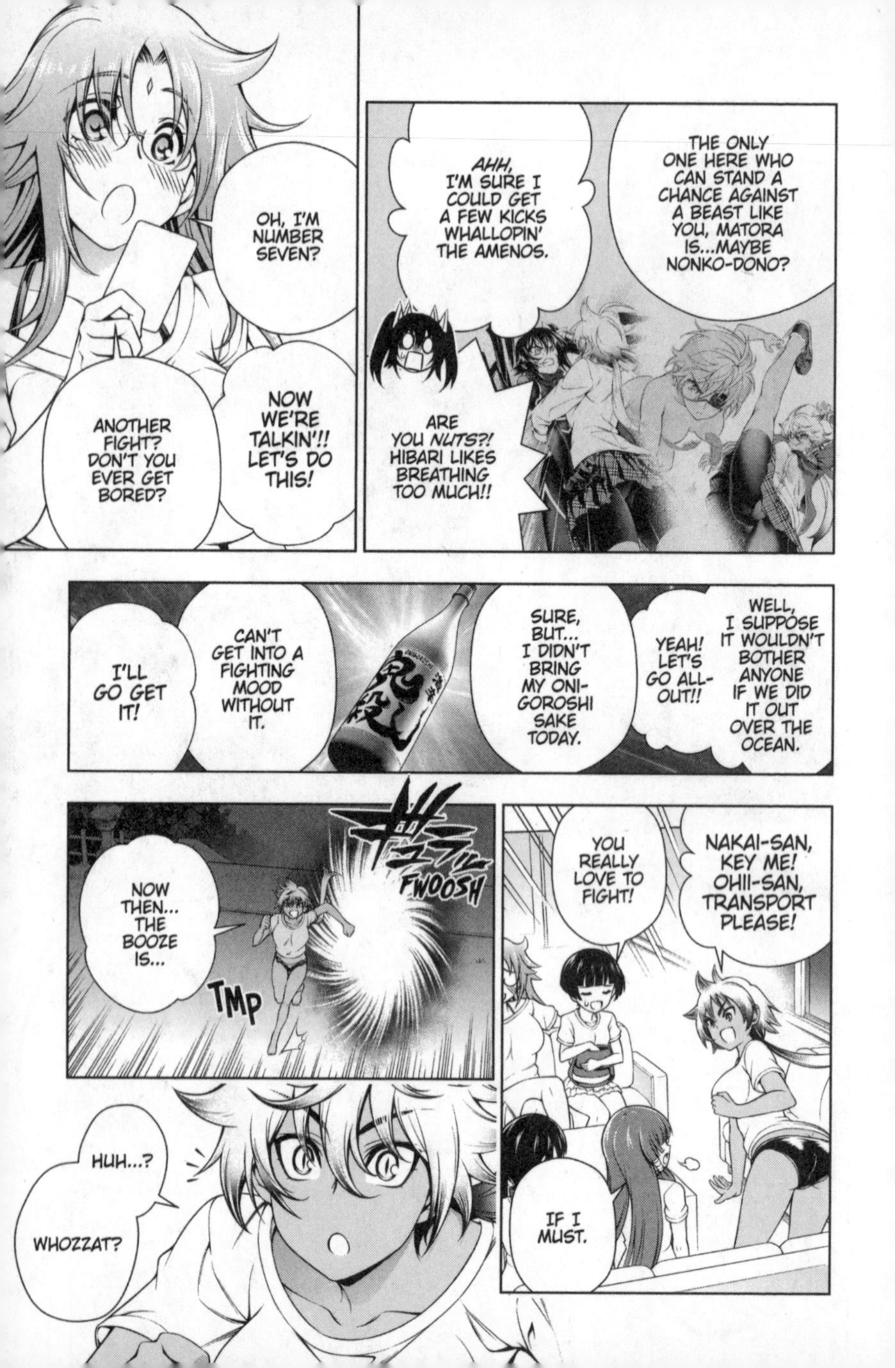
THE ONLY ONE HERE WHO CAN STAND A CHANCE AGAINST A BEAST LIKE YOU, MATORA IS...MAYBE NONKO-DONO?
AHH, I'M SURE I COULD GET A FEW KICKS WHALLOPIN' THE AMENOS.
ARE YOU *NUTS?!* HIBARI LIKES BREATHING TOO MUCH!!
OH, I'M NUMBER SEVEN?
NOW WE'RE TALKIN'!! LET'S DO THIS!
ANOTHER FIGHT? DON'T YOU EVER GET BORED?
WELL, I SUPPOSE IT WOULDN'T BOTHER ANYONE IF WE DID IT OUT OVER THE OCEAN.
YEAH! LET'S GO ALL-OUT!!
SURE, BUT... I DIDN'T BRING MY ONI-GOROSHI SAKE TODAY.
CAN'T GET INTO A FIGHTING MOOD WITHOUT IT.
I'LL GO GET IT!
NAKAI-SAN, KEY ME! OHII-SAN, TRANSPORT PLEASE!
YOU REALLY LOVE TO FIGHT!
IF I MUST.
FWOOSH
NOW THEN... THE BOOZE IS...
TMP
HUH...?
WHOZZAT?

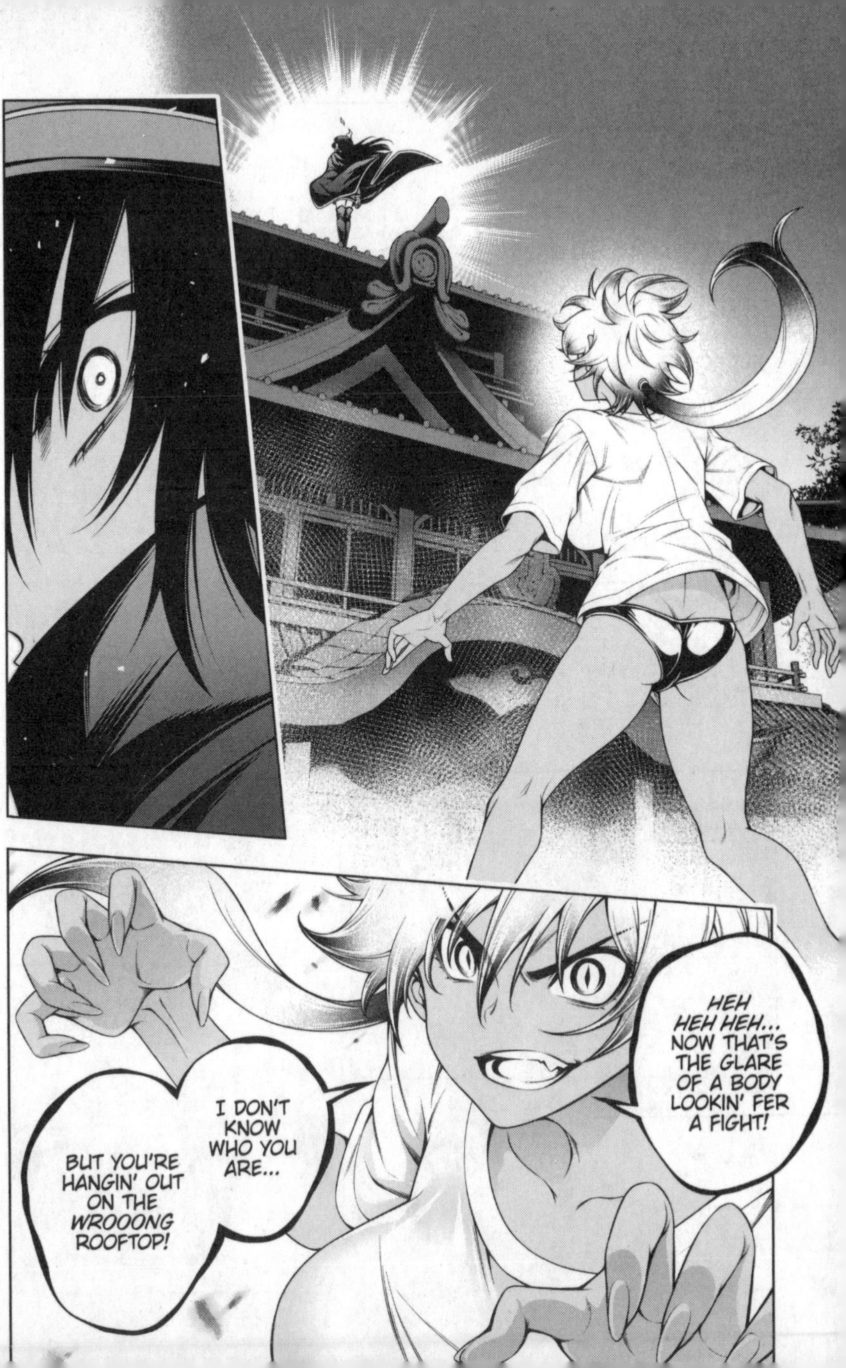
HEH HEH HEH... NOW THAT'S THE GLARE OF A BODY LOOKIN' FER A FIGHT!
I DON'T KNOW WHO YOU ARE...
BUT YOU'RE HANGIN' OUT ON THE *WROOONG* ROOFTOP!

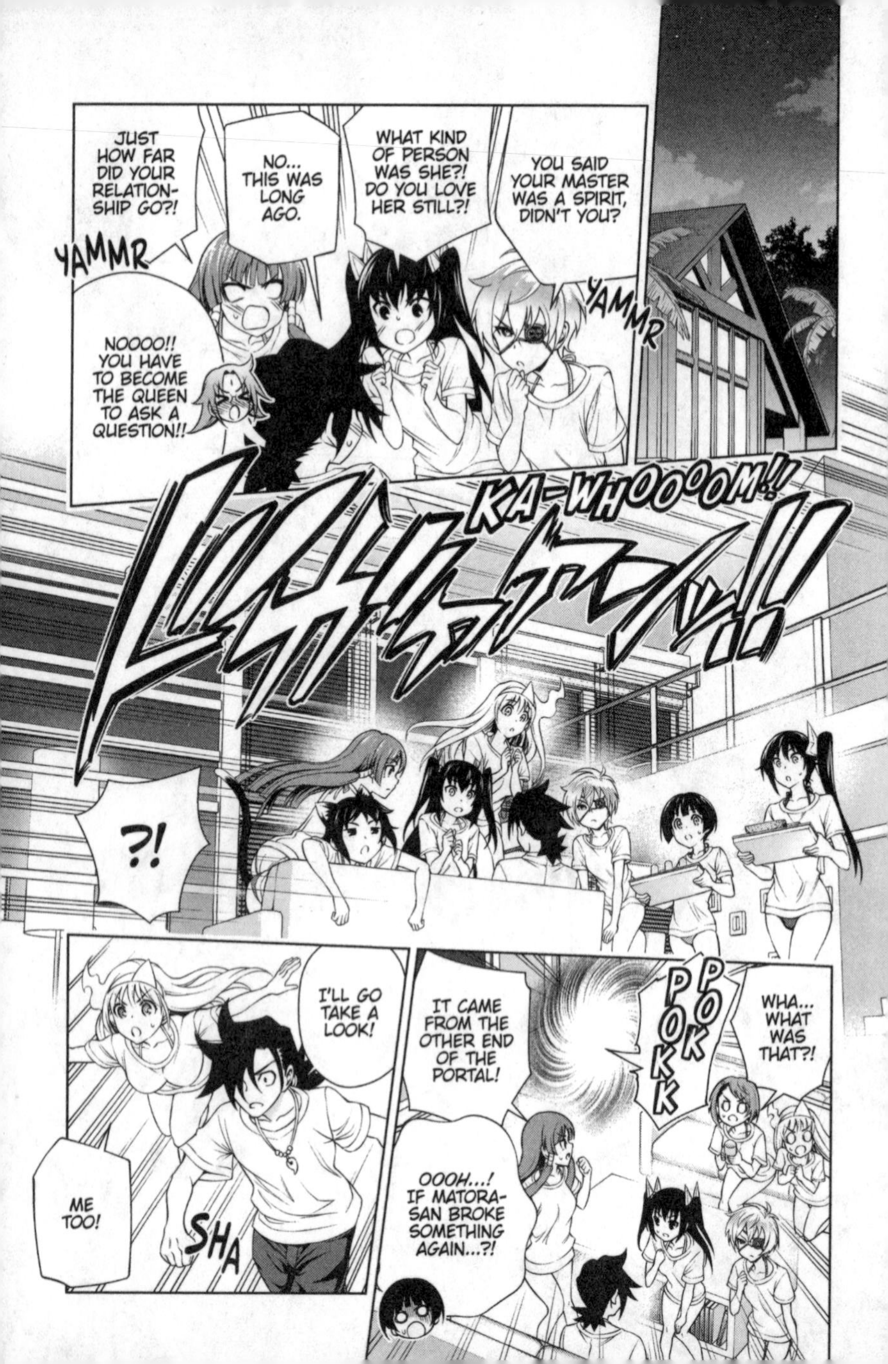
YOU SAID YOUR MASTER WAS A SPIRIT, DIDN'T YOU?
YAMMR
WHAT KIND OF PERSON WAS SHE?! DO YOU LOVE HER STILL?!
NO... THIS WAS LONG AGO.
JUST HOW FAR DID YOUR RELATION-SHIP GO?!
YAMMR
NOOOO!! YOU HAVE TO BECOME THE QUEEN TO ASK A QUESTION!!
KA-WHOOOOOM!!
?!
WHA... WHAT WAS THAT?!
POK POKK
IT CAME FROM THE OTHER END OF THE PORTAL!
OOOH...! IF MATORA-SAN BROKE SOMETHING AGAIN...?!
I'LL GO TAKE A LOOK!
ME TOO!
SHA

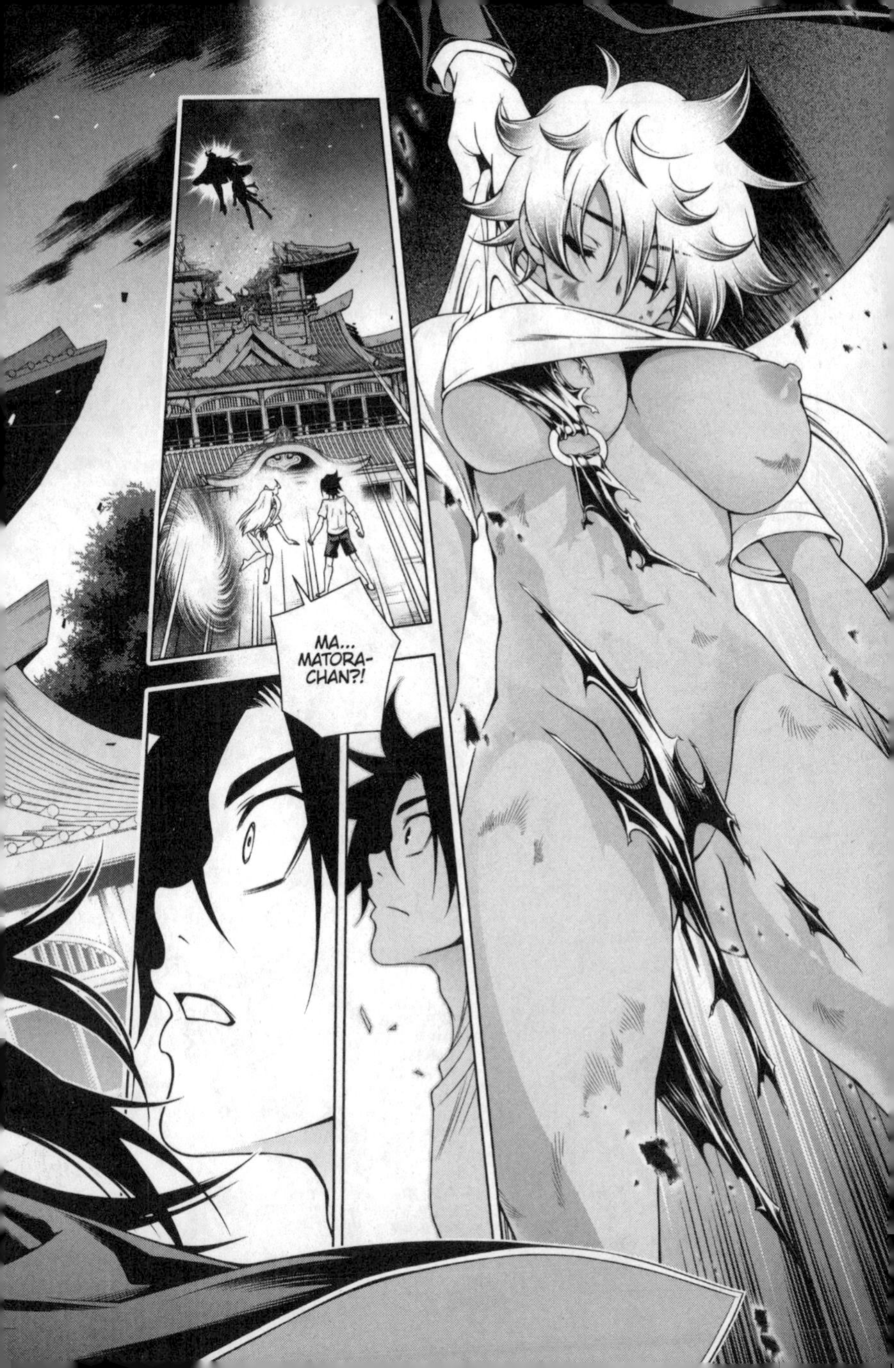
MA... MATORA-CHAN?!

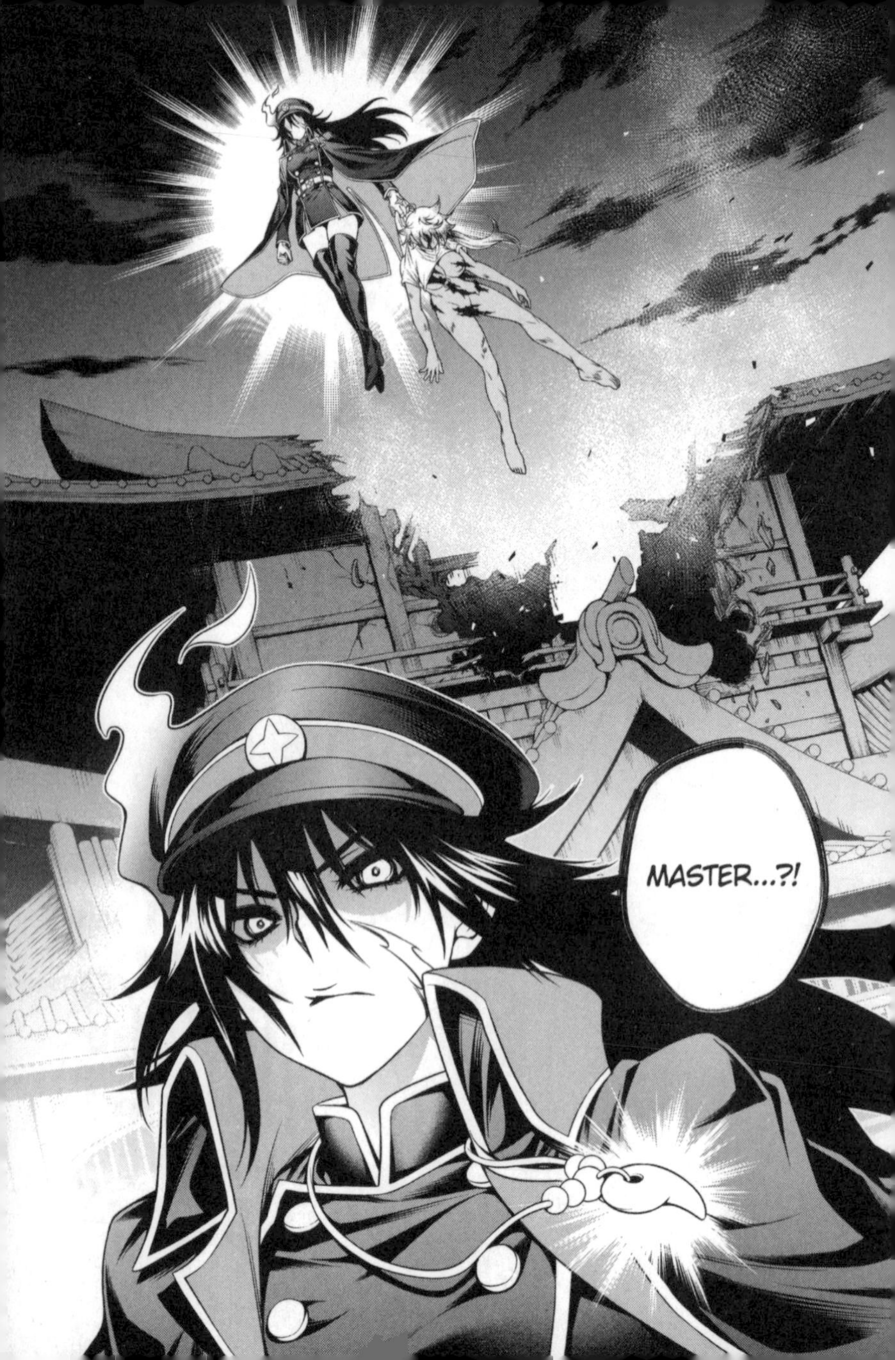
MASTER...?!

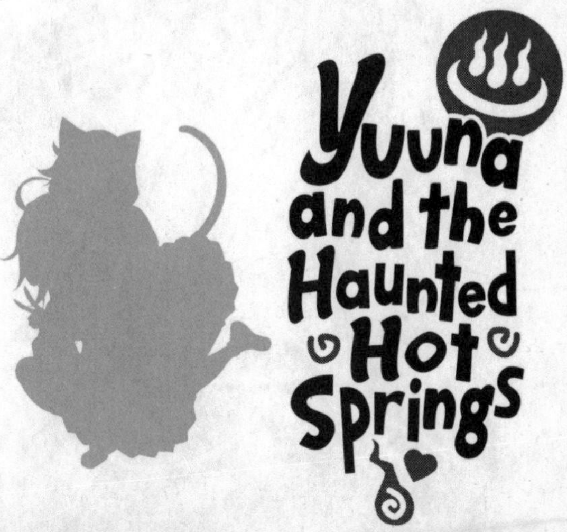

Yuuna and the Haunted Hot Springs

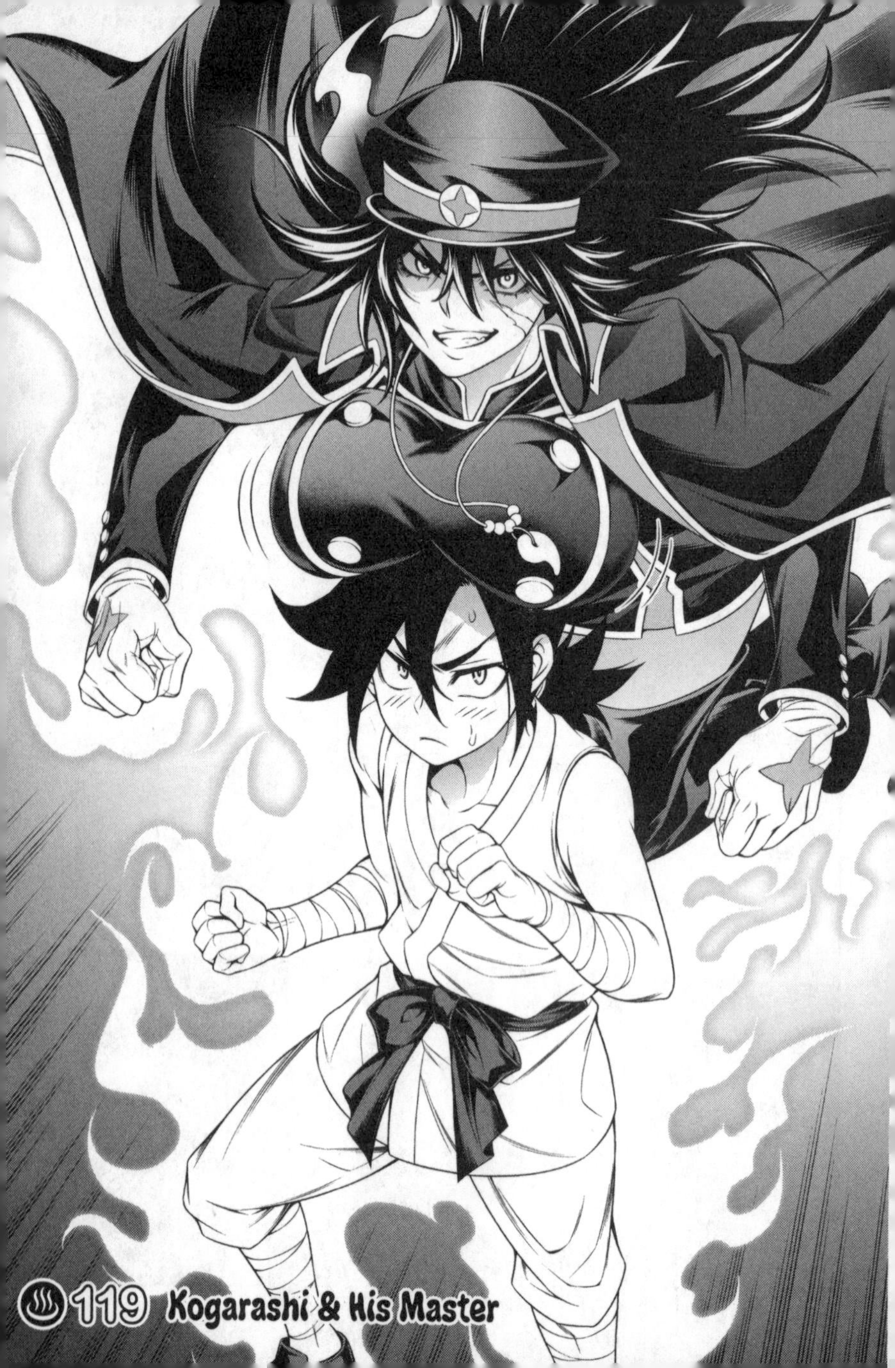
119 Kogarashi & His Master

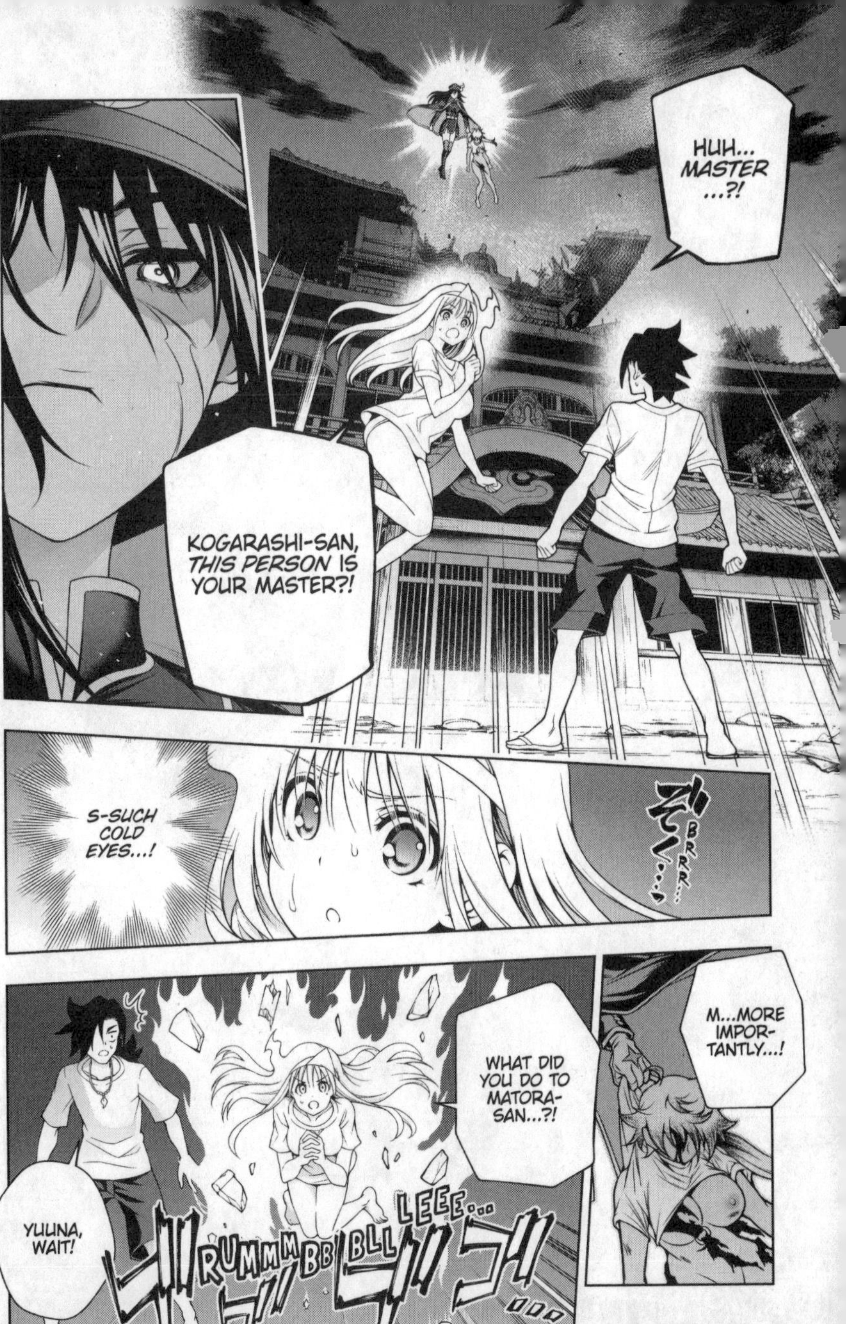
HUH... MASTER ...?!
KOGARASHI-SAN, THIS PERSON IS YOUR MASTER?!
BRRR...
S-SUCH COLD EYES...!
M...MORE IMPOR-TANTLY...!
WHAT DID YOU DO TO MATORA-SAN...?!
YUUNA, WAIT!
RUMMMBBBLLLEEE...

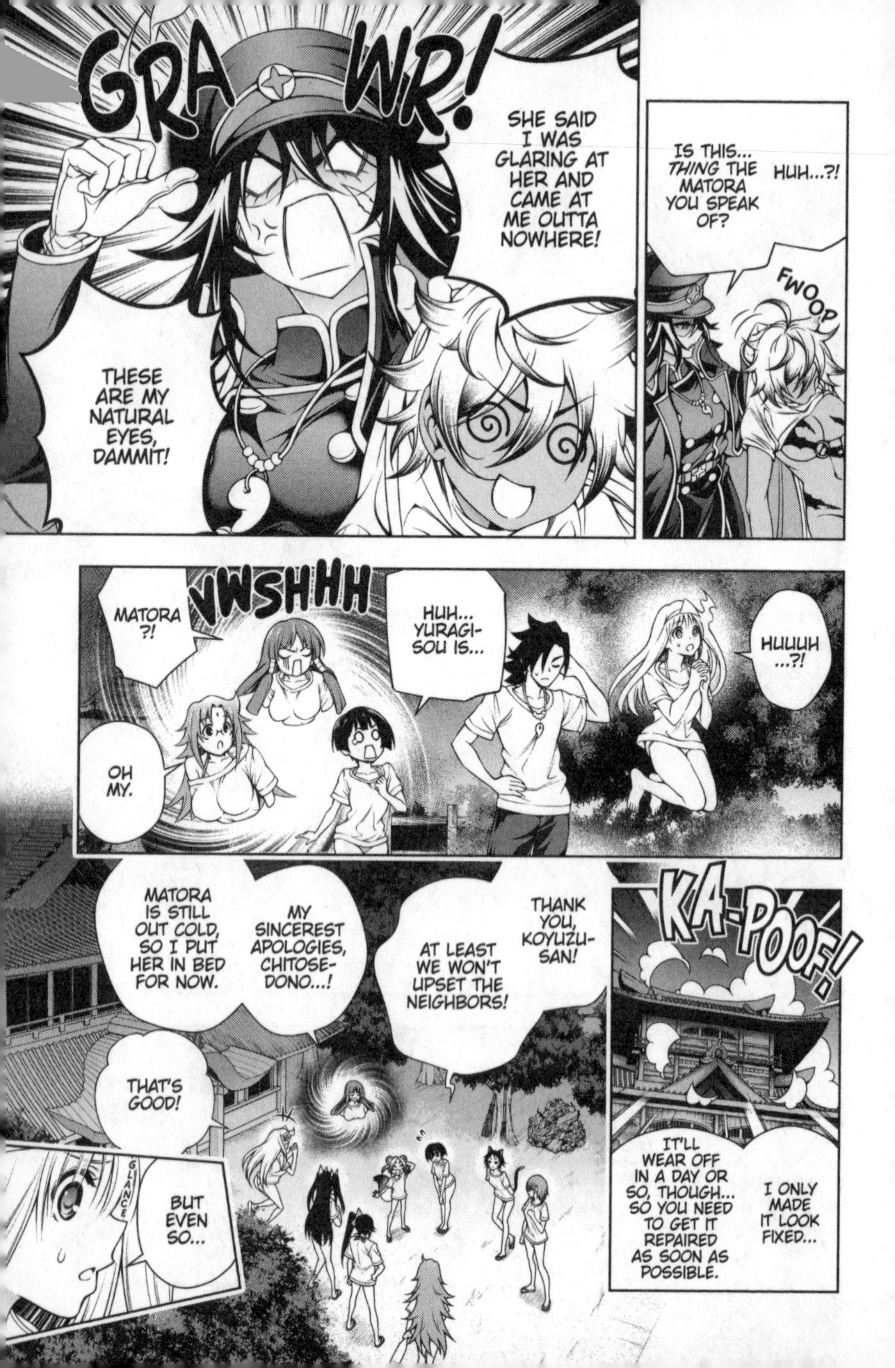
HUH...?!
IS THIS... THING THE MATORA YOU SPEAK OF?
FWOOP
GRAWR!
SHE SAID I WAS GLARING AT HER AND CAME AT ME OUTTA NOWHERE!
THESE ARE MY NATURAL EYES, DAMMIT!
HUUUH ...?!
HUH... YURAGI-SOU IS...
VWSHHH
MATORA ?!
OH MY.
KA-POOF!
I ONLY MADE IT LOOK FIXED...
IT'LL WEAR OFF IN A DAY OR SO, THOUGH... SO YOU NEED TO GET IT REPAIRED AS SOON AS POSSIBLE.
THANK YOU, KOYUZU-SAN!
AT LEAST WE WON'T UPSET THE NEIGHBORS!
MY SINCEREST APOLOGIES, CHITOSE-DONO...!
MATORA IS STILL OUT COLD, SO I PUT HER IN BED FOR NOW.
THAT'S GOOD!
GLANCE
BUT EVEN SO...

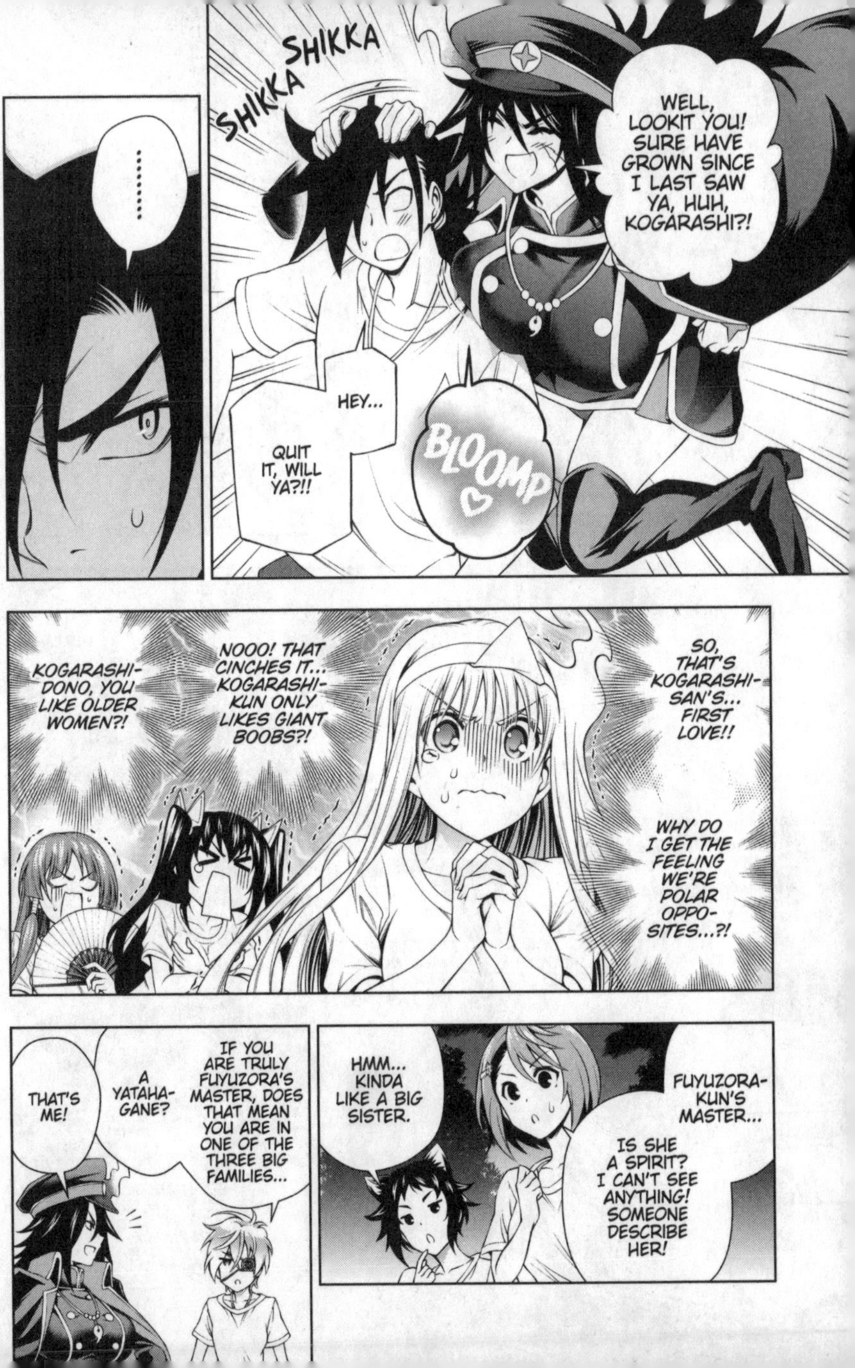
SHIKKA SHIKKA
WELL, LOOKIT YOU! SURE HAVE GROWN SINCE I LAST SAW YA, HUH, KOGARASHI?!
HEY... QUIT IT, WILL YA?!!
BLOOMP
......
SO, THAT'S KOGARASHI-SAN'S... FIRST LOVE!!
WHY DO I GET THE FEELING WE'RE POLAR OPPOSITES...?!
NOOO! THAT CINCHES IT... KOGARASHI-KUN ONLY LIKES GIANT BOOBS?!
KOGARASHI-DONO, YOU LIKE OLDER WOMEN?!
FUYUZORA-KUN'S MASTER...
IS SHE A SPIRIT? I CAN'T SEE ANYTHING! SOMEONE DESCRIBE HER!
HMM... KINDA LIKE A BIG SISTER.
IF YOU ARE TRULY FUYUZORA'S MASTER, DOES THAT MEAN YOU ARE IN ONE OF THE THREE BIG FAMILIES...
A YATAHA-GANE?
THAT'S ME!

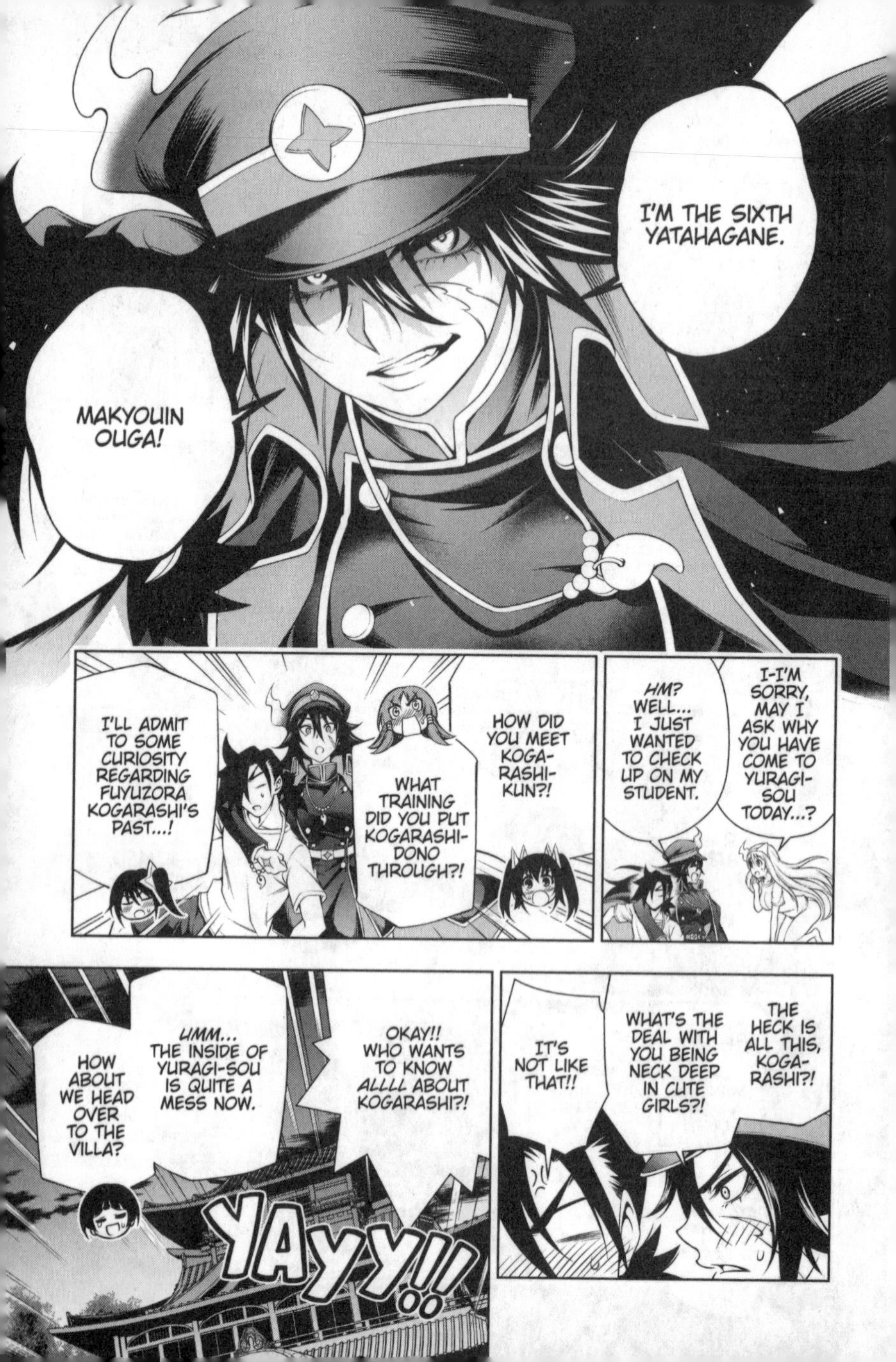
I'M THE SIXTH YATAHAGANE.
MAKYOUIN OUGA!
I-I'M SORRY, MAY I ASK WHY YOU HAVE COME TO YURAGI-SOU TODAY...?
HM? WELL... I JUST WANTED TO CHECK UP ON MY STUDENT.
HOW DID YOU MEET KOGA-RASHI-KUN?!
WHAT TRAINING DID YOU PUT KOGARASHI-DONO THROUGH?!
I'LL ADMIT TO SOME CURIOSITY REGARDING FUYUZORA KOGARASHI'S PAST...!
THE HECK IS ALL THIS, KOGA-RASHI?!
WHAT'S THE DEAL WITH YOU BEING NECK DEEP IN CUTE GIRLS?!
IT'S NOT LIKE THAT!!
OKAY!! WHO WANTS TO KNOW ALLLL ABOUT KOGARASHI?!
UMM... THE INSIDE OF YURAGI-SOU IS QUITE A MESS NOW.
HOW ABOUT WE HEAD OVER TO THE VILLA?
YAYY!!

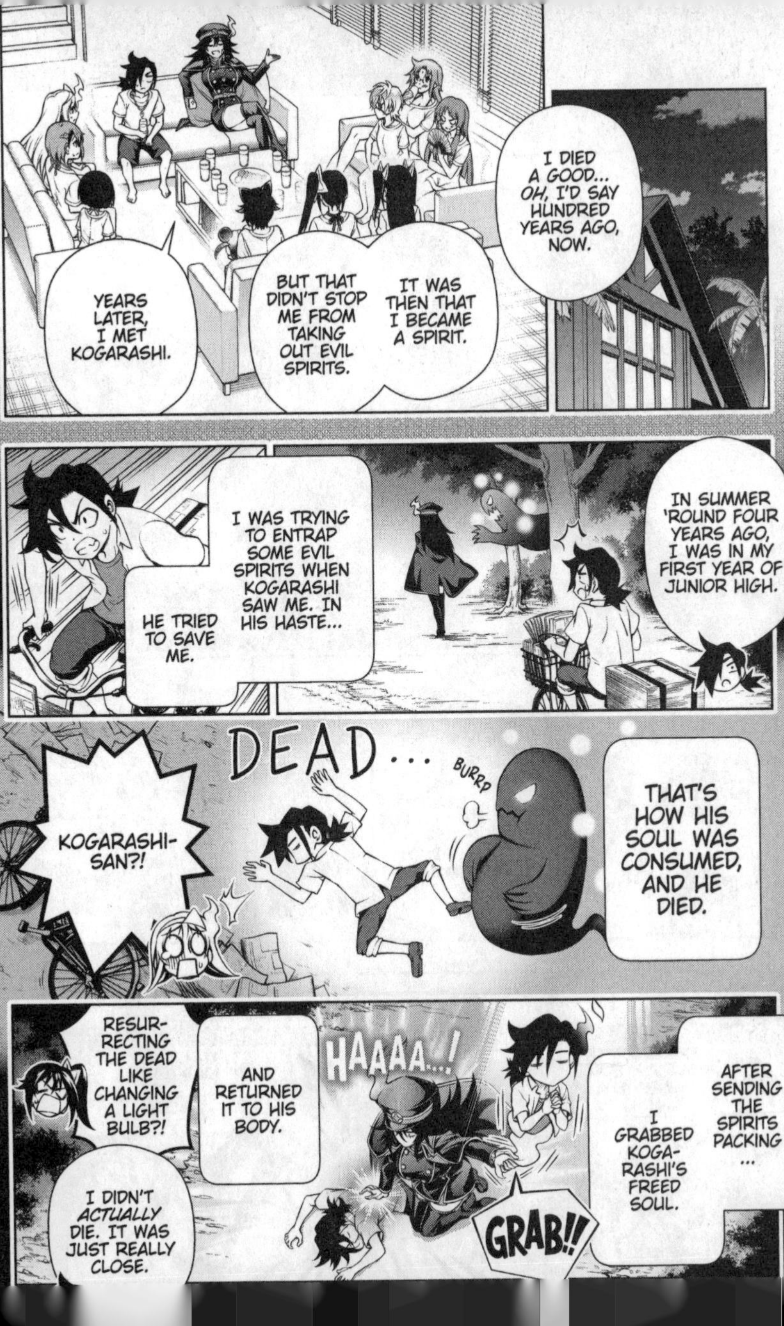
I DIED A GOOD... *OH*, I'D SAY HUNDRED YEARS AGO, NOW.
IT WAS THEN THAT I BECAME A SPIRIT.
BUT THAT DIDN'T STOP ME FROM TAKING OUT EVIL SPIRITS.
YEARS LATER, I MET KOGARASHI.
IN SUMMER 'ROUND FOUR YEARS AGO, I WAS IN MY FIRST YEAR OF JUNIOR HIGH.
I WAS TRYING TO ENTRAP SOME EVIL SPIRITS WHEN KOGARASHI SAW ME. IN HIS HASTE...
HE TRIED TO SAVE ME.
THAT'S HOW HIS SOUL WAS CONSUMED, AND HE DIED.
BURRP
DEAD...
KOGARASHI-SAN?!
AFTER SENDING THE SPIRITS PACKING...
I GRABBED KOGARASHI'S FREED SOUL.
GRAB!!
HAAAA...!
AND RETURNED IT TO HIS BODY.
RESURRECTING THE DEAD LIKE CHANGING A LIGHT BULB?!
I DIDN'T *ACTUALLY* DIE. IT WAS JUST REALLY CLOSE.

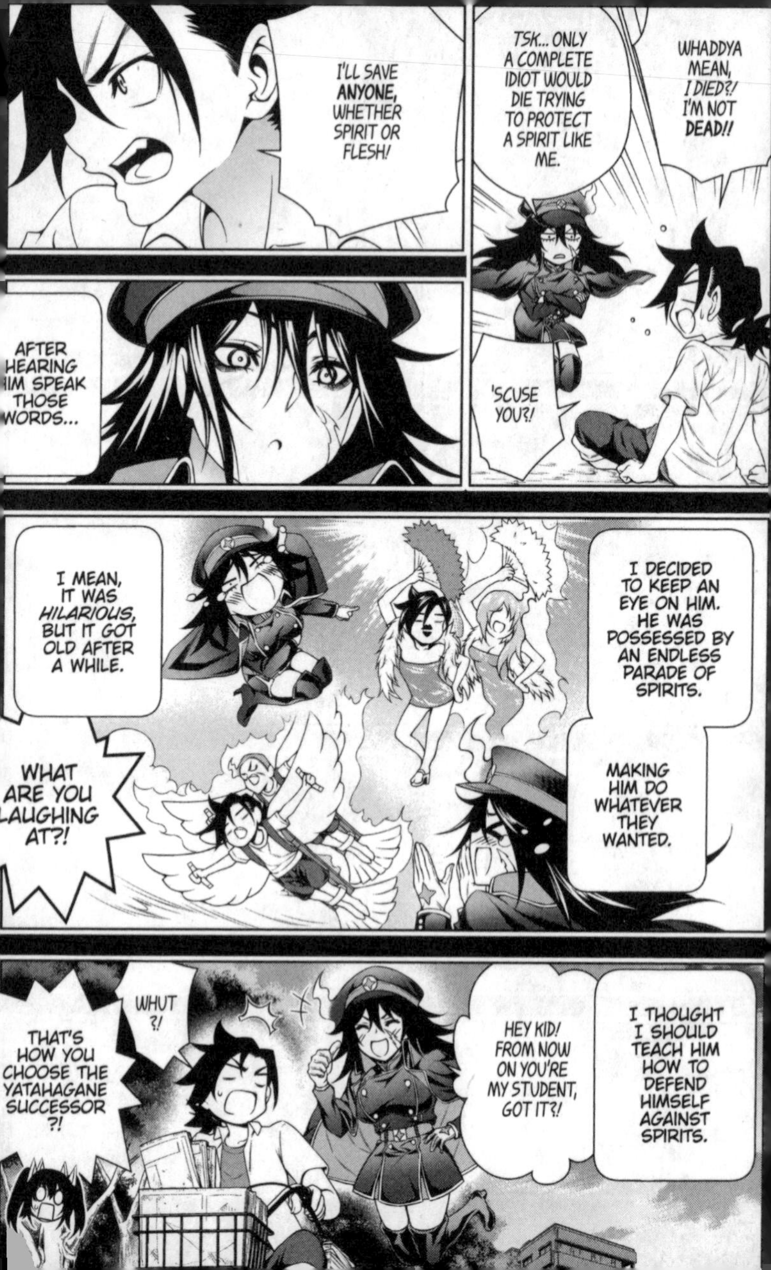
WHADDYA MEAN, I DIED?! I'M NOT DEAD!!
TSK... ONLY A COMPLETE IDIOT WOULD DIE TRYING TO PROTECT A SPIRIT LIKE ME.
'SCUSE YOU?!
I'LL SAVE ANYONE, WHETHER SPIRIT OR FLESH!
AFTER HEARING HIM SPEAK THOSE WORDS...
I DECIDED TO KEEP AN EYE ON HIM. HE WAS POSSESSED BY AN ENDLESS PARADE OF SPIRITS.
MAKING HIM DO WHATEVER THEY WANTED.
I MEAN, IT WAS HILARIOUS, BUT IT GOT OLD AFTER A WHILE.
WHAT ARE YOU LAUGHING AT?!
I THOUGHT I SHOULD TEACH HIM HOW TO DEFEND HIMSELF AGAINST SPIRITS.
HEY KID! FROM NOW ON YOU'RE MY STUDENT, GOT IT?!
WHUT ?!
THAT'S HOW YOU CHOOSE THE YATAHAGANE SUCCESSOR ?!

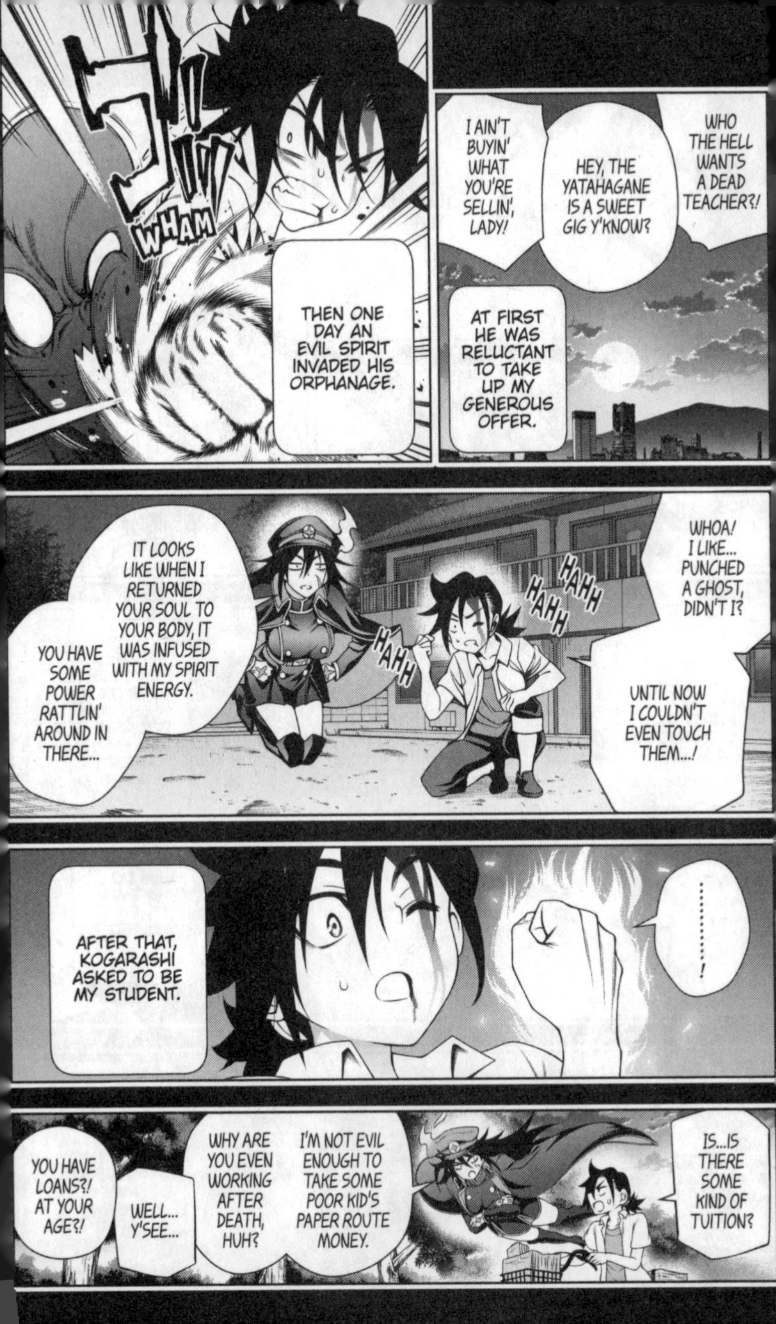
WHO THE HELL WANTS A DEAD TEACHER?!
HEY, THE YATAHAGANE IS A SWEET GIG Y'KNOW?
I AIN'T BUYIN' WHAT YOU'RE SELLIN', LADY!
AT FIRST HE WAS RELUCTANT TO TAKE UP MY GENEROUS OFFER.
WHAM
THEN ONE DAY AN EVIL SPIRIT INVADED HIS ORPHANAGE.
WHOA! I LIKE... PUNCHED A GHOST, DIDN'T I?
HAHH HAHH
UNTIL NOW I COULDN'T EVEN TOUCH THEM...!
HAHH
IT LOOKS LIKE WHEN I RETURNED YOUR SOUL TO YOUR BODY, IT WAS INFUSED WITH MY SPIRIT ENERGY.
YOU HAVE SOME POWER RATTLIN' AROUND IN THERE...
........!
AFTER THAT, KOGARASHI ASKED TO BE MY STUDENT.
IS...IS THERE SOME KIND OF TUITION?
I'M NOT EVIL ENOUGH TO TAKE SOME POOR KID'S PAPER ROUTE MONEY.
WHY ARE YOU EVEN WORKING AFTER DEATH, HUH?
WELL... Y'SEE...
YOU HAVE LOANS?! AT YOUR AGE?!

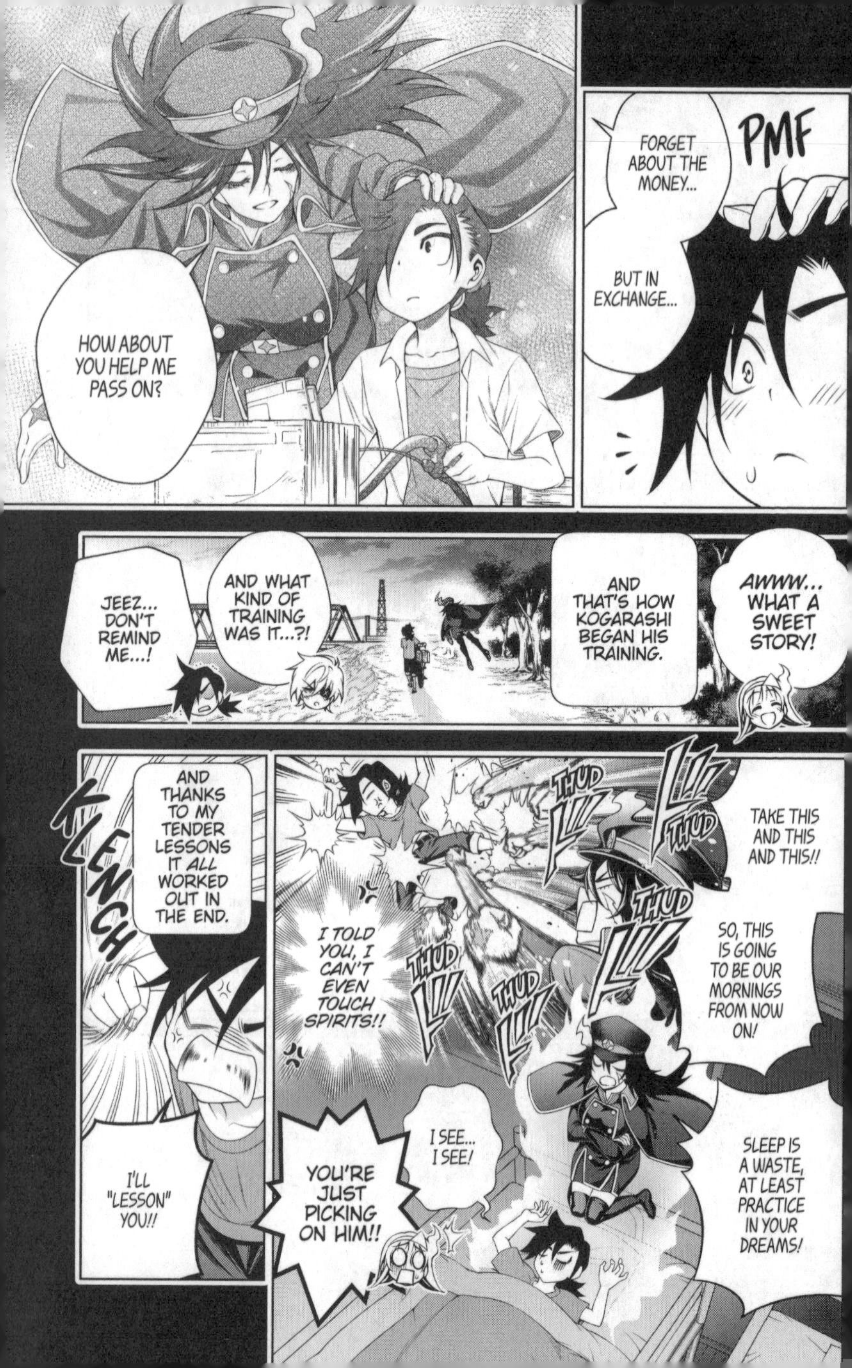
PMF
FORGET ABOUT THE MONEY...
BUT IN EXCHANGE...
HOW ABOUT YOU HELP ME PASS ON?
AWWW... WHAT A SWEET STORY!
AND THAT'S HOW KOGARASHI BEGAN HIS TRAINING.
AND WHAT KIND OF TRAINING WAS IT...?!
JEEZ... DON'T REMIND ME...!
TAKE THIS AND THIS AND THIS!!
THUD
THUD
THUD
THUD
THUD
I TOLD YOU, I CAN'T EVEN TOUCH SPIRITS!!
SO, THIS IS GOING TO BE OUR MORNINGS FROM NOW ON!
SLEEP IS A WASTE, AT LEAST PRACTICE IN YOUR DREAMS!
I SEE... I SEE!
YOU'RE JUST PICKING ON HIM!!
AND THANKS TO MY TENDER LESSONS IT ALL WORKED OUT IN THE END.
KLENCH
I'LL "LESSON" YOU!!

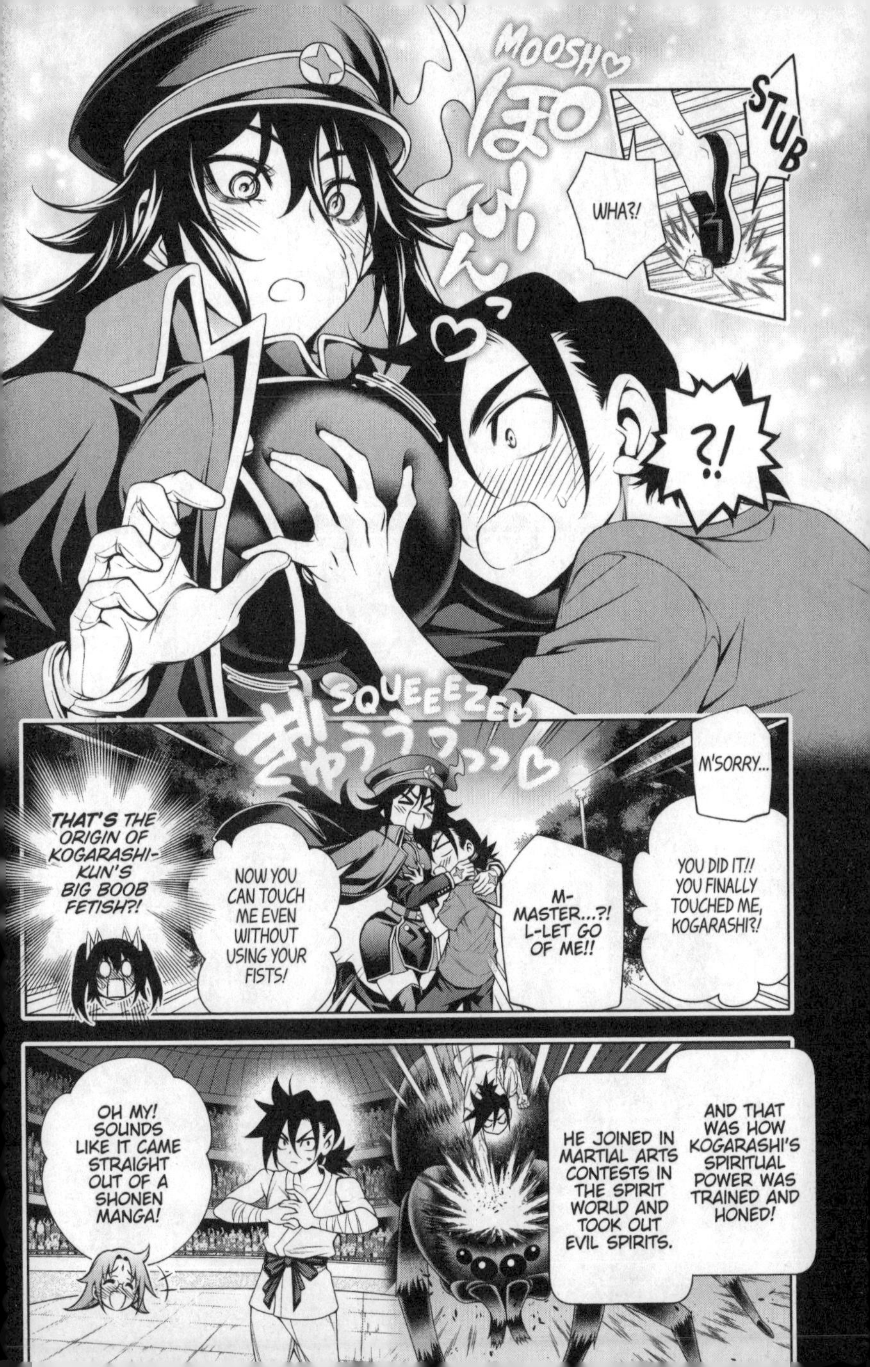
STUB
WHA?!
MOOSH♡
ぽふんっ♡
?!
SQUEEEZE♡
ぎゅううぅっっ♡
M'SORRY...
YOU DID IT!! YOU FINALLY TOUCHED ME, KOGARASHI?!
M-MASTER...?! L-LET GO OF ME!!
NOW YOU CAN TOUCH ME EVEN WITHOUT USING YOUR FISTS!
THAT'S THE ORIGIN OF KOGARASHI-KUN'S BIG BOOB FETISH?!
AND THAT WAS HOW KOGARASHI'S SPIRITUAL POWER WAS TRAINED AND HONED!
HE JOINED IN MARTIAL ARTS CONTESTS IN THE SPIRIT WORLD AND TOOK OUT EVIL SPIRITS.
OH MY! SOUNDS LIKE IT CAME STRAIGHT OUT OF A SHONEN MANGA!

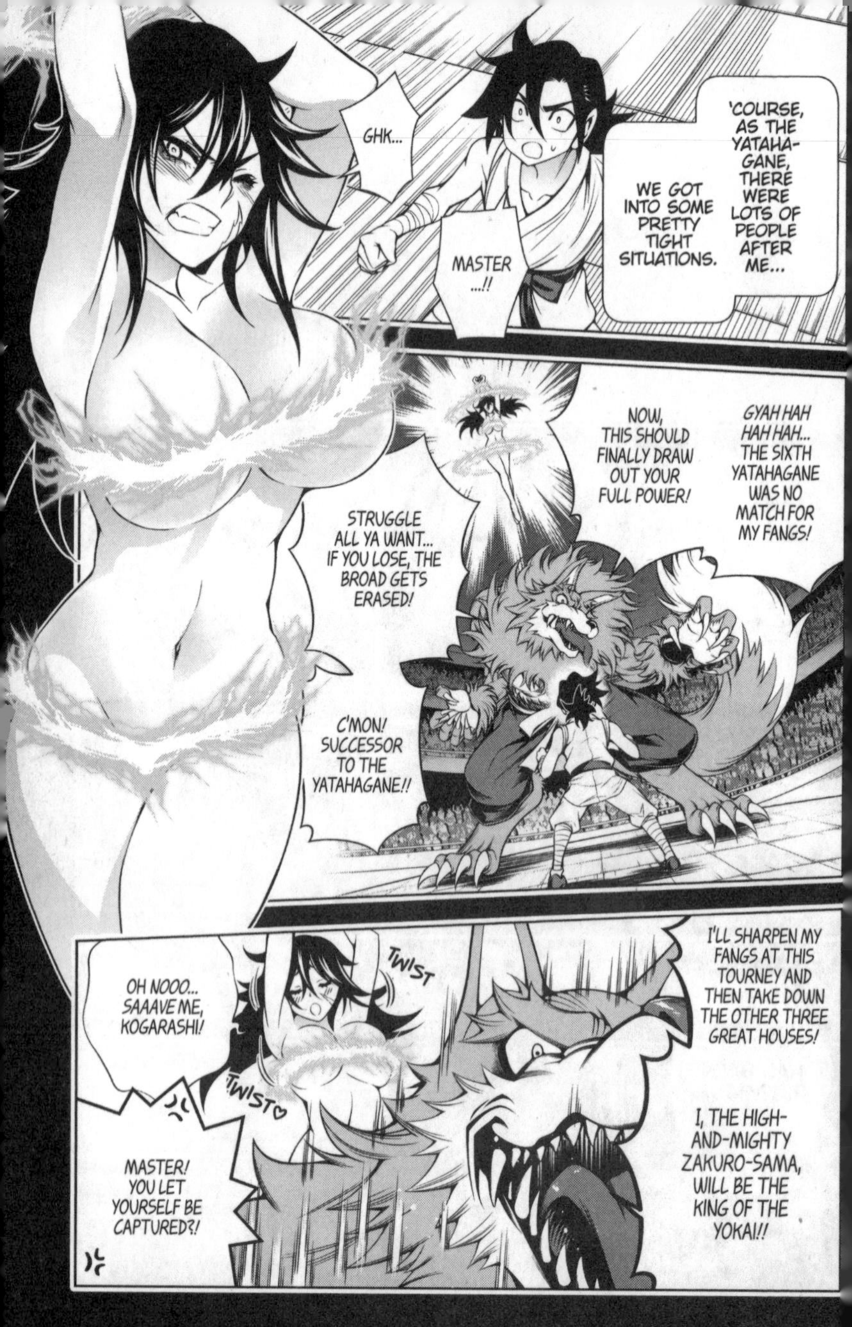
'COURSE, AS THE YATAHA-GANE, THERE WERE LOTS OF PEOPLE AFTER ME...
WE GOT INTO SOME PRETTY TIGHT SITUATIONS.
MASTER ...!!
GYAH HAH HAH HAH... THE SIXTH YATAHAGANE WAS NO MATCH FOR MY FANGS!
NOW, THIS SHOULD FINALLY DRAW OUT YOUR FULL POWER!
STRUGGLE ALL YA WANT... IF YOU LOSE, THE BROAD GETS ERASED!
C'MON! SUCCESSOR TO THE YATAHAGANE!!
GHK...
I'LL SHARPEN MY FANGS AT THIS TOURNEY AND THEN TAKE DOWN THE OTHER THREE GREAT HOUSES!
I, THE HIGH-AND-MIGHTY ZAKURO-SAMA, WILL BE THE KING OF THE YOKAI!!
TWIST
OH NOOO... SAAAVE ME, KOGARASHI!
TWIST♡
MASTER! YOU LET YOURSELF BE CAPTURED?!

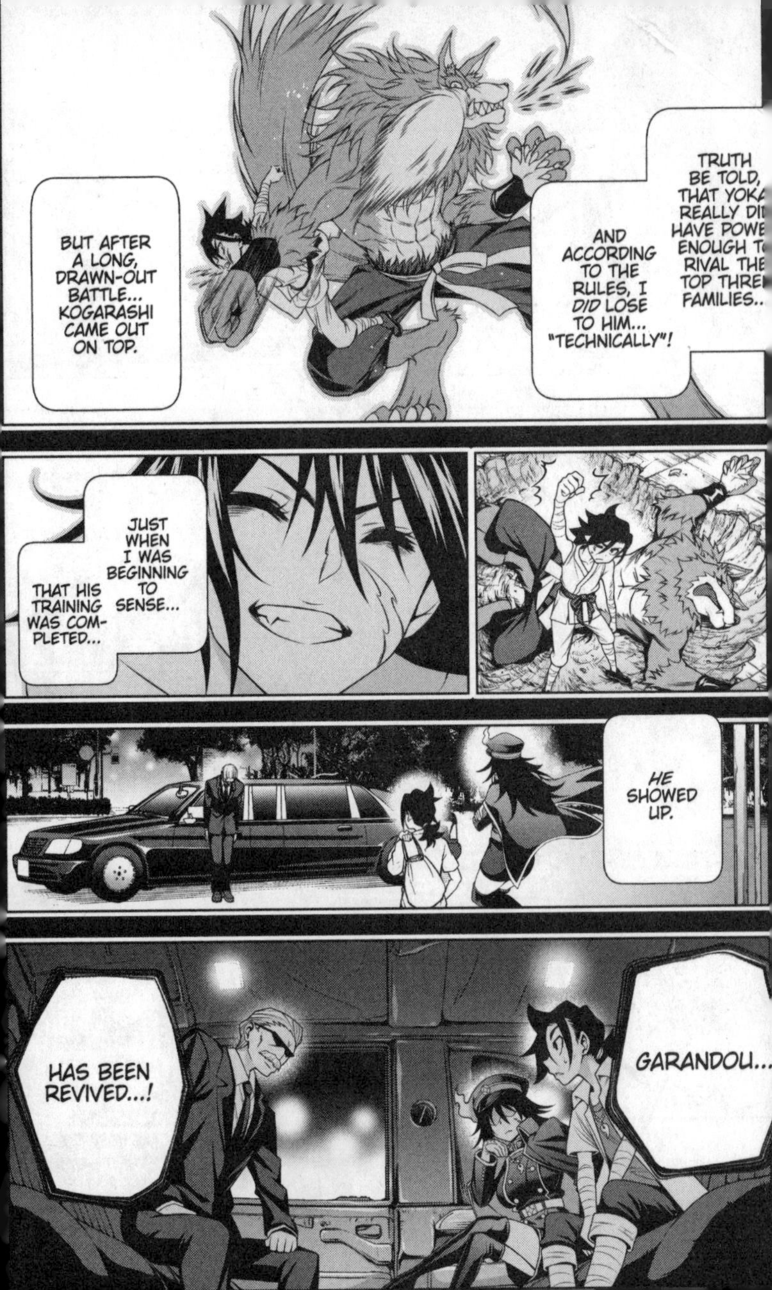
TRUTH BE TOLD, THAT YOKA REALLY DID HAVE POWE ENOUGH T RIVAL THE TOP THRE FAMILIES..
AND ACCORDING TO THE RULES, I *DID* LOSE TO HIM... "TECHNICALLY"!
BUT AFTER A LONG, DRAWN-OUT BATTLE... KOGARASHI CAME OUT ON TOP.
JUST WHEN I WAS BEGINNING TO SENSE...
THAT HIS TRAINING WAS COMPLETED...
HE SHOWED UP.
GARANDOU...
HAS BEEN REVIVED...!

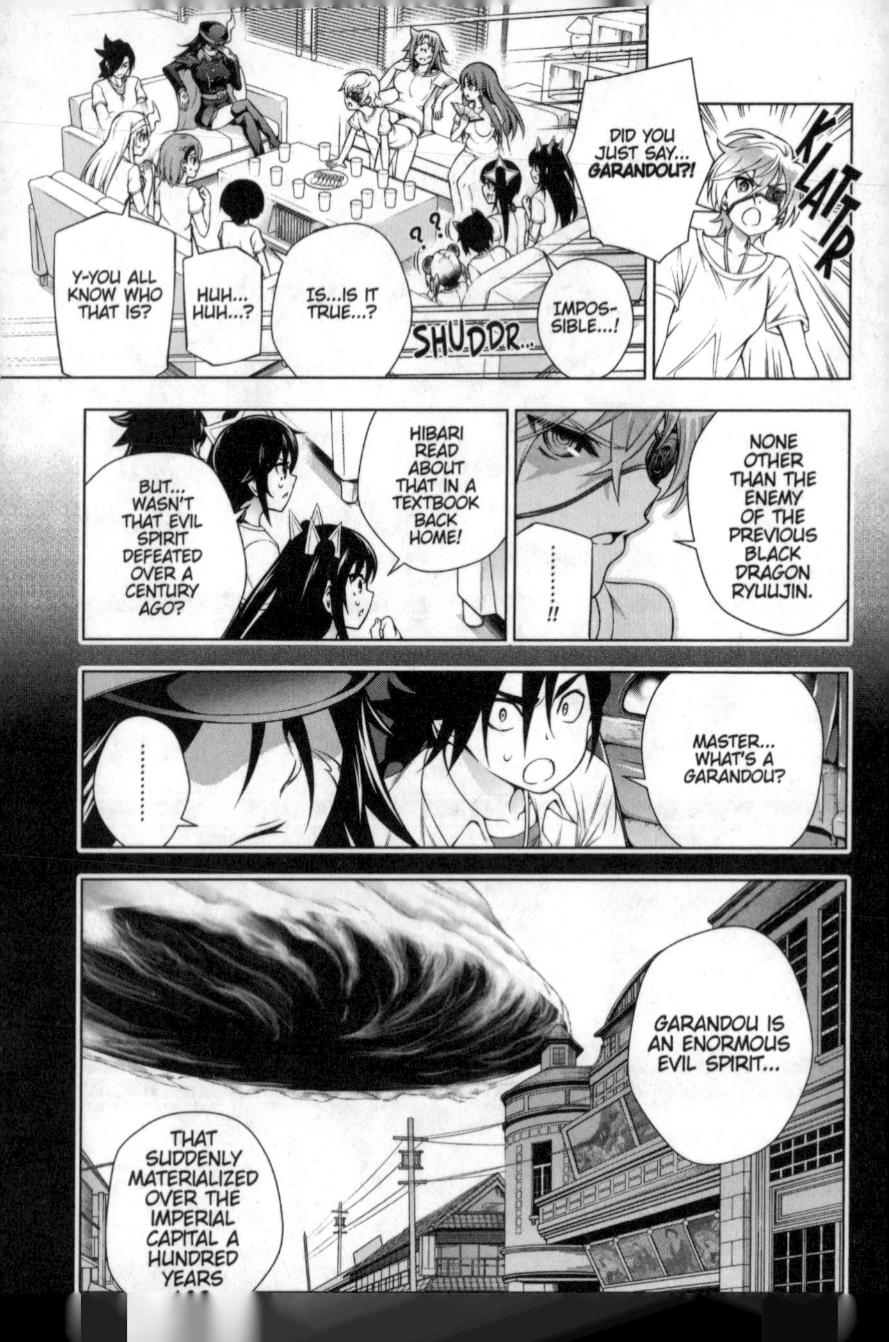

DID YOU JUST SAY... GARANDOU?!
KLATTR
IMPOS-SIBLE...!
SHUDDR...
? ?
IS...IS IT TRUE...?
HUH... HUH...?
Y-YOU ALL KNOW WHO THAT IS?
NONE OTHER THAN THE ENEMY OF THE PREVIOUS BLACK DRAGON RYUUJIN.
......!!
HIBARI READ ABOUT THAT IN A TEXTBOOK BACK HOME!
BUT... WASN'T THAT EVIL SPIRIT DEFEATED OVER A CENTURY AGO?
MASTER... WHAT'S A GARANDOU?
....
GARANDOU IS AN ENORMOUS EVIL SPIRIT...
THAT SUDDENLY MATERIALIZED OVER THE IMPERIAL CAPITAL A HUNDRED YEARS

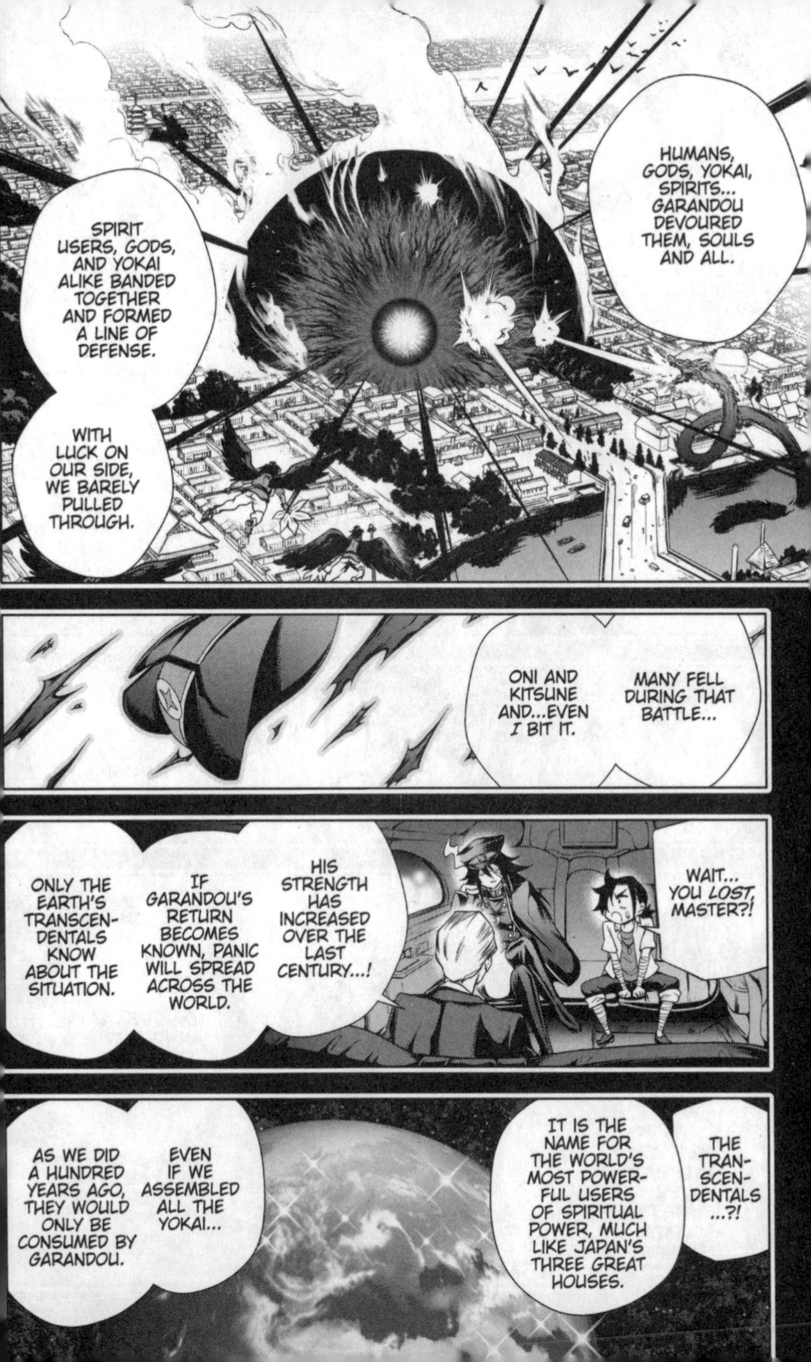
HUMANS, GODS, YOKAI, SPIRITS... GARANDOU DEVOURED THEM, SOULS AND ALL.
SPIRIT USERS, GODS, AND YOKAI ALIKE BANDED TOGETHER AND FORMED A LINE OF DEFENSE.
WITH LUCK ON OUR SIDE, WE BARELY PULLED THROUGH.
MANY FELL DURING THAT BATTLE...
ONI AND KITSUNE AND...EVEN *I* BIT IT.
WAIT... YOU *LOST*, MASTER?!
HIS STRENGTH HAS INCREASED OVER THE LAST CENTURY...!
IF GARANDOU'S RETURN BECOMES KNOWN, PANIC WILL SPREAD ACROSS THE WORLD.
ONLY THE EARTH'S TRANSCEN-DENTALS KNOW ABOUT THE SITUATION.
THE TRAN-SCEN-DENTALS ...?!
IT IS THE NAME FOR THE WORLD'S MOST POWER-FUL USERS OF SPIRITUAL POWER, MUCH LIKE JAPAN'S THREE GREAT HOUSES.
EVEN IF WE ASSEMBLED ALL THE YOKAI...
AS WE DID A HUNDRED YEARS AGO, THEY WOULD ONLY BE CONSUMED BY GARANDOU.

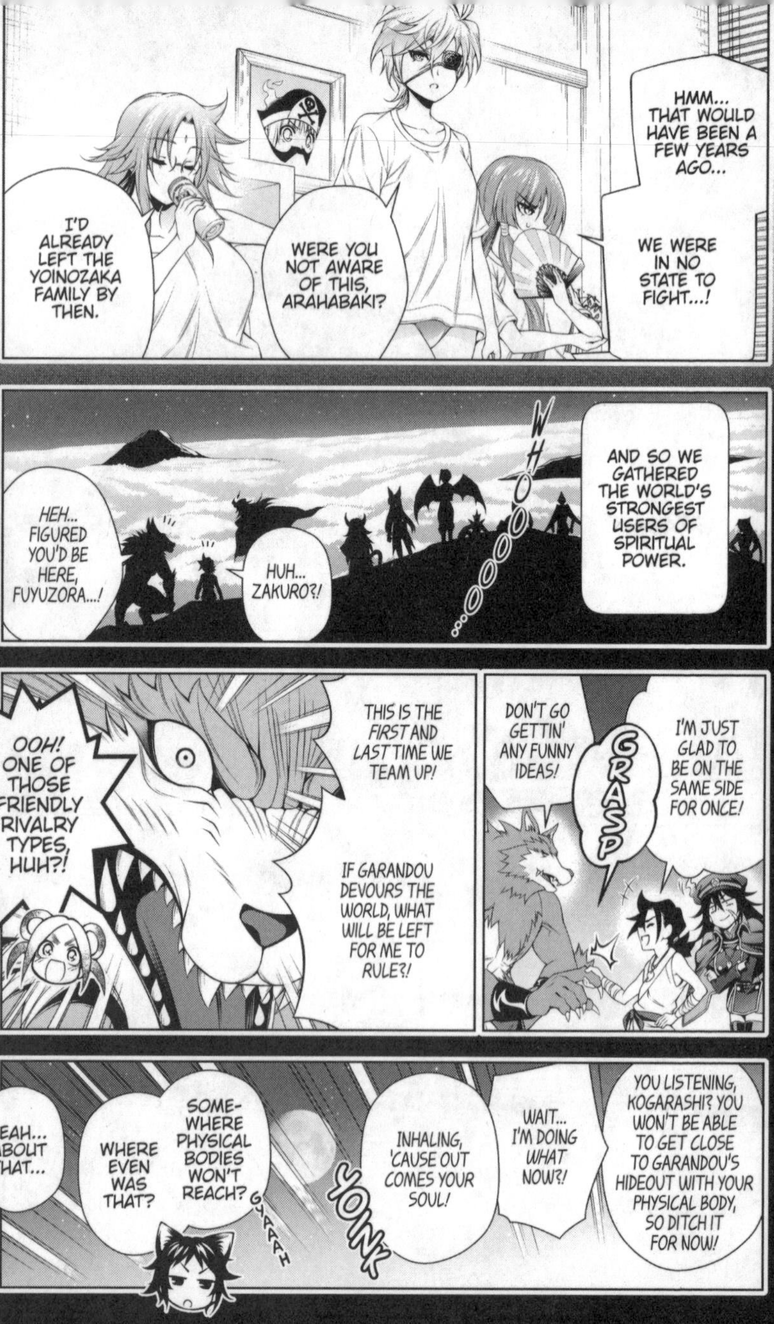
HMM... THAT WOULD HAVE BEEN A FEW YEARS AGO...
WE WERE IN NO STATE TO FIGHT...!
WERE YOU NOT AWARE OF THIS, ARAHABAKI?
I'D ALREADY LEFT THE YOINOZAKA FAMILY BY THEN.
AND SO WE GATHERED THE WORLD'S STRONGEST USERS OF SPIRITUAL POWER.
WHOOOOOOOOO...
HUH... ZAKURO?!
HEH... FIGURED YOU'D BE HERE, FUYUZORA...!
I'M JUST GLAD TO BE ON THE SAME SIDE FOR ONCE!
GRASP
DON'T GO GETTIN' ANY FUNNY IDEAS!
THIS IS THE FIRST AND LAST TIME WE TEAM UP!
IF GARANDOU DEVOURS THE WORLD, WHAT WILL BE LEFT FOR ME TO RULE?!
OOH! ONE OF THOSE FRIENDLY RIVALRY TYPES, HUH?!
YOU LISTENING, KOGARASHI? YOU WON'T BE ABLE TO GET CLOSE TO GARANDOU'S HIDEOUT WITH YOUR PHYSICAL BODY, SO DITCH IT FOR NOW!
WAIT... I'M DOING WHAT NOW?!
INHALING, 'CAUSE OUT COMES YOUR SOUL!
YOINK
SOME-WHERE PHYSICAL BODIES WON'T REACH?
GYAAAH
WHERE EVEN WAS THAT?
YEAH... ABOUT THAT...

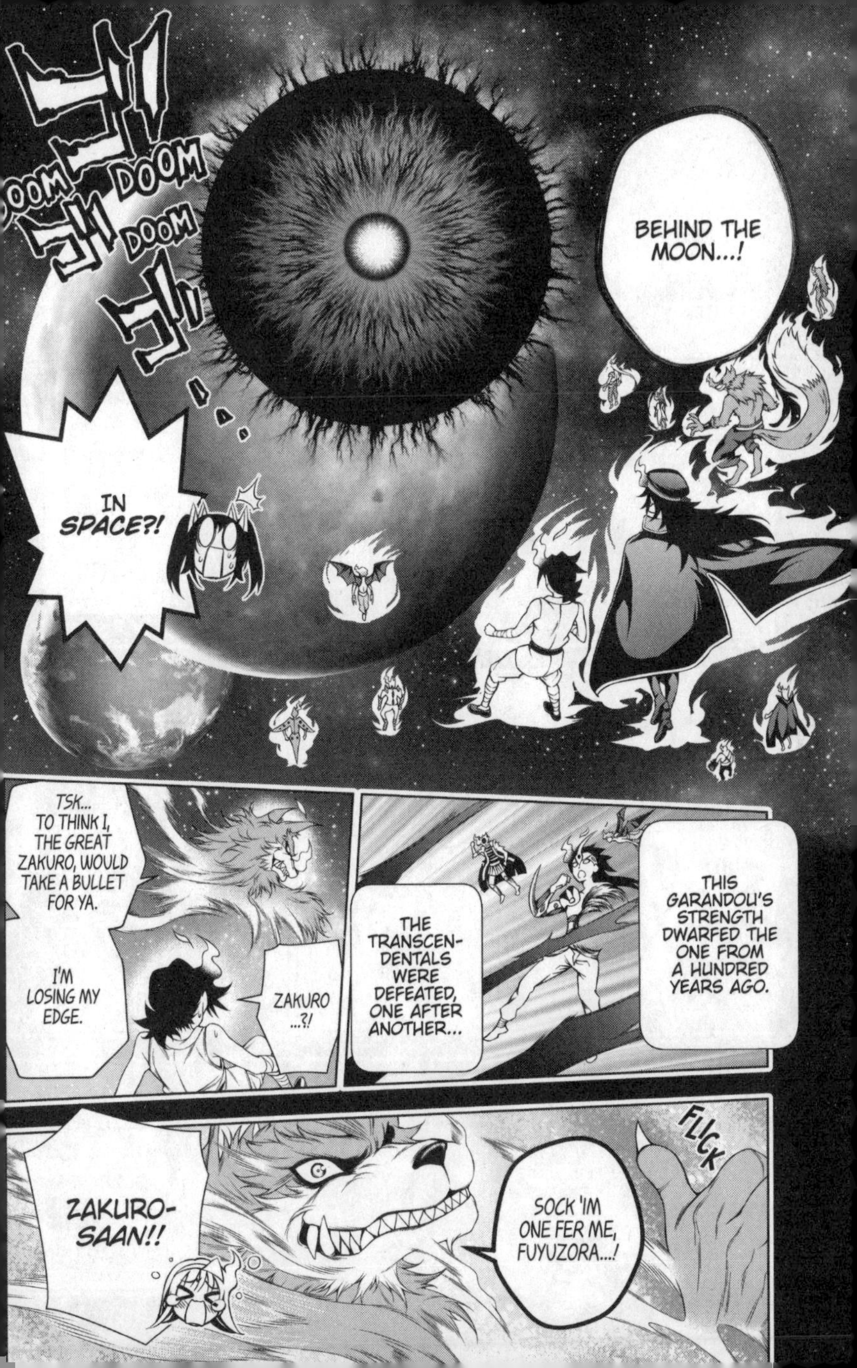
BEHIND THE MOON...!
DOOM DOOM DOOM DOOM
IN SPACE?!
THIS GARANDOU'S STRENGTH DWARFED THE ONE FROM A HUNDRED YEARS AGO.
THE TRANSCEN-DENTALS WERE DEFEATED, ONE AFTER ANOTHER...
TSK... TO THINK I, THE GREAT ZAKURO, WOULD TAKE A BULLET FOR YA.
ZAKURO ...?!
I'M LOSING MY EDGE.
FLICK
SOCK 'IM ONE FER ME, FUYUZORA...!
ZAKURO-SAAN!!

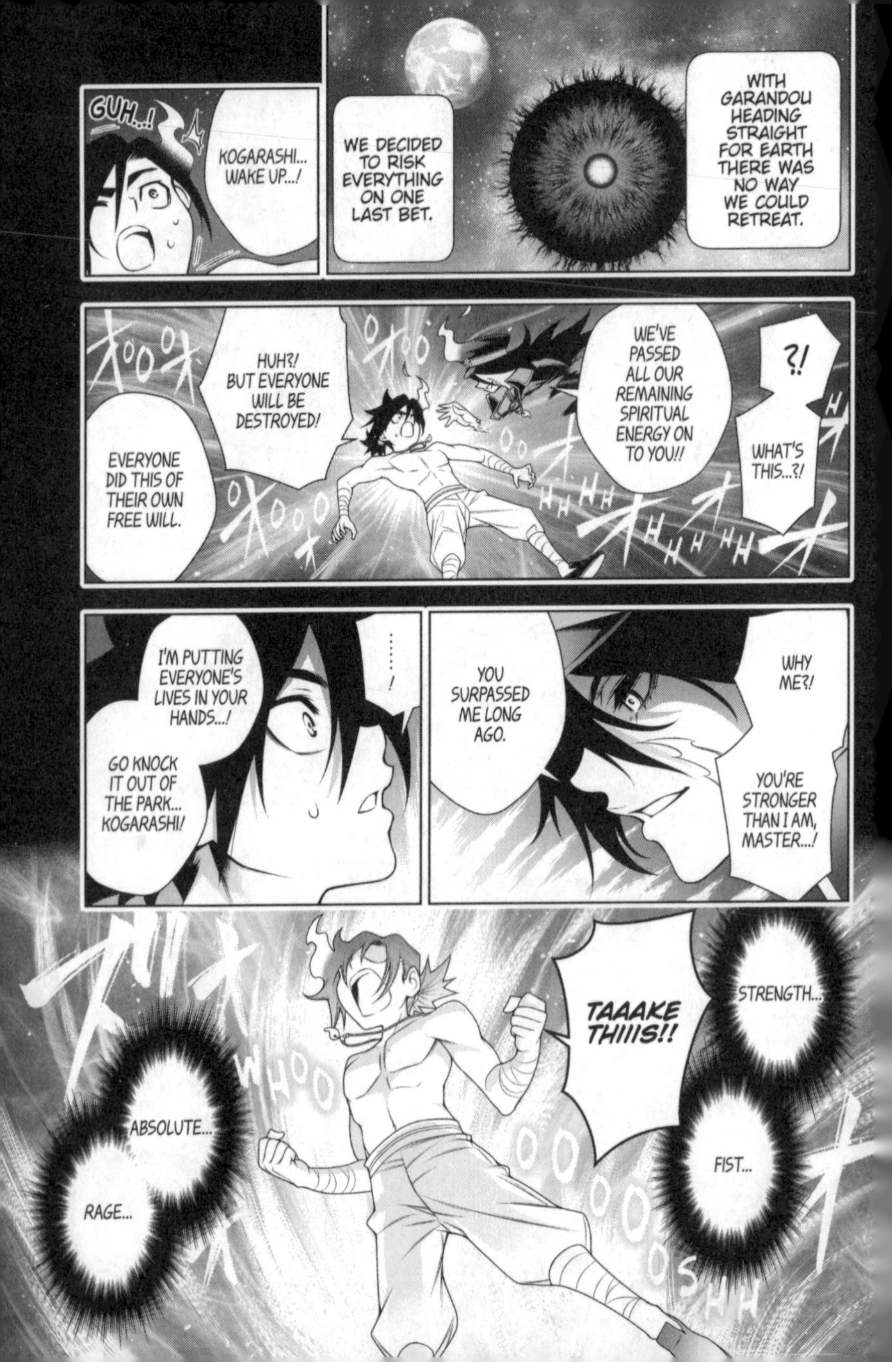
WITH GARANDOU HEADING STRAIGHT FOR EARTH THERE WAS NO WAY WE COULD RETREAT.
WE DECIDED TO RISK EVERYTHING ON ONE LAST BET.
GUH...!
KOGARASHI... WAKE UP...!
?!
WHAT'S THIS...?!
WE'VE PASSED ALL OUR REMAINING SPIRITUAL ENERGY ON TO YOU!!
HUH?! BUT EVERYONE WILL BE DESTROYED!
EVERYONE DID THIS OF THEIR OWN FREE WILL.
WHY ME?!
YOU'RE STRONGER THAN I AM, MASTER...!
YOU SURPASSED ME LONG AGO.
......!
I'M PUTTING EVERYONE'S LIVES IN YOUR HANDS...!
GO KNOCK IT OUT OF THE PARK... KOGARASHI!
STRENGTH...
FIST...
TAAAKE THIIIS!!
WHOOOOOOOOOSHH
ABSOLUTE...
RAGE...

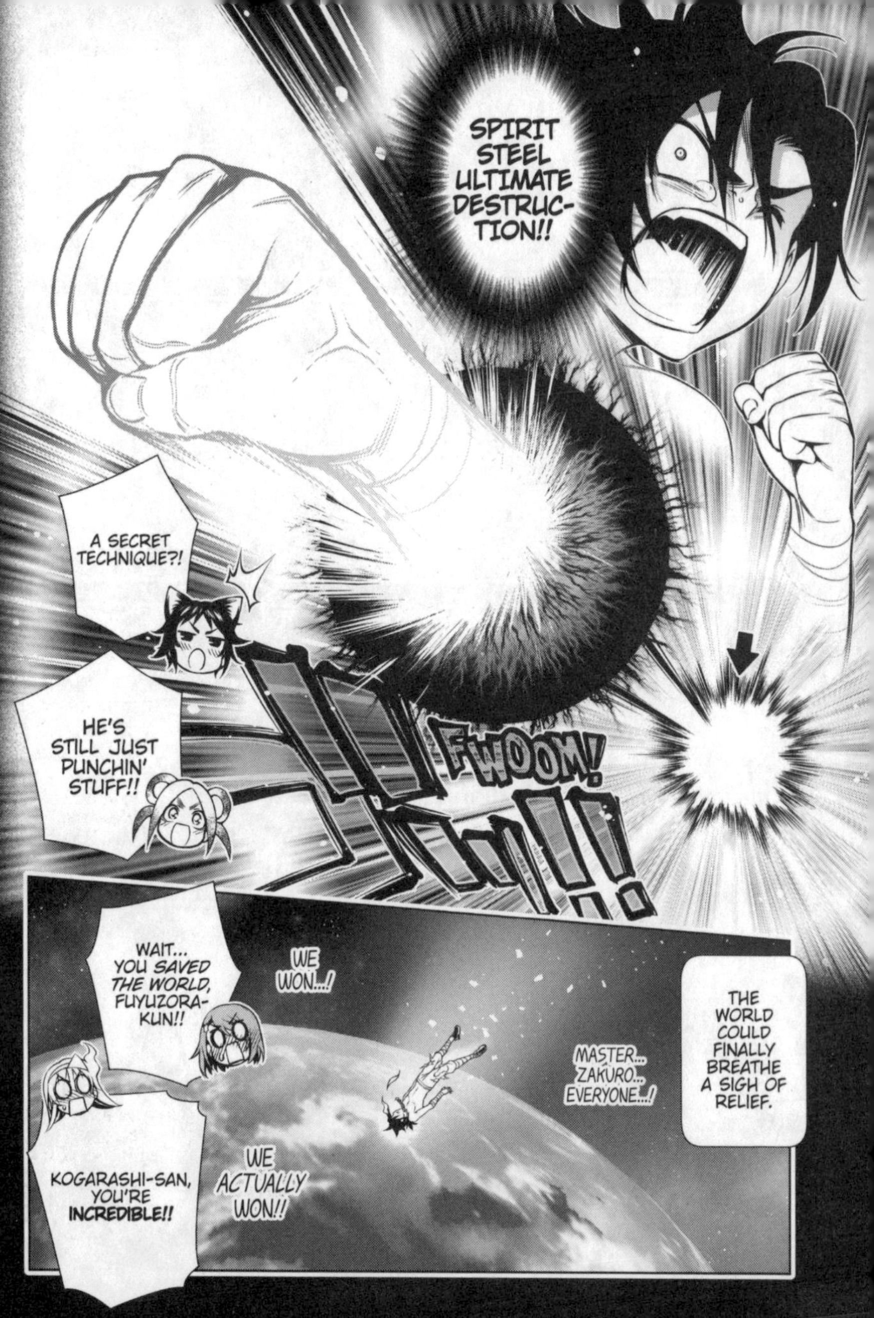
SPIRIT STEEL ULTIMATE DESTRUCTION!!
A SECRET TECHNIQUE?!
HE'S STILL JUST PUNCHIN' STUFF!!
FWOOM!
THE WORLD COULD FINALLY BREATHE A SIGH OF RELIEF.
MASTER... ZAKURO... EVERYONE...!
WE WON...!
WE ACTUALLY WON!!
WAIT... YOU SAVED THE WORLD, FUYUZORA-KUN!!
KOGARASHI-SAN, YOU'RE INCREDIBLE!!

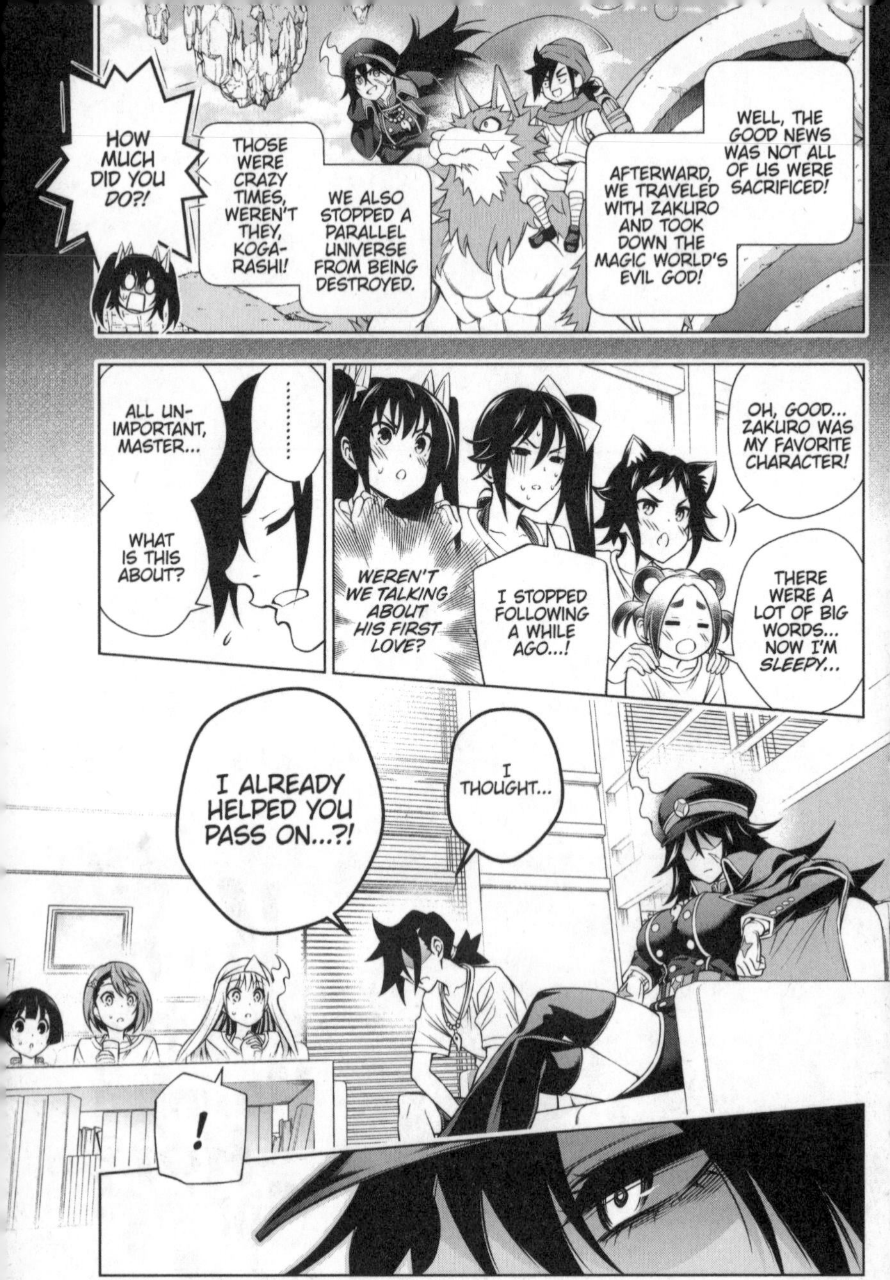
WELL, THE GOOD NEWS WAS NOT ALL OF US WERE SACRIFICED!
AFTERWARD, WE TRAVELED WITH ZAKURO AND TOOK DOWN THE MAGIC WORLD'S EVIL GOD!
WE ALSO STOPPED A PARALLEL UNIVERSE FROM BEING DESTROYED.
THOSE WERE CRAZY TIMES, WEREN'T THEY, KOGA-RASHI!
HOW MUCH DID YOU DO?!
OH, GOOD... ZAKURO WAS MY FAVORITE CHARACTER!
THERE WERE A LOT OF BIG WORDS... NOW I'M SLEEPY...
I STOPPED FOLLOWING A WHILE AGO...!
WEREN'T WE TALKING ABOUT HIS FIRST LOVE?
......
ALL UN-IMPORTANT, MASTER...
WHAT IS THIS ABOUT?
I THOUGHT...
I ALREADY HELPED YOU PASS ON...?!
!

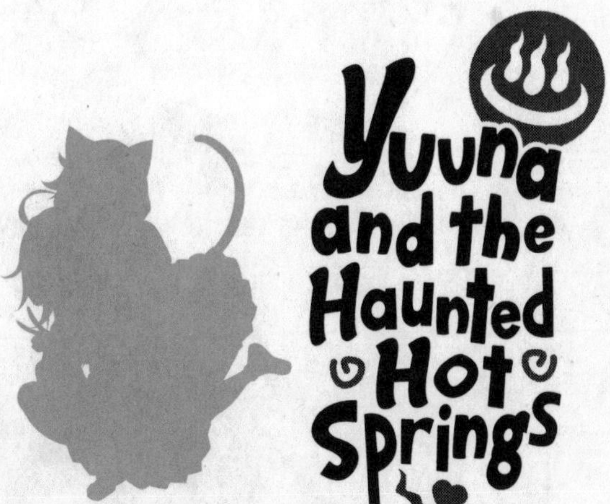

Yuuna and the Haunted Hot Springs

♨ 120 Ouga-san's Regrets

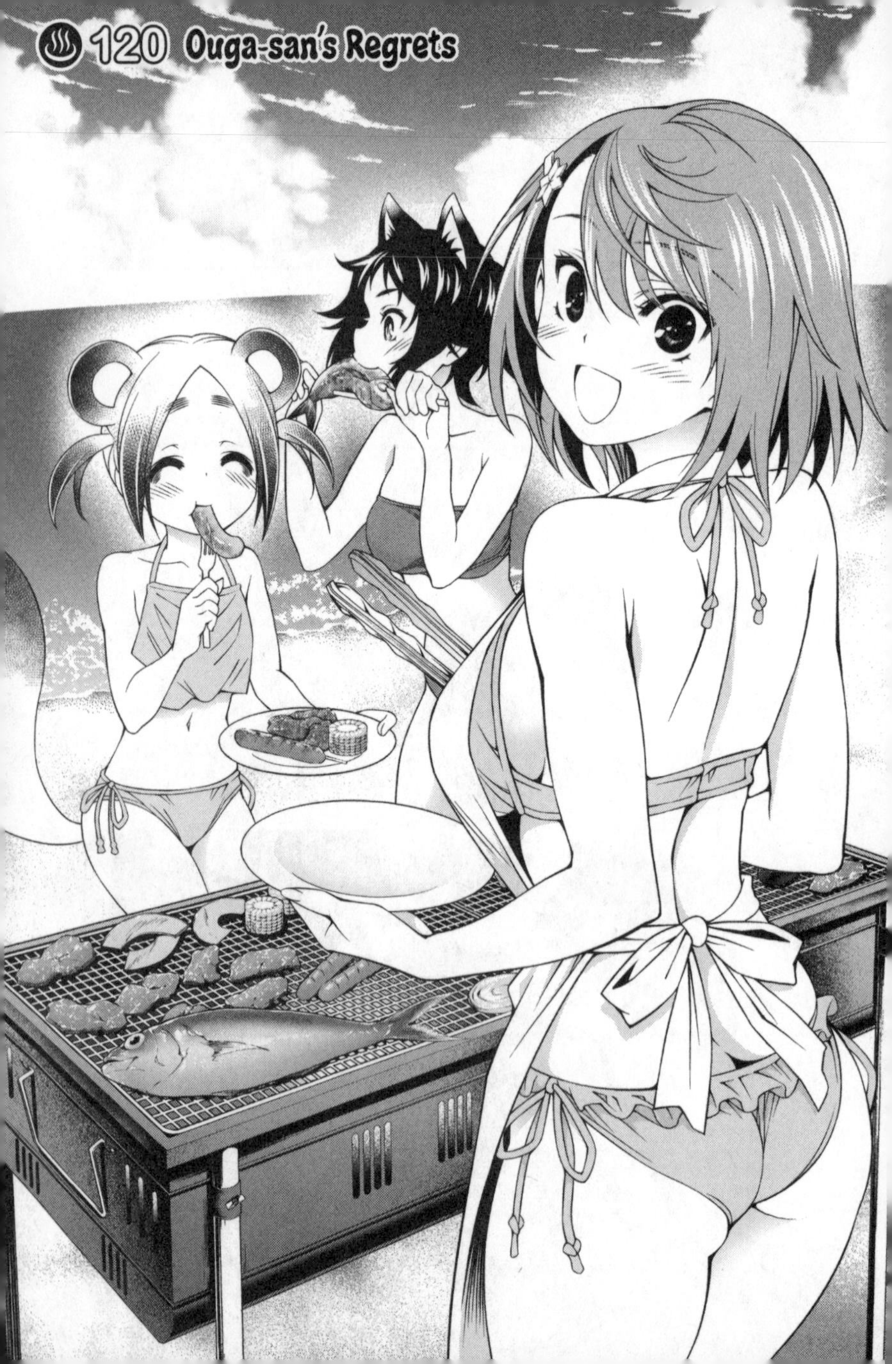

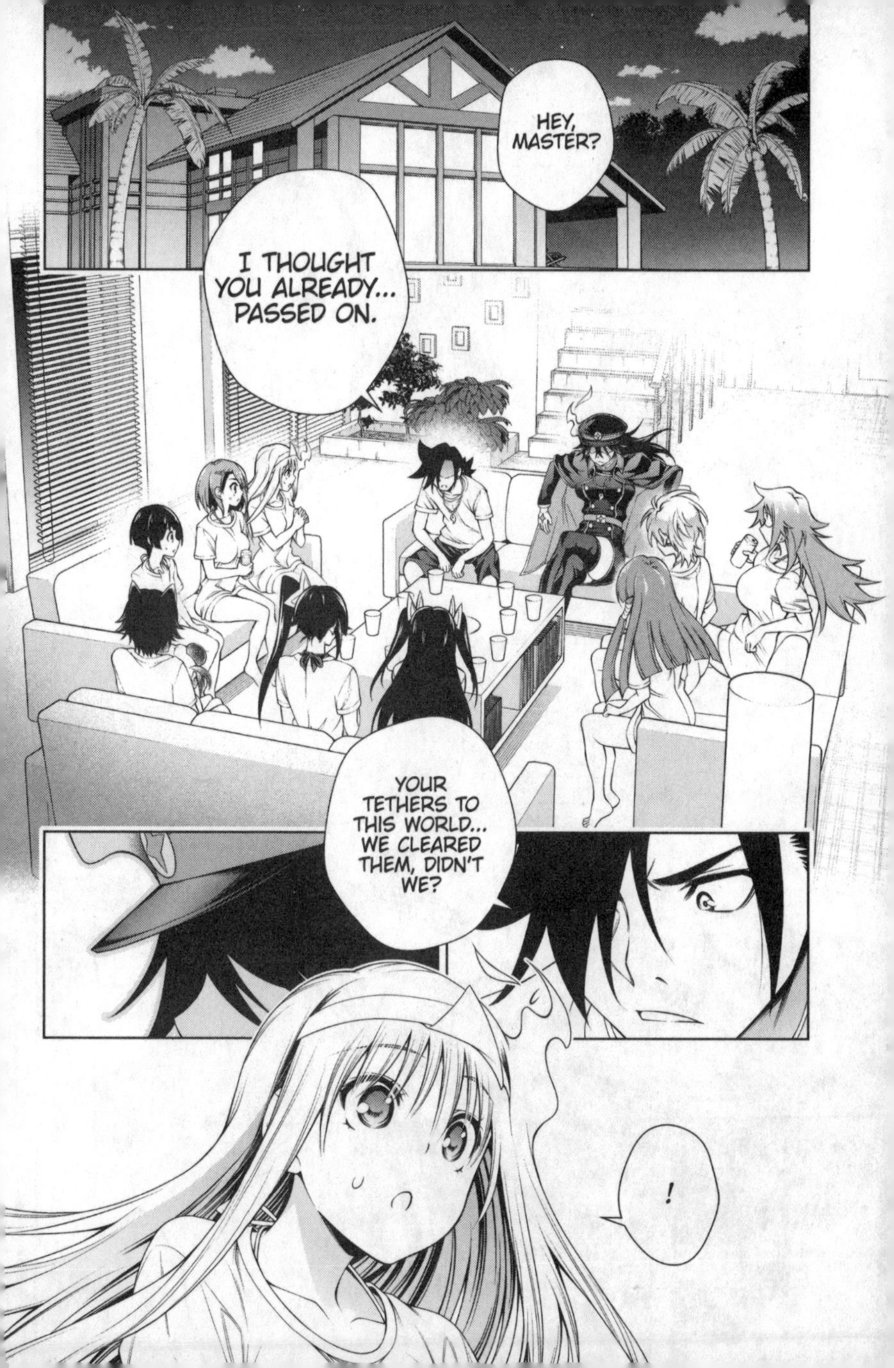
HEY, MASTER?
I THOUGHT YOU ALREADY... PASSED ON.
YOUR TETHERS TO THIS WORLD... WE CLEARED THEM, DIDN'T WE?
!

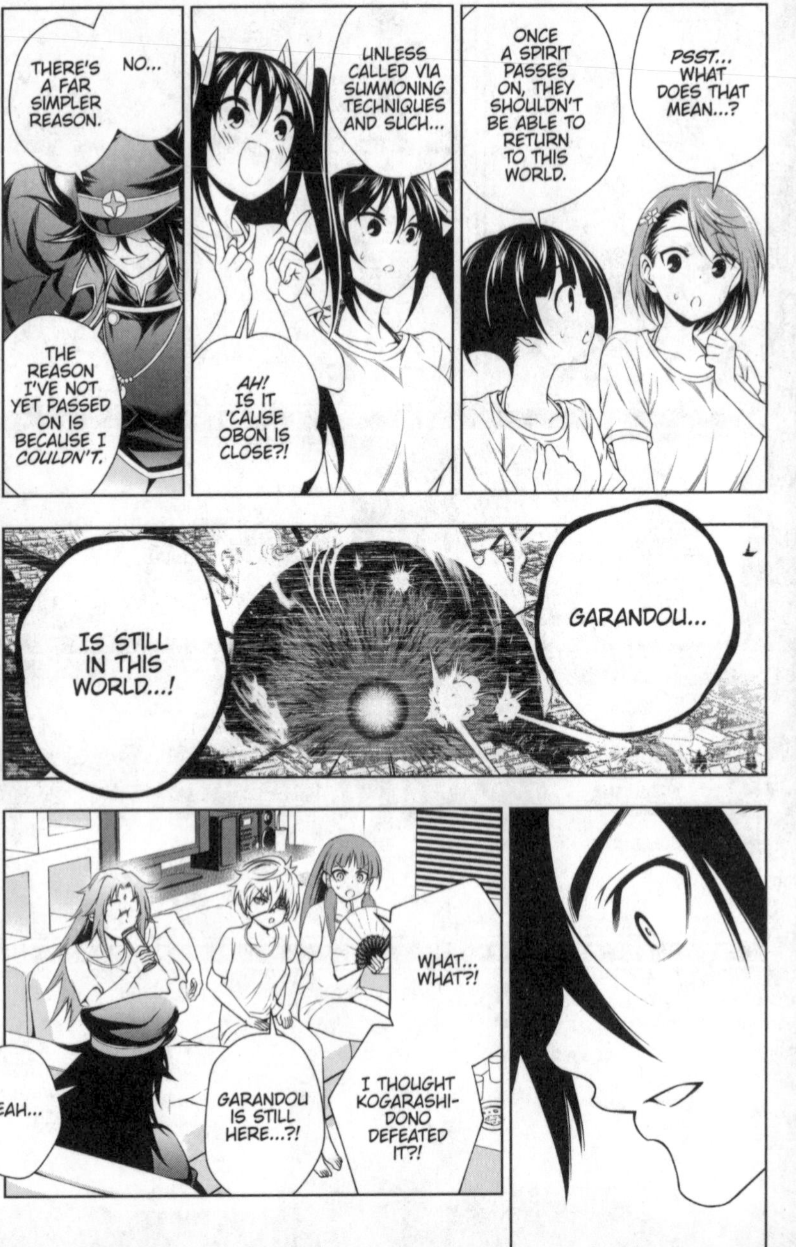
PSST... WHAT DOES THAT MEAN...?
ONCE A SPIRIT PASSES ON, THEY SHOULDN'T BE ABLE TO RETURN TO THIS WORLD.
UNLESS CALLED VIA SUMMONING TECHNIQUES AND SUCH...
AH! IS IT 'CAUSE OBON IS CLOSE?!
NO...
THERE'S A FAR SIMPLER REASON.
THE REASON I'VE NOT YET PASSED ON IS BECAUSE I COULDN'T.
GARANDOU...
IS STILL IN THIS WORLD...!
WHAT... WHAT?!
I THOUGHT KOGARASHI-DONO DEFEATED IT?!
GARANDOU IS STILL HERE...?!
YEAH...

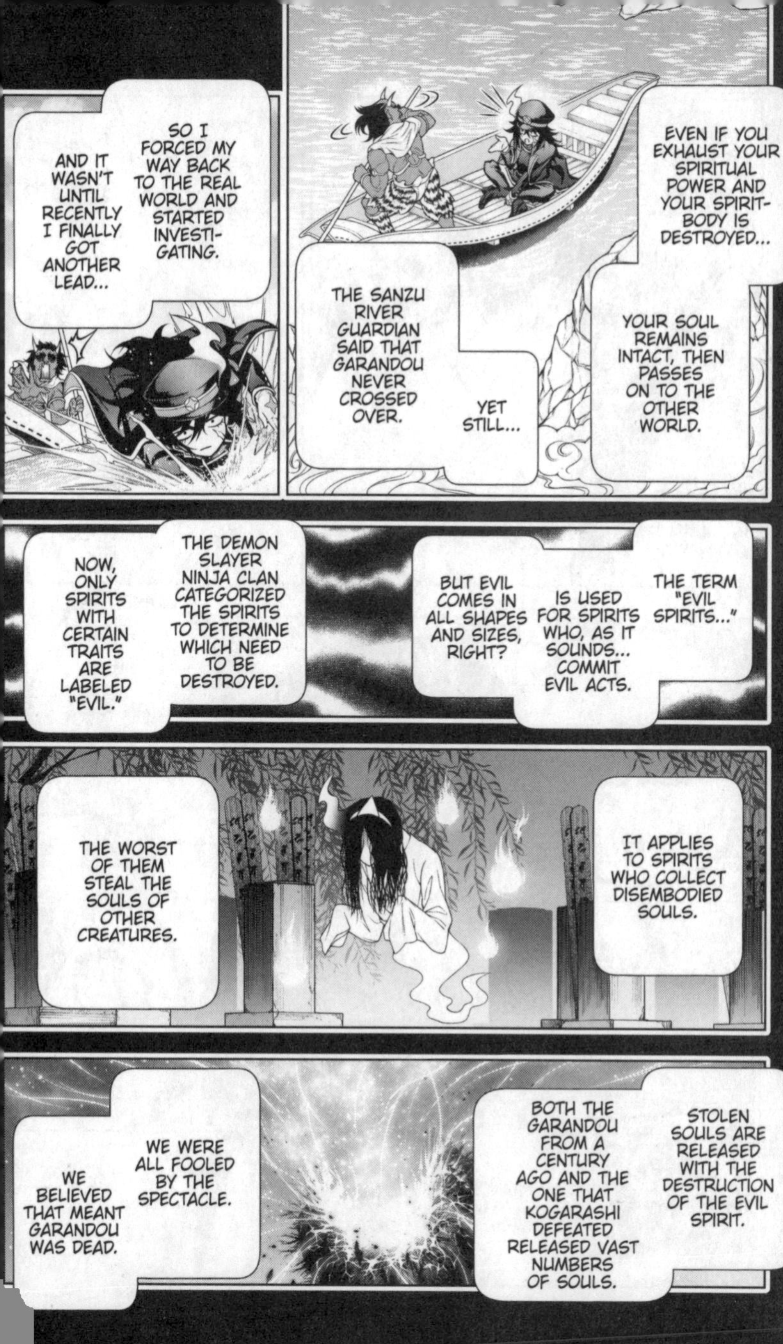
EVEN IF YOU EXHAUST YOUR SPIRITUAL POWER AND YOUR SPIRIT-BODY IS DESTROYED...
YOUR SOUL REMAINS INTACT, THEN PASSES ON TO THE OTHER WORLD.
YET STILL...
THE SANZU RIVER GUARDIAN SAID THAT GARANDOU NEVER CROSSED OVER.
SO I FORCED MY WAY BACK TO THE REAL WORLD AND STARTED INVESTI-GATING.
AND IT WASN'T UNTIL RECENTLY I FINALLY GOT ANOTHER LEAD...
THE TERM "EVIL SPIRITS..."
IS USED FOR SPIRITS WHO, AS IT SOUNDS... COMMIT EVIL ACTS.
BUT EVIL COMES IN ALL SHAPES AND SIZES, RIGHT?
THE DEMON SLAYER NINJA CLAN CATEGORIZED THE SPIRITS TO DETERMINE WHICH NEED TO BE DESTROYED.
NOW, ONLY SPIRITS WITH CERTAIN TRAITS ARE LABELED "EVIL."
IT APPLIES TO SPIRITS WHO COLLECT DISEMBODIED SOULS.
THE WORST OF THEM STEAL THE SOULS OF OTHER CREATURES.
STOLEN SOULS ARE RELEASED WITH THE DESTRUCTION OF THE EVIL SPIRIT.
BOTH THE GARANDOU FROM A CENTURY AGO AND THE ONE THAT KOGARASHI DEFEATED RELEASED VAST NUMBERS OF SOULS.
WE WERE ALL FOOLED BY THE SPECTACLE.
WE BELIEVED THAT MEANT GARANDOU WAS DEAD.

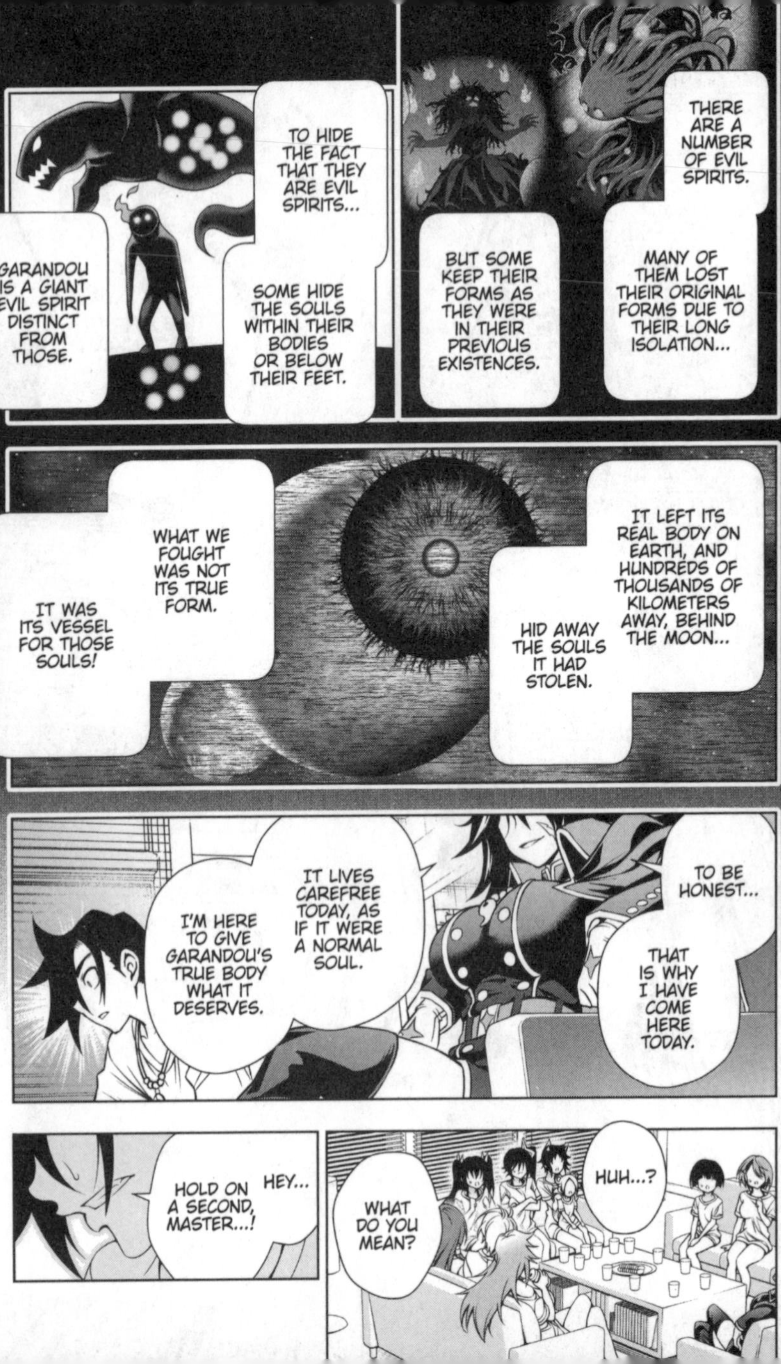
THERE ARE A NUMBER OF EVIL SPIRITS.
MANY OF THEM LOST THEIR ORIGINAL FORMS DUE TO THEIR LONG ISOLATION...
BUT SOME KEEP THEIR FORMS AS THEY WERE IN THEIR PREVIOUS EXISTENCES.
TO HIDE THE FACT THAT THEY ARE EVIL SPIRITS...
SOME HIDE THE SOULS WITHIN THEIR BODIES OR BELOW THEIR FEET.
GARANDOU IS A GIANT EVIL SPIRIT DISTINCT FROM THOSE.
IT LEFT ITS REAL BODY ON EARTH, AND HUNDREDS OF THOUSANDS OF KILOMETERS AWAY, BEHIND THE MOON...
HID AWAY THE SOULS IT HAD STOLEN.
WHAT WE FOUGHT WAS NOT ITS TRUE FORM.
IT WAS ITS VESSEL FOR THOSE SOULS!
TO BE HONEST...
THAT IS WHY I HAVE COME HERE TODAY.
IT LIVES CAREFREE TODAY, AS IF IT WERE A NORMAL SOUL.
I'M HERE TO GIVE GARANDOU'S TRUE BODY WHAT IT DESERVES.
HUH...?
WHAT DO YOU MEAN?
HEY...
HOLD ON A SECOND, MASTER...!

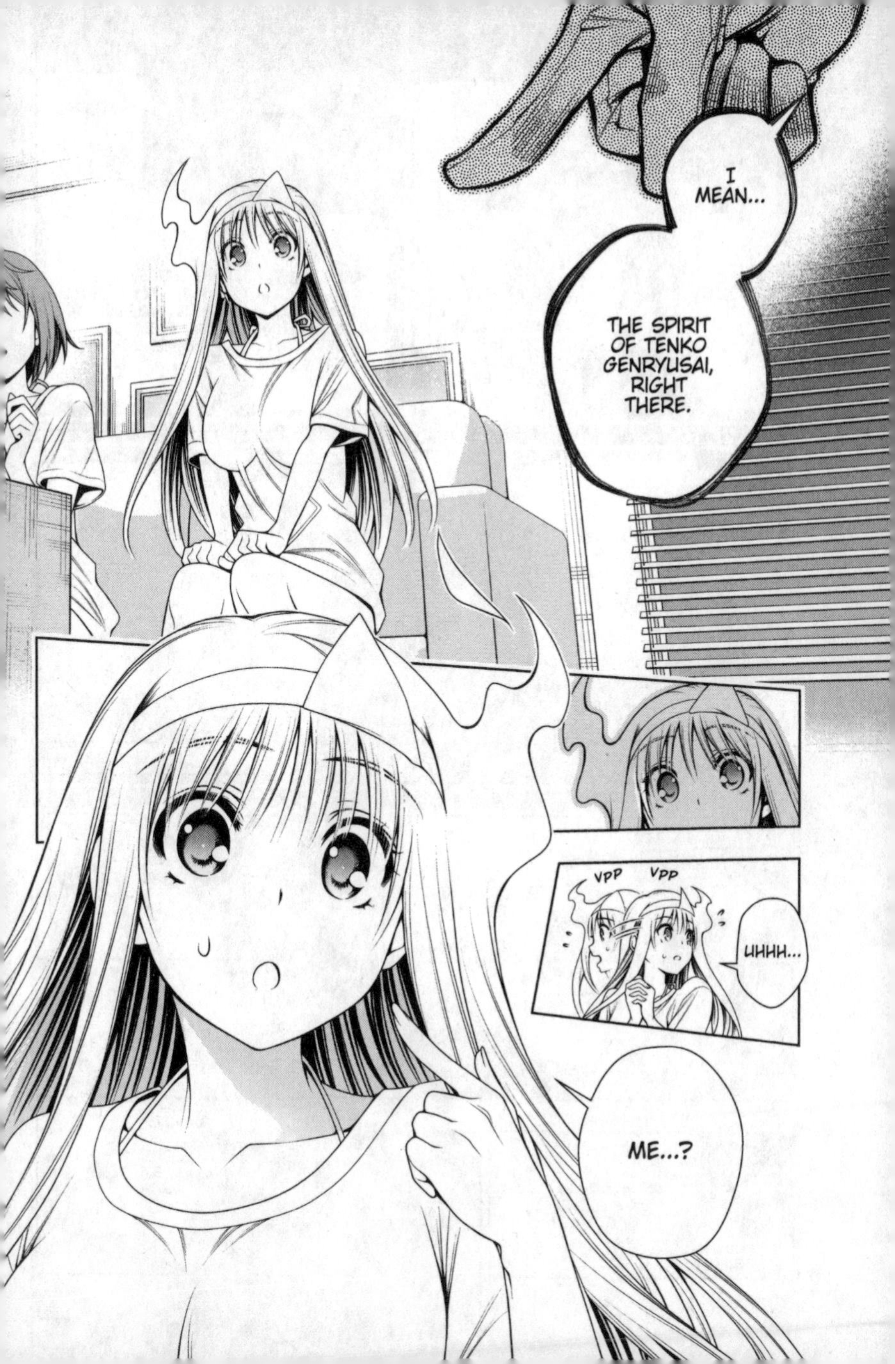
I MEAN...
THE SPIRIT OF TENKO GENRYUSAI, RIGHT THERE.
VPP VPP
UHHH...
ME...?

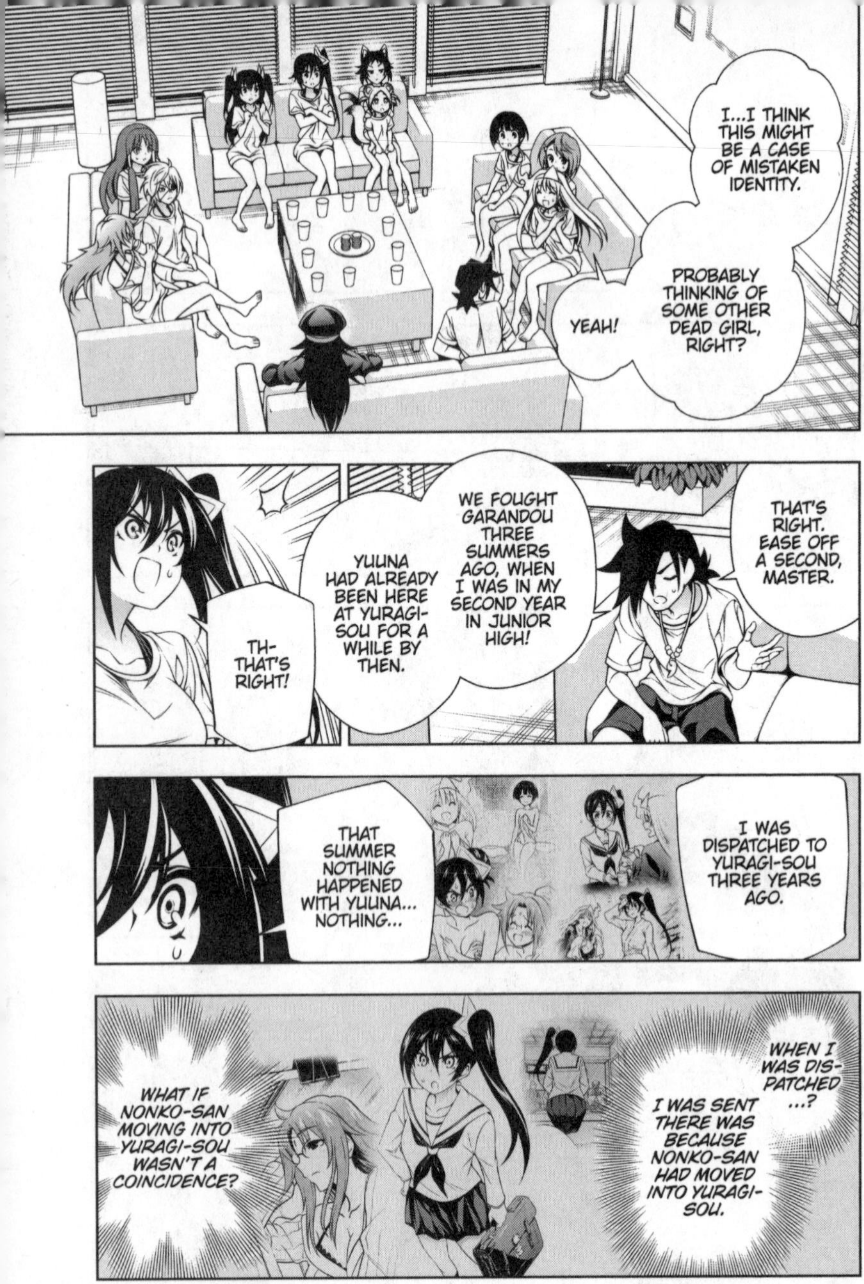

I...I THINK THIS MIGHT BE A CASE OF MISTAKEN IDENTITY.
PROBABLY THINKING OF SOME OTHER DEAD GIRL, RIGHT?
YEAH!
THAT'S RIGHT. EASE OFF A SECOND, MASTER.
WE FOUGHT GARANDOU THREE SUMMERS AGO, WHEN I WAS IN MY SECOND YEAR IN JUNIOR HIGH!
YUUNA HAD ALREADY BEEN HERE AT YURAGI-SOU FOR A WHILE BY THEN.
TH-THAT'S RIGHT!
I WAS DISPATCHED TO YURAGI-SOU THREE YEARS AGO.
THAT SUMMER NOTHING HAPPENED WITH YUUNA... NOTHING...
WHEN I WAS DIS-PATCHED ...?
I WAS SENT THERE WAS BECAUSE NONKO-SAN HAD MOVED INTO YURAGI-SOU.
WHAT IF NONKO-SAN MOVING INTO YURAGI-SOU WASN'T A COINCIDENCE?

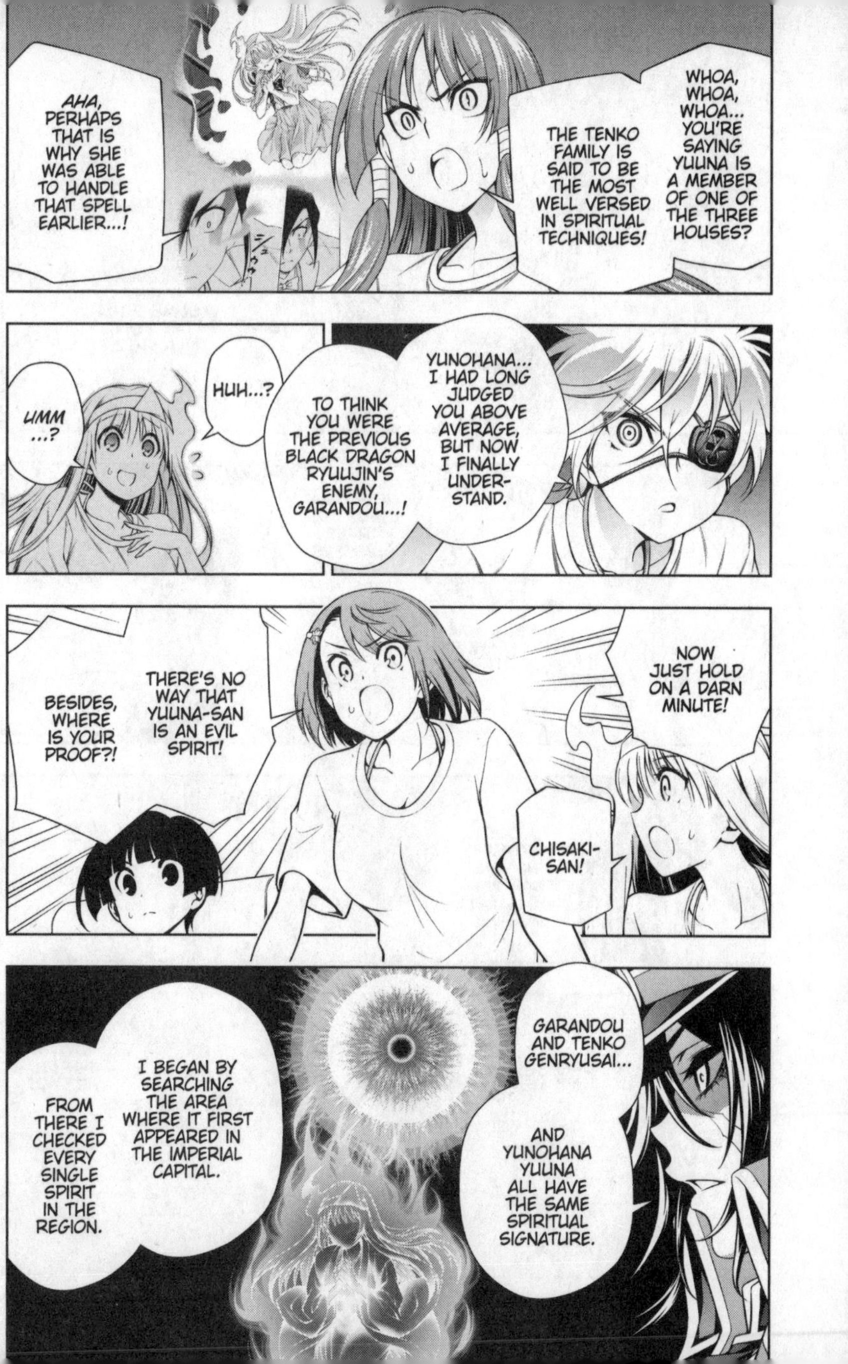
WHOA, WHOA, WHOA... YOU'RE SAYING YUUNA IS A MEMBER OF ONE OF THE THREE HOUSES?
THE TENKO FAMILY IS SAID TO BE THE MOST WELL VERSED IN SPIRITUAL TECHNIQUES!
AHA, PERHAPS THAT IS WHY SHE WAS ABLE TO HANDLE THAT SPELL EARLIER...!
YUNOHANA... I HAD LONG JUDGED YOU ABOVE AVERAGE, BUT NOW I FINALLY UNDER-STAND.
TO THINK YOU WERE THE PREVIOUS BLACK DRAGON RYUUJIN'S ENEMY, GARANDOU...!
HUH...?
UMM ...?
NOW JUST HOLD ON A DARN MINUTE!
CHISAKI-SAN!
THERE'S NO WAY THAT YUUNA-SAN IS AN EVIL SPIRIT!
BESIDES, WHERE IS YOUR PROOF?!
GARANDOU AND TENKO GENRYUSAI...
AND YUNOHANA YUUNA ALL HAVE THE SAME SPIRITUAL SIGNATURE.
I BEGAN BY SEARCHING THE AREA WHERE IT FIRST APPEARED IN THE IMPERIAL CAPITAL.
FROM THERE I CHECKED EVERY SINGLE SPIRIT IN THE REGION.

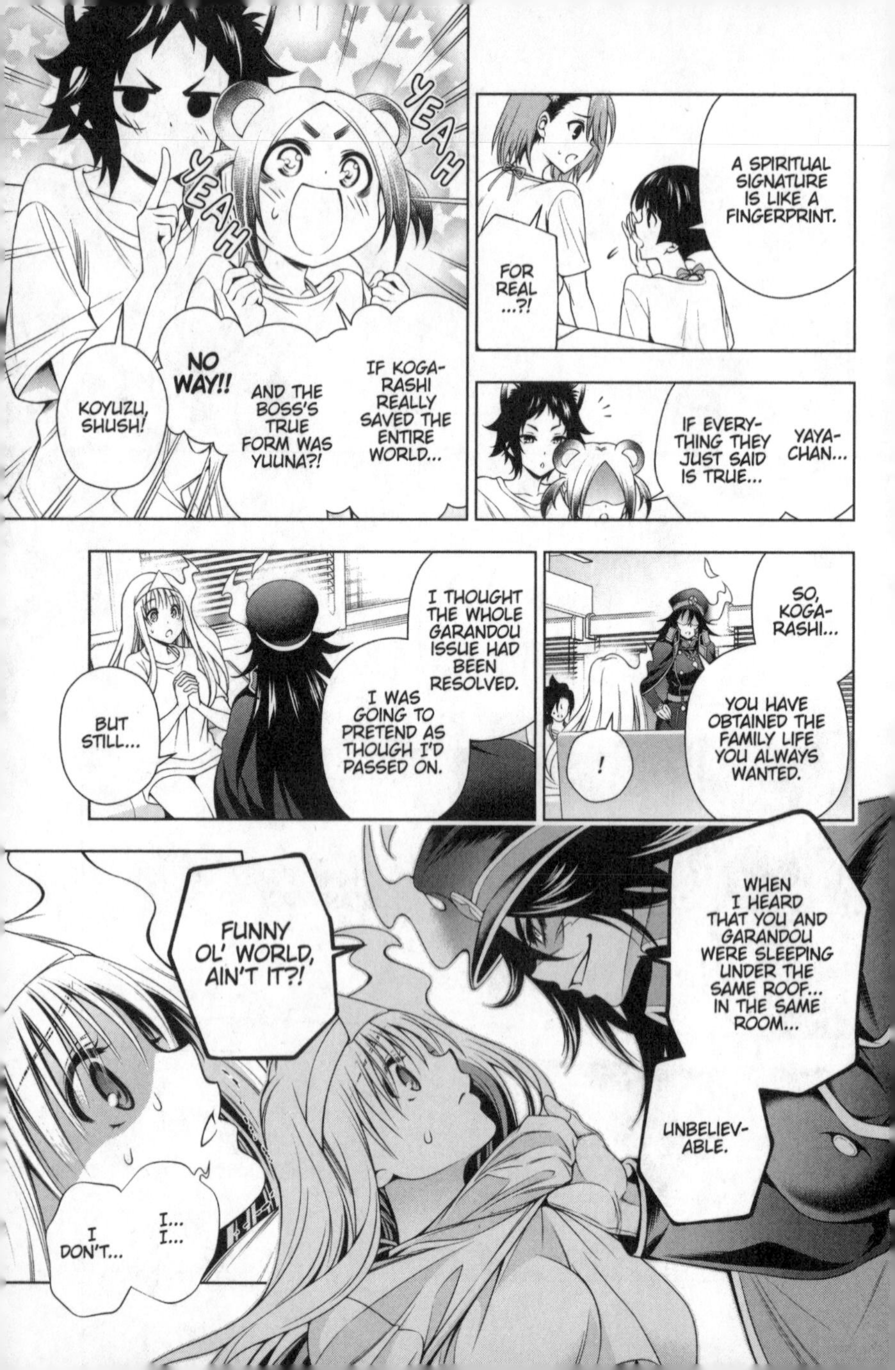
A SPIRITUAL SIGNATURE IS LIKE A FINGERPRINT.
FOR REAL ...?!
YAYA-CHAN...
IF EVERY-THING THEY JUST SAID IS TRUE...
YEAH
YEAH
IF KOGA-RASHI REALLY SAVED THE ENTIRE WORLD...
AND THE BOSS'S TRUE FORM WAS YUUNA?!
NO WAY!!
KOYUZU, SHUSH!
SO, KOGA-RASHI...
YOU HAVE OBTAINED THE FAMILY LIFE YOU ALWAYS WANTED.
!
I THOUGHT THE WHOLE GARANDOU ISSUE HAD BEEN RESOLVED.
I WAS GOING TO PRETEND AS THOUGH I'D PASSED ON.
BUT STILL...
WHEN I HEARD THAT YOU AND GARANDOU WERE SLEEPING UNDER THE SAME ROOF... IN THE SAME ROOM...
UNBELIEV-ABLE.
FUNNY OL' WORLD, AIN'T IT?!
I... I...
I DON'T...

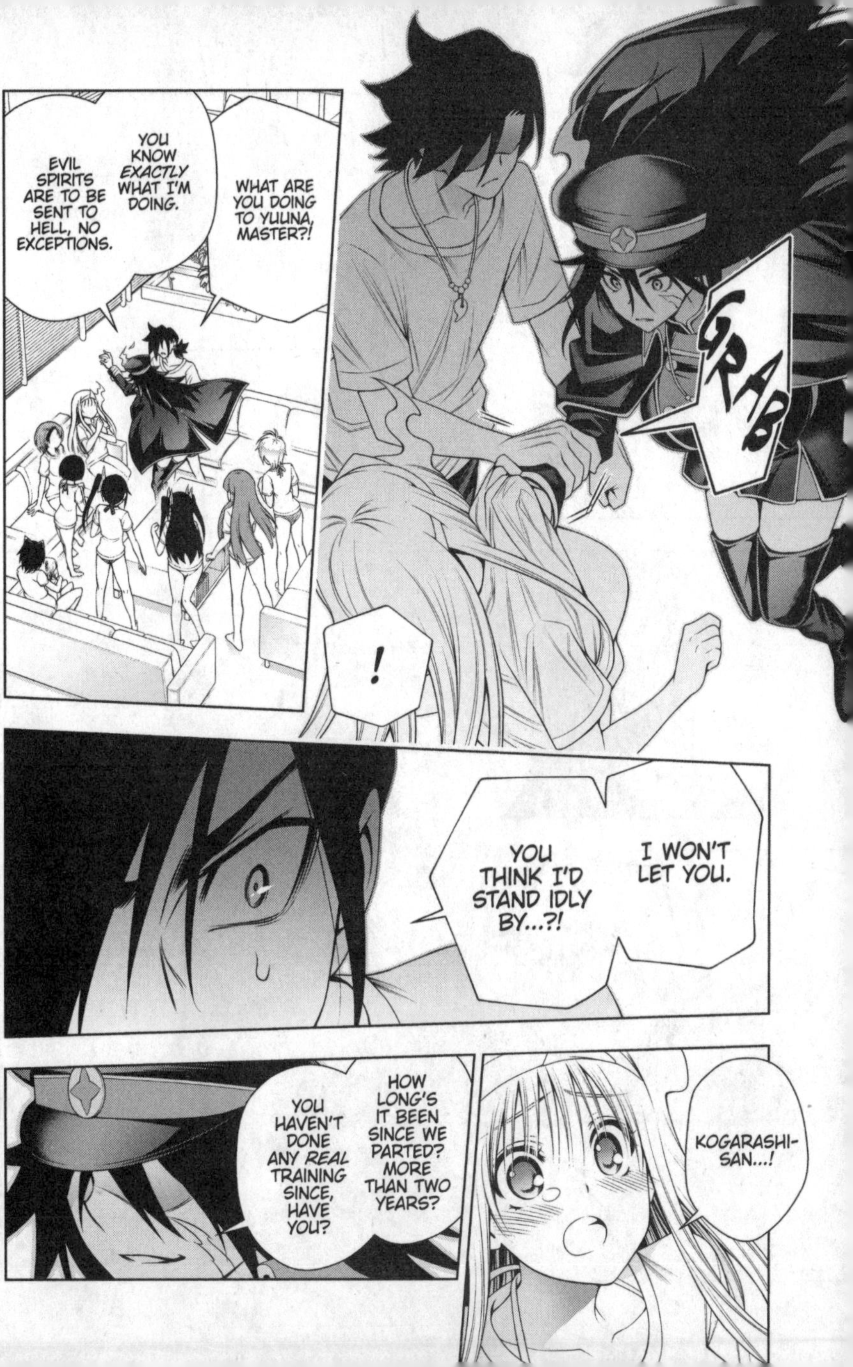
GRAB
!
WHAT ARE YOU DOING TO YUUNA, MASTER?!
YOU KNOW *EXACTLY* WHAT I'M DOING.
EVIL SPIRITS ARE TO BE SENT TO HELL, NO EXCEPTIONS.
I WON'T LET YOU.
YOU THINK I'D STAND IDLY BY...?!
KOGARASHI-SAN...!
HOW LONG'S IT BEEN SINCE WE PARTED? MORE THAN TWO YEARS?
YOU HAVEN'T DONE ANY *REAL* TRAINING SINCE, HAVE YOU?

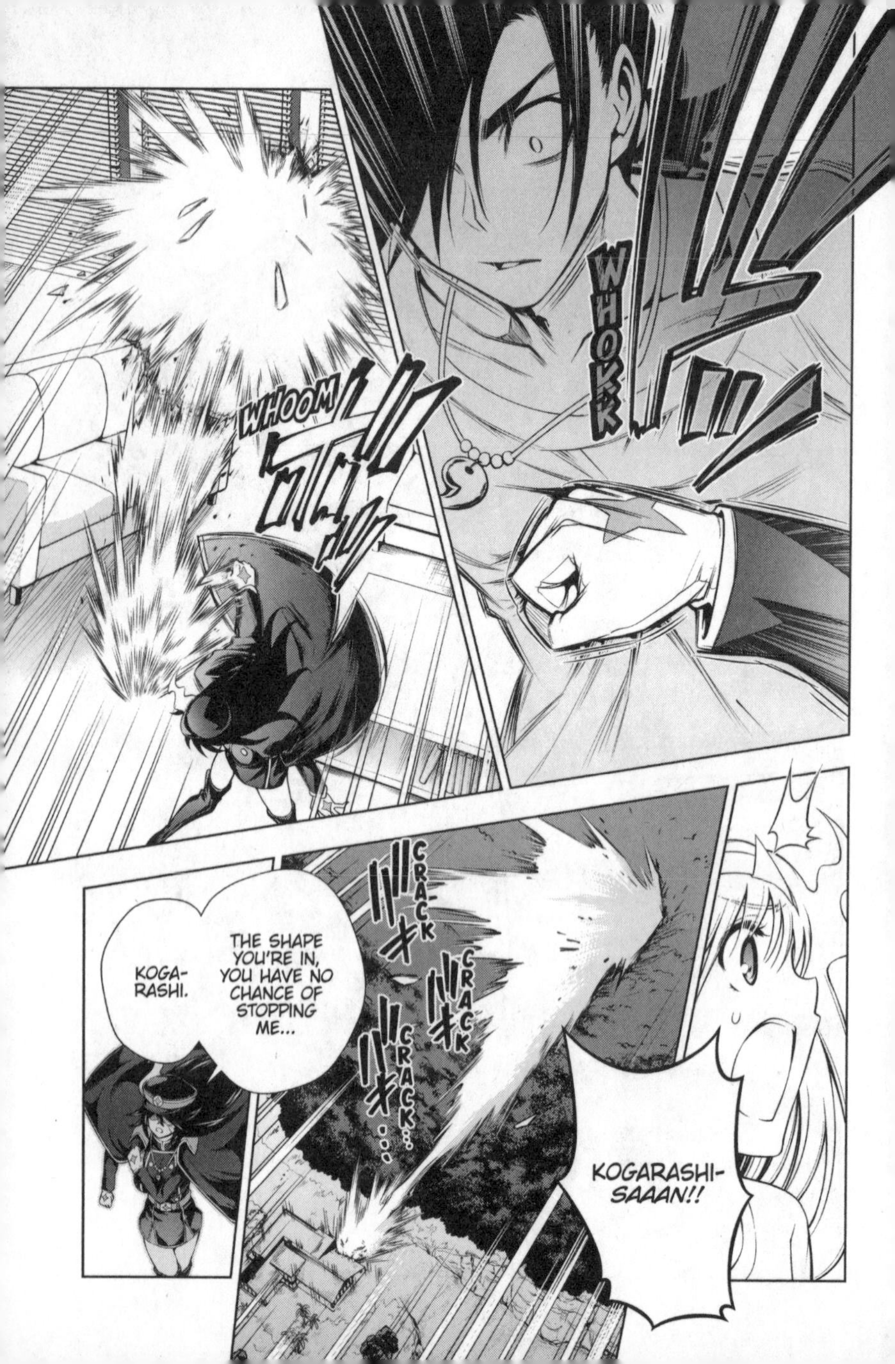
WHOKK
WHOOM
KOGARASHI-SAAAN!!
CRACK
CRACK
CRACK...
THE SHAPE YOU'RE IN, YOU HAVE NO CHANCE OF STOPPING ME...
KOGA-RASHI.

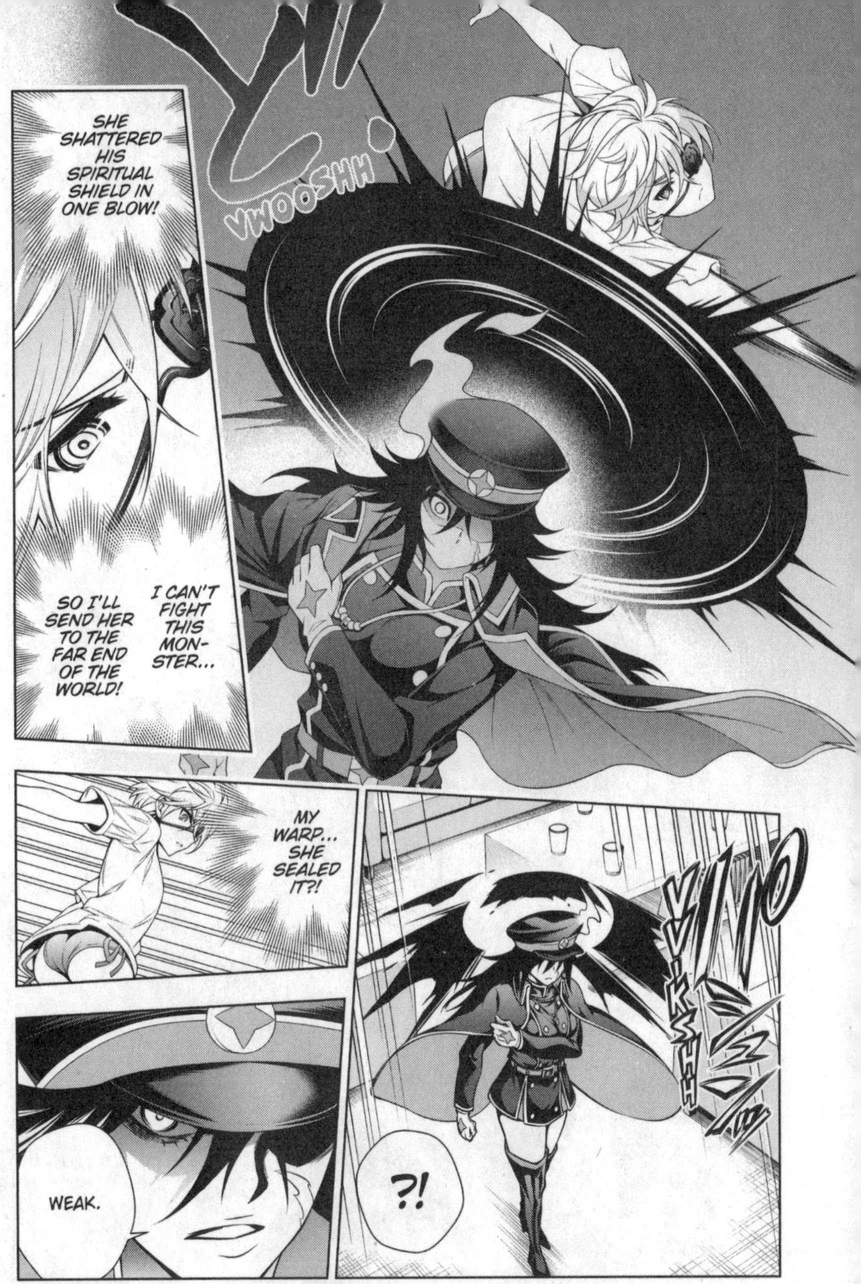
VWOOSHH
SHE SHATTERED HIS SPIRITUAL SHIELD IN ONE BLOW!
I CAN'T FIGHT THIS MONSTER...
SO I'LL SEND HER TO THE FAR END OF THE WORLD!
VVIKSHH
?!
MY WARP... SHE SEALED IT?!
WEAK.

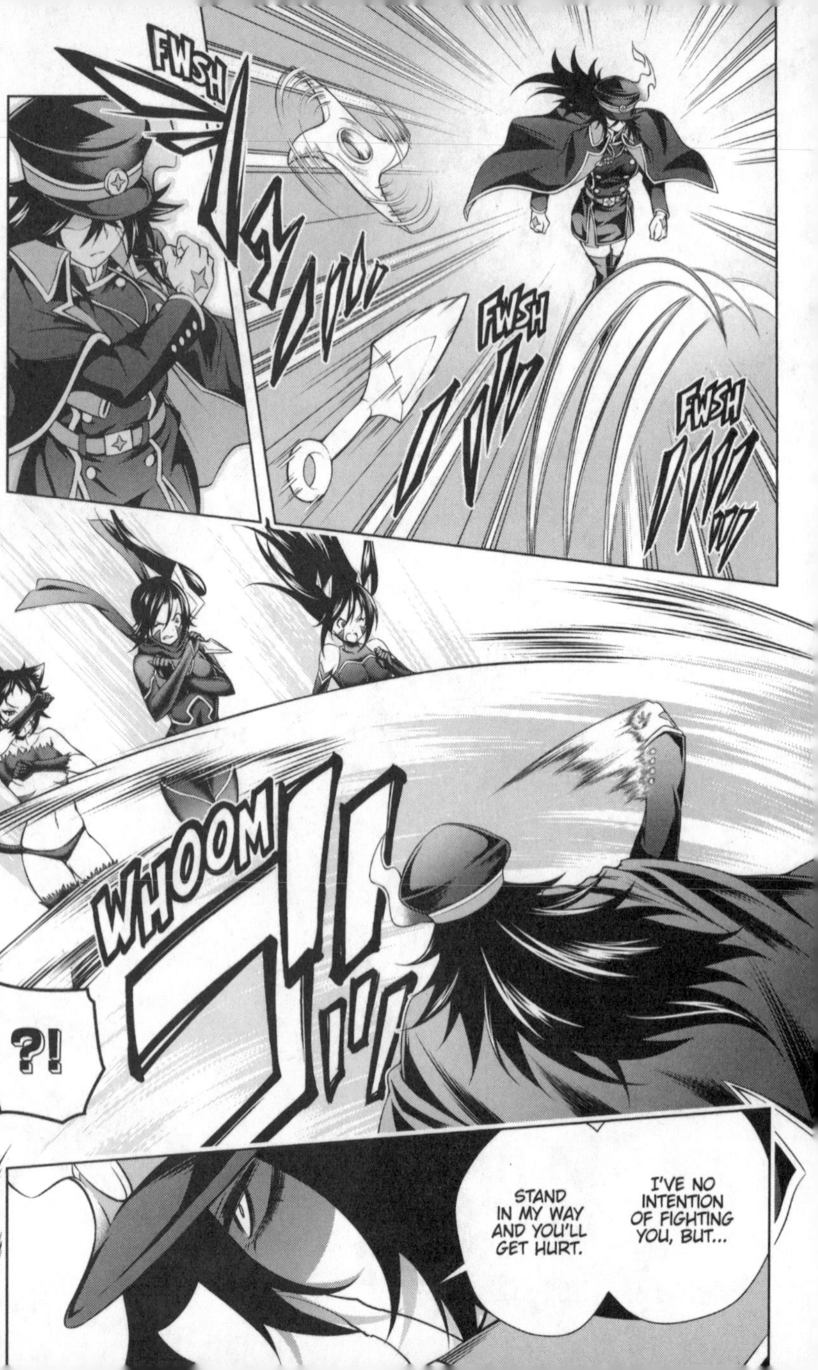
FWSH
FWSH
FWSH
WHOOM
?!
I'VE NO INTENTION OF FIGHTING YOU, BUT...
STAND IN MY WAY AND YOU'LL GET HURT.

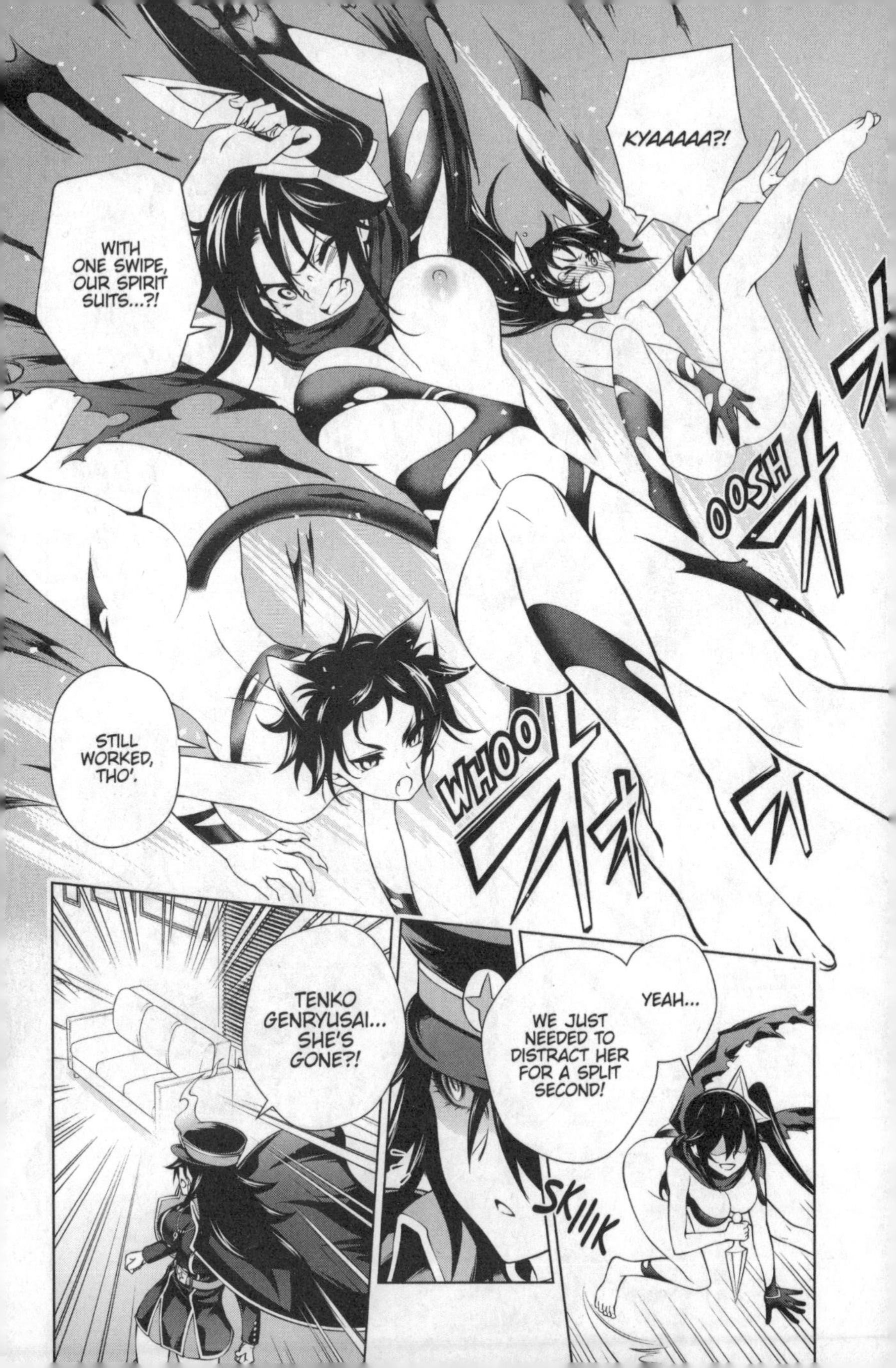
KYAAAAA?!
WITH ONE SWIPE, OUR SPIRIT SUITS...?!
OOSH
WHOO
STILL WORKED, THO'.
YEAH...
WE JUST NEEDED TO DISTRACT HER FOR A SPLIT SECOND!
SKIIIK
TENKO GENRYUSAI... SHE'S GONE?!

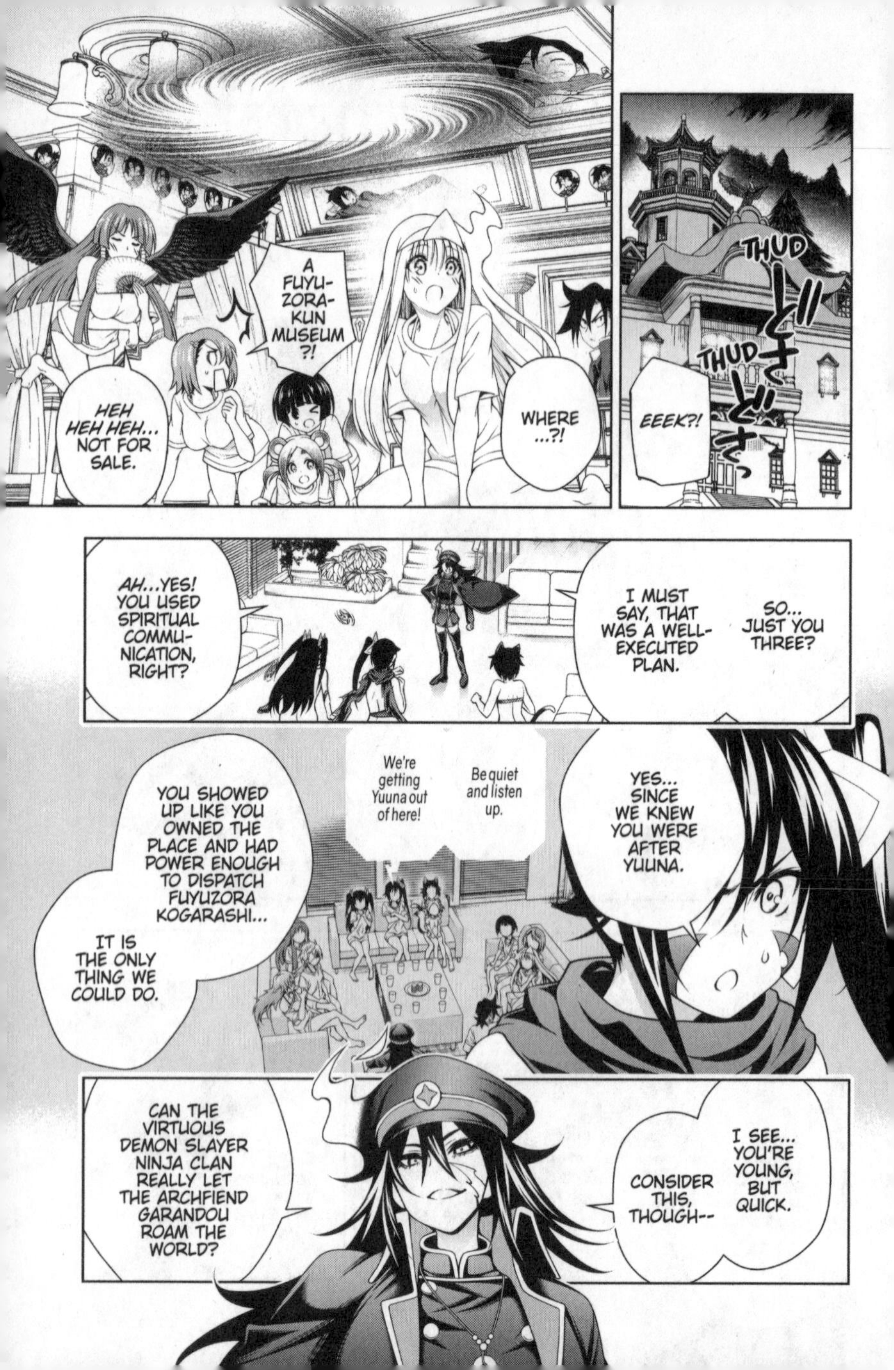
THUD
どさ
THUD
どさっ
EEEK?!
WHERE ...?!
A FUYUZORA-KUN MUSEUM ?!
HEH HEH HEH... NOT FOR SALE.
SO... JUST YOU THREE?
I MUST SAY, THAT WAS A WELL-EXECUTED PLAN.
AH...YES! YOU USED SPIRITUAL COMMUNICATION, RIGHT?
YES... SINCE WE KNEW YOU WERE AFTER YUUNA.
Be quiet and listen up.
We're getting Yuuna out of here!
YOU SHOWED UP LIKE YOU OWNED THE PLACE AND HAD POWER ENOUGH TO DISPATCH FUYUZORA KOGARASHI...
IT IS THE ONLY THING WE COULD DO.
I SEE... YOU'RE YOUNG, BUT QUICK.
CONSIDER THIS, THOUGH--
CAN THE VIRTUOUS DEMON SLAYER NINJA CLAN REALLY LET THE ARCHFIEND GARANDOU ROAM THE WORLD?

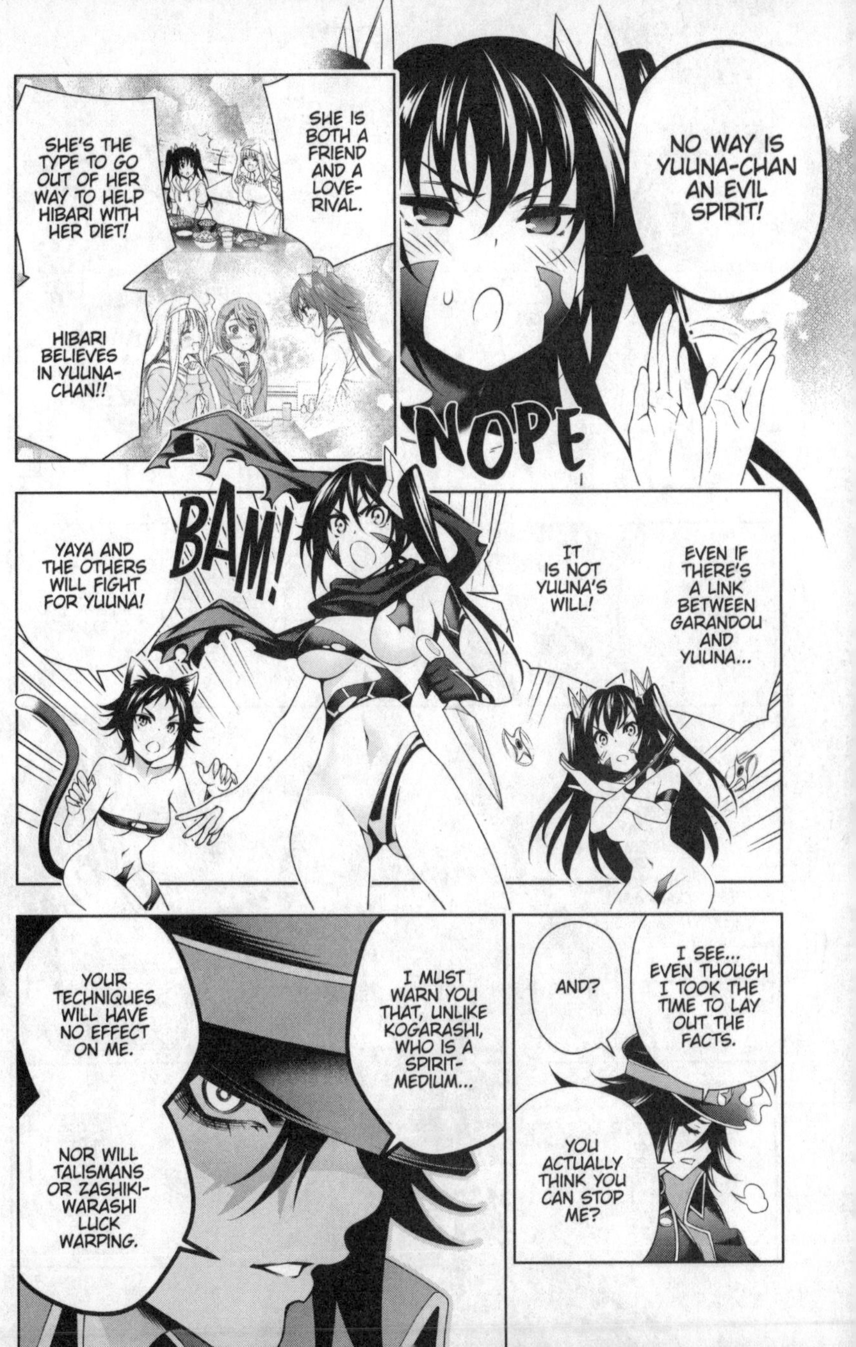
NO WAY IS YUUNA-CHAN AN EVIL SPIRIT!
NOPE
SHE IS BOTH A FRIEND AND A LOVE-RIVAL.
SHE'S THE TYPE TO GO OUT OF HER WAY TO HELP HIBARI WITH HER DIET!
HIBARI BELIEVES IN YUUNA-CHAN!!
EVEN IF THERE'S A LINK BETWEEN GARANDOU AND YUUNA...
IT IS NOT YUUNA'S WILL!
BAM!
YAYA AND THE OTHERS WILL FIGHT FOR YUUNA!
I SEE... EVEN THOUGH I TOOK THE TIME TO LAY OUT THE FACTS.
AND?
YOU ACTUALLY THINK YOU CAN STOP ME?
I MUST WARN YOU THAT, UNLIKE KOGARASHI, WHO IS A SPIRIT-MEDIUM...
YOUR TECHNIQUES WILL HAVE NO EFFECT ON ME.
NOR WILL TALISMANS OR ZASHIKI-WARASHI LUCK WARPING.

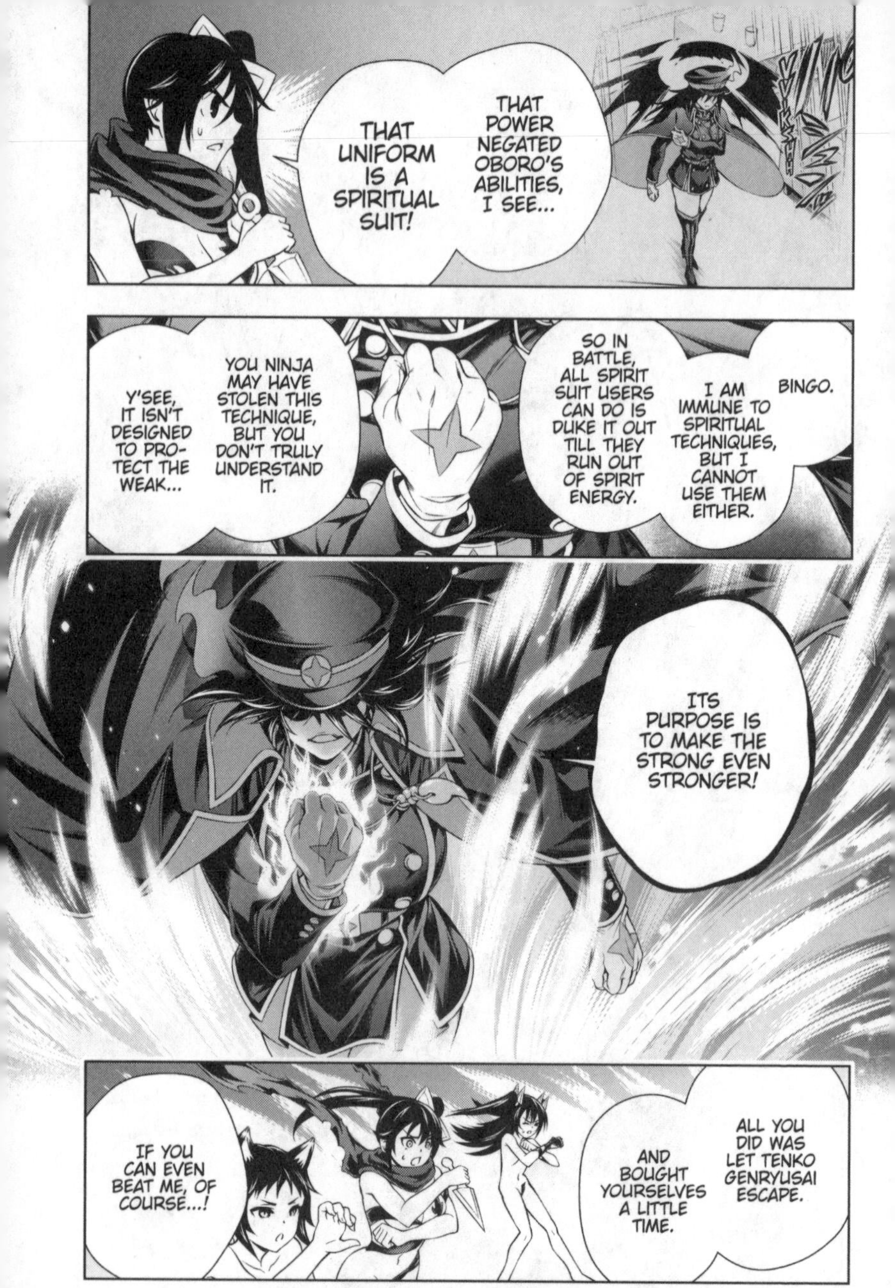
THAT POWER NEGATED OBORO'S ABILITIES, I SEE...
THAT UNIFORM IS A SPIRITUAL SUIT!
BINGO.
I AM IMMUNE TO SPIRITUAL TECHNIQUES, BUT I CANNOT USE THEM EITHER.
SO IN BATTLE, ALL SPIRIT SUIT USERS CAN DO IS DUKE IT OUT TILL THEY RUN OUT OF SPIRIT ENERGY.
YOU NINJA MAY HAVE STOLEN THIS TECHNIQUE, BUT YOU DON'T TRULY UNDERSTAND IT.
Y'SEE, IT ISN'T DESIGNED TO PRO-TECT THE WEAK...
ITS PURPOSE IS TO MAKE THE STRONG EVEN STRONGER!
ALL YOU DID WAS LET TENKO GENRYUSAI ESCAPE.
AND BOUGHT YOURSELVES A LITTLE TIME.
IF YOU CAN EVEN BEAT ME, OF COURSE...!

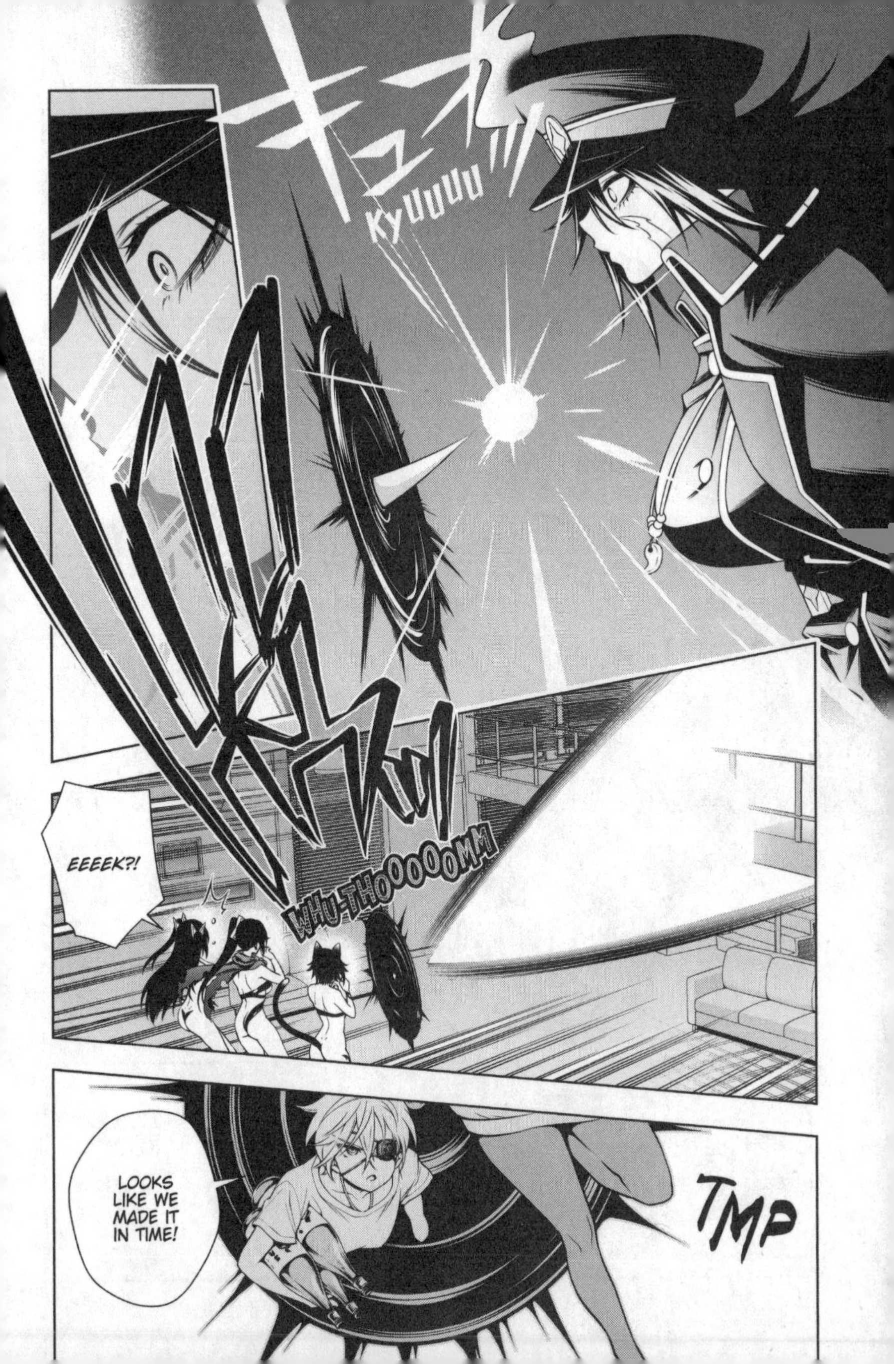
キュオ
KYUUUU
WHU-THOOOOOMM
EEEEK?!
TMP
LOOKS LIKE WE MADE IT IN TIME!

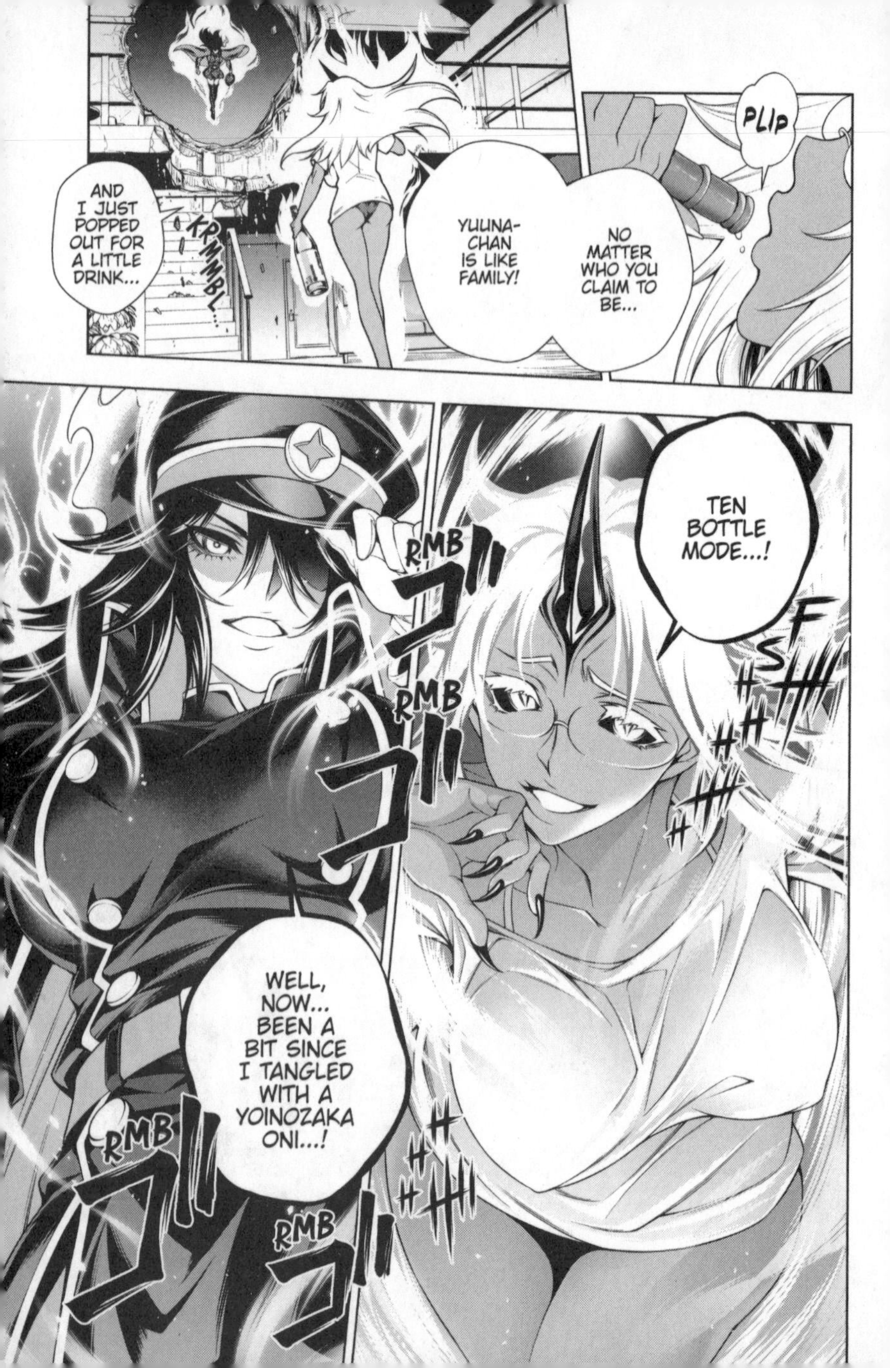
PLIP
NO MATTER WHO YOU CLAIM TO BE...
YUUNA-CHAN IS LIKE FAMILY!
KRMMBL...
AND I JUST POPPED OUT FOR A LITTLE DRINK...
TEN BOTTLE MODE...!
FSHHH
RMB
RMB
WELL, NOW... BEEN A BIT SINCE I TANGLED WITH A YOINOZAKA ONI...!
RMB
RMB

Yuuna
and the
Haunted
Hot
Springs

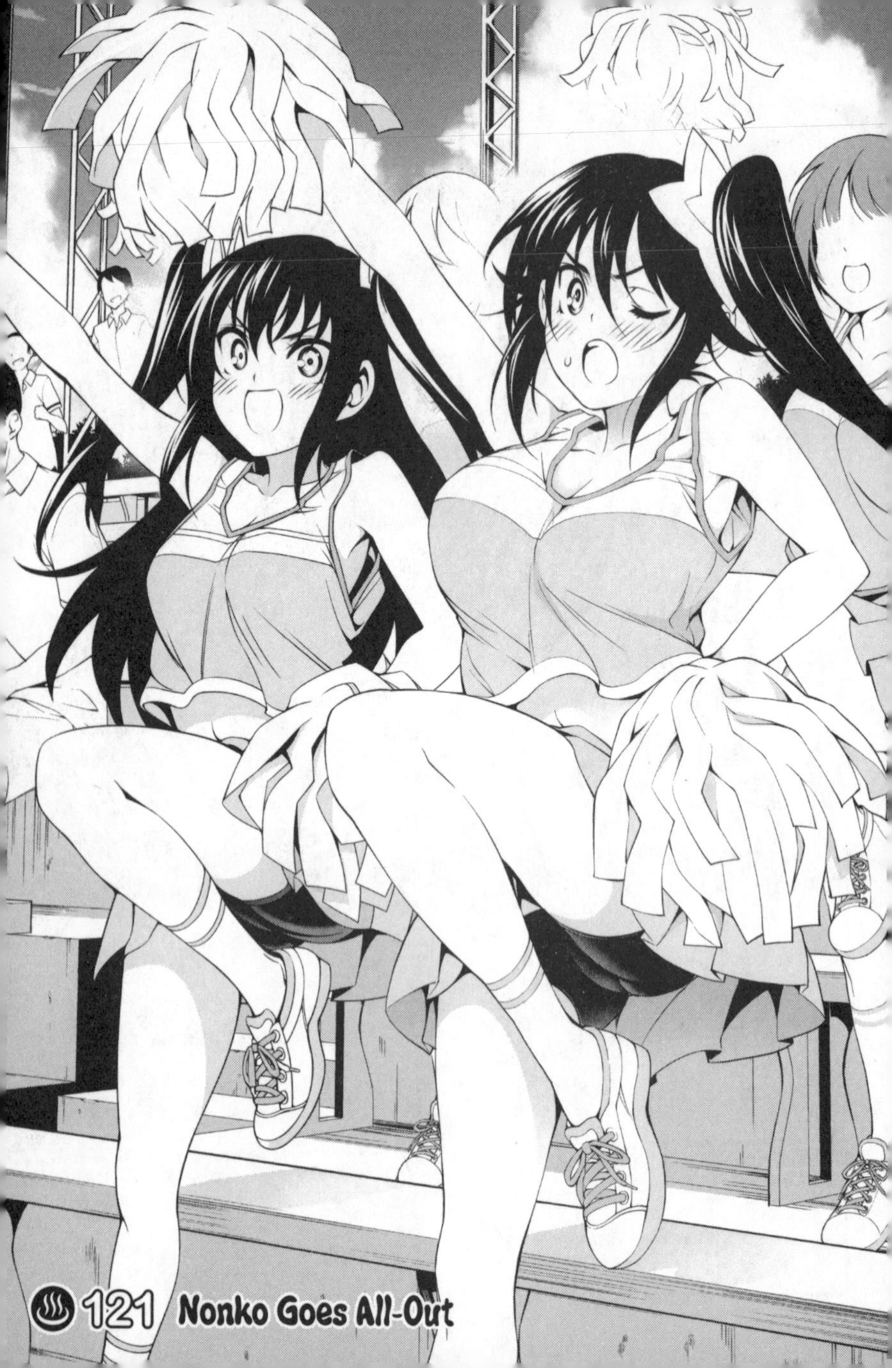
121 Nonko Goes All-Out

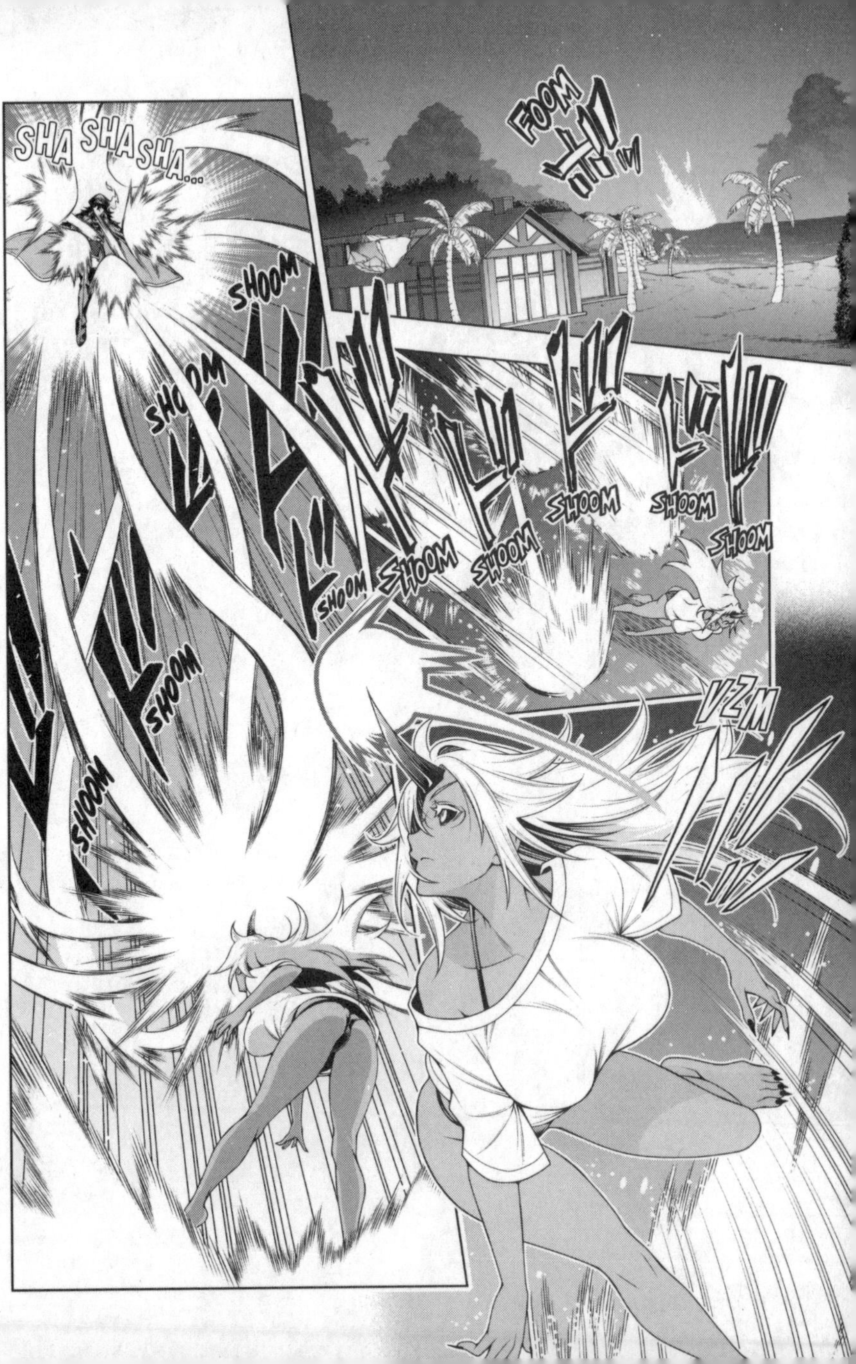
FOOM
SHOOM
SHOOM
SHOOM
SHOOM
SHOOM
SHOOM
VZM
SHA SHA SHA...
SHOOM
SHOOM
SHOOM
SHOOM
SHOOM
SHOOM

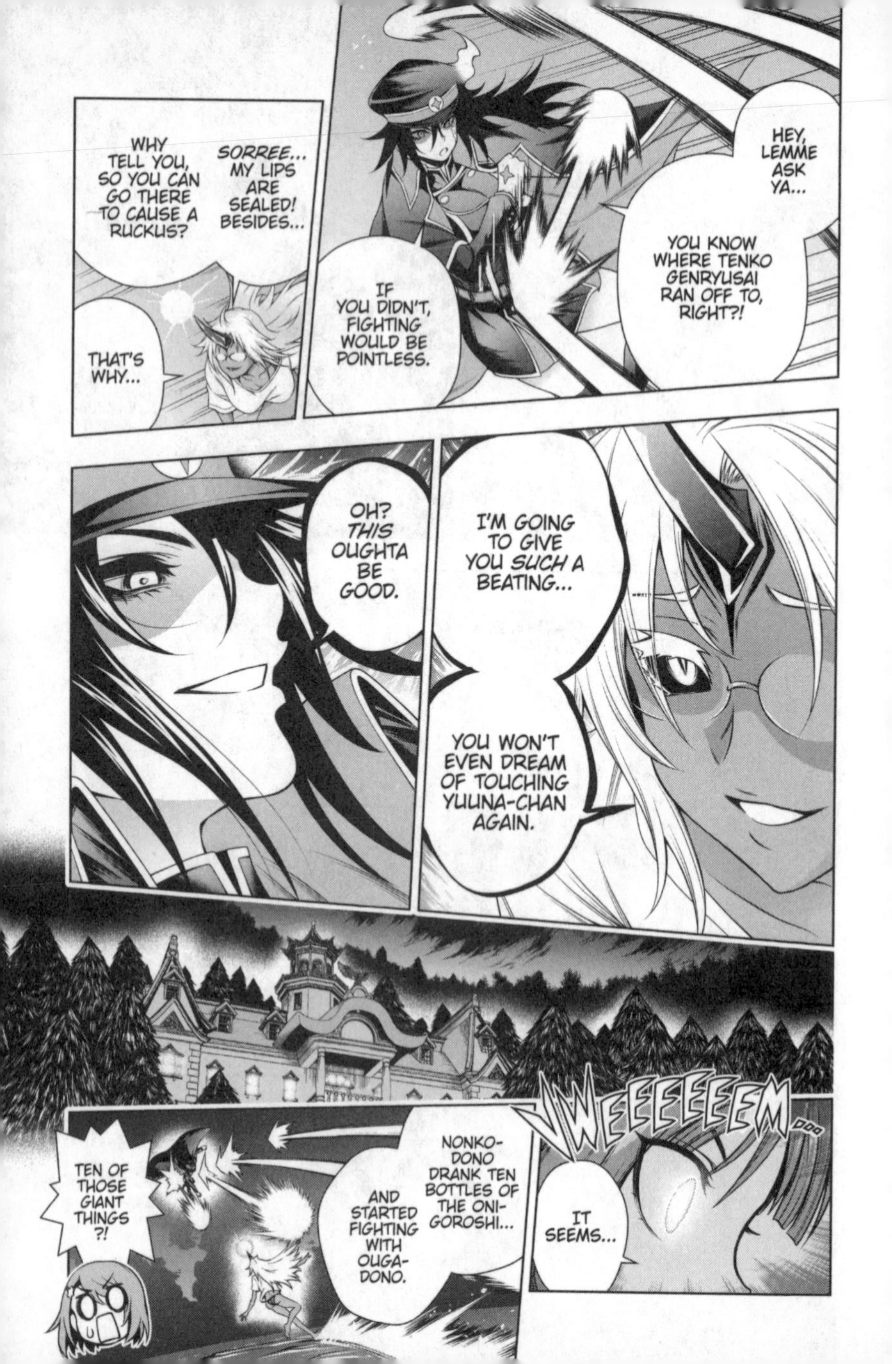
HEY, LEMME ASK YA...
YOU KNOW WHERE TENKO GENRYUSAI RAN OFF TO, RIGHT?!
IF YOU DIDN'T, FIGHTING WOULD BE POINTLESS.
SORREE... MY LIPS ARE SEALED! BESIDES...
WHY TELL YOU, SO YOU CAN GO THERE TO CAUSE A RUCKUS?
THAT'S WHY...
I'M GOING TO GIVE YOU SUCH A BEATING...
YOU WON'T EVEN DREAM OF TOUCHING YUUNA-CHAN AGAIN.
OH? THIS OUGHTA BE GOOD.
VWEEEEEEM...
IT SEEMS...
NONKO-DONO DRANK TEN BOTTLES OF THE ONI-GOROSHI...
AND STARTED FIGHTING WITH OUGA-DONO.
TEN OF THOSE GIANT THINGS?!

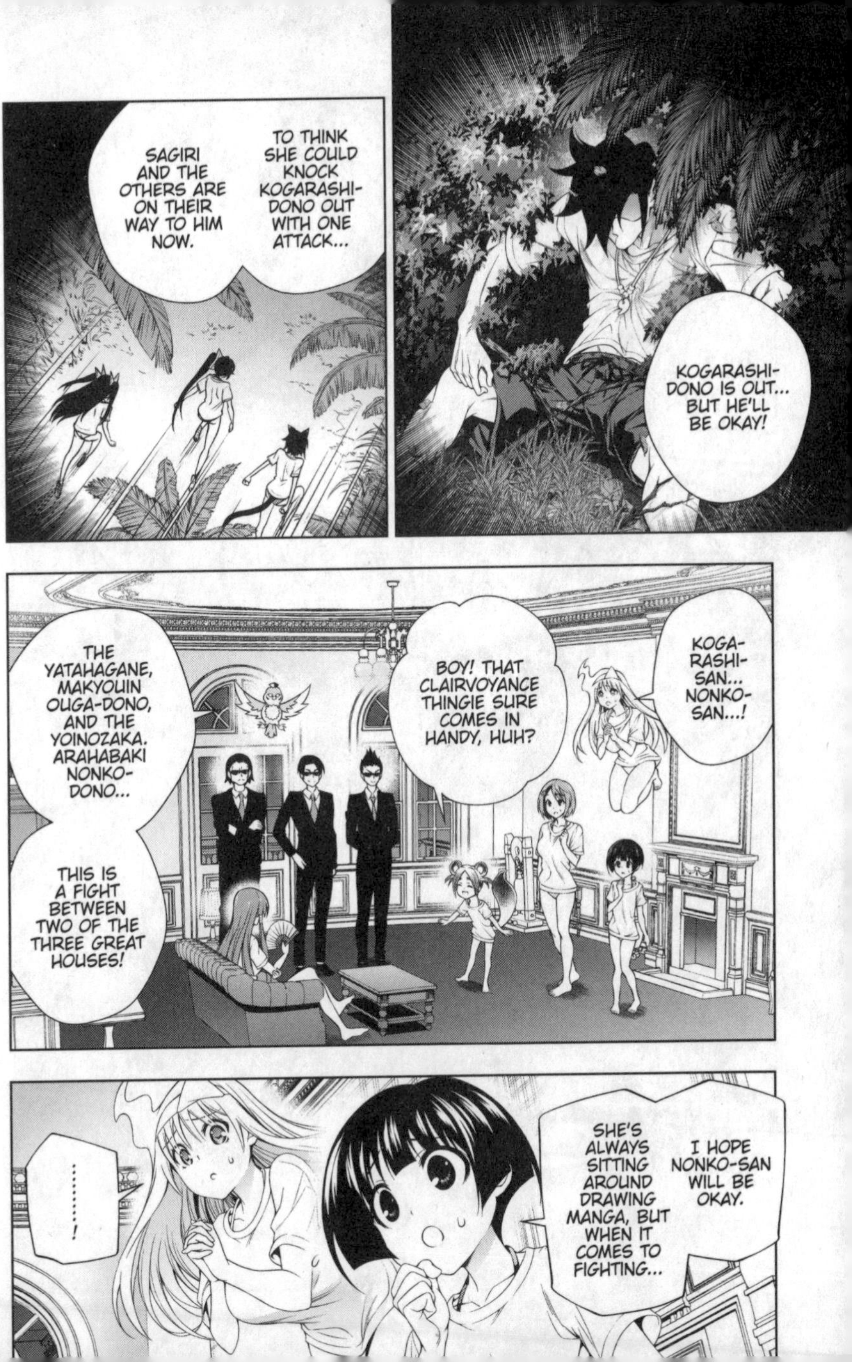
KOGARASHI-DONO IS OUT... BUT HE'LL BE OKAY!
TO THINK SHE COULD KNOCK KOGARASHI-DONO OUT WITH ONE ATTACK...
SAGIRI AND THE OTHERS ARE ON THEIR WAY TO HIM NOW.
KOGA-RASHI-SAN... NONKO-SAN...!
BOY! THAT CLAIRVOYANCE THINGIE SURE COMES IN HANDY, HUH?
THE YATAHAGANE, MAKYOUIN OUGA-DONO, AND THE YOINOZAKA. ARAHABAKI NONKO-DONO...
THIS IS A FIGHT BETWEEN TWO OF THE THREE GREAT HOUSES!
I HOPE NONKO-SAN WILL BE OKAY.
SHE'S ALWAYS SITTING AROUND DRAWING MANGA, BUT WHEN IT COMES TO FIGHTING...
......!

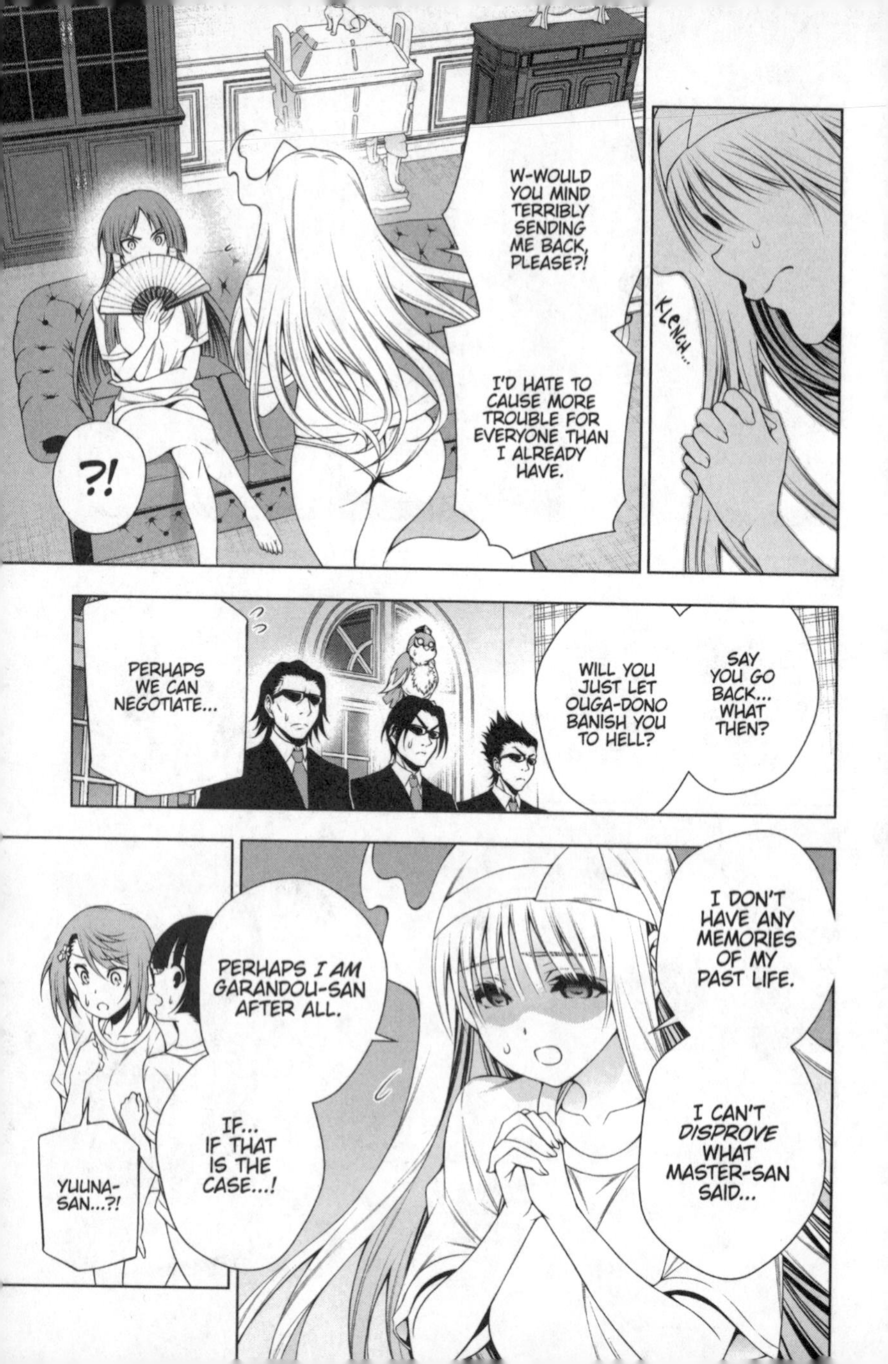
KLENCH...
W-WOULD YOU MIND TERRIBLY SENDING ME BACK, PLEASE?!
I'D HATE TO CAUSE MORE TROUBLE FOR EVERYONE THAN I ALREADY HAVE.
?!
SAY YOU GO BACK... WHAT THEN?
WILL YOU JUST LET OUGA-DONO BANISH YOU TO HELL?
PERHAPS WE CAN NEGOTIATE...
I DON'T HAVE ANY MEMORIES OF MY PAST LIFE.
I CAN'T *DISPROVE* WHAT MASTER-SAN SAID...
PERHAPS *I AM* GARANDOU-SAN AFTER ALL.
IF... IF THAT IS THE CASE...!
YUUNA-SAN...?!

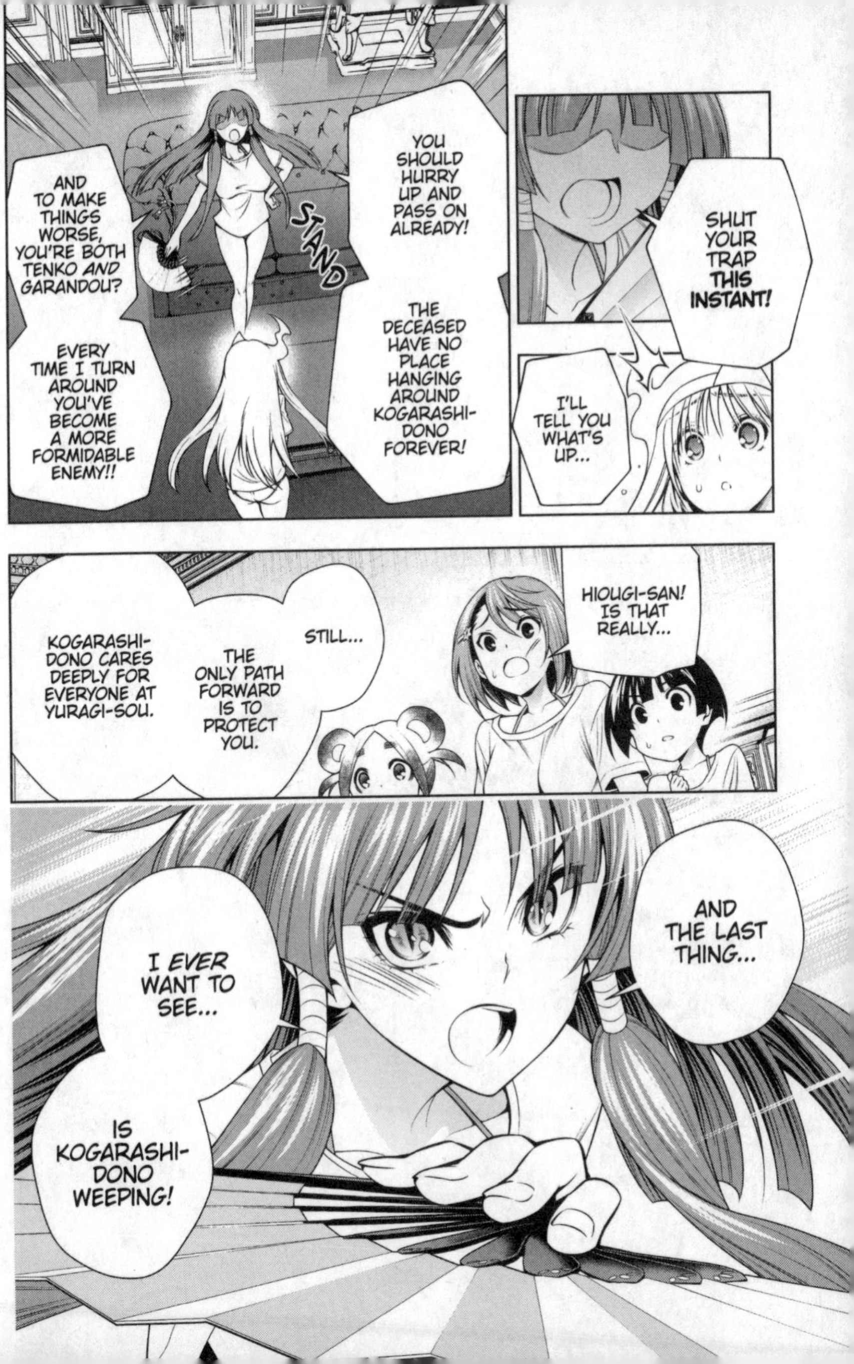
SHUT YOUR TRAP THIS INSTANT!
I'LL TELL YOU WHAT'S UP...
YOU SHOULD HURRY UP AND PASS ON ALREADY!
THE DECEASED HAVE NO PLACE HANGING AROUND KOGARASHI-DONO FOREVER!
STAND
AND TO MAKE THINGS WORSE, YOU'RE BOTH TENKO AND GARANDOU?
EVERY TIME I TURN AROUND YOU'VE BECOME A MORE FORMIDABLE ENEMY!!
HIOUGI-SAN! IS THAT REALLY...
STILL...
THE ONLY PATH FORWARD IS TO PROTECT YOU.
KOGARASHI-DONO CARES DEEPLY FOR EVERYONE AT YURAGI-SOU.
AND THE LAST THING...
I EVER WANT TO SEE...
IS KOGARASHI-DONO WEEPING!

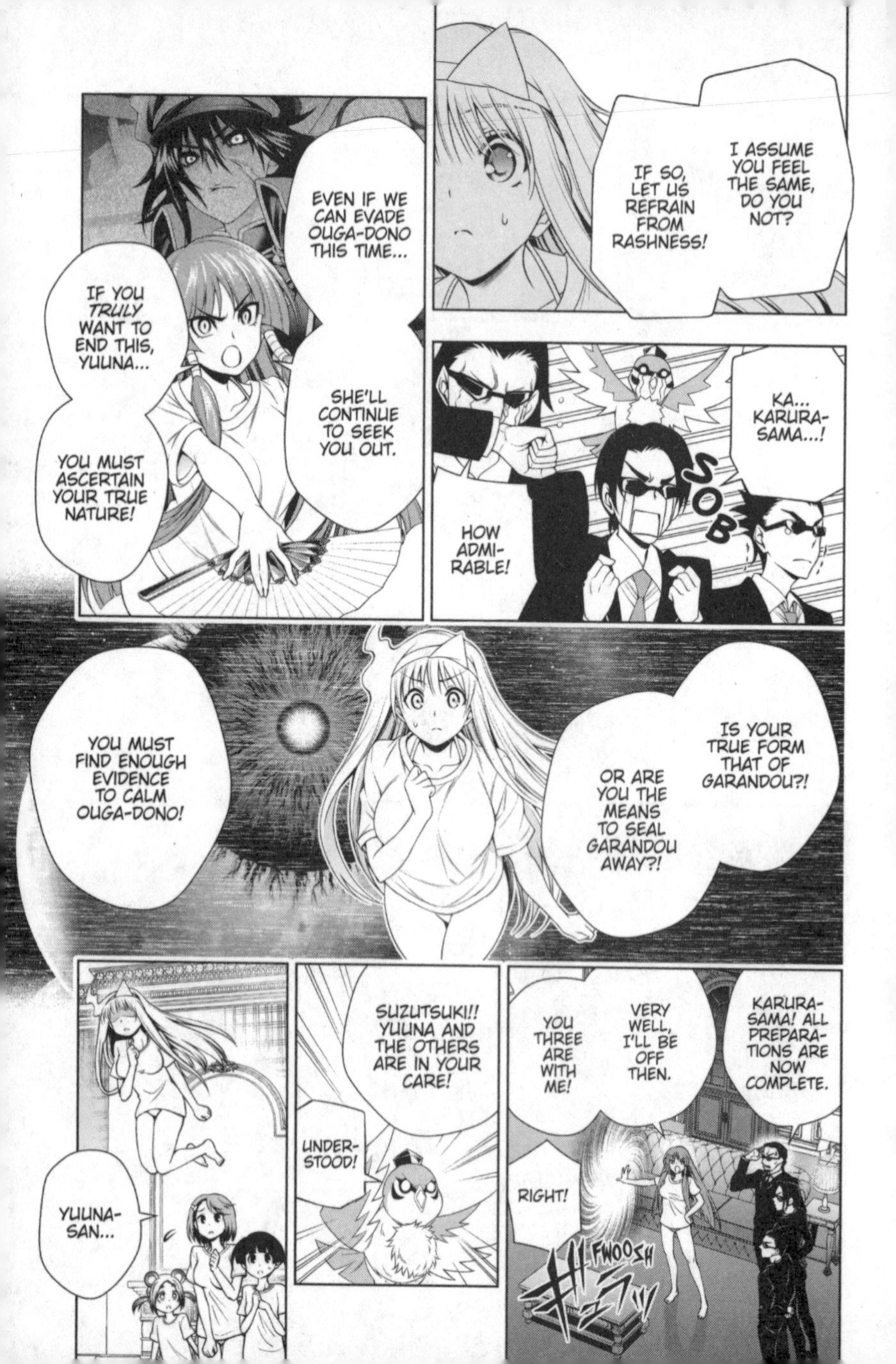
I ASSUME YOU FEEL THE SAME, DO YOU NOT?
IF SO, LET US REFRAIN FROM RASHNESS!
KA... KARURA-SAMA...!
SOB
HOW ADMIRABLE!
EVEN IF WE CAN EVADE OUGA-DONO THIS TIME...
SHE'LL CONTINUE TO SEEK YOU OUT.
IF YOU *TRULY* WANT TO END THIS, YUUNA...
YOU MUST ASCERTAIN YOUR TRUE NATURE!
IS YOUR TRUE FORM THAT OF GARANDOU?!
OR ARE YOU THE MEANS TO SEAL GARANDOU AWAY?!
YOU MUST FIND ENOUGH EVIDENCE TO CALM OUGA-DONO!
KARURA-SAMA! ALL PREPARA-TIONS ARE NOW COMPLETE.
VERY WELL, I'LL BE OFF THEN.
YOU THREE ARE WITH ME!
RIGHT!
FWOOSH
SUZUTSUKI!! YUUNA AND THE OTHERS ARE IN YOUR CARE!
UNDER-STOOD!
YUUNA-SAN...

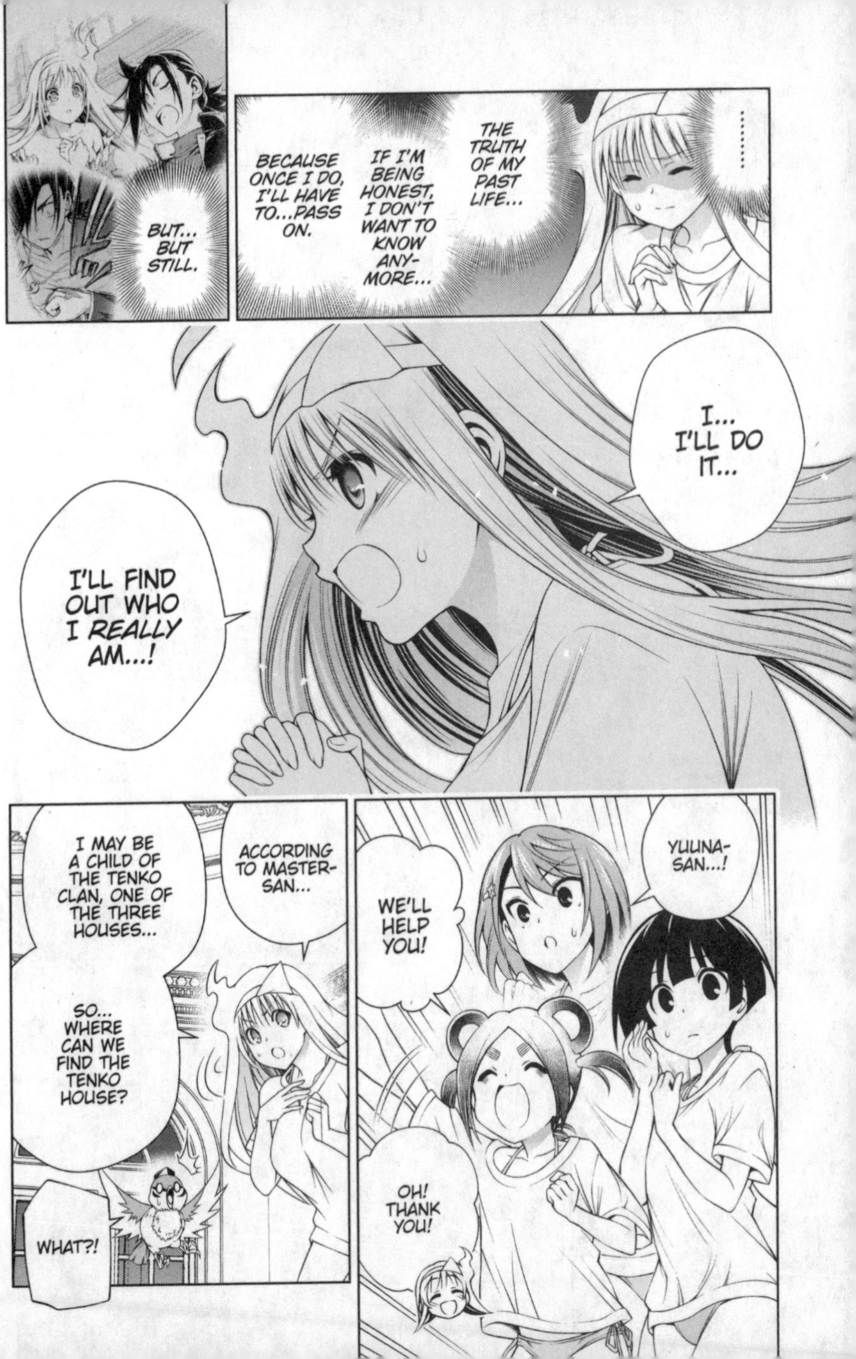
......
THE TRUTH OF MY PAST LIFE...
IF I'M BEING HONEST, I DON'T WANT TO KNOW ANYMORE...
BECAUSE ONCE I DO, I'LL HAVE TO...PASS ON.
BUT... BUT STILL.
I... I'LL DO IT...
I'LL FIND OUT WHO I *REALLY* AM...!
YUUNA-SAN...!
WE'LL HELP YOU!
OH! THANK YOU!
ACCORDING TO MASTER-SAN...
I MAY BE A CHILD OF THE TENKO CLAN, ONE OF THE THREE HOUSES...
SO... WHERE CAN WE FIND THE TENKO HOUSE?
WHAT?!

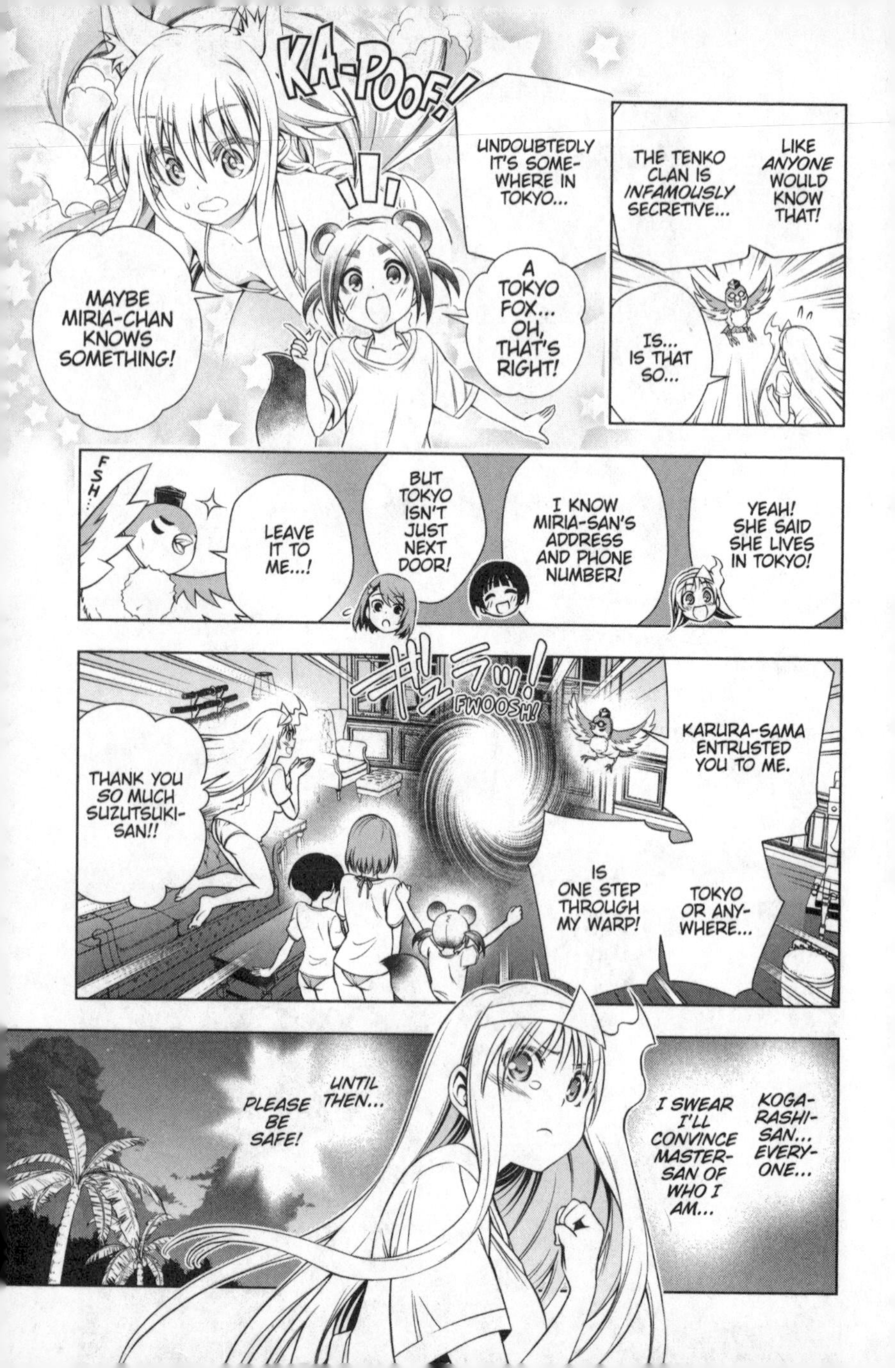

LIKE ANYONE WOULD KNOW THAT!
THE TENKO CLAN IS INFAMOUSLY SECRETIVE...
IS... IS THAT SO...
UNDOUBTEDLY IT'S SOME-WHERE IN TOKYO...
KA-POOF!
A TOKYO FOX... OH, THAT'S RIGHT!
MAYBE MIRIA-CHAN KNOWS SOMETHING!
YEAH! SHE SAID SHE LIVES IN TOKYO!
I KNOW MIRIA-SAN'S ADDRESS AND PHONE NUMBER!
BUT TOKYO ISN'T JUST NEXT DOOR!
LEAVE IT TO ME...!
FSH...
FWOOSH!
KARURA-SAMA ENTRUSTED YOU TO ME.
TOKYO OR ANY-WHERE...
IS ONE STEP THROUGH MY WARP!
THANK YOU SO MUCH SUZUTSUKI-SAN!!
KOGA-RASHI-SAN... EVERY-ONE...
I SWEAR I'LL CONVINCE MASTER-SAN OF WHO I AM...
UNTIL THEN...
PLEASE BE SAFE!

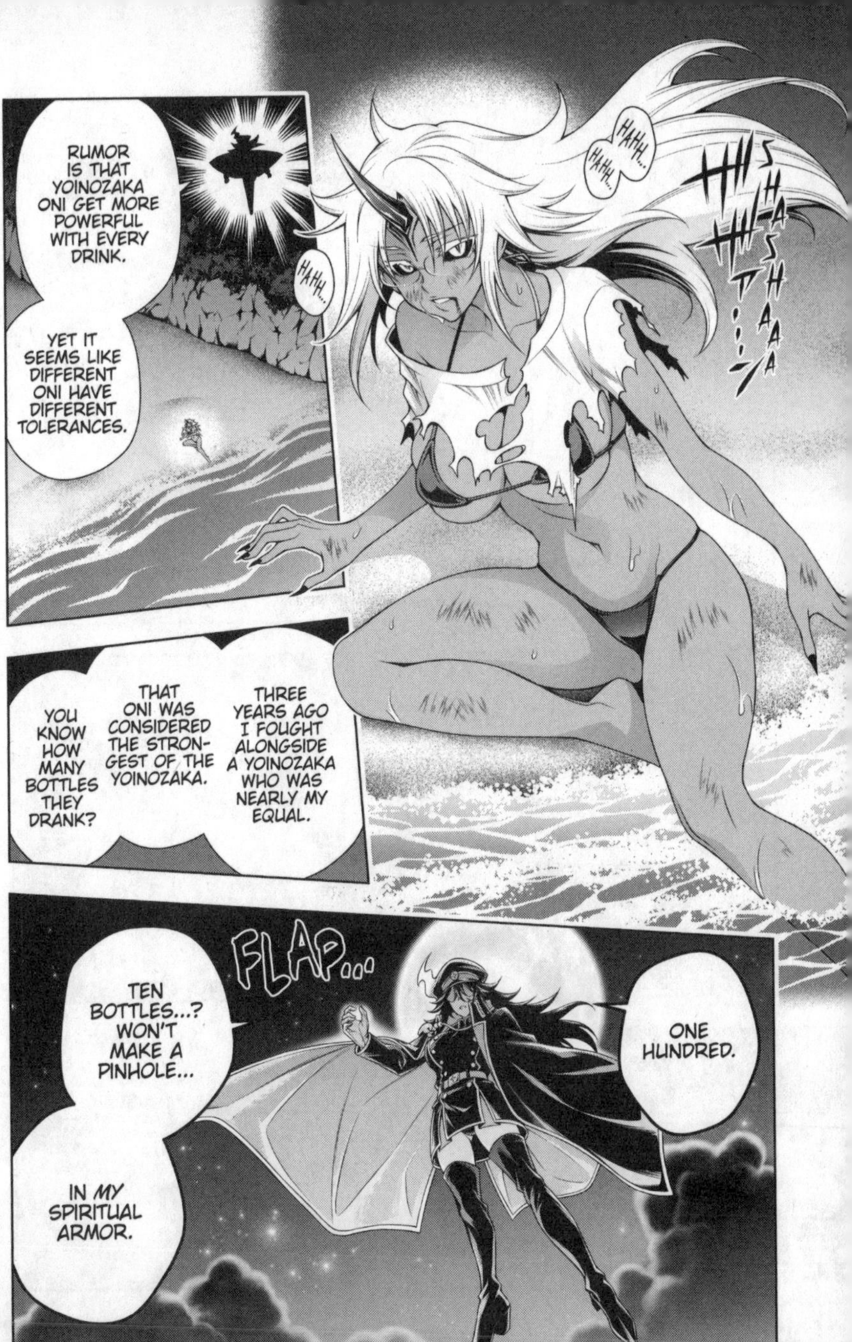
HAHH...
HAHH...
SHASHAAA
HAHH...
RUMOR IS THAT YOINOZAKA ONI GET MORE POWERFUL WITH EVERY DRINK.
YET IT SEEMS LIKE DIFFERENT ONI HAVE DIFFERENT TOLERANCES.
THREE YEARS AGO I FOUGHT ALONGSIDE A YOINOZAKA WHO WAS NEARLY MY EQUAL.
THAT ONI WAS CONSIDERED THE STRONGEST OF THE YOINOZAKA.
YOU KNOW HOW MANY BOTTLES THEY DRANK?
FLAP...
ONE HUNDRED.
TEN BOTTLES...? WON'T MAKE A PINHOLE...
IN MY SPIRITUAL ARMOR.

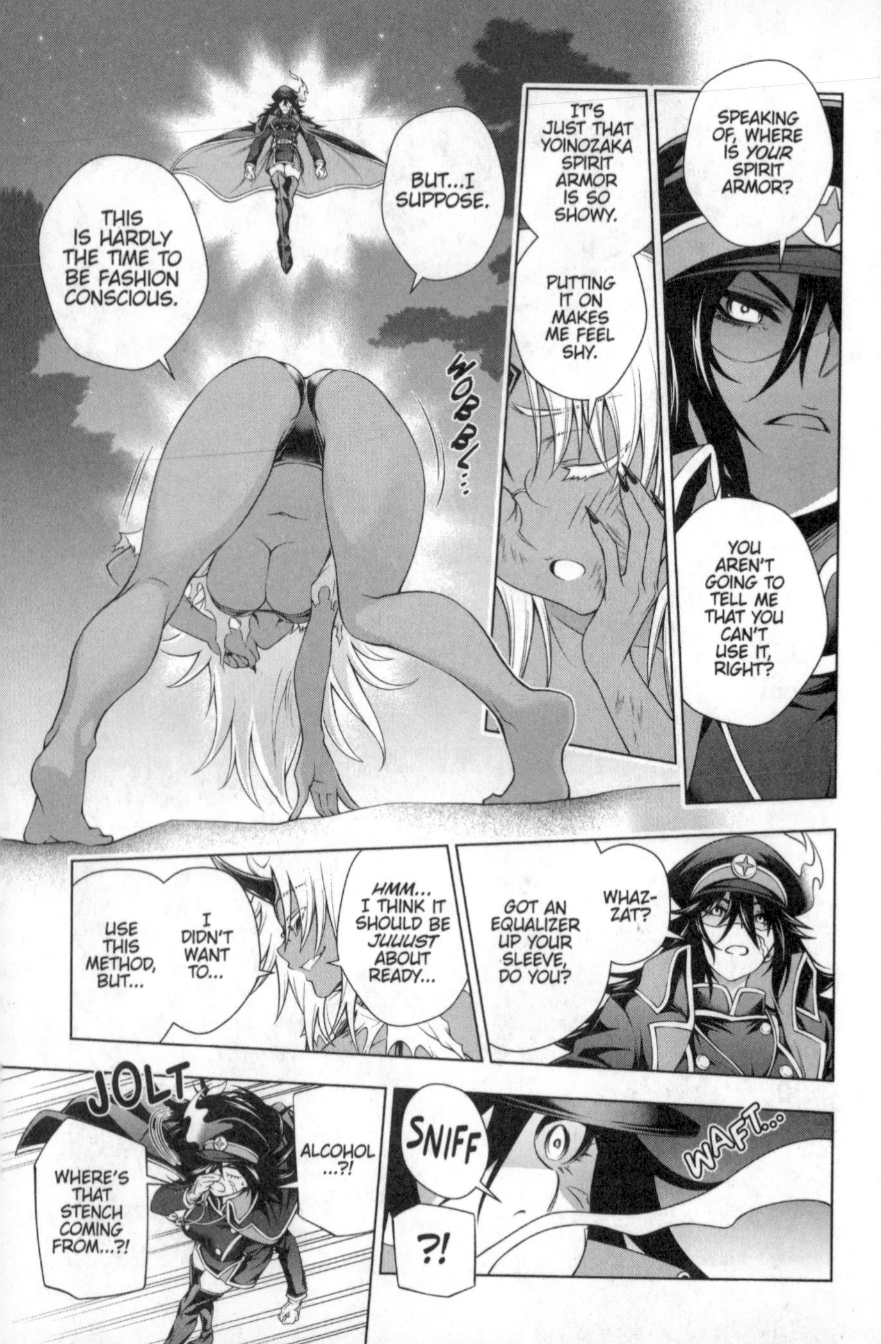
SPEAKING OF, WHERE IS YOUR SPIRIT ARMOR?
YOU AREN'T GOING TO TELL ME THAT YOU CAN'T USE IT, RIGHT?
IT'S JUST THAT YOINOZAKA SPIRIT ARMOR IS SO SHOWY.
PUTTING IT ON MAKES ME FEEL SHY.
BUT...I SUPPOSE.
THIS IS HARDLY THE TIME TO BE FASHION CONSCIOUS.
WOBBL...
WHAZ-ZAT?
GOT AN EQUALIZER UP YOUR SLEEVE, DO YOU?
HMM... I THINK IT SHOULD BE JUUUST ABOUT READY...
I DIDN'T WANT TO...
USE THIS METHOD, BUT...
WAFT...
SNIFF
?!
JOLT
ALCOHOL ...?!
WHERE'S THAT STENCH COMING FROM...?!

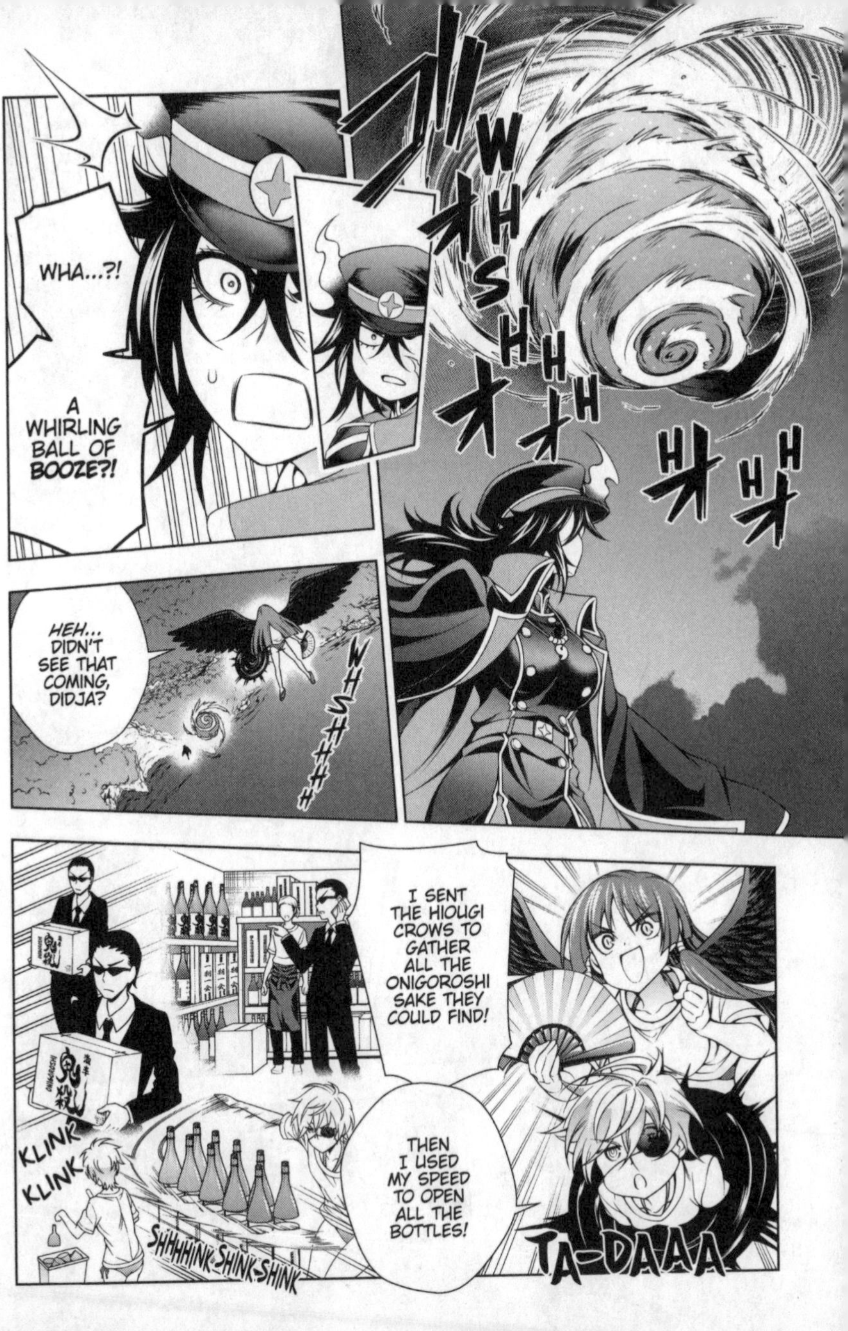
WHSHHHH
HHH
WHA...?!
A WHIRLING BALL OF BOOZE?!
HEH... DIDN'T SEE THAT COMING, DIDJA?
WHSHHHHH
I SENT THE HIOUGI CROWS TO GATHER ALL THE ONIGOROSHI SAKE THEY COULD FIND!
THEN I USED MY SPEED TO OPEN ALL THE BOTTLES!
TA-DAAA
KLINK
KLINK
SHHHHINK-SHINK-SHINK

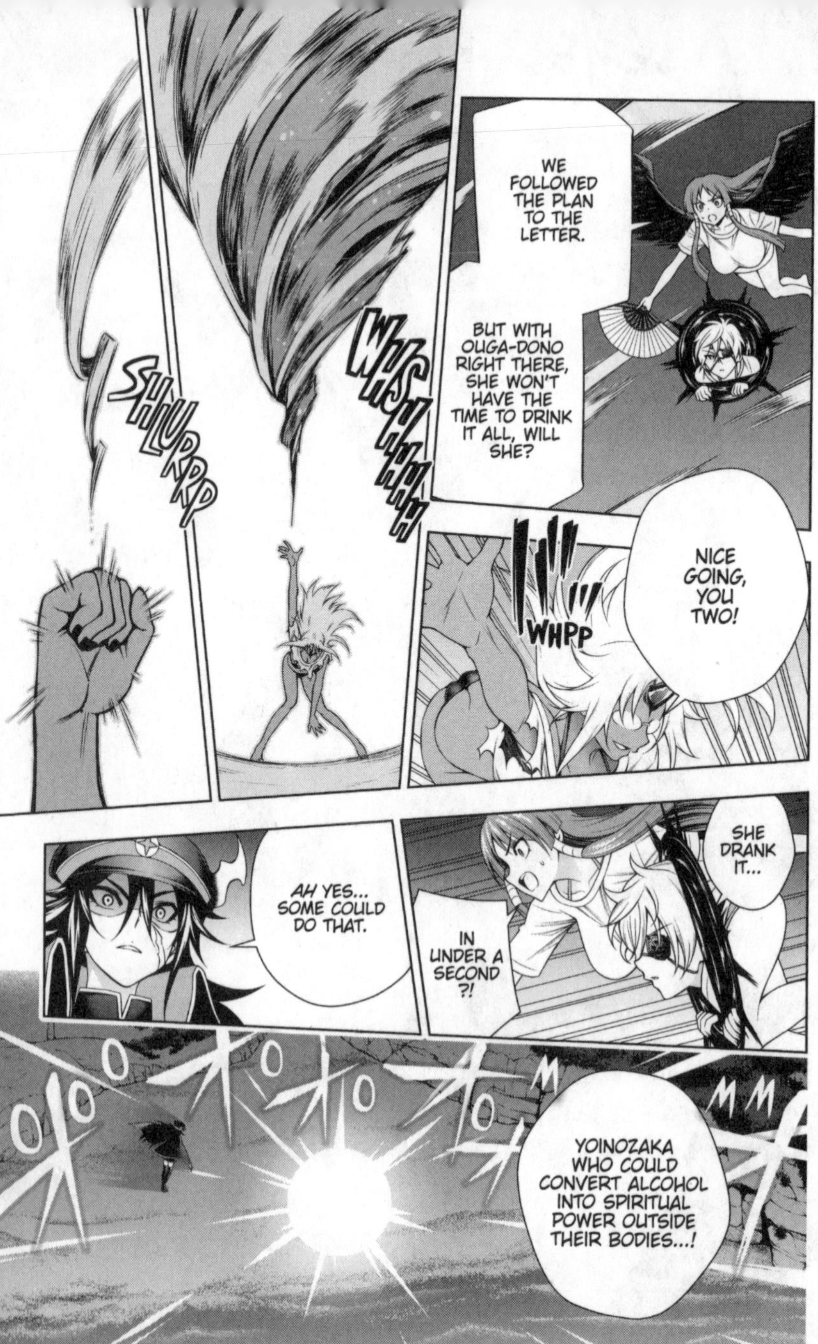
WE FOLLOWED THE PLAN TO THE LETTER.
BUT WITH OUGA-DONO RIGHT THERE, SHE WON'T HAVE THE TIME TO DRINK IT ALL, WILL SHE?
NICE GOING, YOU TWO!
WHPP
SHLURRP
SHE DRANK IT...
IN UNDER A SECOND?!
AH YES... SOME COULD DO THAT.
YOINOZAKA WHO COULD CONVERT ALCOHOL INTO SPIRITUAL POWER OUTSIDE THEIR BODIES...!

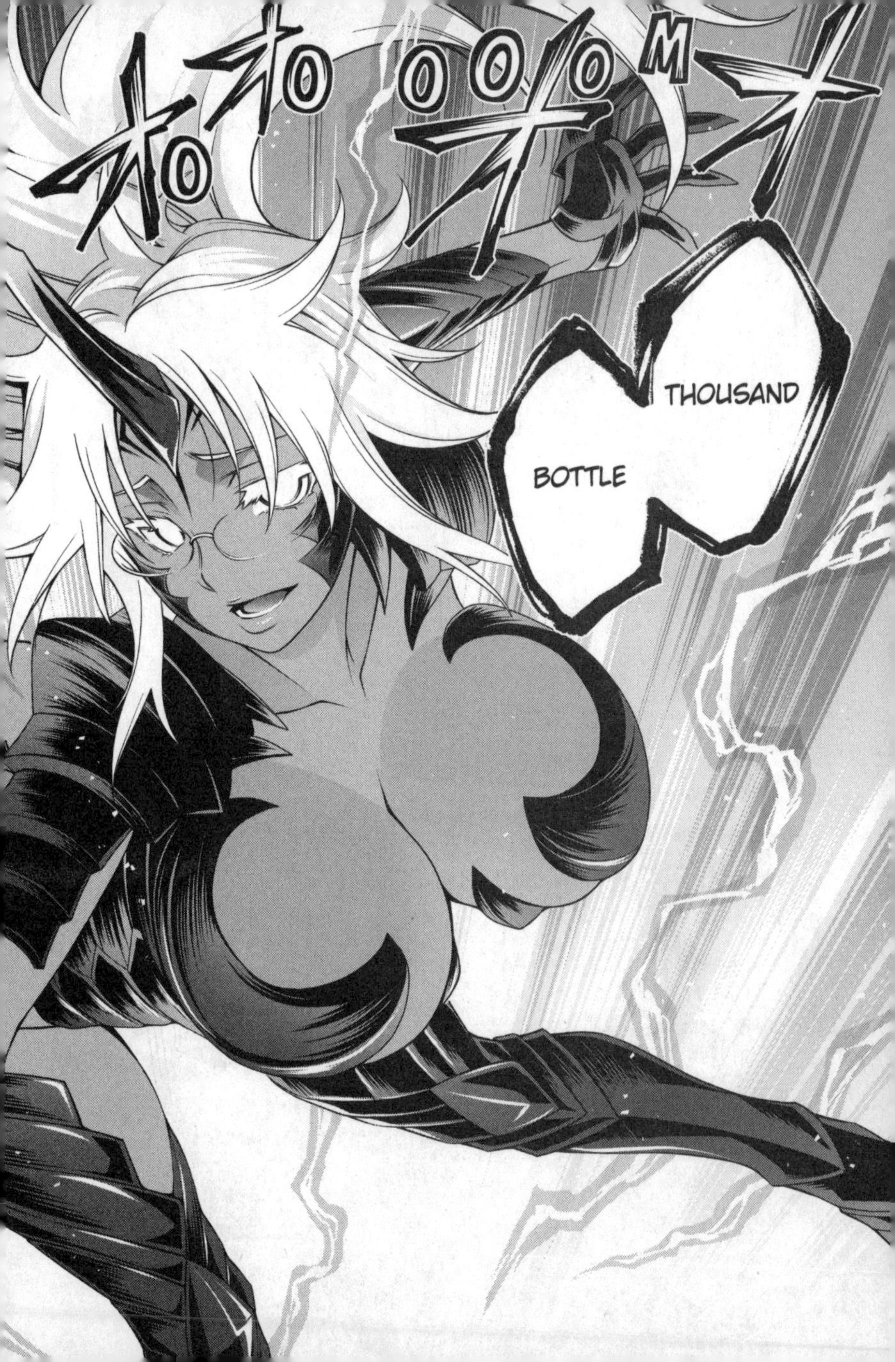
OOOOOM
THOUSAND
BOTTLE

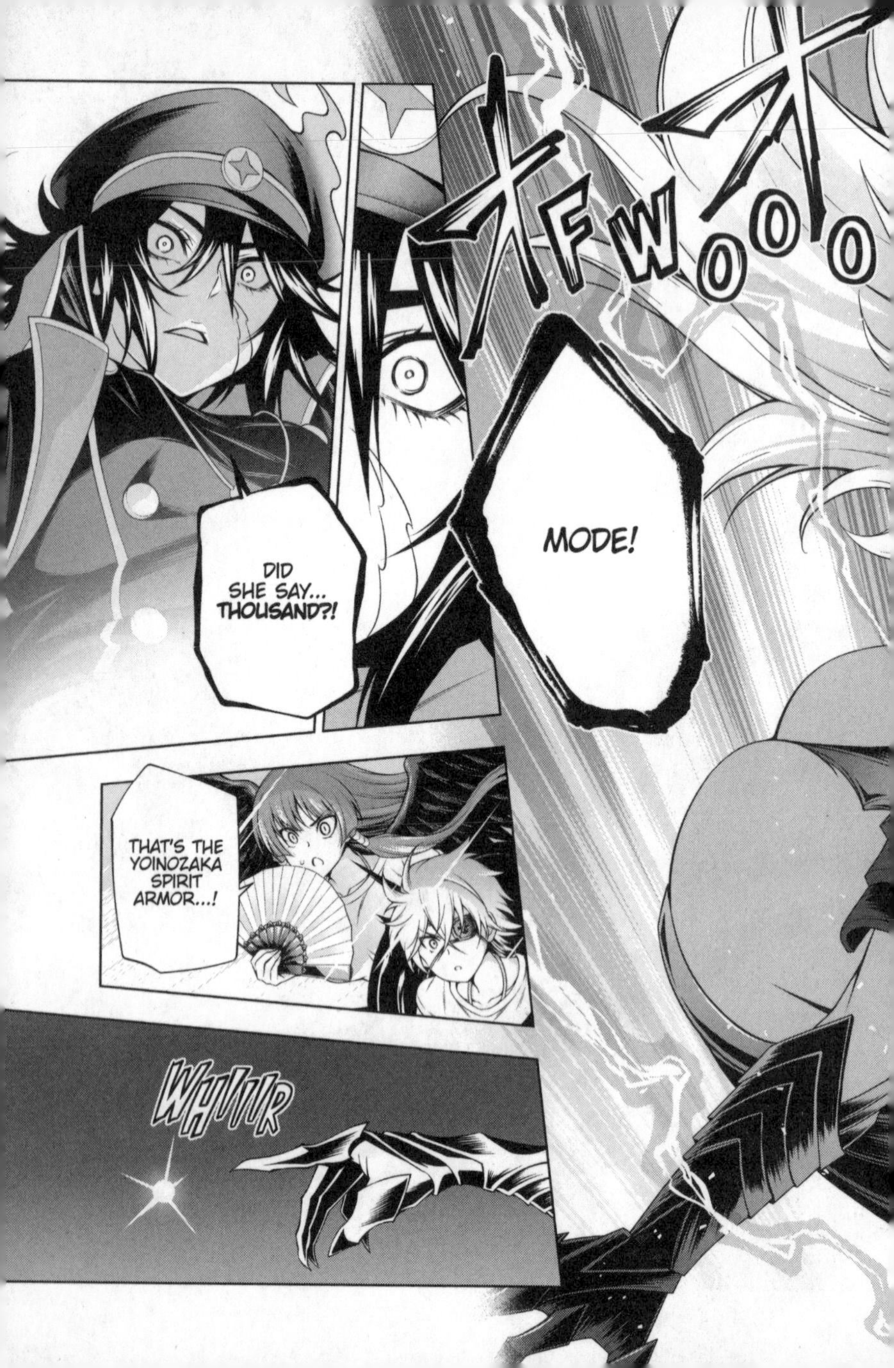
FWOOO
MODE!
DID SHE SAY... THOUSAND?!
THAT'S THE YOINOZAKA SPIRIT ARMOR...!
WHIRR

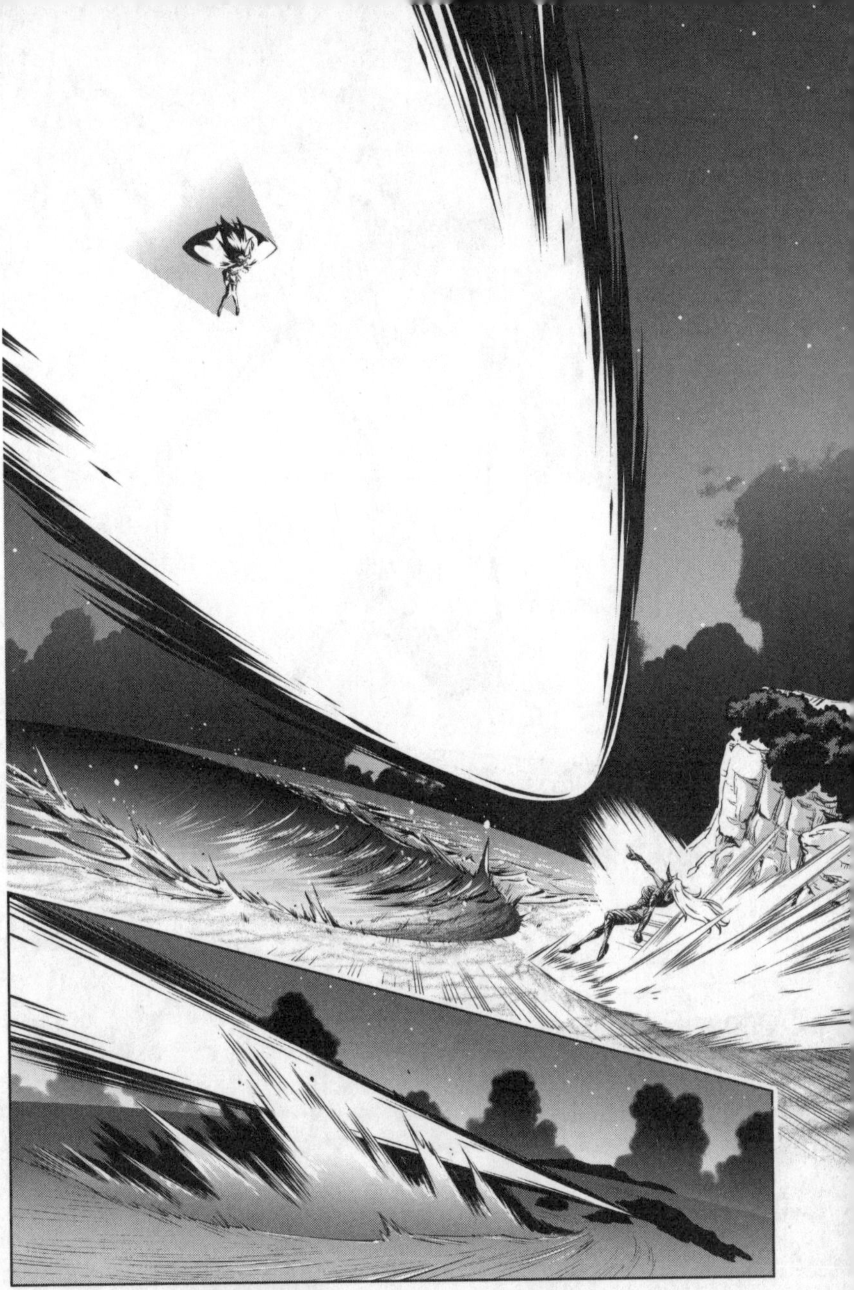

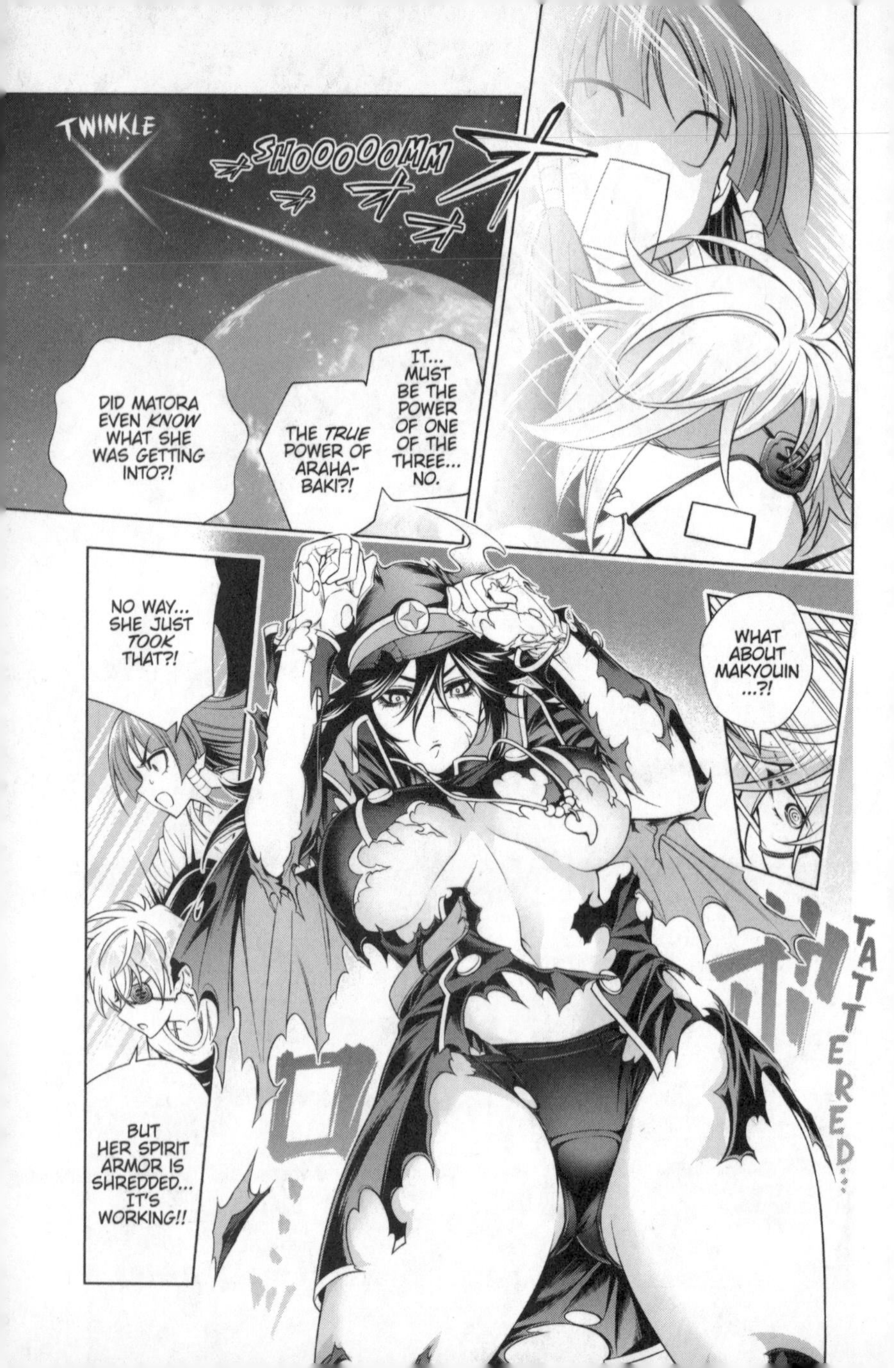
SHOOOOOMM
TWINKLE
IT... MUST BE THE POWER OF ONE OF THE THREE... NO.
THE *TRUE* POWER OF ARAHA-BAKI?!
DID MATORA EVEN *KNOW* WHAT SHE WAS GETTING INTO?!
WHAT ABOUT MAKYOUIN ...?!
TATTERED...
NO WAY... SHE JUST *TOOK* THAT?!
BUT HER SPIRIT ARMOR IS SHREDDED... IT'S WORKING!!

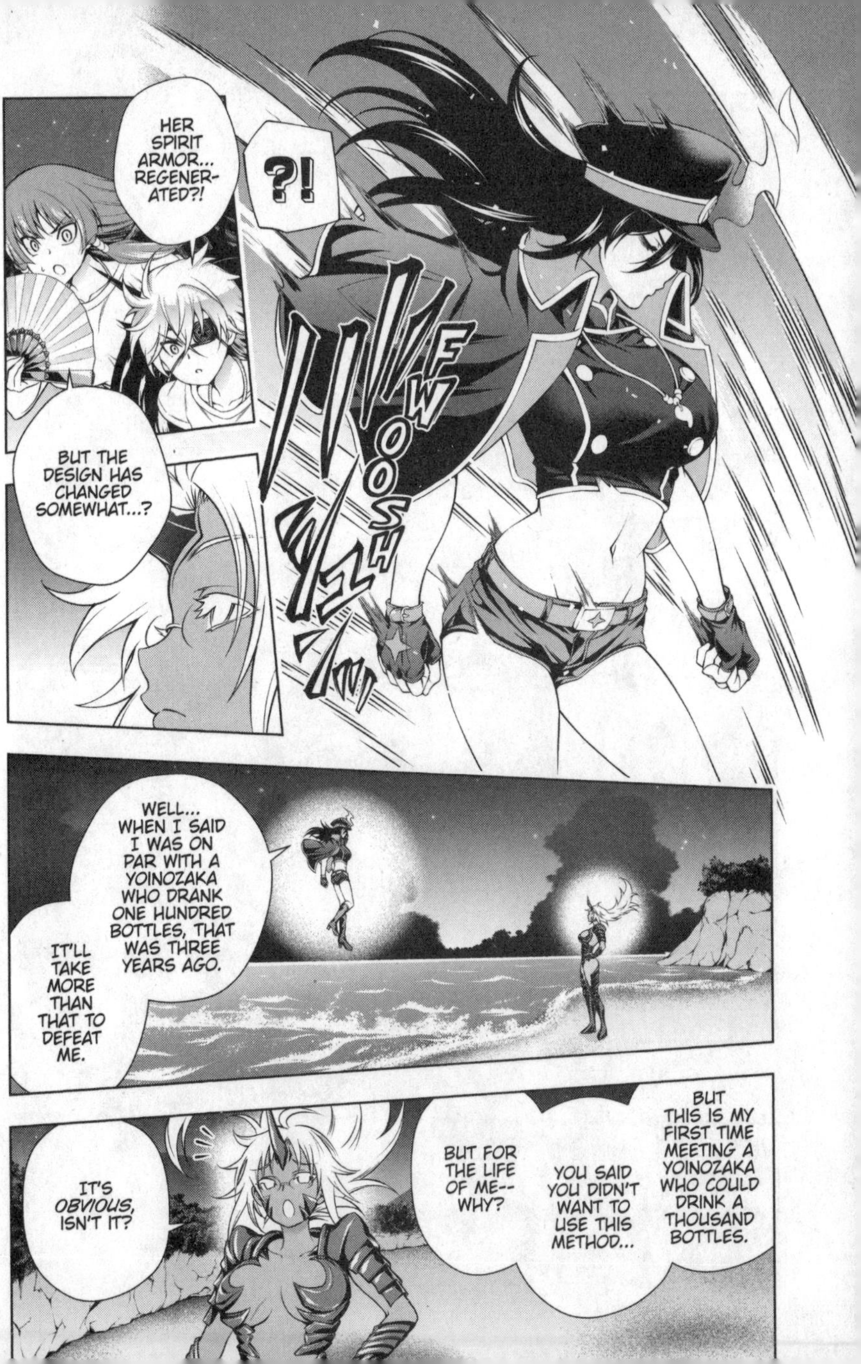
?!
WOOSH
HER SPIRIT ARMOR... REGENER-ATED?!
BUT THE DESIGN HAS CHANGED SOMEWHAT...?
WELL... WHEN I SAID I WAS ON PAR WITH A YOINOZAKA WHO DRANK ONE HUNDRED BOTTLES, THAT WAS THREE YEARS AGO.
IT'LL TAKE MORE THAN THAT TO DEFEAT ME.
BUT THIS IS MY FIRST TIME MEETING A YOINOZAKA WHO COULD DRINK A THOUSAND BOTTLES.
YOU SAID YOU DIDN'T WANT TO USE THIS METHOD...
BUT FOR THE LIFE OF ME-- WHY?
IT'S *OBVIOUS*, ISN'T IT?

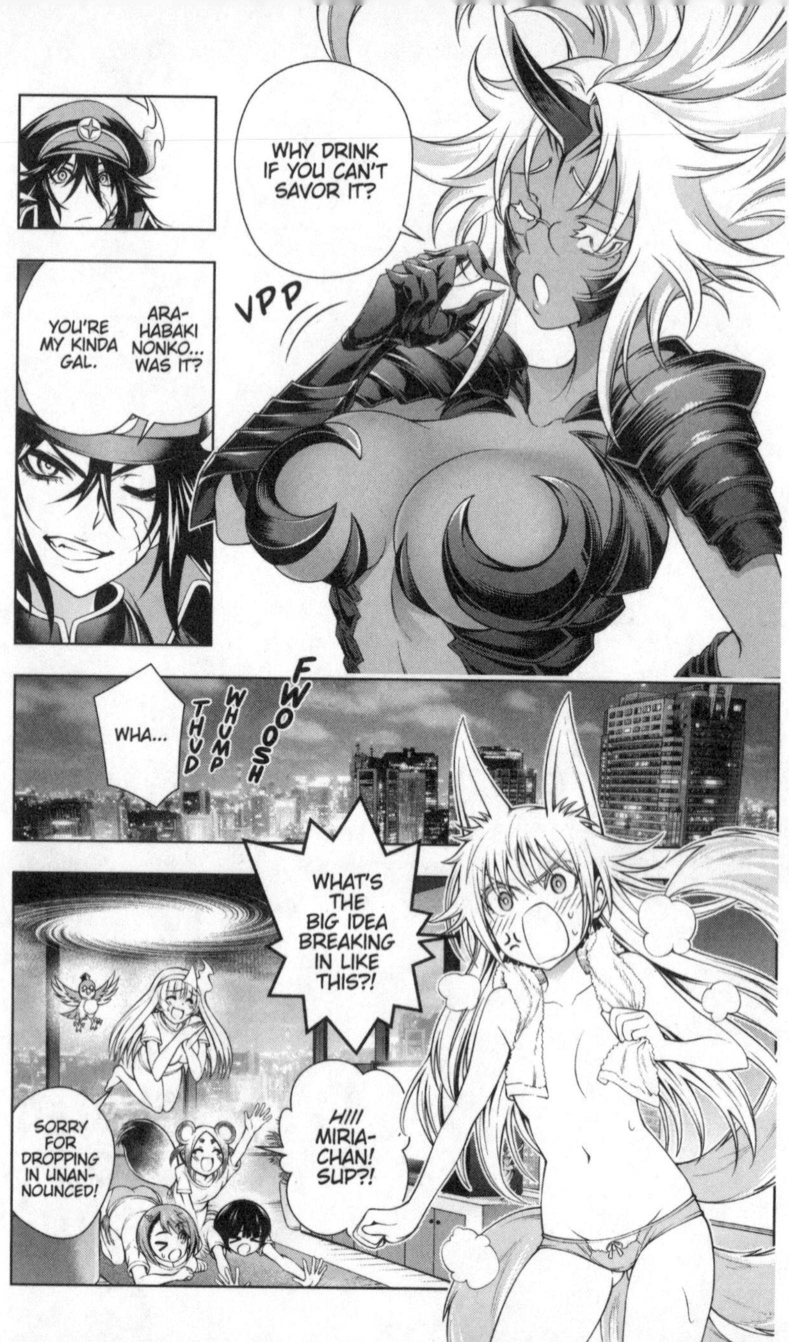
WHY DRINK IF YOU CAN'T SAVOR IT?
VPP
ARA-HABAKI NONKO... WAS IT?
YOU'RE MY KINDA GAL.
FWOOSH
WHUMP
THUD
WHA...
WHAT'S THE BIG IDEA BREAKING IN LIKE THIS?!
HI!! MIRIA-CHAN! SUP?!
SORRY FOR DROPPING IN UNAN-NOUNCED!

Yuuna
and the
Haunted
Hot
Springs

122 Up Close with Sagiri & Hibari...

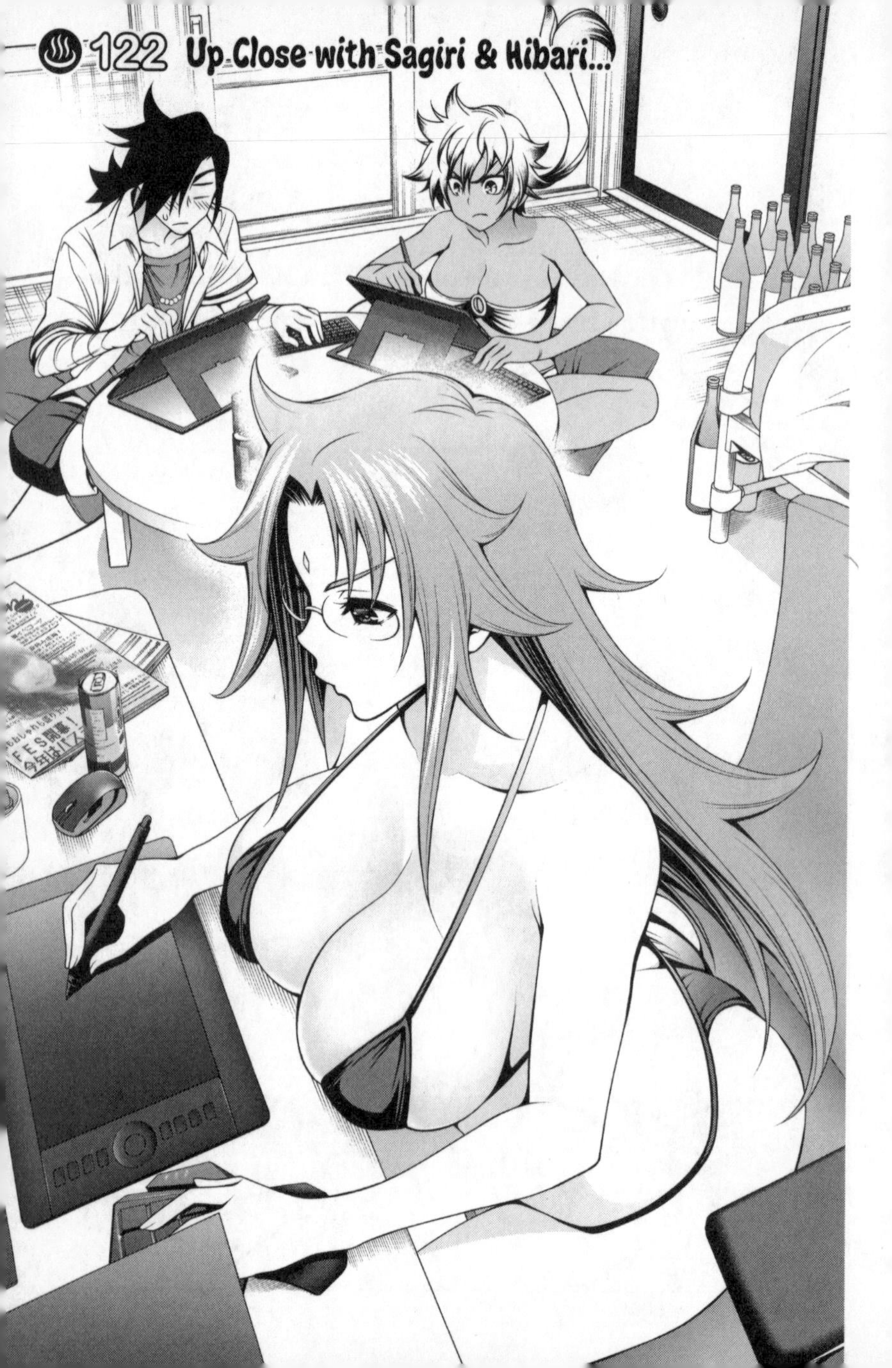

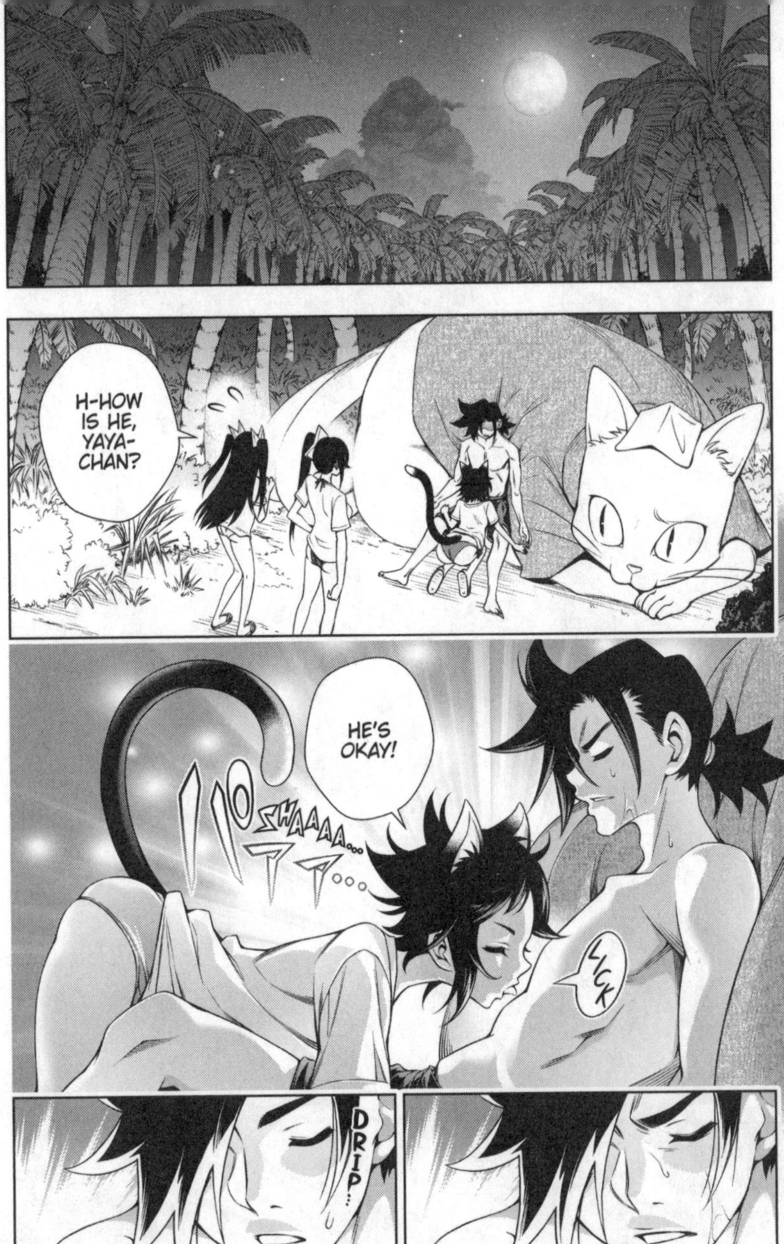
H-HOW IS HE, YAYA-CHAN?
HE'S OKAY!
SHAAAA...
LICK
DRIP...

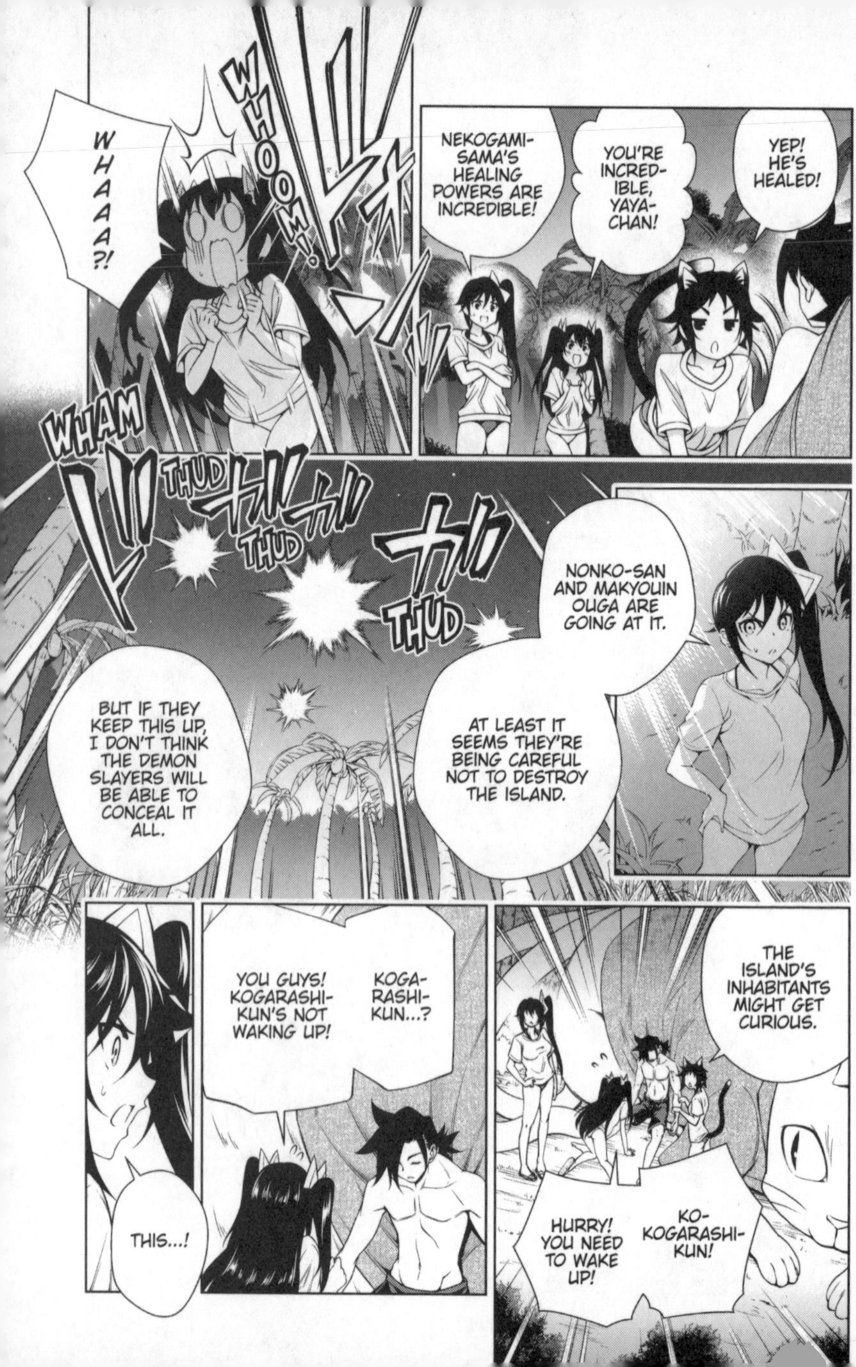
YEP! HE'S HEALED!
YOU'RE INCREDIBLE, YAYA-CHAN!
NEKOGAMI-SAMA'S HEALING POWERS ARE INCREDIBLE!
WHOOOM!
WHAAAAA?!
NONKO-SAN AND MAKYOUIN OUGA ARE GOING AT IT.
WHAM
THUD
THUD
THUD
AT LEAST IT SEEMS THEY'RE BEING CAREFUL NOT TO DESTROY THE ISLAND.
BUT IF THEY KEEP THIS UP, I DON'T THINK THE DEMON SLAYERS WILL BE ABLE TO CONCEAL IT ALL.
THE ISLAND'S INHABITANTS MIGHT GET CURIOUS.
KO-KOGARASHI-KUN!
HURRY! YOU NEED TO WAKE UP!
KOGA-RASHI-KUN...?
YOU GUYS! KOGARASHI-KUN'S NOT WAKING UP!
THIS...!

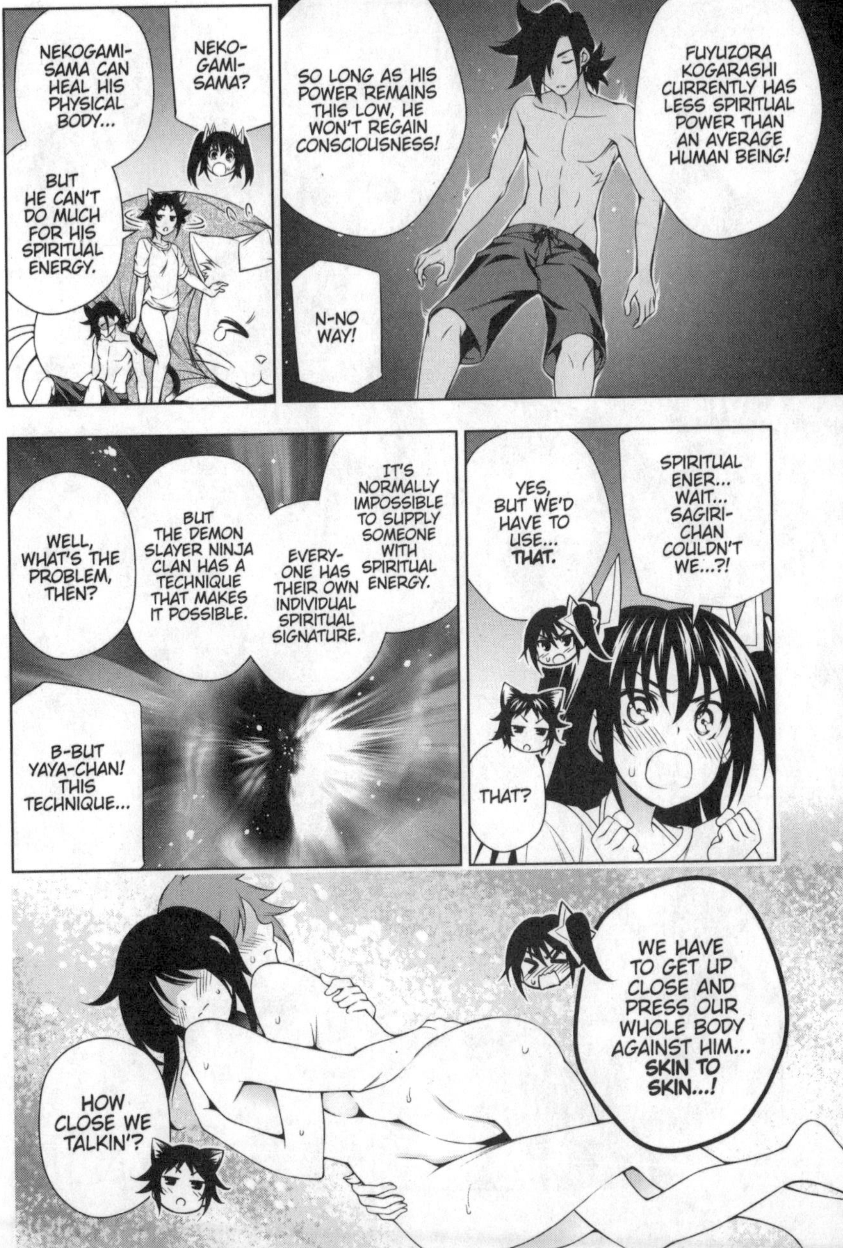
FUYUZORA KOGARASHI CURRENTLY HAS LESS SPIRITUAL POWER THAN AN AVERAGE HUMAN BEING!
SO LONG AS HIS POWER REMAINS THIS LOW, HE WON'T REGAIN CONSCIOUSNESS!
N-NO WAY!
NEKO-GAMI-SAMA?
NEKOGAMI-SAMA CAN HEAL HIS PHYSICAL BODY...
BUT HE CAN'T DO MUCH FOR HIS SPIRITUAL ENERGY.
SPIRITUAL ENER... WAIT... SAGIRI-CHAN COULDN'T WE...?!
YES, BUT WE'D HAVE TO USE... **THAT.**
THAT?
IT'S NORMALLY IMPOSSIBLE TO SUPPLY SOMEONE WITH SPIRITUAL ENERGY.
EVERY-ONE HAS THEIR OWN INDIVIDUAL SPIRITUAL SIGNATURE.
BUT THE DEMON SLAYER NINJA CLAN HAS A TECHNIQUE THAT MAKES IT POSSIBLE.
WELL, WHAT'S THE PROBLEM, THEN?
B-BUT YAYA-CHAN! THIS TECHNIQUE...
WE HAVE TO GET UP CLOSE AND PRESS OUR WHOLE BODY AGAINST HIM... **SKIN TO SKIN...!**
HOW CLOSE WE TALKIN'?

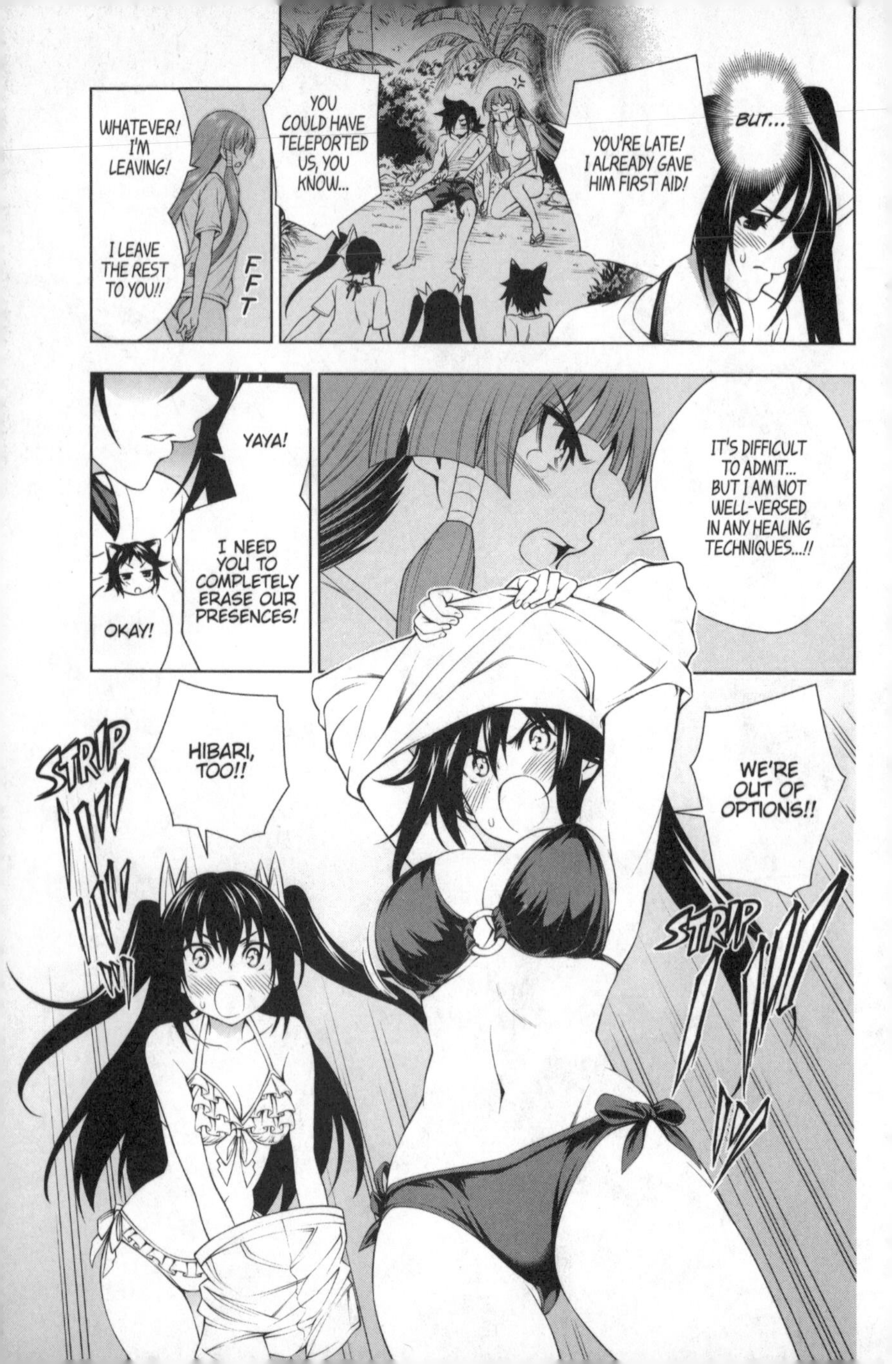

BUT...
YOU'RE LATE! I ALREADY GAVE HIM FIRST AID!
YOU COULD HAVE TELEPORTED US, YOU KNOW...
WHATEVER! I'M LEAVING!
I LEAVE THE REST TO YOU!!
FFT
IT'S DIFFICULT TO ADMIT... BUT I AM NOT WELL-VERSED IN ANY HEALING TECHNIQUES...!!
YAYA!
I NEED YOU TO COMPLETELY ERASE OUR PRESENCES!
OKAY!
WE'RE OUT OF OPTIONS!!
STRIP
HIBARI, TOO!!
STRIP

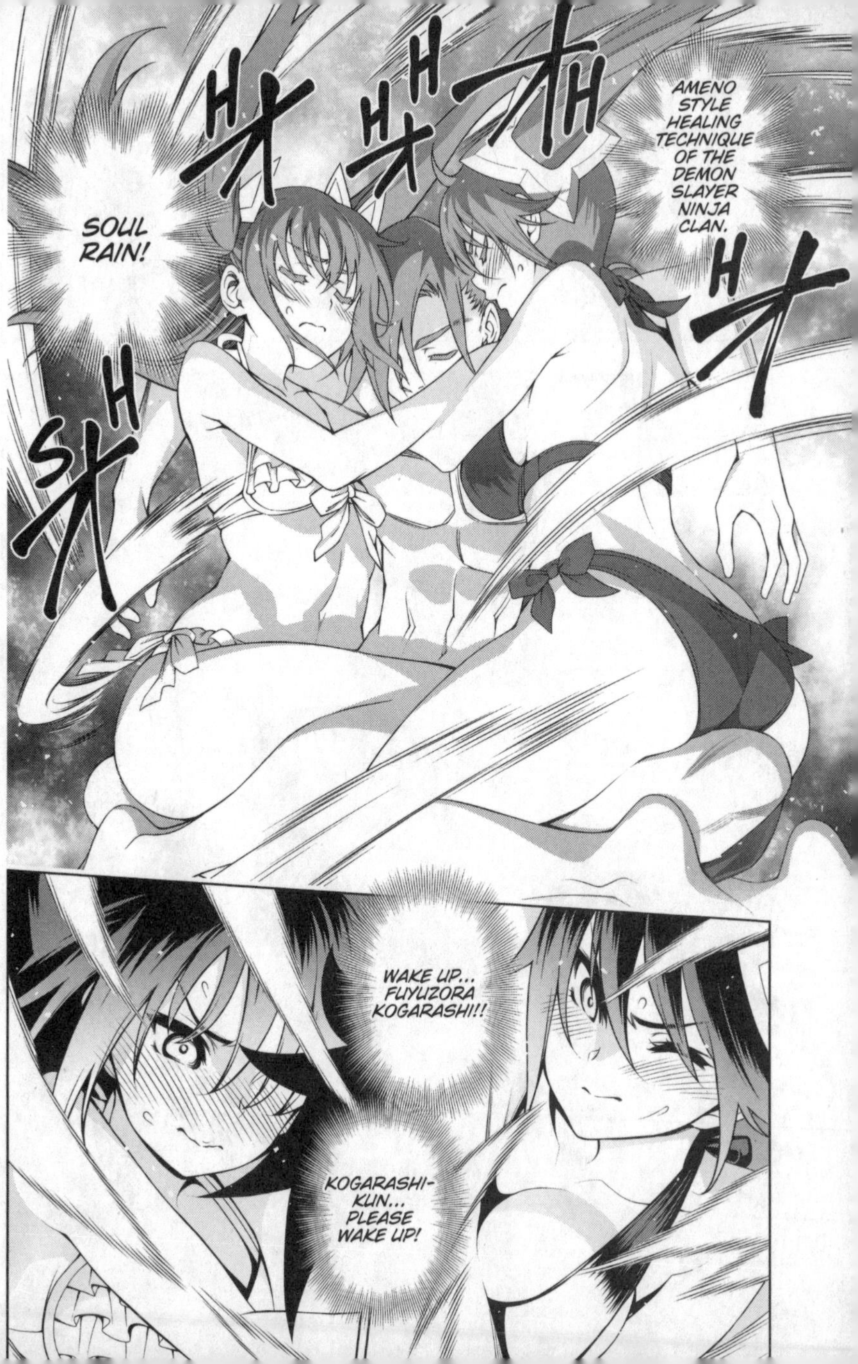
AMENO STYLE HEALING TECHNIQUE OF THE DEMON SLAYER NINJA CLAN.
SOUL RAIN!
WAKE UP... FUYUZORA KOGARASHI!!
KOGARASHI-KUN... PLEASE WAKE UP!

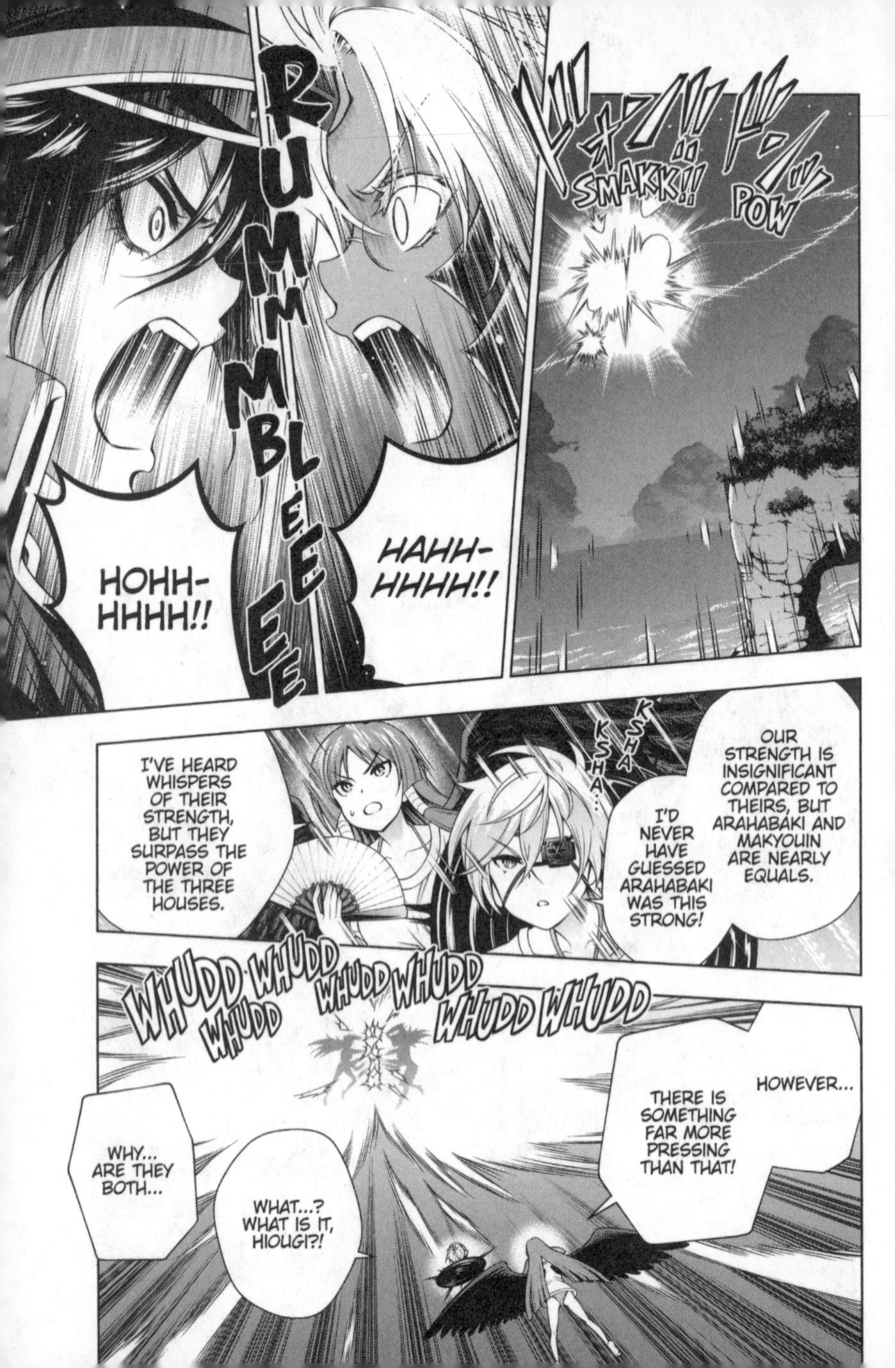
SMAKK!!
POW
RUMMMBLEEE
HAHH-HHHH!!
HOHH-HHHH!!
OUR STRENGTH IS INSIGNIFICANT COMPARED TO THEIRS, BUT ARAHABAKI AND MAKYOUIN ARE NEARLY EQUALS.
KSHA KSHA...
I'D NEVER HAVE GUESSED ARAHABAKI WAS THIS STRONG!
I'VE HEARD WHISPERS OF THEIR STRENGTH, BUT THEY SURPASS THE POWER OF THE THREE HOUSES.
WHUDD WHUDD WHUDD WHUDD WHUDD WHUDD WHUDD
HOWEVER...
THERE IS SOMETHING FAR MORE PRESSING THAN THAT!
WHAT...? WHAT IS IT, HIOUGI?!
WHY... ARE THEY BOTH...

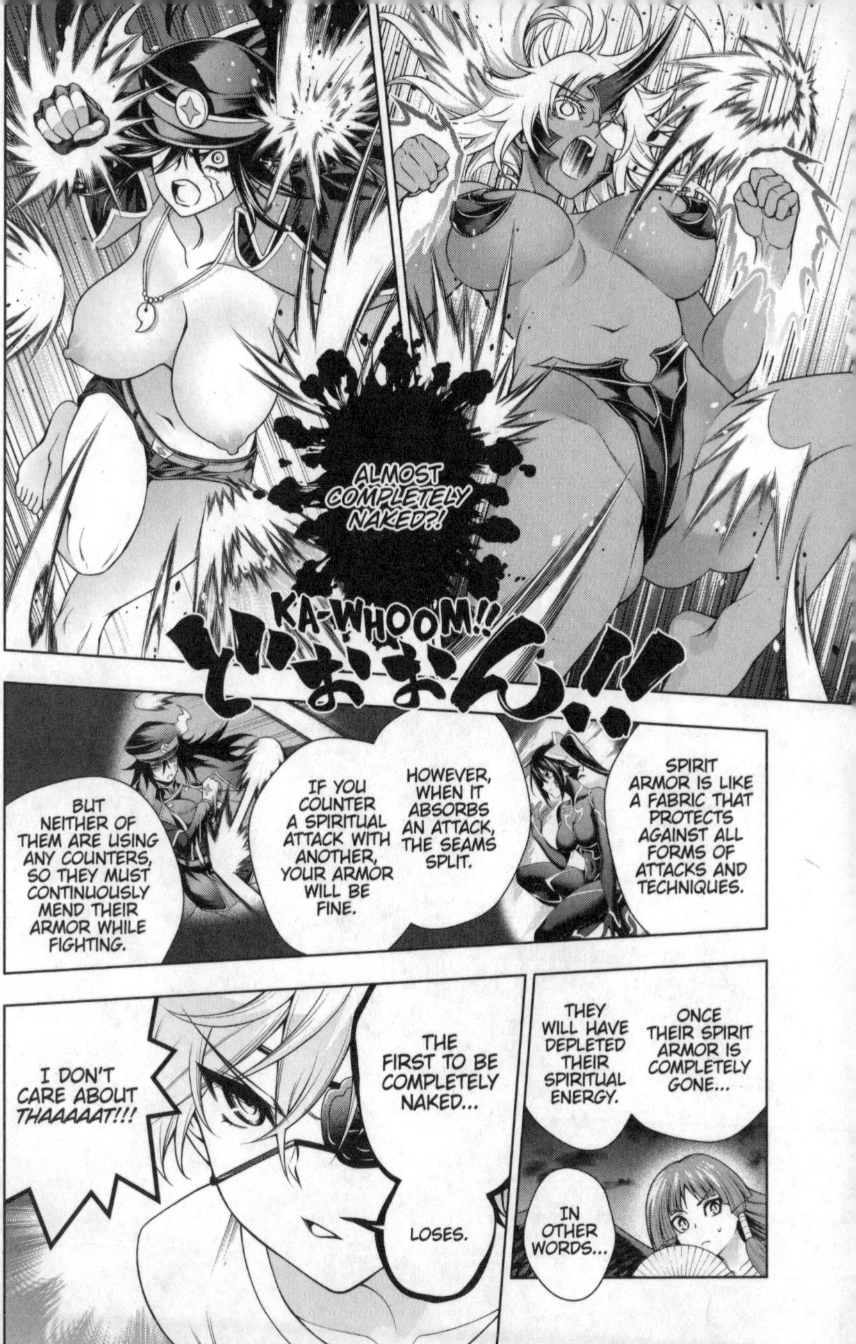
ALMOST COMPLETELY NAKED?!
KA-WHOOM!!
SPIRIT ARMOR IS LIKE A FABRIC THAT PROTECTS AGAINST ALL FORMS OF ATTACKS AND TECHNIQUES.
HOWEVER, WHEN IT ABSORBS AN ATTACK, THE SEAMS SPLIT.
IF YOU COUNTER A SPIRITUAL ATTACK WITH ANOTHER, YOUR ARMOR WILL BE FINE.
BUT NEITHER OF THEM ARE USING ANY COUNTERS, SO THEY MUST CONTINUOUSLY MEND THEIR ARMOR WHILE FIGHTING.
ONCE THEIR SPIRIT ARMOR IS COMPLETELY GONE...
THEY WILL HAVE DEPLETED THEIR SPIRITUAL ENERGY.
IN OTHER WORDS...
THE FIRST TO BE COMPLETELY NAKED...
LOSES.
I DON'T CARE ABOUT *THAAAAAT!!!*

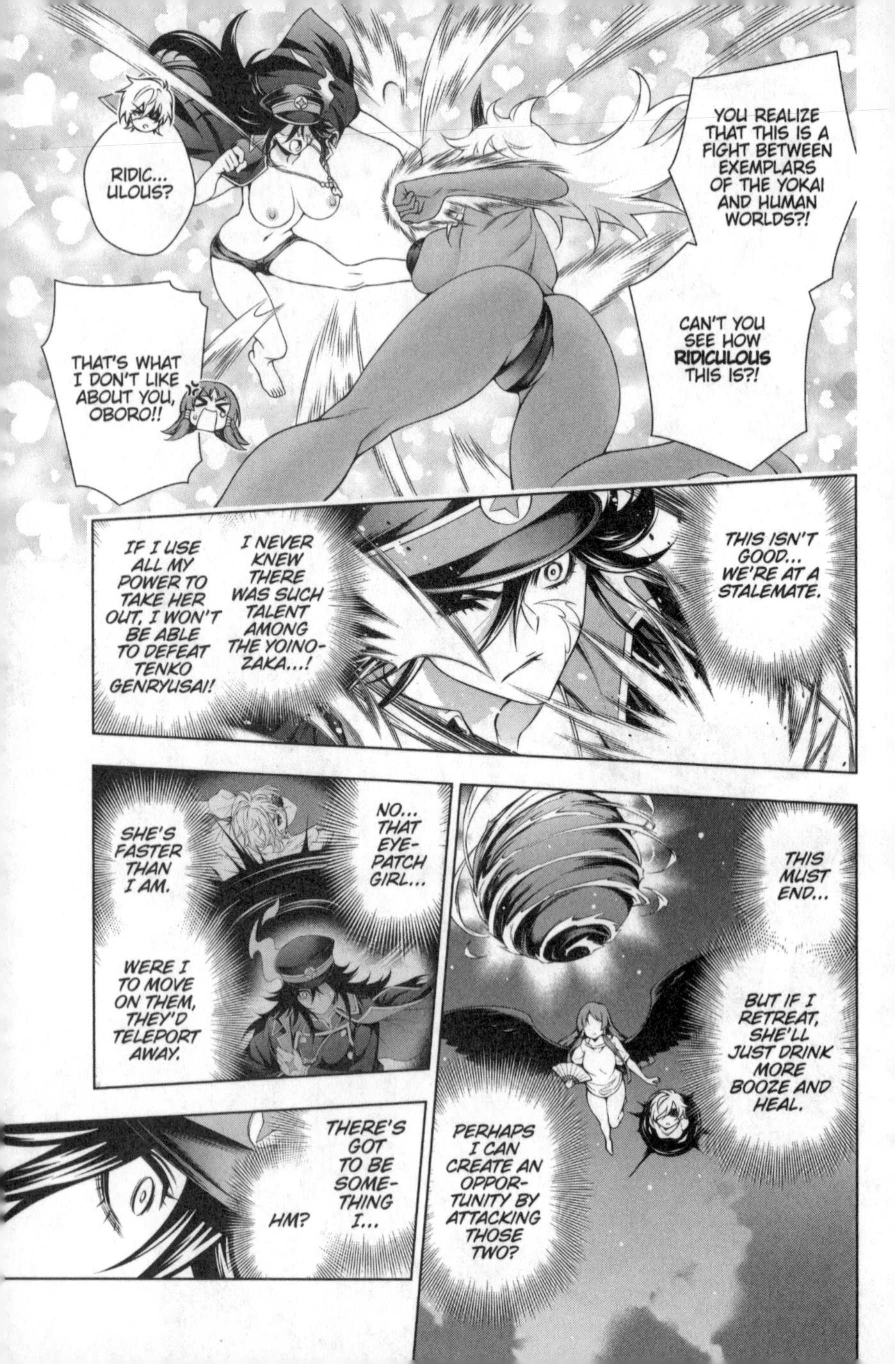
YOU REALIZE THAT THIS IS A FIGHT BETWEEN EXEMPLARS OF THE YOKAI AND HUMAN WORLDS?!
CAN'T YOU SEE HOW **RIDICULOUS** THIS IS?!
RIDIC... ULOUS?
THAT'S WHAT I DON'T LIKE ABOUT YOU, OBORO!!
THIS ISN'T GOOD... WE'RE AT A STALEMATE.
I NEVER KNEW THERE WAS SUCH TALENT AMONG THE YOINO-ZAKA...!
IF I USE ALL MY POWER TO TAKE HER OUT, I WON'T BE ABLE TO DEFEAT TENKO GENRYUSAI!
THIS MUST END...
BUT IF I RETREAT, SHE'LL JUST DRINK MORE BOOZE AND HEAL.
PERHAPS I CAN CREATE AN OPPOR-TUNITY BY ATTACKING THOSE TWO?
NO... THAT EYE-PATCH GIRL...
SHE'S FASTER THAN I AM.
WERE I TO MOVE ON THEM, THEY'D TELEPORT AWAY.
THERE'S GOT TO BE SOME-THING I...
HM?

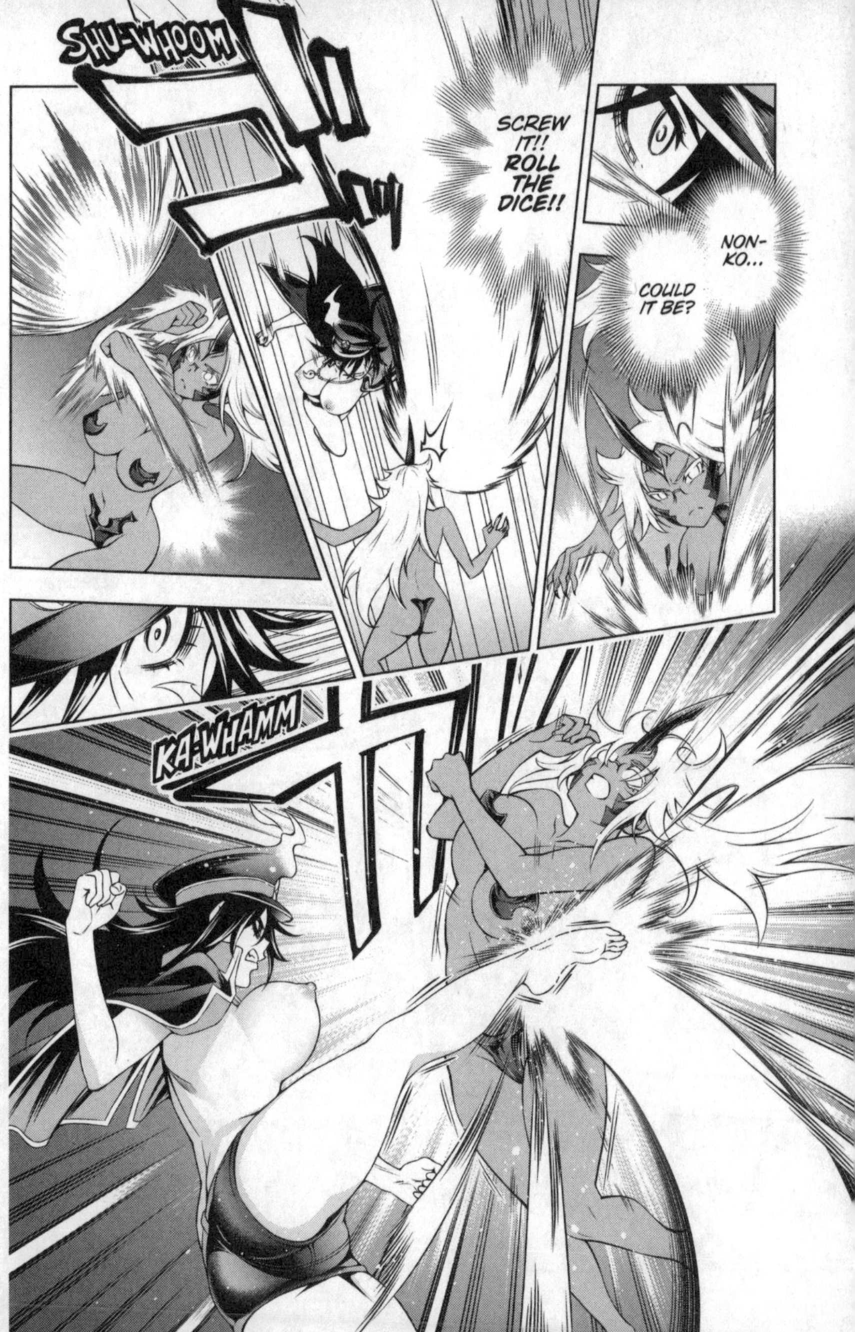
NON-KO...
COULD IT BE?
SCREW IT!! ROLL THE DICE!!
SHU-WHOOM
KA-WHAMM

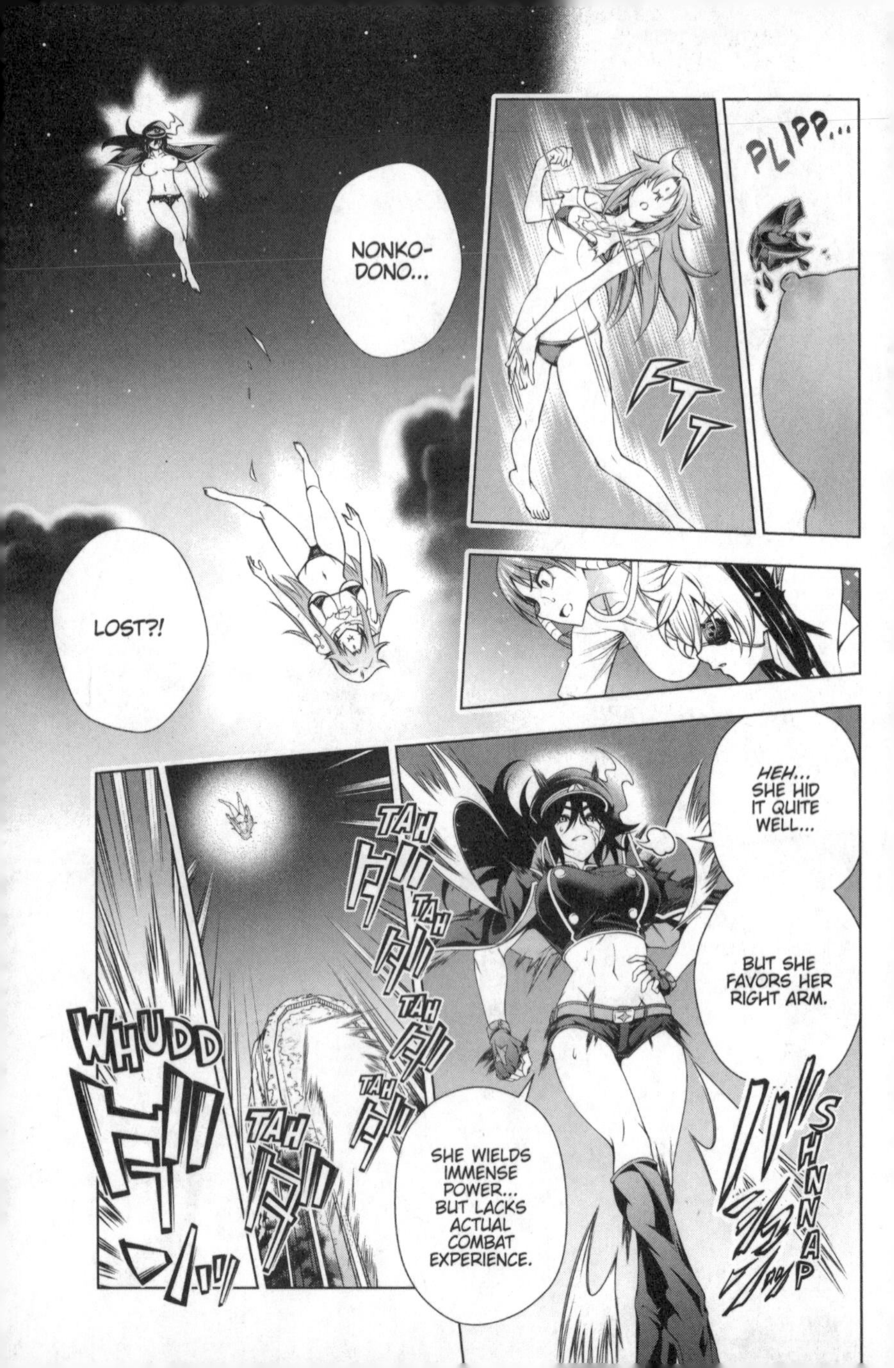
PLIPP...
FTT
NONKO-DONO...
LOST?!
HEH... SHE HID IT QUITE WELL...
BUT SHE FAVORS HER RIGHT ARM.
SHNNAP
TAH
TAH
TAH
TAH
SHE WIELDS IMMENSE POWER... BUT LACKS ACTUAL COMBAT EXPERIENCE.
TAH
WHUDD

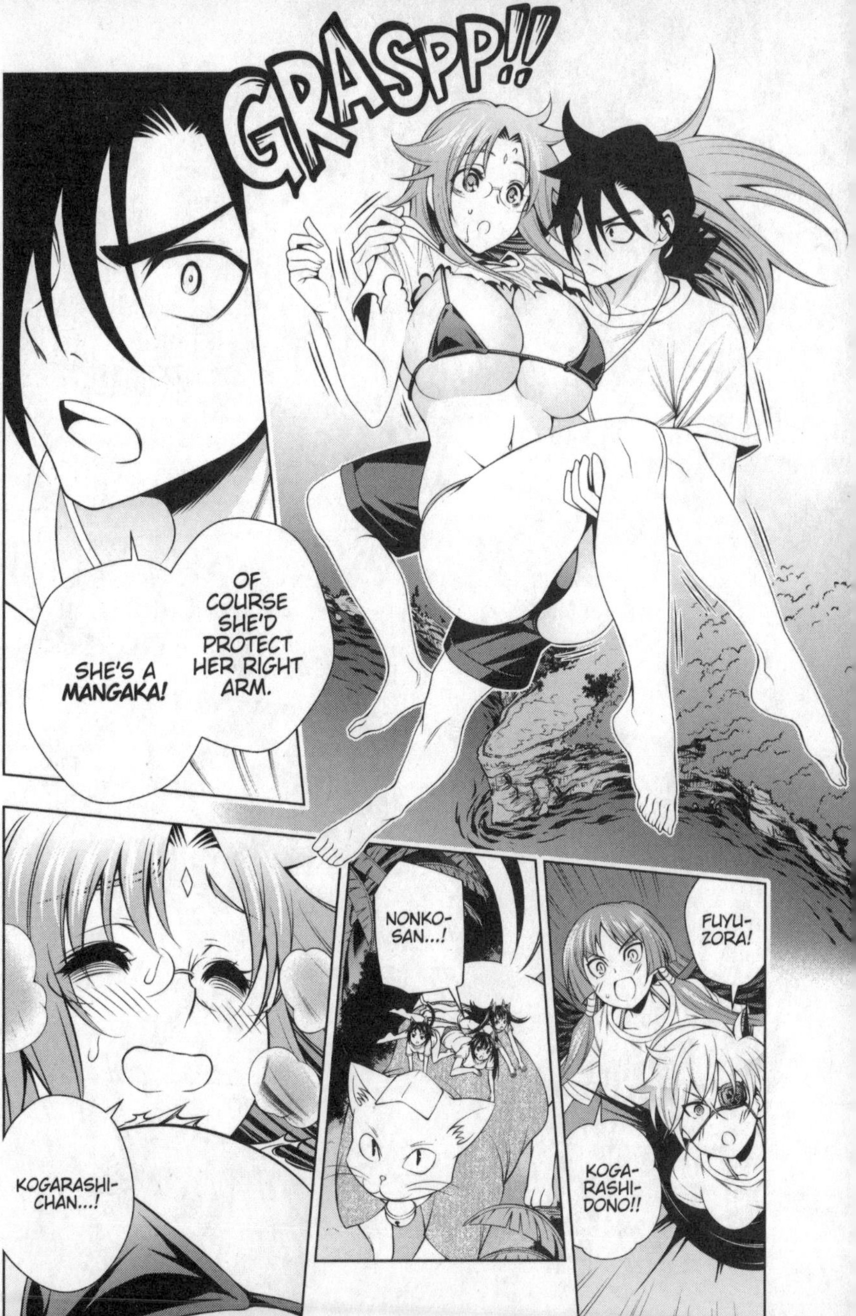
GRASPP!!
OF COURSE SHE'D PROTECT HER RIGHT ARM.
SHE'S A MANGAKA!
FUYU-ZORA!
KOGA-RASHI-DONO!!
NONKO-SAN...!
KOGARASHI-CHAN...!

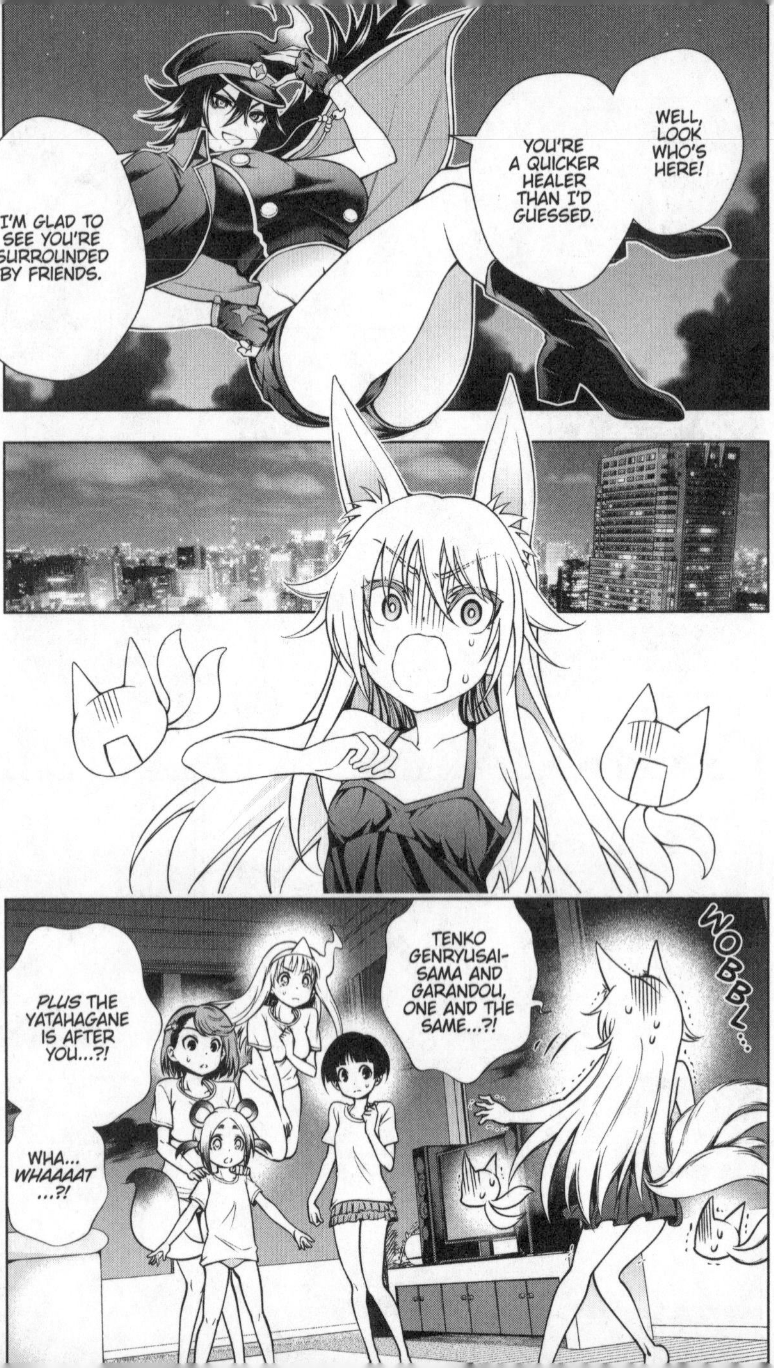
WELL, LOOK WHO'S HERE!
YOU'RE A QUICKER HEALER THAN I'D GUESSED.
I'M GLAD TO SEE YOU'RE SURROUNDED BY FRIENDS.
WOBBL...
TENKO GENRYUSAI-SAMA AND GARANDOU, ONE AND THE SAME...?!
PLUS THE YATAHAGANE IS AFTER YOU...?!
WHA... *WHAAAAT* ...?!

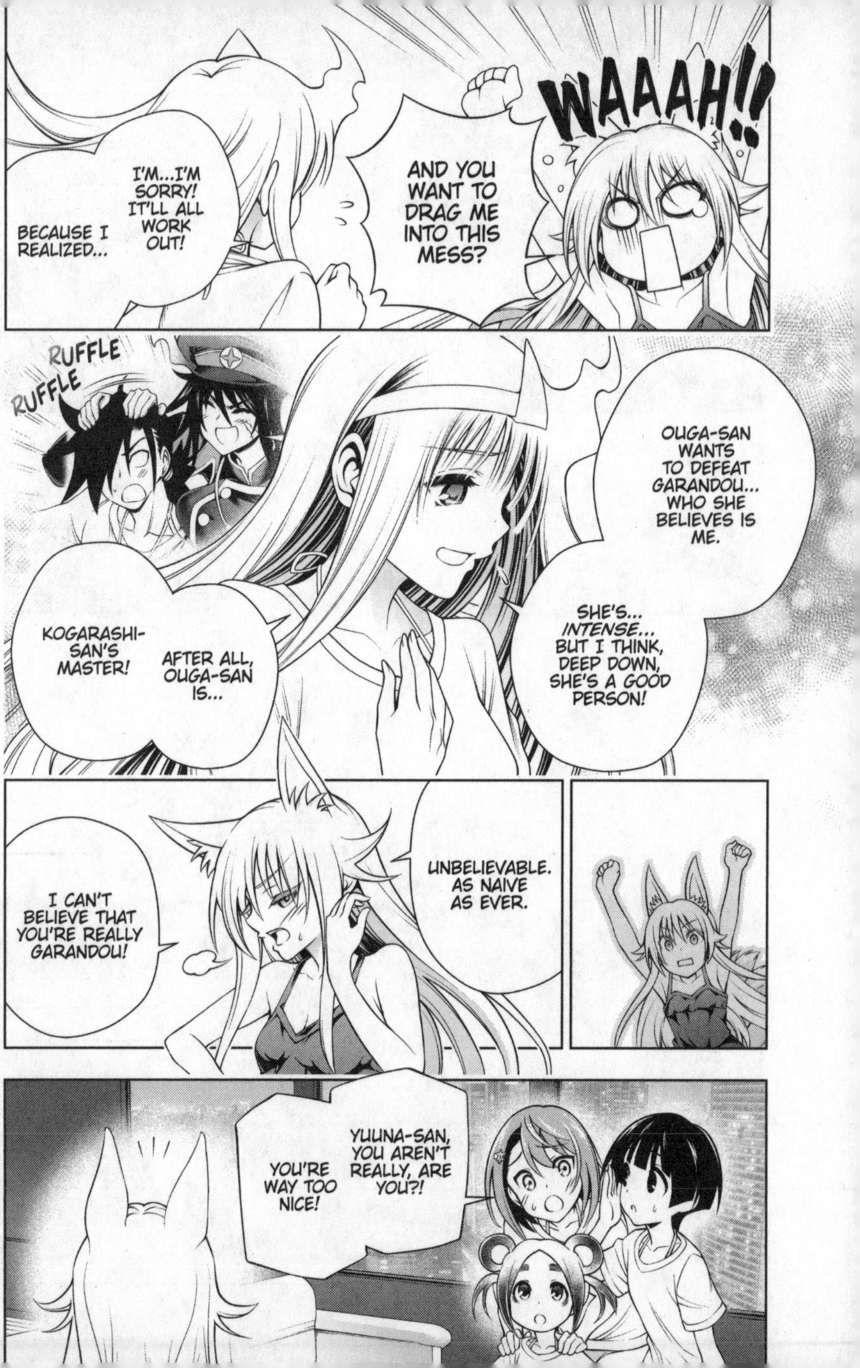
WAAAH!!
AND YOU WANT TO DRAG ME INTO THIS MESS?
I'M...I'M SORRY! IT'LL ALL WORK OUT!
BECAUSE I REALIZED...
OUGA-SAN WANTS TO DEFEAT GARANDOU... WHO SHE BELIEVES IS ME.
SHE'S... *INTENSE*... BUT I THINK, DEEP DOWN, SHE'S A GOOD PERSON!
RUFFLE RUFFLE
AFTER ALL, OUGA-SAN IS...
KOGARASHI-SAN'S MASTER!
UNBELIEVABLE. AS NAIVE AS EVER.
I CAN'T BELIEVE THAT YOU'RE REALLY GARANDOU!
YUUNA-SAN, YOU AREN'T REALLY, ARE YOU?!
YOU'RE WAY TOO NICE!

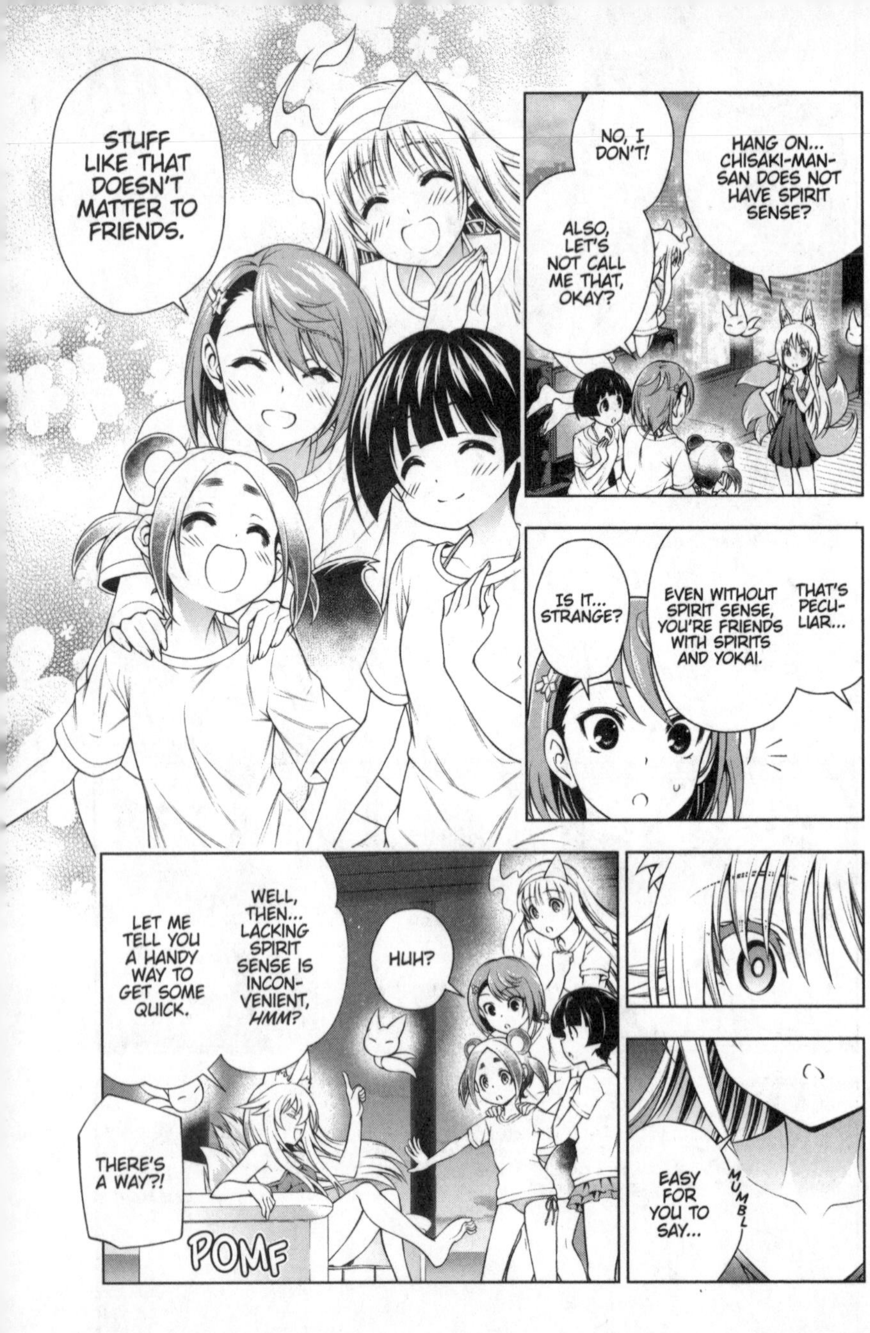
HANG ON... CHISAKI-MAN-SAN DOES NOT HAVE SPIRIT SENSE?
NO, I DON'T!
ALSO, LET'S NOT CALL ME THAT, OKAY?
THAT'S PECULIAR...
EVEN WITHOUT SPIRIT SENSE, YOU'RE FRIENDS WITH SPIRITS AND YOKAI.
IS IT... STRANGE?
STUFF LIKE THAT DOESN'T MATTER TO FRIENDS.
EASY FOR YOU TO SAY...
MUMBL
WELL, THEN... LACKING SPIRIT SENSE IS INCONVENIENT, *HMM?*
LET ME TELL YOU A HANDY WAY TO GET SOME QUICK.
HUH?
THERE'S A WAY?!
POMF

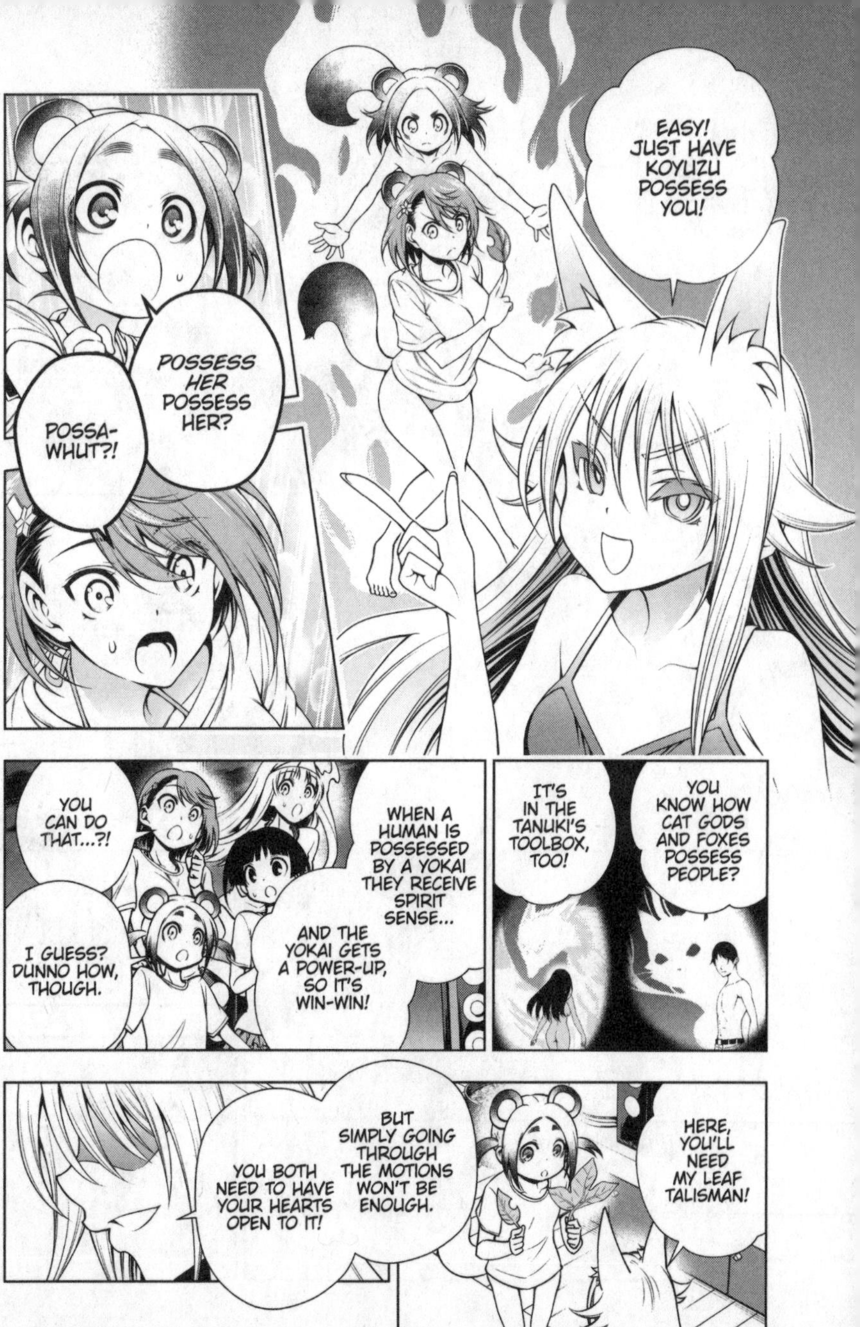
EASY! JUST HAVE KOYUZU POSSESS YOU!
POSSESS HER POSSESS HER?
POSSA-WHUT?!
YOU KNOW HOW CAT GODS AND FOXES POSSESS PEOPLE?
IT'S IN THE TANUKI'S TOOLBOX, TOO!
WHEN A HUMAN IS POSSESSED BY A YOKAI THEY RECEIVE SPIRIT SENSE...
AND THE YOKAI GETS A POWER-UP, SO IT'S WIN-WIN!
YOU CAN DO THAT...?!
I GUESS? DUNNO HOW, THOUGH.
HERE, YOU'LL NEED MY LEAF TALISMAN!
BUT SIMPLY GOING THROUGH THE MOTIONS WON'T BE ENOUGH.
YOU BOTH NEED TO HAVE YOUR HEARTS OPEN TO IT!

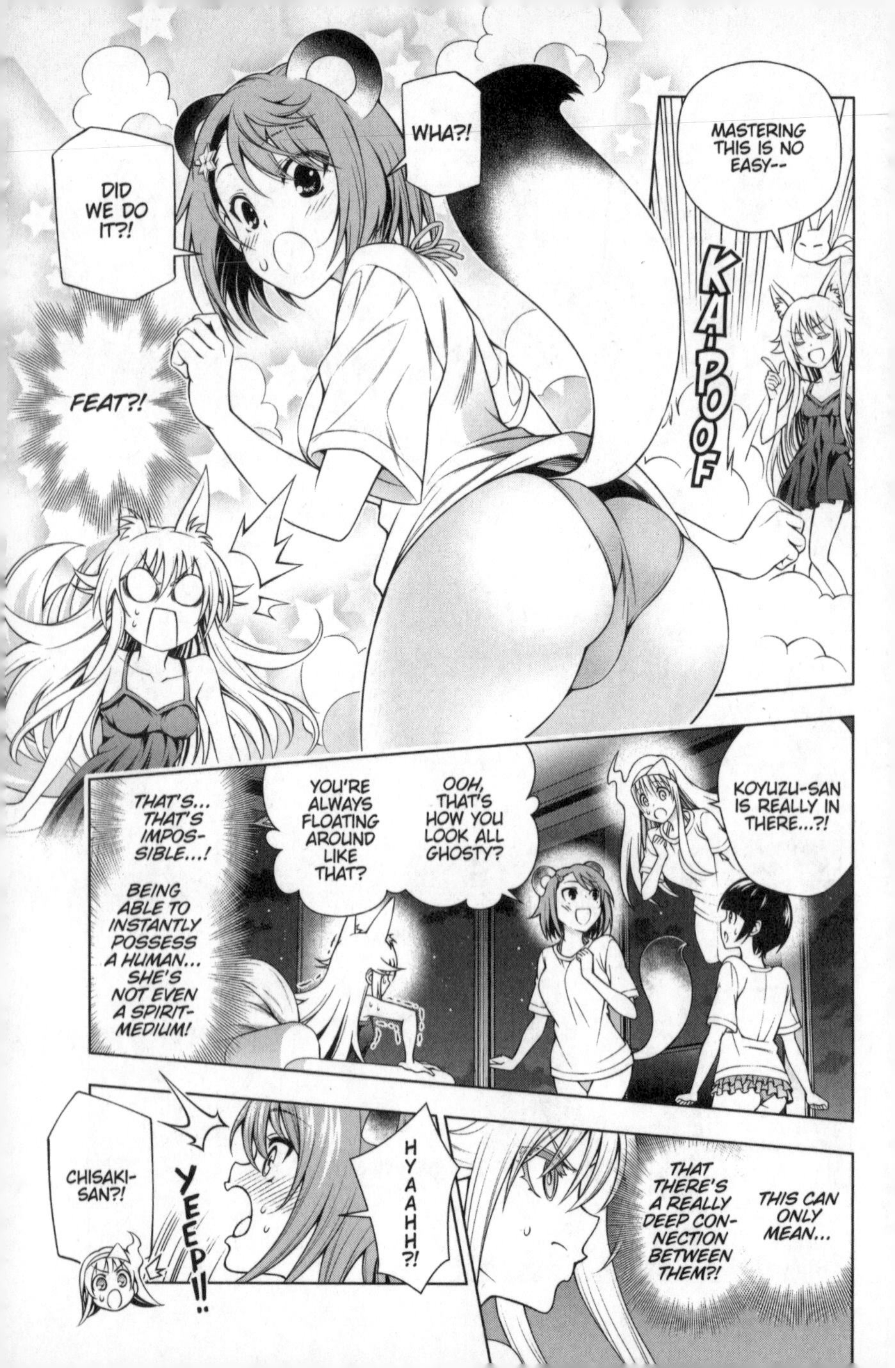
MASTERING THIS IS NO EASY--
KA-POOF
WHA?!
DID WE DO IT?!
FEAT?!
KOYUZU-SAN IS REALLY IN THERE...?!
OOH, THAT'S HOW YOU LOOK ALL GHOSTY?
YOU'RE ALWAYS FLOATING AROUND LIKE THAT?
THAT'S... THAT'S IMPOSSIBLE...!
BEING ABLE TO INSTANTLY POSSESS A HUMAN... SHE'S NOT EVEN A SPIRIT-MEDIUM!
THIS CAN ONLY MEAN...
THAT THERE'S A REALLY DEEP CONNECTION BETWEEN THEM?!
HYAAHH?!
YEEP!!
CHISAKI-SAN?!

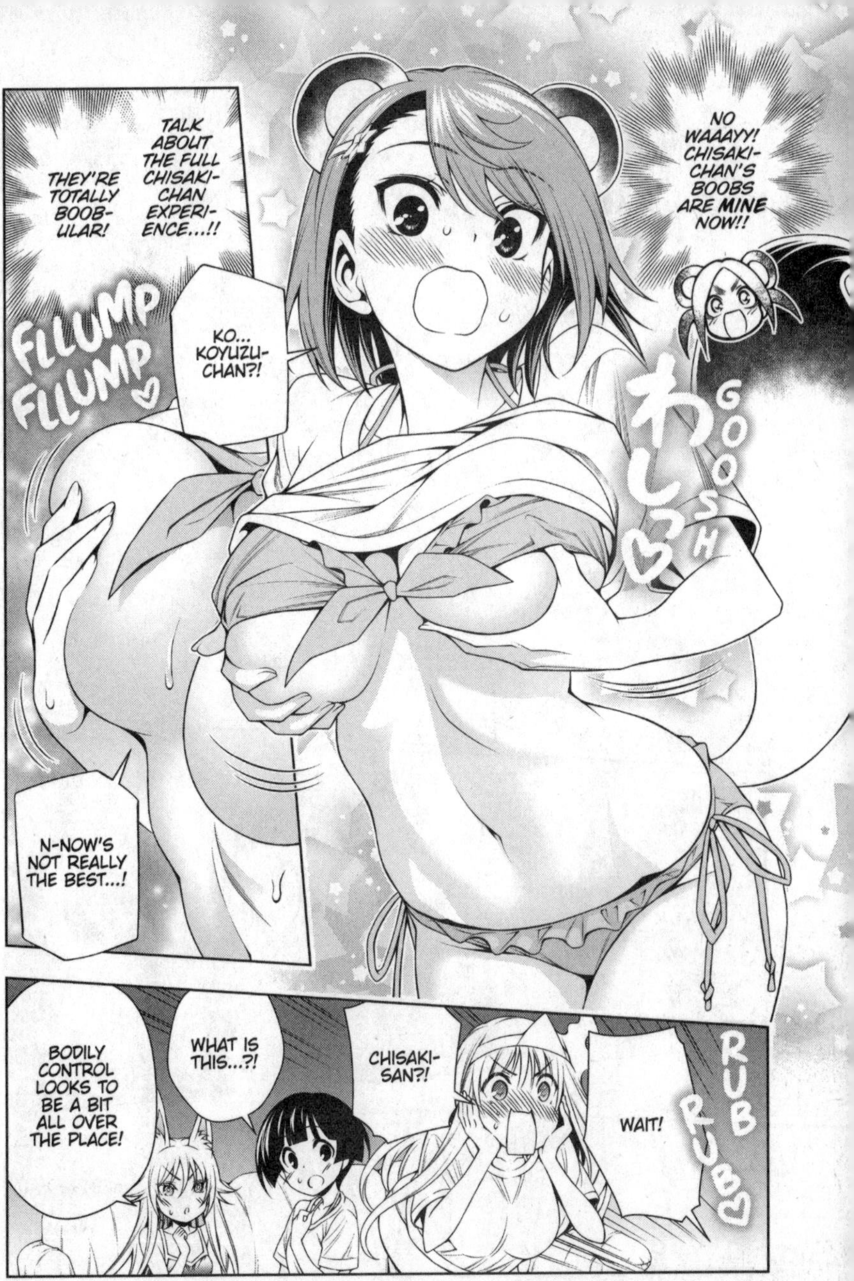
NO WAAAYY! CHISAKI-CHAN'S BOOBS ARE MINE NOW!!
わしっ GOOSH
TALK ABOUT THE FULL CHISAKI-CHAN EXPERIENCE...!!
THEY'RE TOTALLY BOOB-ULAR!
KO... KOYUZU-CHAN?!
FLLUMP FLLUMP
N-NOW'S NOT REALLY THE BEST...!
RUB RUB
WAIT!
CHISAKI-SAN?!
WHAT IS THIS...?!
BODILY CONTROL LOOKS TO BE A BIT ALL OVER THE PLACE!

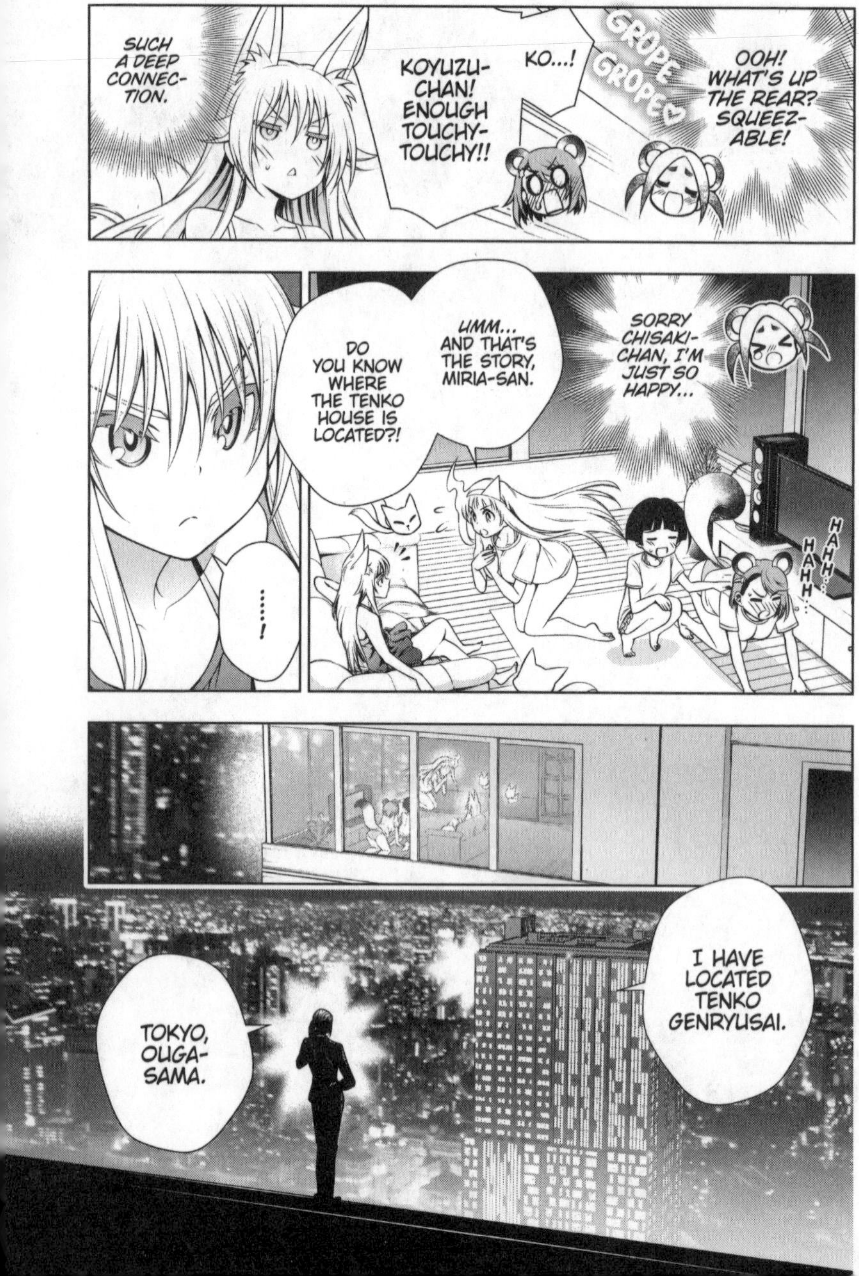
OOH! WHAT'S UP THE REAR? SQUEEZ-ABLE!
GROPE GROPE♡
KO...!
KOYUZU-CHAN! ENOUGH TOUCHY-TOUCHY!!
SUCH A DEEP CONNEC-TION.
SORRY CHISAKI-CHAN, I'M JUST SO HAPPY...
UMM... AND THAT'S THE STORY, MIRIA-SAN.
DO YOU KNOW WHERE THE TENKO HOUSE IS LOCATED?!
HAHH HAHH...
......!
I HAVE LOCATED TENKO GENRYUSAI.
TOKYO, OUGA-SAMA.

123 Yuuna-san Closes in on the Tenko Clan

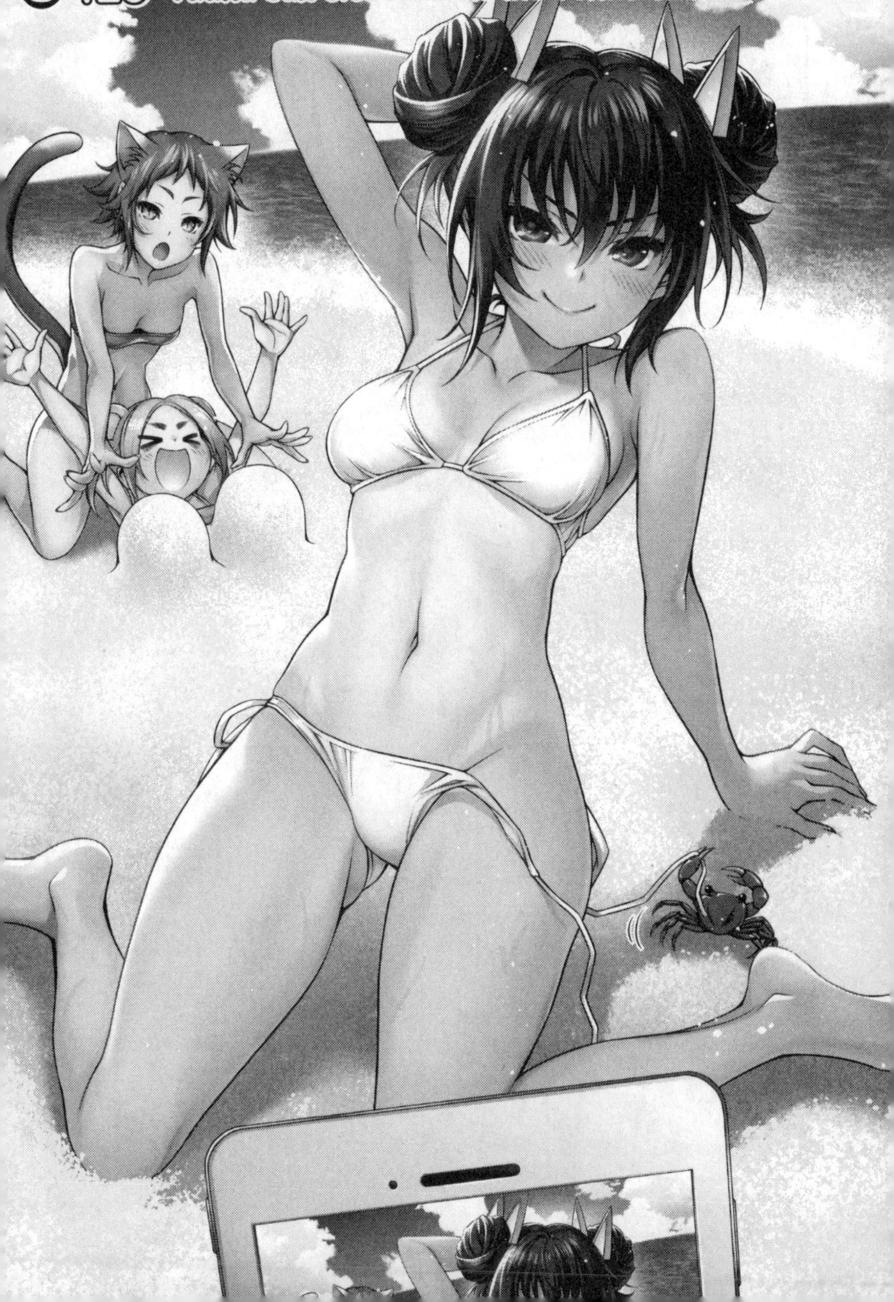

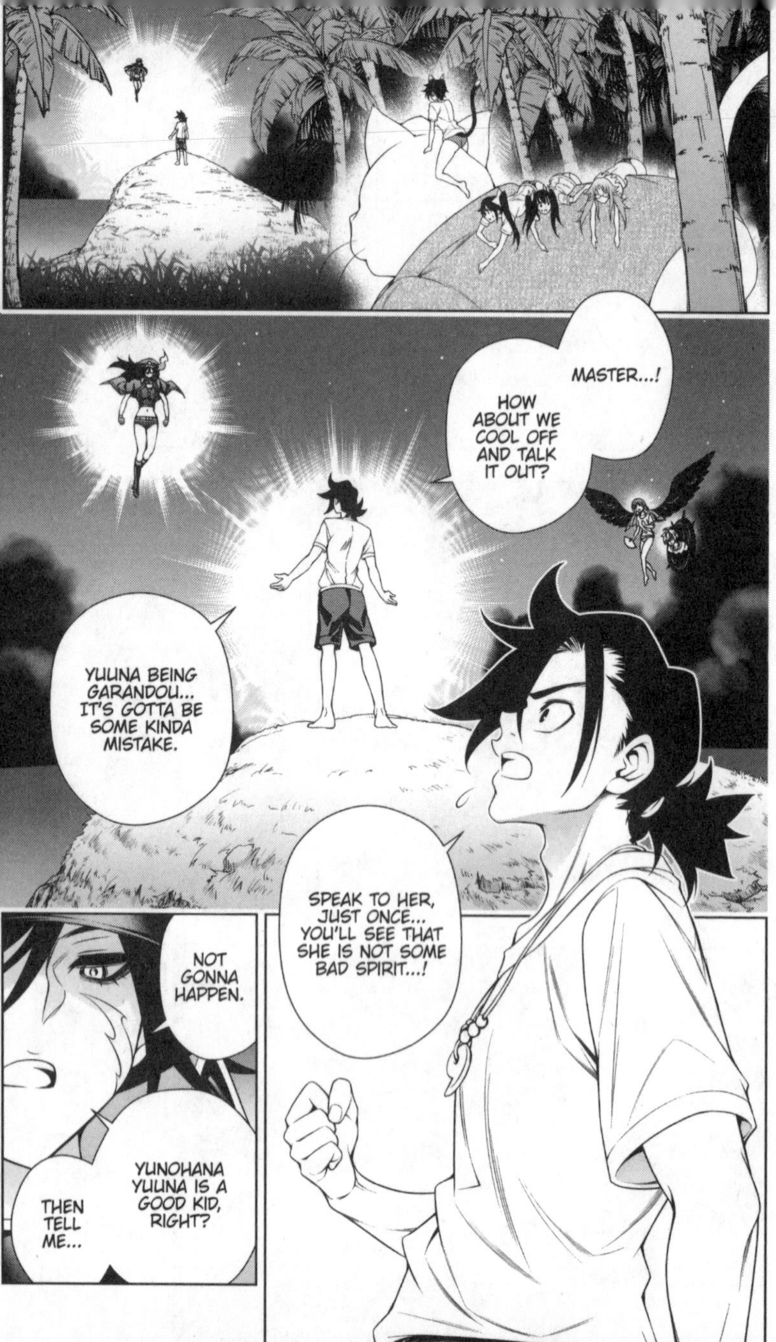
MASTER...!
HOW ABOUT WE COOL OFF AND TALK IT OUT?
YUUNA BEING GARANDOU... IT'S GOTTA BE SOME KINDA MISTAKE.
SPEAK TO HER, JUST ONCE... YOU'LL SEE THAT SHE IS NOT SOME BAD SPIRIT...!
NOT GONNA HAPPEN.
YUNOHANA YUUNA IS A GOOD KID, RIGHT?
THEN TELL ME...

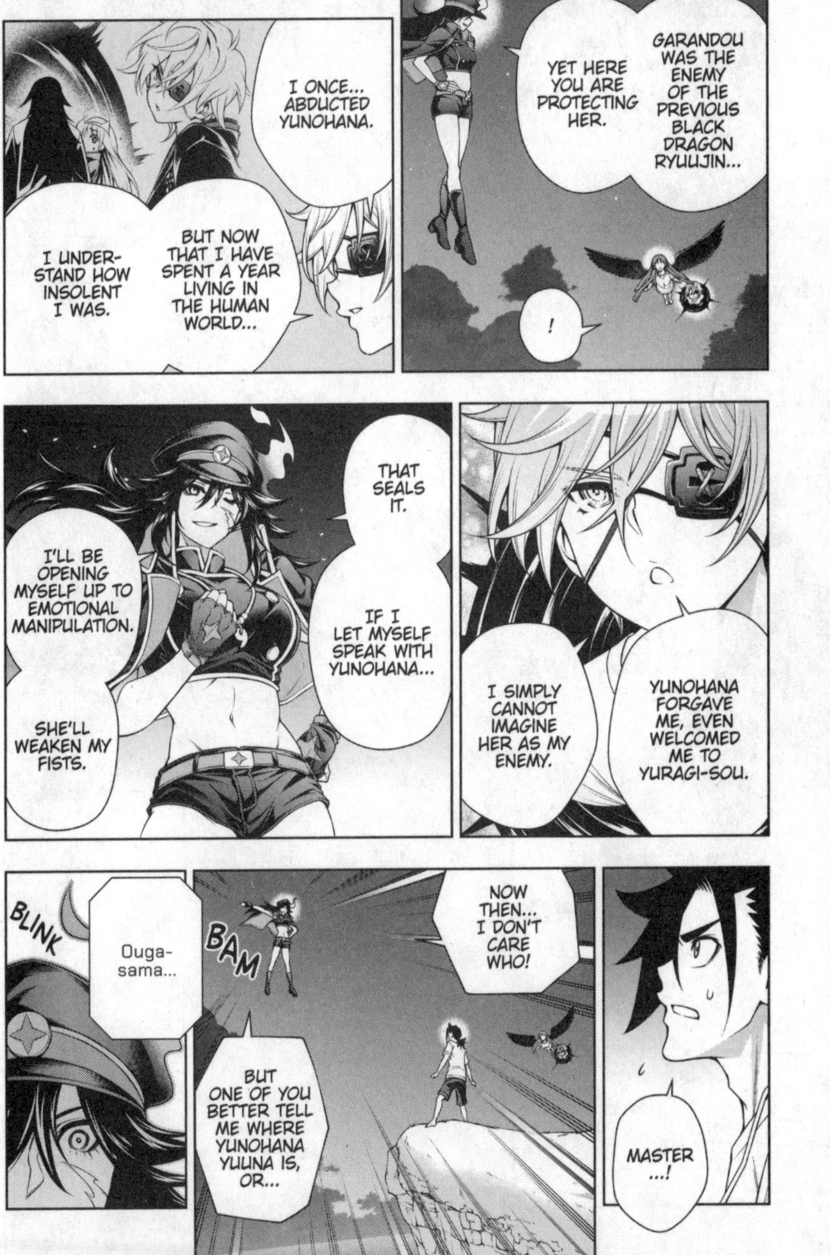
GARANDOU WAS THE ENEMY OF THE PREVIOUS BLACK DRAGON RYUUJIN...
YET HERE YOU ARE PROTECTING HER.
!
I ONCE... ABDUCTED YUNOHANA.
BUT NOW THAT I HAVE SPENT A YEAR LIVING IN THE HUMAN WORLD...
I UNDER-STAND HOW INSOLENT I WAS.
YUNOHANA FORGAVE ME, EVEN WELCOMED ME TO YURAGI-SOU.
I SIMPLY CANNOT IMAGINE HER AS MY ENEMY.
THAT SEALS IT.
IF I LET MYSELF SPEAK WITH YUNOHANA...
I'LL BE OPENING MYSELF UP TO EMOTIONAL MANIPULATION.
SHE'LL WEAKEN MY FISTS.
MASTER ...!
NOW THEN... I DON'T CARE WHO!
BAM
BUT ONE OF YOU BETTER TELL ME WHERE YUNOHANA YUUNA IS, OR...
BLINK
Ouga-sama...

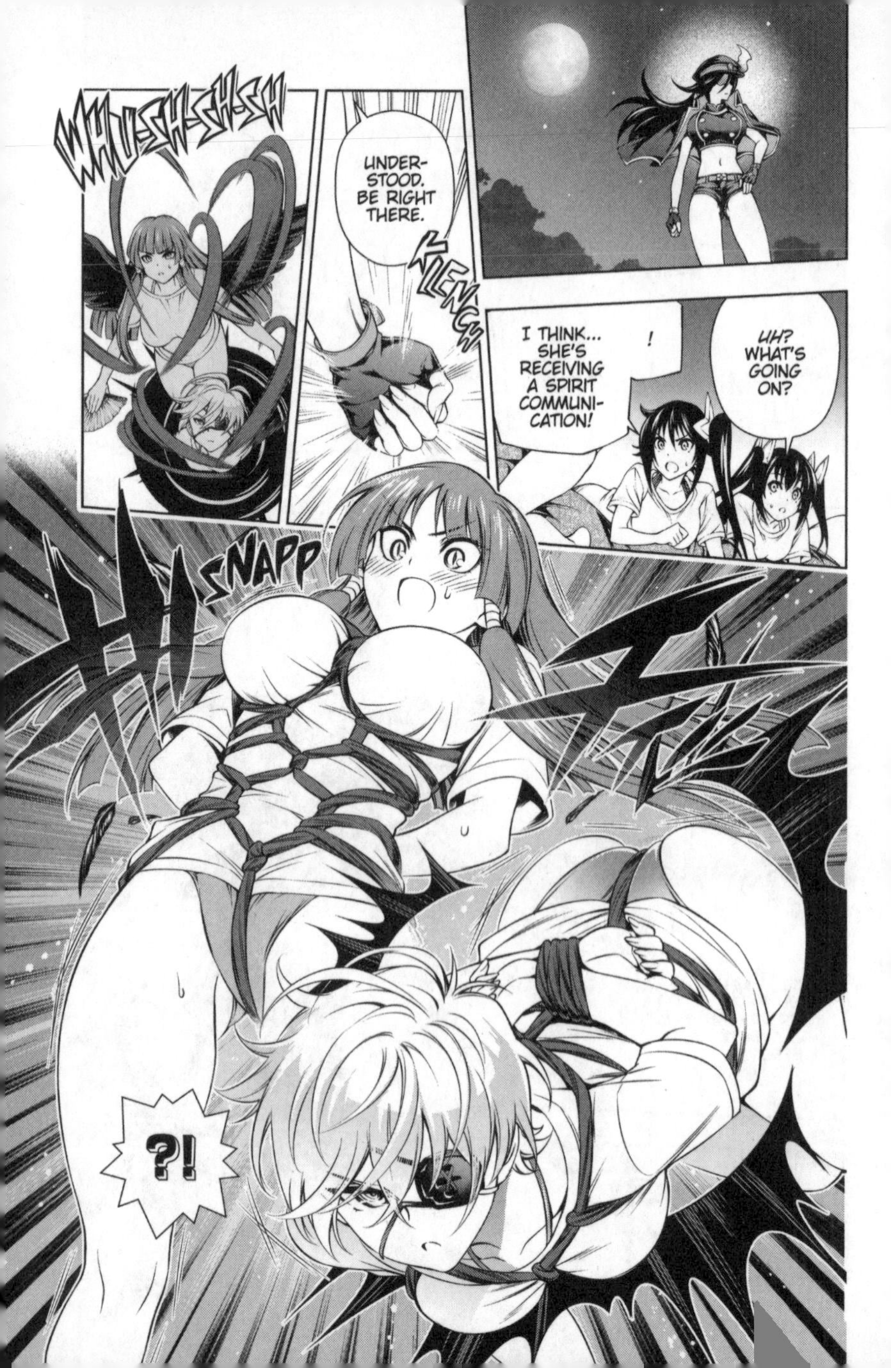
UH? WHAT'S GOING ON?
!
I THINK... SHE'S RECEIVING A SPIRIT COMMUNI-CATION!
UNDER-STOOD. BE RIGHT THERE.
KLENCH
WHUSH-SH-SH
SNAPP
?!

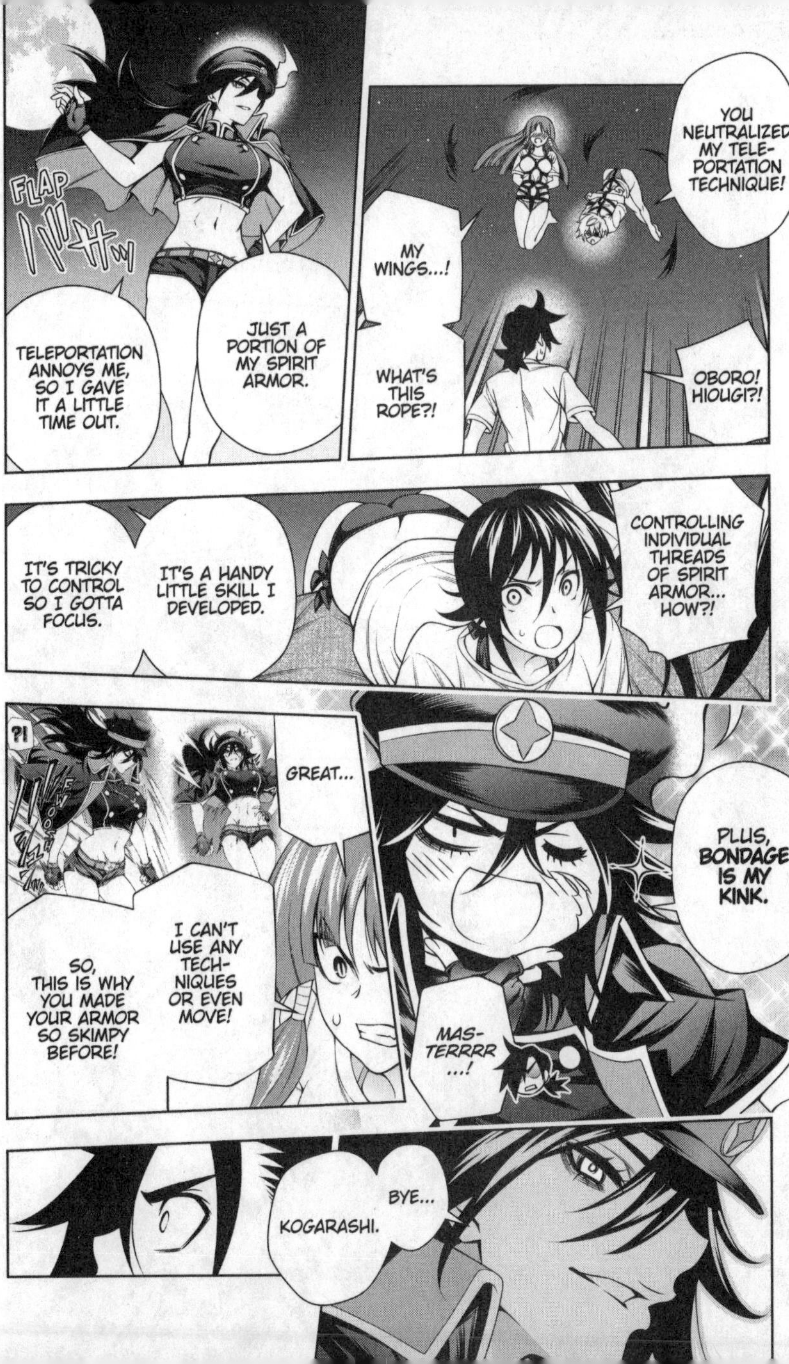
YOU NEUTRALIZED MY TELE-PORTATION TECHNIQUE!
MY WINGS...!
OBORO! HIOUGI?!
WHAT'S THIS ROPE?!
FLAP
JUST A PORTION OF MY SPIRIT ARMOR.
TELEPORTATION ANNOYS ME, SO I GAVE IT A LITTLE TIME OUT.
CONTROLLING INDIVIDUAL THREADS OF SPIRIT ARMOR... HOW?!
IT'S A HANDY LITTLE SKILL I DEVELOPED.
IT'S TRICKY TO CONTROL SO I GOTTA FOCUS.
PLUS, BONDAGE IS MY KINK.
MAS-TERRRR...!
GREAT...
?!
FWOOSH
I CAN'T USE ANY TECH-NIQUES OR EVEN MOVE!
SO, THIS IS WHY YOU MADE YOUR ARMOR SO SKIMPY BEFORE!
BYE...
KOGARASHI.

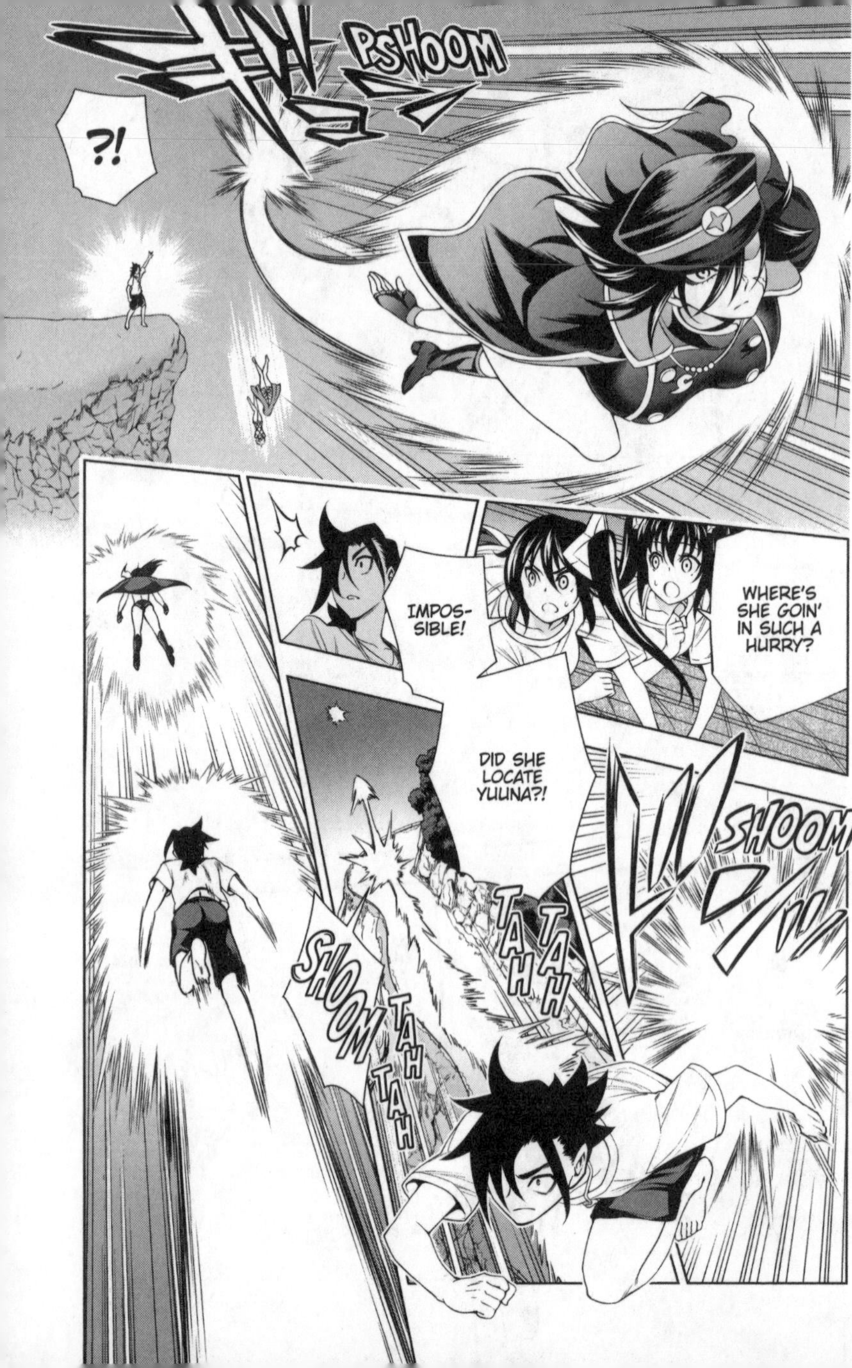
PSHOOM
?!
WHERE'S SHE GOIN' IN SUCH A HURRY?
IMPOS-SIBLE!
DID SHE LOCATE YUUNA?!
SHOOM
TAH TAH
SHOOM
TAH TAH

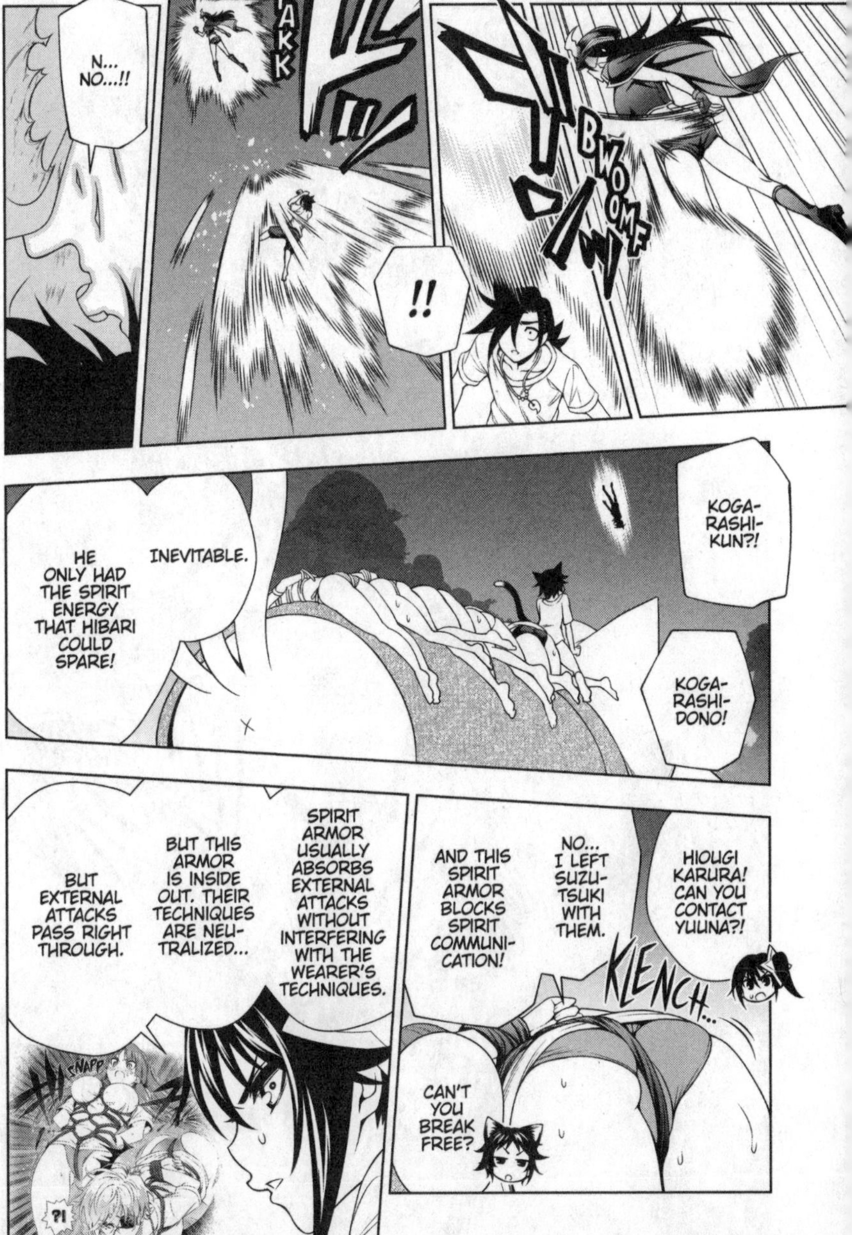
BWOOMF
!!
SPAKK
N... NO...!!
KOGA-RASHI-KUN?!
KOGA-RASHI-DONO!
INEVITABLE.
HE ONLY HAD THE SPIRIT ENERGY THAT HIBARI COULD SPARE!
HIOUGI KARURA! CAN YOU CONTACT YUUNA?!
KLENCH...
NO... I LEFT SUZU-TSUKI WITH THEM.
AND THIS SPIRIT ARMOR BLOCKS SPIRIT COMMUNI-CATION!
CAN'T YOU BREAK FREE?
SPIRIT ARMOR USUALLY ABSORBS EXTERNAL ATTACKS WITHOUT INTERFERING WITH THE WEARER'S TECHNIQUES.
BUT THIS ARMOR IS INSIDE OUT. THEIR TECHNIQUES ARE NEU-TRALIZED...
BUT EXTERNAL ATTACKS PASS RIGHT THROUGH.
SNAPP
?!

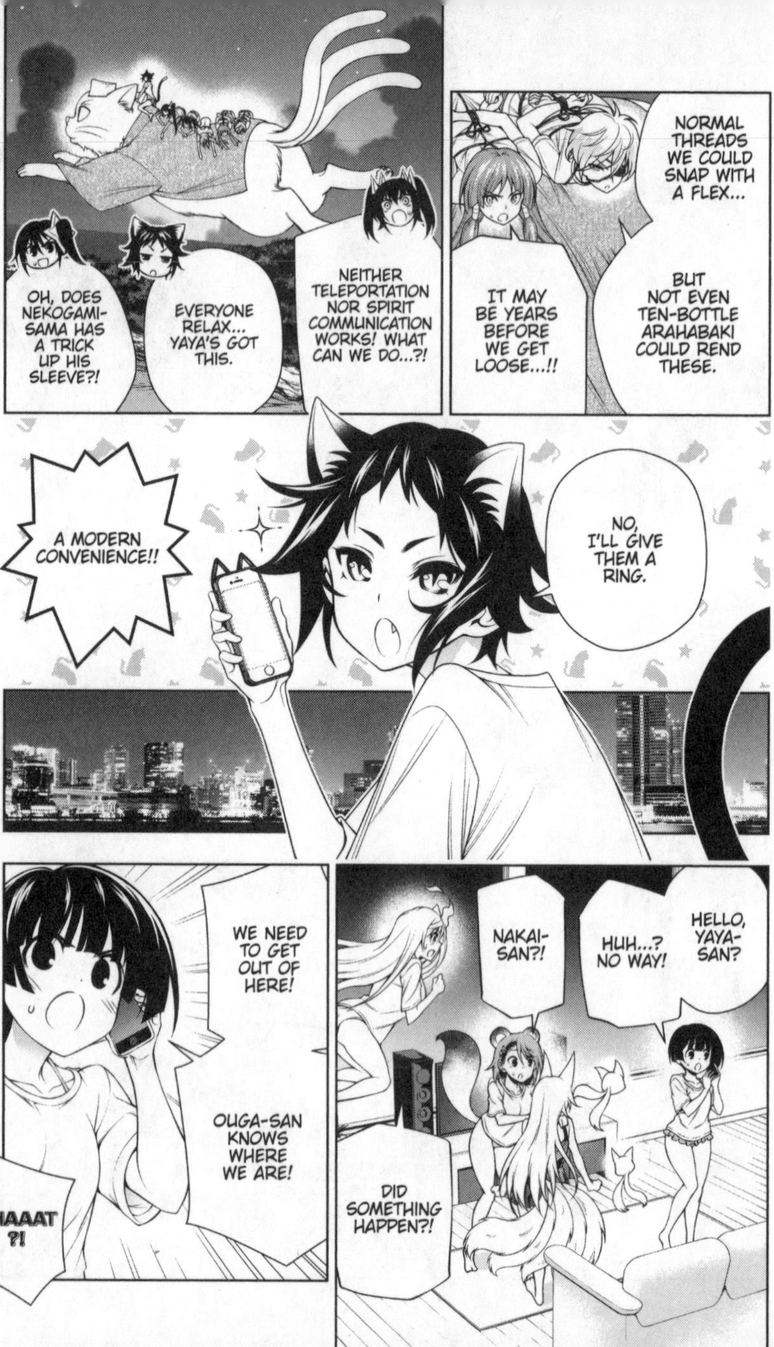
NORMAL THREADS WE COULD SNAP WITH A FLEX...
BUT NOT EVEN TEN-BOTTLE ARAHABAKI COULD REND THESE.
IT MAY BE YEARS BEFORE WE GET LOOSE...!!
NEITHER TELEPORTATION NOR SPIRIT COMMUNICATION WORKS! WHAT CAN WE DO...?!
EVERYONE RELAX... YAYA'S GOT THIS.
OH, DOES NEKOGAMI-SAMA HAS A TRICK UP HIS SLEEVE?!
NO, I'LL GIVE THEM A RING.
A MODERN CONVENIENCE!!
HELLO, YAYA-SAN?
HUH...? NO WAY!
NAKAI-SAN?!
DID SOMETHING HAPPEN?!
WE NEED TO GET OUT OF HERE!
OUGA-SAN KNOWS WHERE WE ARE!
WHAAAT?!

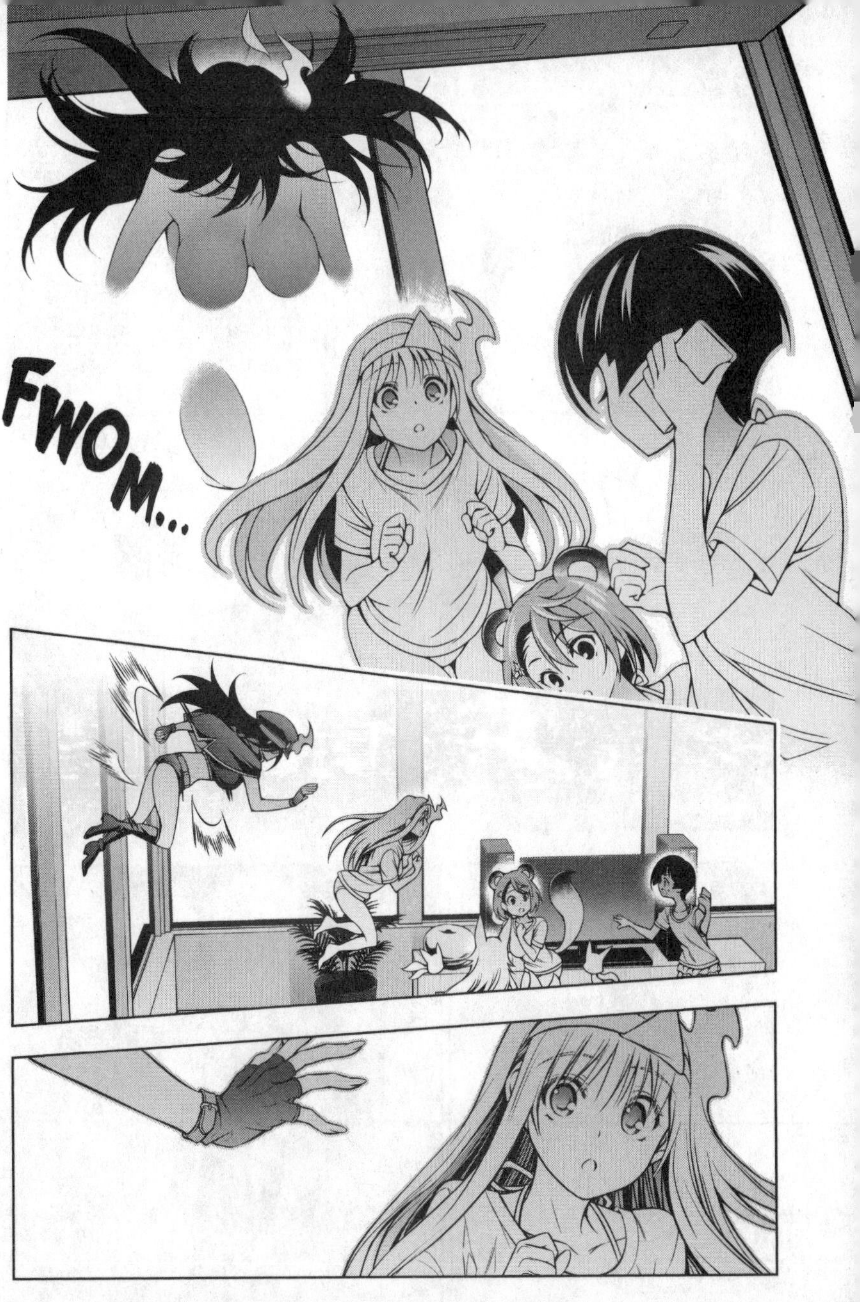
FWOM...

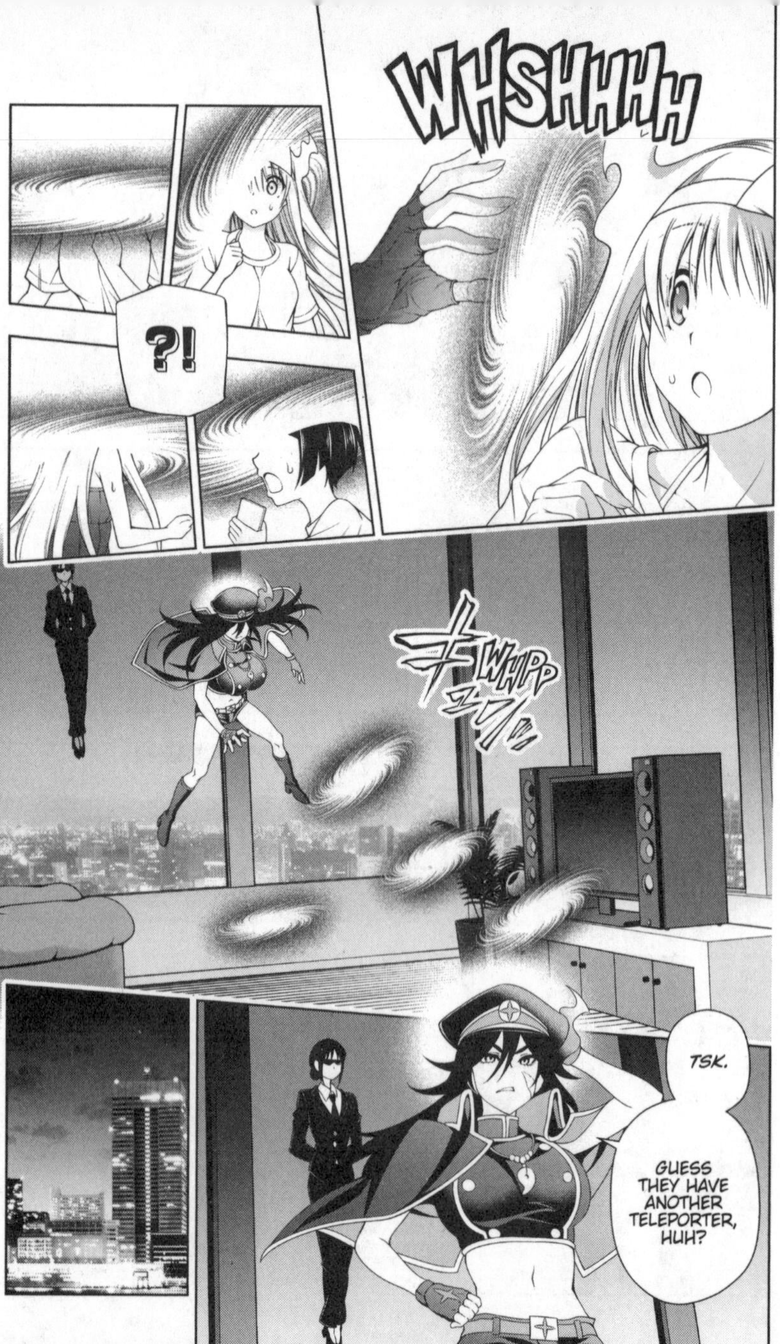
WHSHHHH
?!
WHPP
TSK.
GUESS THEY HAVE ANOTHER TELEPORTER, HUH?

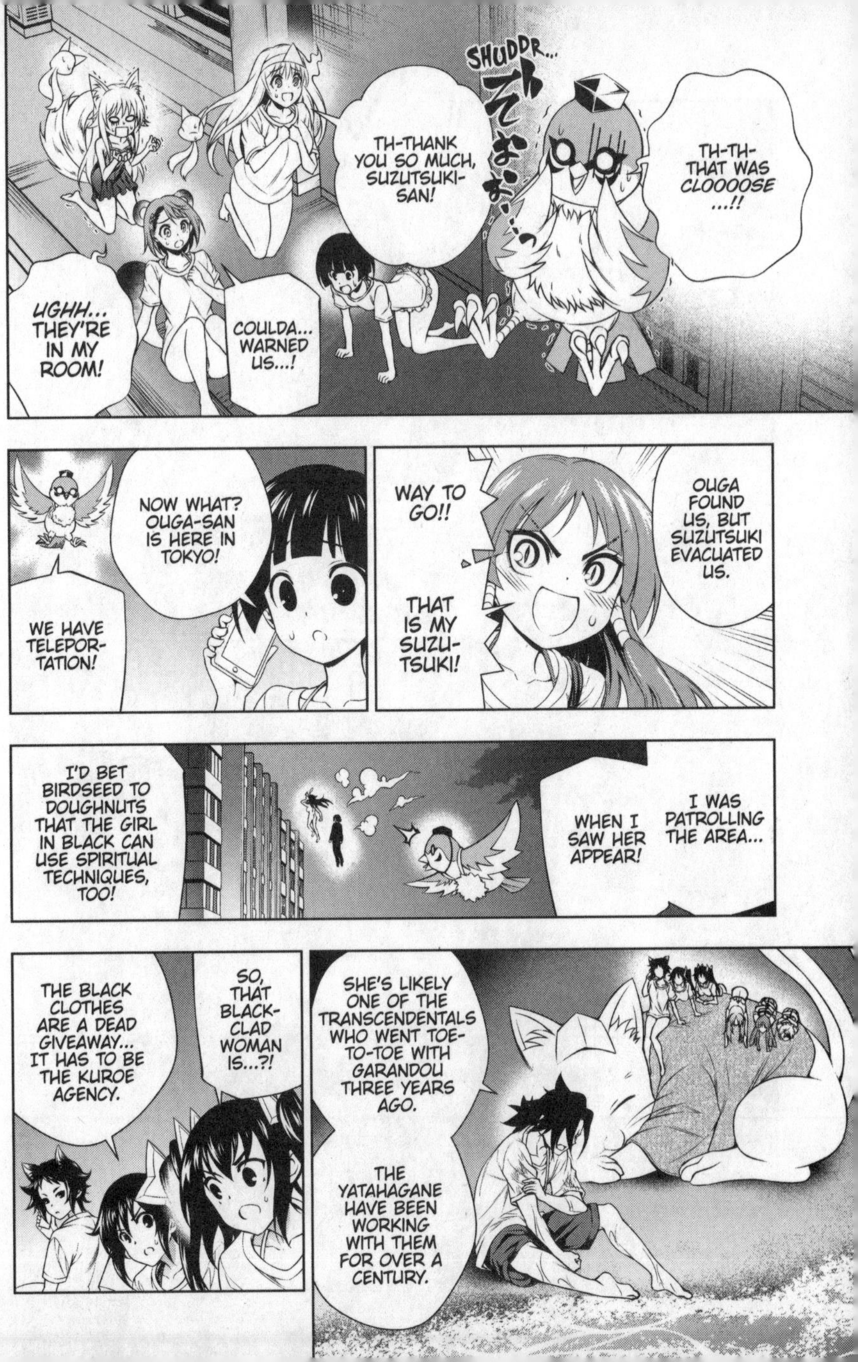
TH-TH-THAT WAS CLOOOOSE ...!!
SHUDDR...
TH-THANK YOU SO MUCH, SUZUTSUKI-SAN!
COULDA... WARNED US...!
UGHH... THEY'RE IN MY ROOM!
OUGA FOUND US, BUT SUZUTSUKI EVACUATED US.
WAY TO GO!!
THAT IS MY SUZU-TSUKI!
NOW WHAT? OUGA-SAN IS HERE IN TOKYO!
WE HAVE TELEPOR-TATION!
I WAS PATROLLING THE AREA...
WHEN I SAW HER APPEAR!
I'D BET BIRDSEED TO DOUGHNUTS THAT THE GIRL IN BLACK CAN USE SPIRITUAL TECHNIQUES, TOO!
SHE'S LIKELY ONE OF THE TRANSCENDENTALS WHO WENT TOE-TO-TOE WITH GARANDOU THREE YEARS AGO.
THE YATAHAGANE HAVE BEEN WORKING WITH THEM FOR OVER A CENTURY.
SO, THAT BLACK-CLAD WOMAN IS...?!
THE BLACK CLOTHES ARE A DEAD GIVEAWAY... IT HAS TO BE THE KUROE AGENCY.

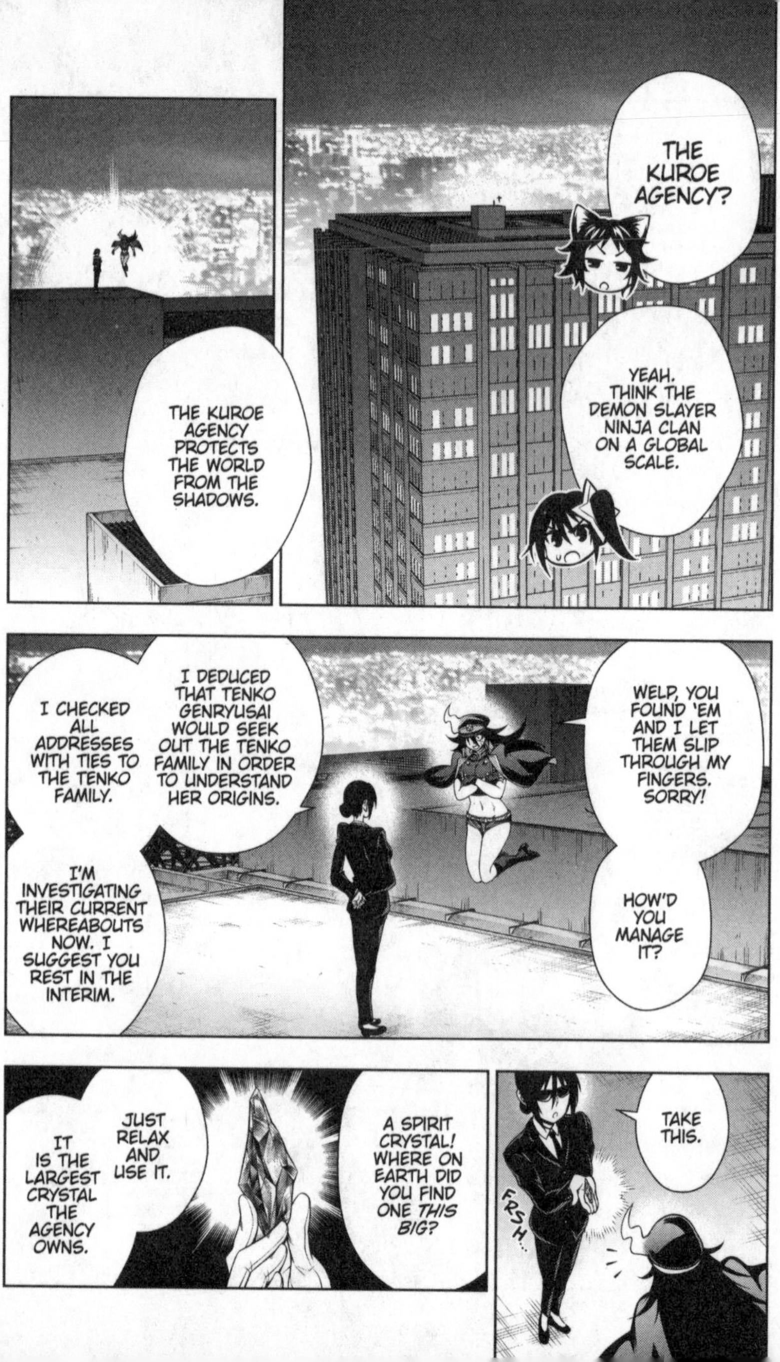
THE KUROE AGENCY?
YEAH. THINK THE DEMON SLAYER NINJA CLAN ON A GLOBAL SCALE.
THE KUROE AGENCY PROTECTS THE WORLD FROM THE SHADOWS.
WELP, YOU FOUND 'EM AND I LET THEM SLIP THROUGH MY FINGERS. SORRY!
HOW'D YOU MANAGE IT?
I DEDUCED THAT TENKO GENRYUSAI WOULD SEEK OUT THE TENKO FAMILY IN ORDER TO UNDERSTAND HER ORIGINS.
I CHECKED ALL ADDRESSES WITH TIES TO THE TENKO FAMILY.
I'M INVESTIGATING THEIR CURRENT WHEREABOUTS NOW. I SUGGEST YOU REST IN THE INTERIM.
TAKE THIS.
FRSH...
A SPIRIT CRYSTAL! WHERE ON EARTH DID YOU FIND ONE *THIS* BIG?
JUST RELAX AND USE IT.
IT IS THE LARGEST CRYSTAL THE AGENCY OWNS.

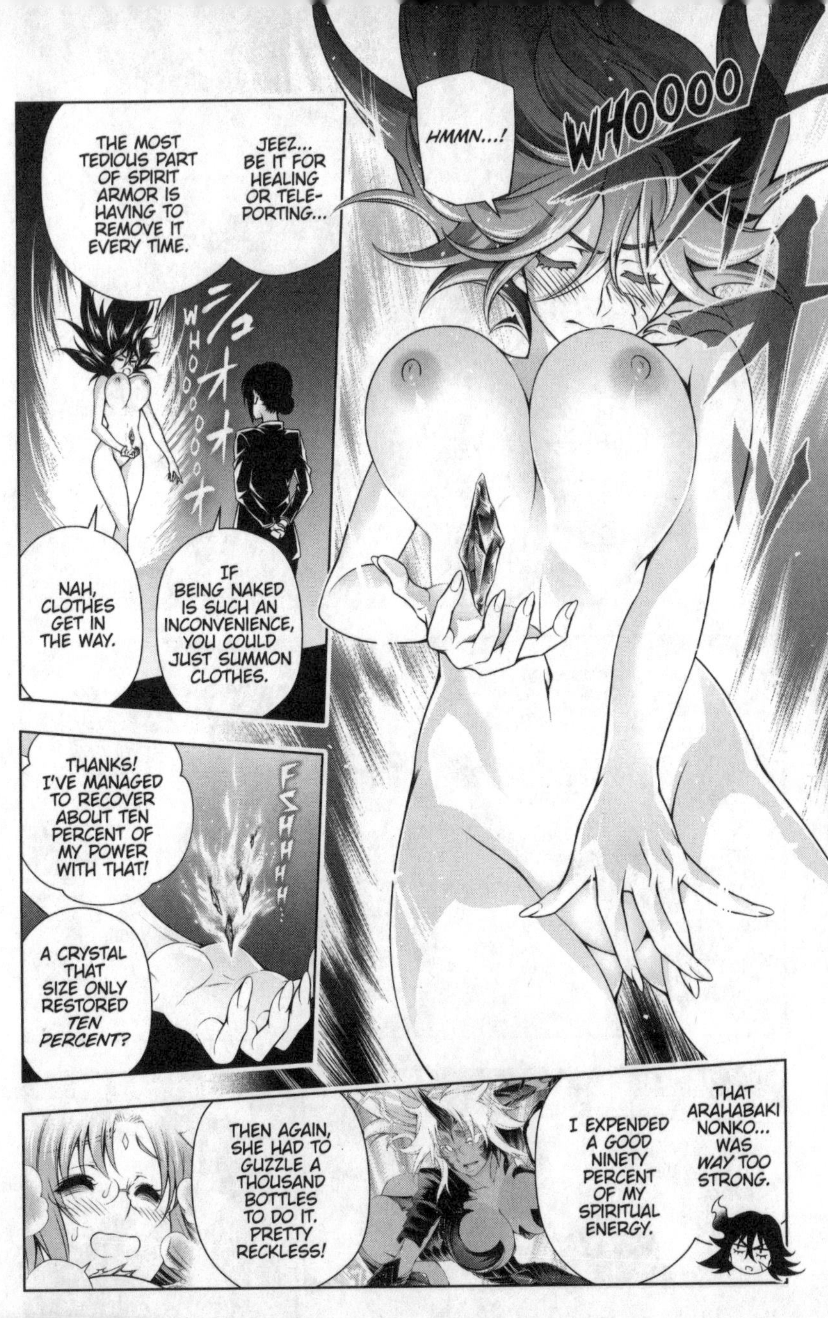
HMMN...!
WHOOOO
JEEZ... BE IT FOR HEALING OR TELE-PORTING...
THE MOST TEDIOUS PART OF SPIRIT ARMOR IS HAVING TO REMOVE IT EVERY TIME.
シュオオオオ
WHOOOOOOOO
IF BEING NAKED IS SUCH AN INCONVENIENCE, YOU COULD JUST SUMMON CLOTHES.
NAH, CLOTHES GET IN THE WAY.
THANKS! I'VE MANAGED TO RECOVER ABOUT TEN PERCENT OF MY POWER WITH THAT!
FSHHHH...
A CRYSTAL THAT SIZE ONLY RESTORED TEN PERCENT?
THAT ARAHABAKI NONKO... WAS WAY TOO STRONG.
I EXPENDED A GOOD NINETY PERCENT OF MY SPIRITUAL ENERGY.
THEN AGAIN, SHE HAD TO GUZZLE A THOUSAND BOTTLES TO DO IT. PRETTY RECKLESS!

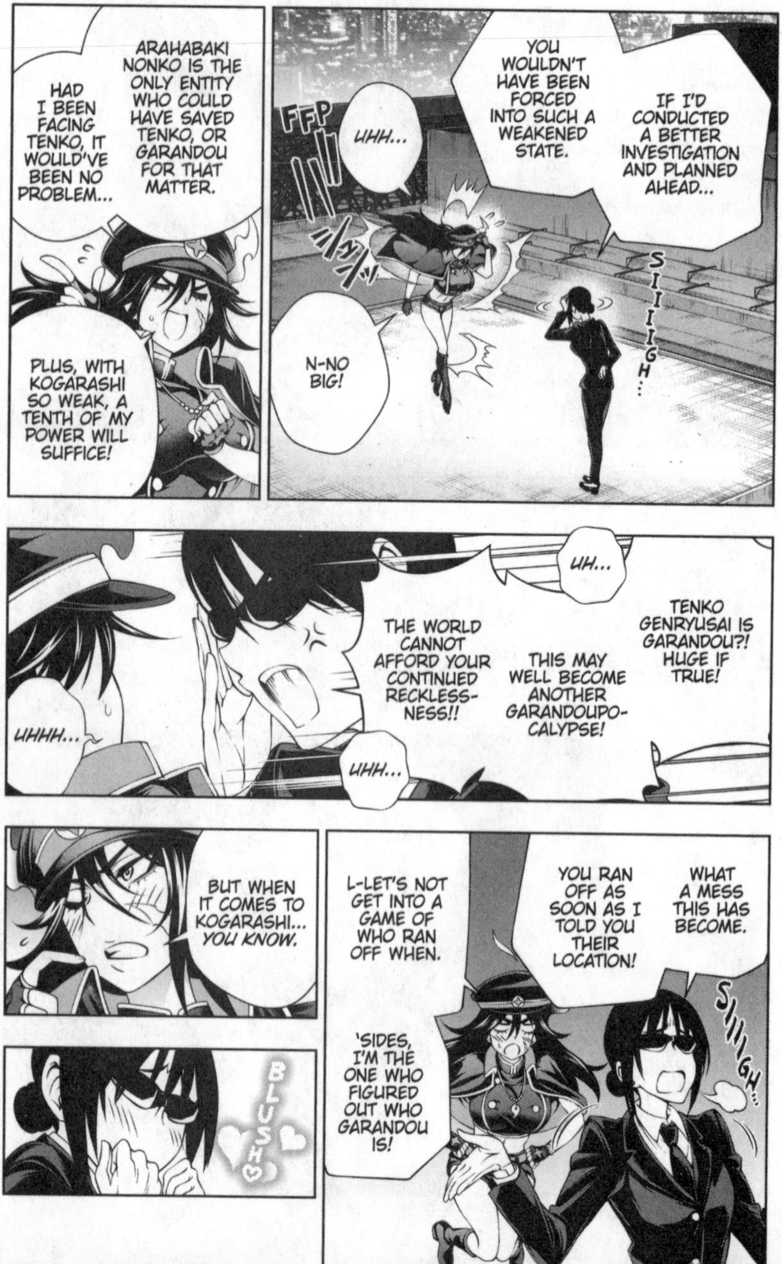
IF I'D CONDUCTED A BETTER INVESTIGATION AND PLANNED AHEAD...
YOU WOULDN'T HAVE BEEN FORCED INTO SUCH A WEAKENED STATE.
SIIIIGH...
UHH...
FFP
N-NO BIG!
ARAHABAKI NONKO IS THE ONLY ENTITY WHO COULD HAVE SAVED TENKO, OR GARANDOU FOR THAT MATTER.
HAD I BEEN FACING TENKO, IT WOULD'VE BEEN NO PROBLEM...
PLUS, WITH KOGARASHI SO WEAK, A TENTH OF MY POWER WILL SUFFICE!
UH...
TENKO GENRYUSAI IS GARANDOU?! HUGE IF TRUE!
THIS MAY WELL BECOME ANOTHER GARANDOUPO-CALYPSE!
THE WORLD CANNOT AFFORD YOUR CONTINUED RECKLESS-NESS!!
UHH...
UHHH...
WHAT A MESS THIS HAS BECOME.
YOU RAN OFF AS SOON AS I TOLD YOU THEIR LOCATION!
L-LET'S NOT GET INTO A GAME OF WHO RAN OFF WHEN.
SIIIGH...
'SIDES, I'M THE ONE WHO FIGURED OUT WHO GARANDOU IS!
BUT WHEN IT COMES TO KOGARASHI... YOU KNOW.
BLUSH

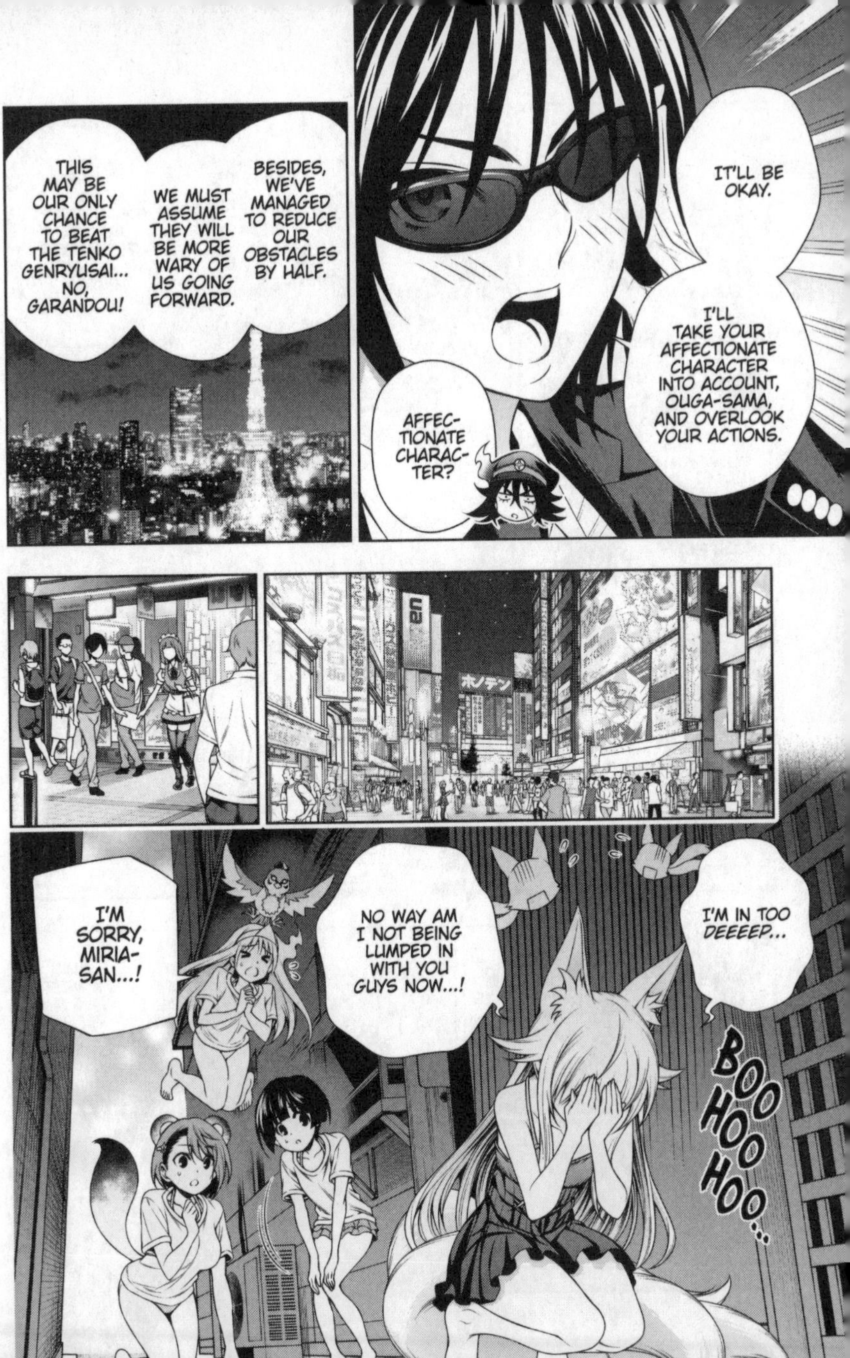
IT'LL BE OKAY.
I'LL TAKE YOUR AFFECTIONATE CHARACTER INTO ACCOUNT, OUGA-SAMA, AND OVERLOOK YOUR ACTIONS.
AFFECTIONATE CHARACTER?
THIS MAY BE OUR ONLY CHANCE TO BEAT THE TENKO GENRYUSAI... NO, GARANDOU!
WE MUST ASSUME THEY WILL BE MORE WARY OF US GOING FORWARD.
BESIDES, WE'VE MANAGED TO REDUCE OUR OBSTACLES BY HALF.
I'M IN TOO DEEEEP...
BOO HOO HOO HOO...
NO WAY AM I NOT BEING LUMPED IN WITH YOU GUYS NOW...!
I'M SORRY, MIRIA-SAN...!

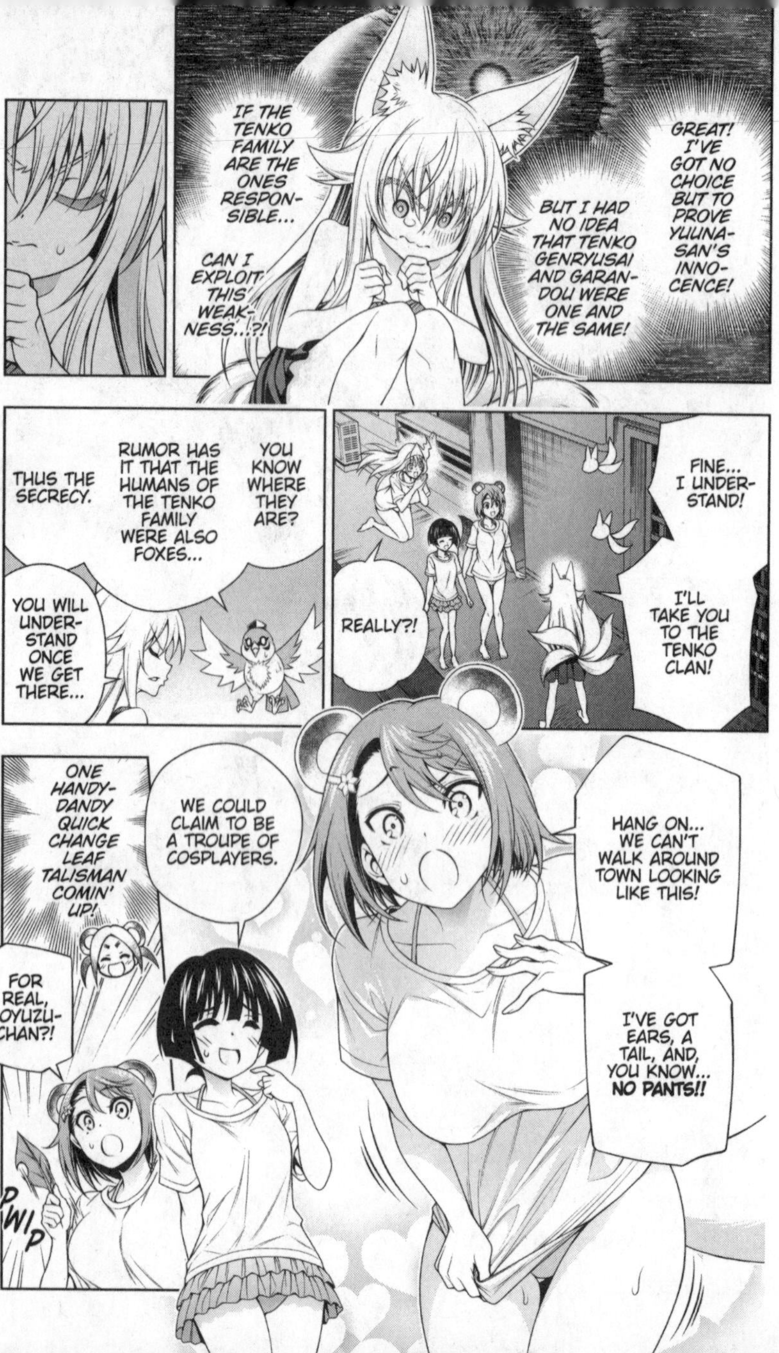
GREAT! I'VE GOT NO CHOICE BUT TO PROVE YUUNA-SAN'S INNOCENCE!
BUT I HAD NO IDEA THAT TENKO GENRYUSAI AND GARANDOU WERE ONE AND THE SAME!
IF THE TENKO FAMILY ARE THE ONES RESPONSIBLE...
CAN I EXPLOIT THIS WEAKNESS...?!
FINE... I UNDERSTAND!
I'LL TAKE YOU TO THE TENKO CLAN!
REALLY?!
YOU KNOW WHERE THEY ARE?
RUMOR HAS IT THAT THE HUMANS OF THE TENKO FAMILY WERE ALSO FOXES...
THUS THE SECRECY.
YOU WILL UNDERSTAND ONCE WE GET THERE...
HANG ON... WE CAN'T WALK AROUND TOWN LOOKING LIKE THIS!
I'VE GOT EARS, A TAIL, AND, YOU KNOW... **NO PANTS!!**
WE COULD CLAIM TO BE A TROUPE OF COSPLAYERS.
ONE HANDY-DANDY QUICK CHANGE LEAF TALISMAN COMIN' UP!
FOR REAL, KOYUZU-CHAN?!
PWIP

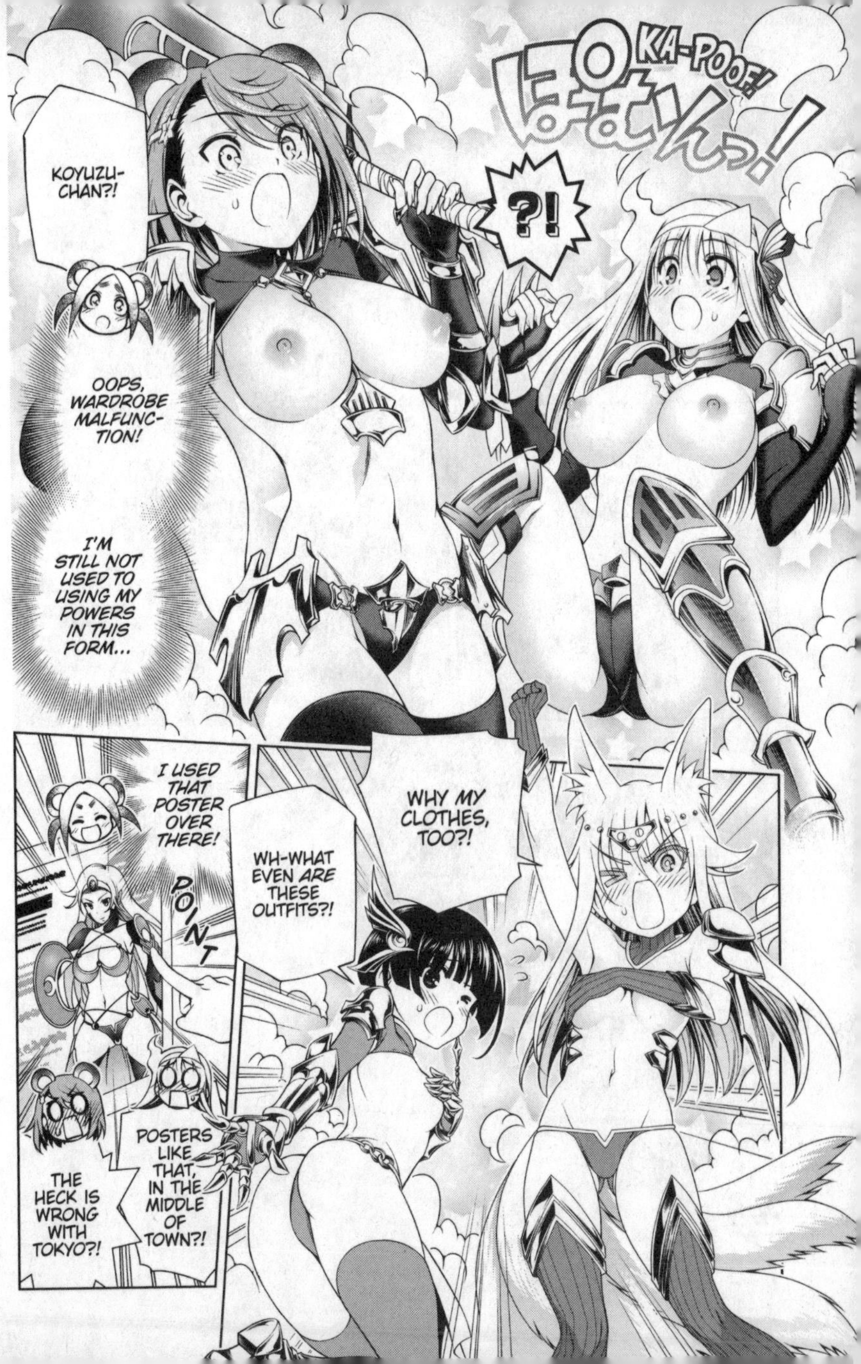
KA-POOF!
?!
KOYUZU-CHAN?!
OOPS, WARDROBE MALFUNCTION!
I'M STILL NOT USED TO USING MY POWERS IN THIS FORM...
WHY MY CLOTHES, TOO?!
WH-WHAT EVEN ARE THESE OUTFITS?!
I USED THAT POSTER OVER THERE!
POINT
POSTERS LIKE THAT, IN THE MIDDLE OF TOWN?!
THE HECK IS WRONG WITH TOKYO?!

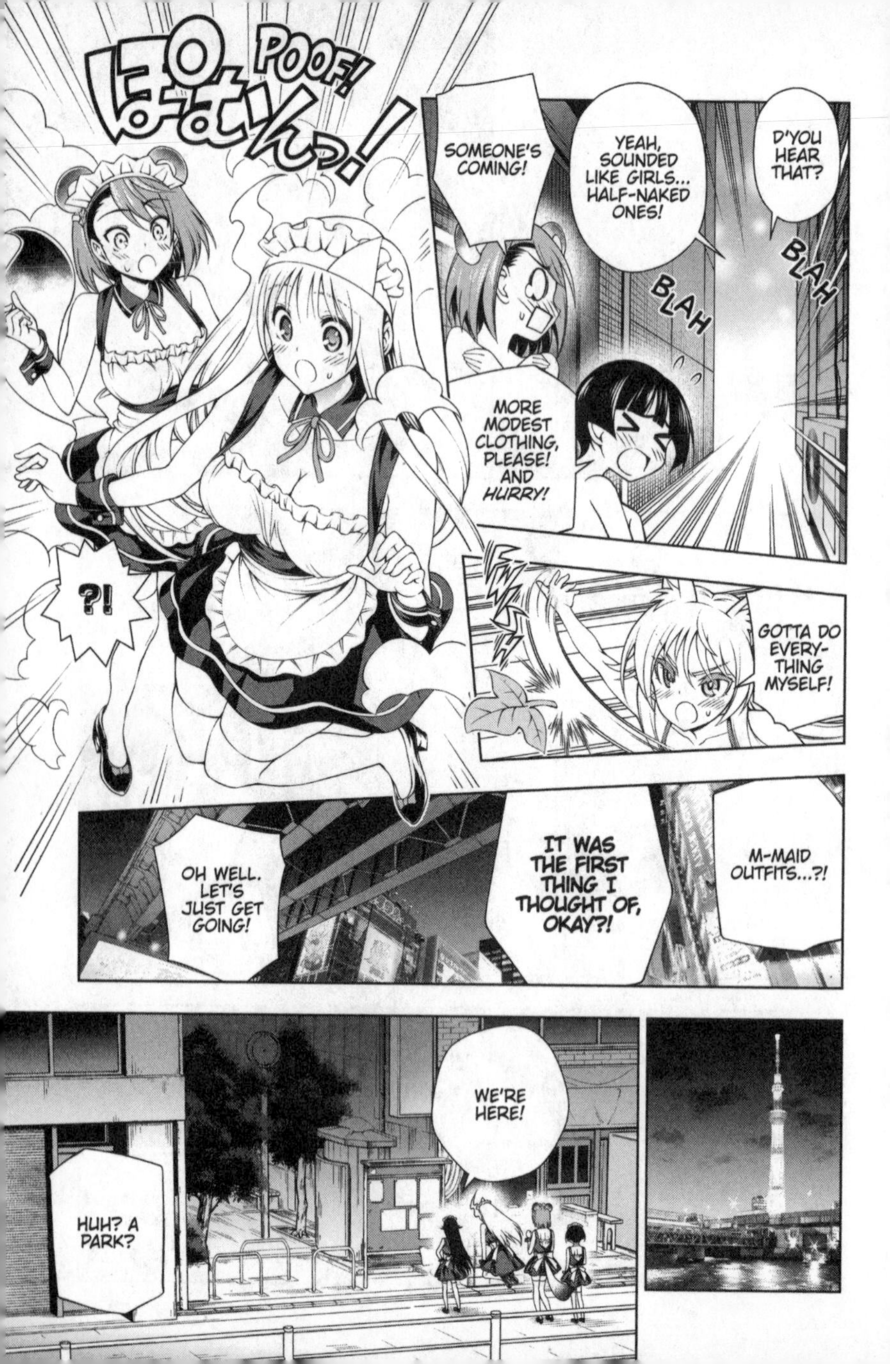
D'YOU HEAR THAT?
BLAH
BLAH
YEAH, SOUNDED LIKE GIRLS... HALF-NAKED ONES!
SOMEONE'S COMING!
MORE MODEST CLOTHING, PLEASE! AND *HURRY!*
GOTTA DO EVERY-THING MYSELF!
ぼわんっ!
POOF!
?!
M-MAID OUTFITS...?!
IT WAS THE FIRST THING I THOUGHT OF, OKAY?!
OH WELL. LET'S JUST GET GOING!
WE'RE HERE!
HUH? A PARK?

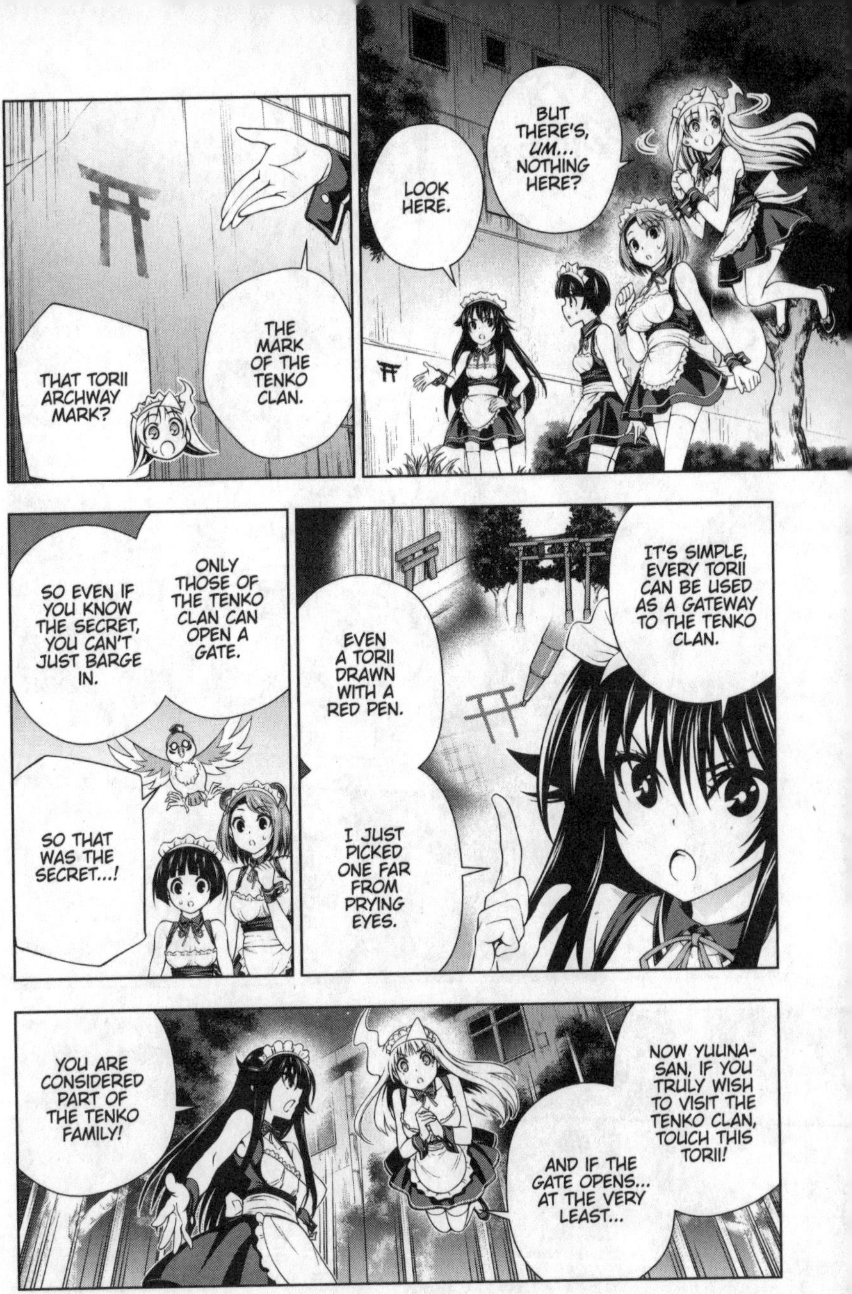
BUT THERE'S, *UM*... NOTHING HERE?
LOOK HERE.
THE MARK OF THE TENKO CLAN.
THAT TORII ARCHWAY MARK?
IT'S SIMPLE, EVERY TORII CAN BE USED AS A GATEWAY TO THE TENKO CLAN.
EVEN A TORII DRAWN WITH A RED PEN.
I JUST PICKED ONE FAR FROM PRYING EYES.
ONLY THOSE OF THE TENKO CLAN CAN OPEN A GATE.
SO EVEN IF YOU KNOW THE SECRET, YOU CAN'T JUST BARGE IN.
SO THAT WAS THE SECRET...!
NOW YUUNA-SAN, IF YOU TRULY WISH TO VISIT THE TENKO CLAN, TOUCH THIS TORII!
AND IF THE GATE OPENS... AT THE VERY LEAST...
YOU ARE CONSIDERED PART OF THE TENKO FAMILY!

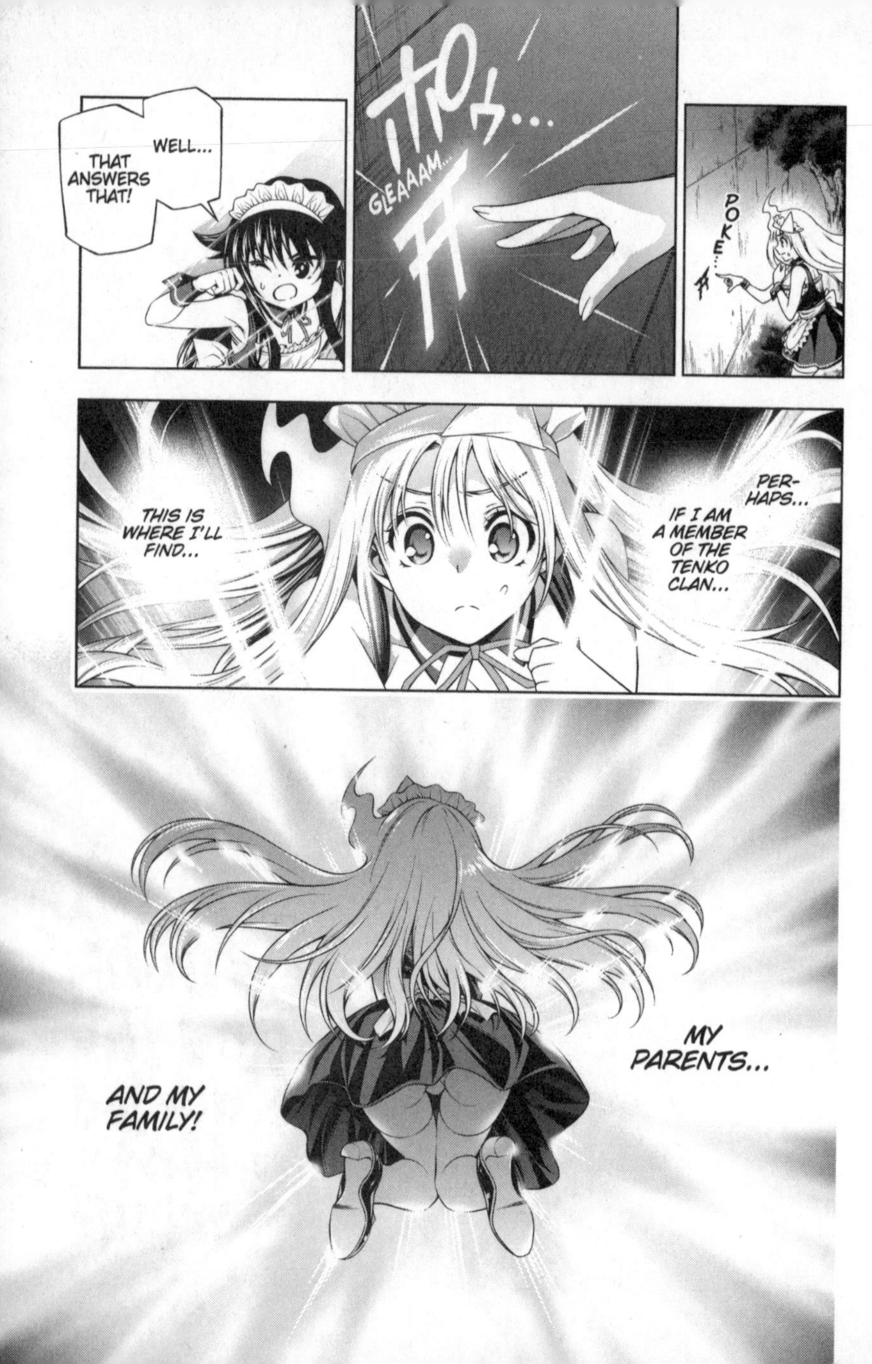

POKE...
GLEAAAM...
WELL... THAT ANSWERS THAT!
PER-HAPS...
IF I AM A MEMBER OF THE TENKO CLAN...
THIS IS WHERE I'LL FIND...
MY PARENTS...
AND MY FAMILY!

Yuuna
and the
Haunted
Hot
Springs

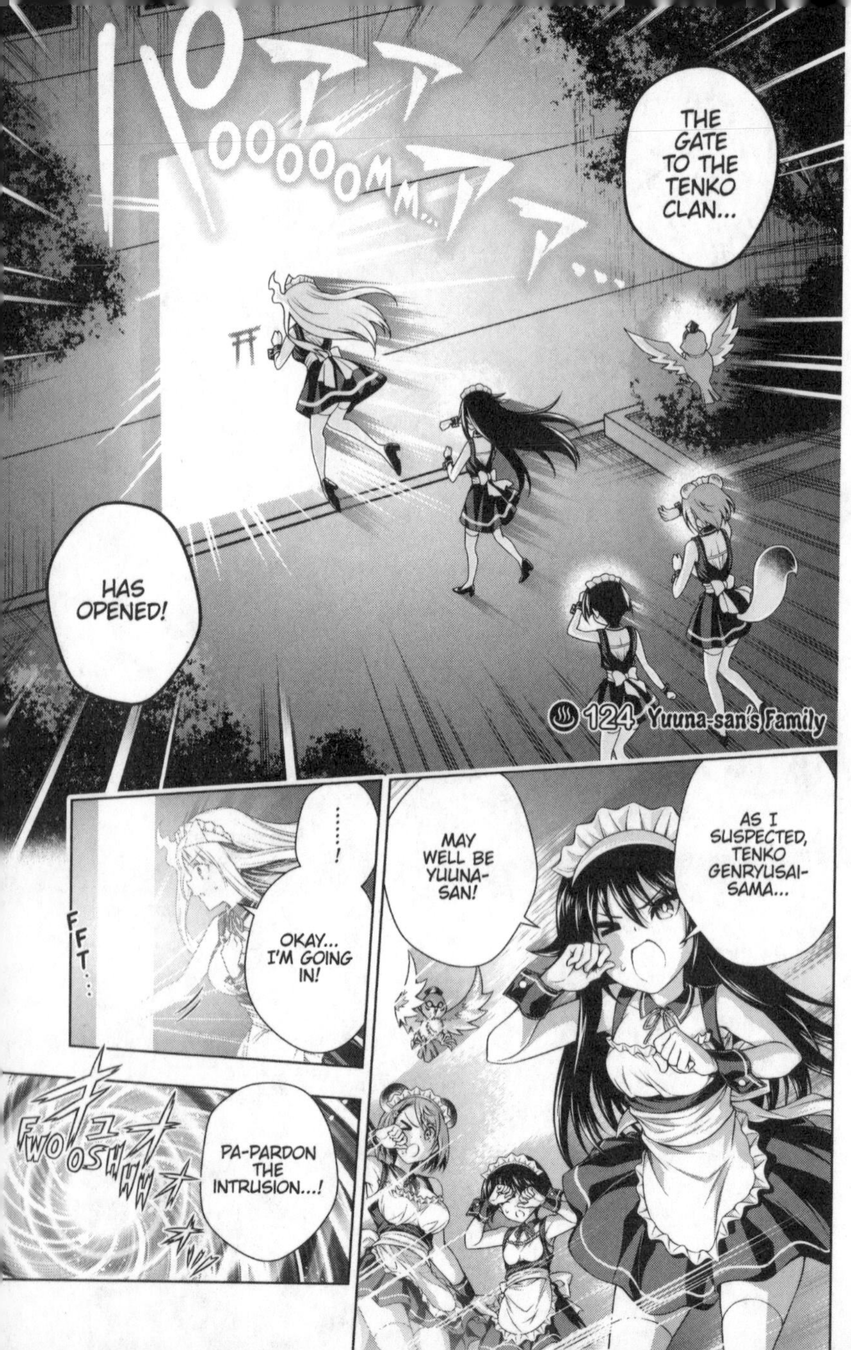
OOOOOMM...
THE GATE TO THE TENKO CLAN...
HAS OPENED!
124 Yuuna-san's Family
AS I SUSPECTED, TENKO GENRYUSAI-SAMA...
MAY WELL BE YUUNA-SAN!
......!
OKAY... I'M GOING IN!
FFT...
FWOOSHHH
PA-PARDON THE INTRUSION...!

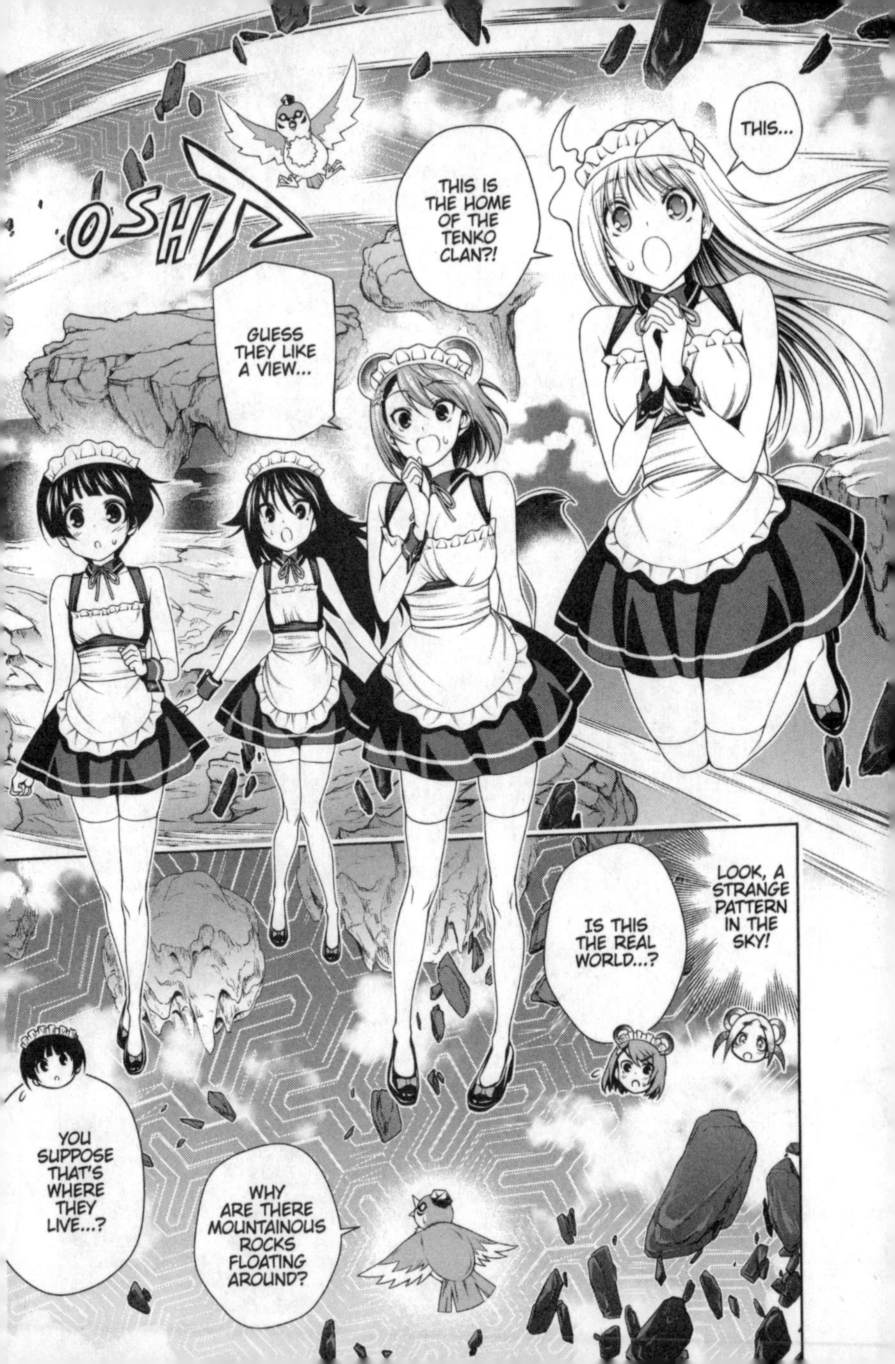
THIS...
THIS IS THE HOME OF THE TENKO CLAN?!
OSH
GUESS THEY LIKE A VIEW...
LOOK, A STRANGE PATTERN IN THE SKY!
IS THIS THE REAL WORLD...?
WHY ARE THERE MOUNTAINOUS ROCKS FLOATING AROUND?
YOU SUPPOSE THAT'S WHERE THEY LIVE...?

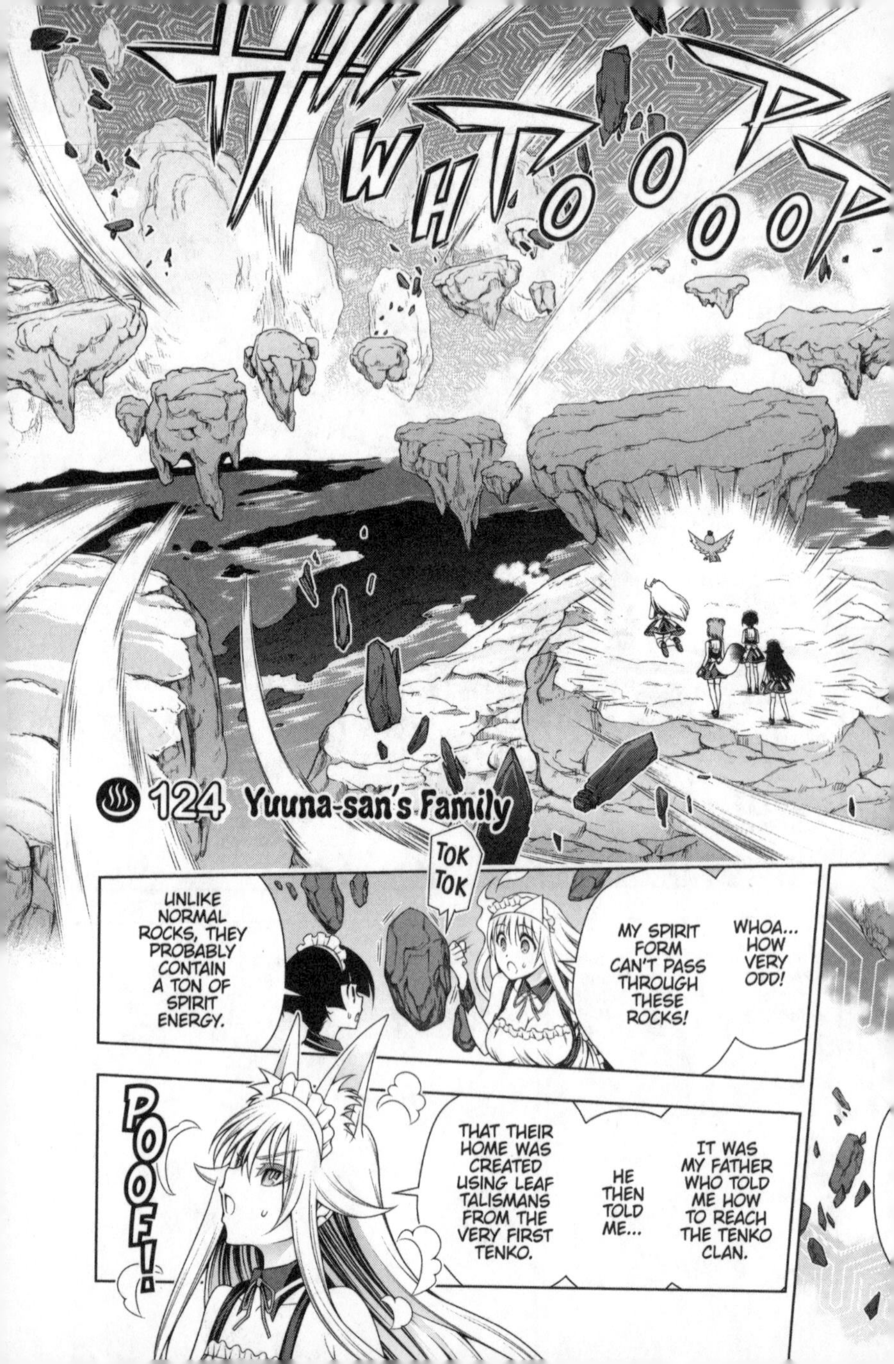
WHOOOOP
124 Yuuna-san's Family
WHOA... HOW VERY ODD!
MY SPIRIT FORM CAN'T PASS THROUGH THESE ROCKS!
TOK TOK
UNLIKE NORMAL ROCKS, THEY PROBABLY CONTAIN A TON OF SPIRIT ENERGY.
IT WAS MY FATHER WHO TOLD ME HOW TO REACH THE TENKO CLAN.
HE THEN TOLD ME...
THAT THEIR HOME WAS CREATED USING LEAF TALISMANS FROM THE VERY FIRST TENKO.
POOF!

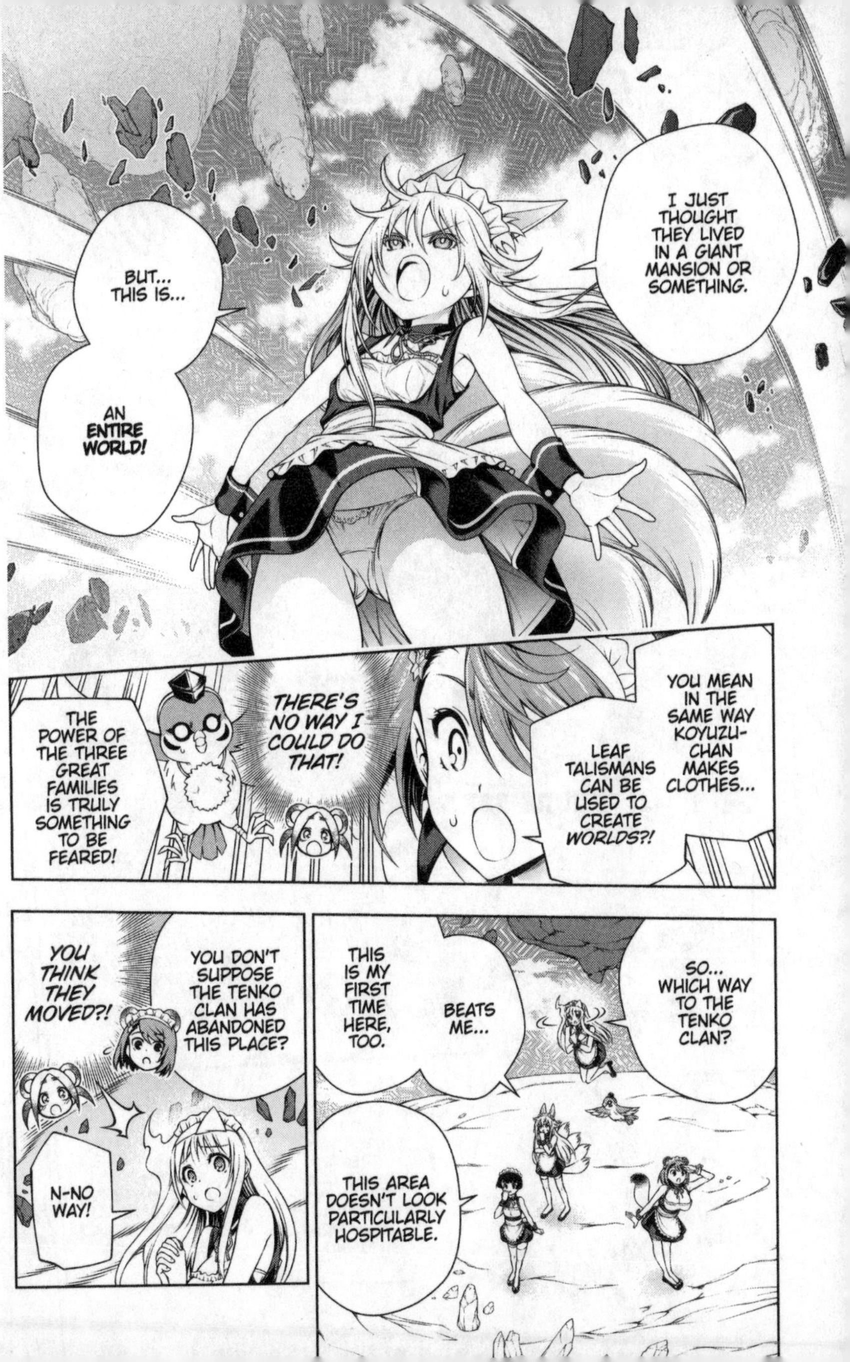
I JUST THOUGHT THEY LIVED IN A GIANT MANSION OR SOMETHING.
BUT... THIS IS...
AN ENTIRE WORLD!
YOU MEAN IN THE SAME WAY KOYUZU-CHAN MAKES CLOTHES...
LEAF TALISMANS CAN BE USED TO CREATE WORLDS?!
THERE'S NO WAY I COULD DO THAT!
THE POWER OF THE THREE GREAT FAMILIES IS TRULY SOMETHING TO BE FEARED!
SO... WHICH WAY TO THE TENKO CLAN?
BEATS ME...
THIS IS MY FIRST TIME HERE, TOO.
THIS AREA DOESN'T LOOK PARTICULARLY HOSPITABLE.
YOU DON'T SUPPOSE THE TENKO CLAN HAS ABANDONED THIS PLACE?
YOU THINK THEY MOVED?!
N-NO WAY!

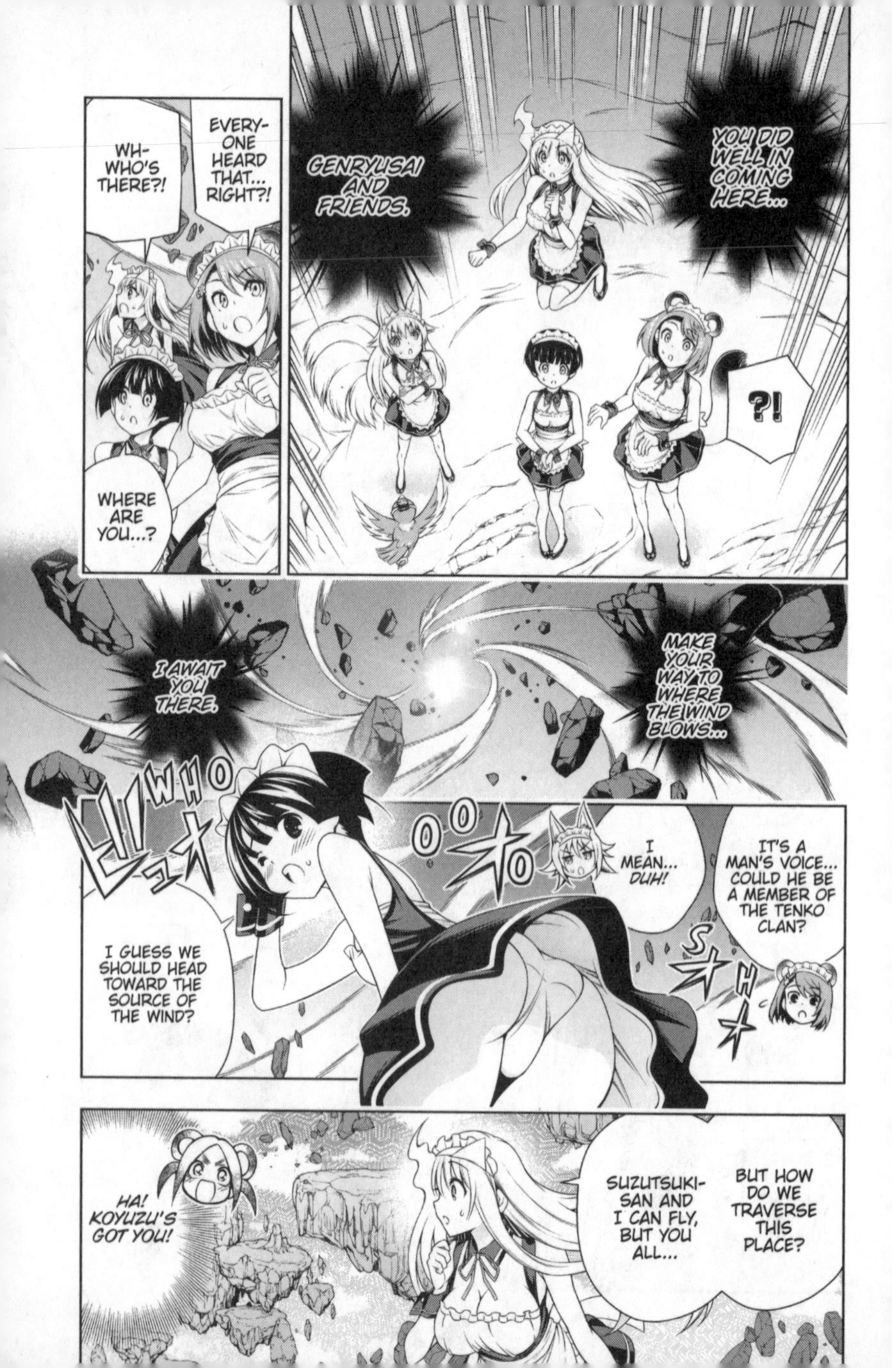
YOU DID WELL IN COMING HERE...
GENRYUSAI AND FRIENDS.
?!
EVERY-ONE HEARD THAT... RIGHT?!
WH-WHO'S THERE?!
WHERE ARE YOU...?
MAKE YOUR WAY TO WHERE THE WIND BLOWS...
I AWAIT YOU THERE.
IT'S A MAN'S VOICE... COULD HE BE A MEMBER OF THE TENKO CLAN?
I MEAN... DUH!
SHH
WHOOOOO
I GUESS WE SHOULD HEAD TOWARD THE SOURCE OF THE WIND?
BUT HOW DO WE TRAVERSE THIS PLACE?
SUZUTSUKI-SAN AND I CAN FLY, BUT YOU ALL...
HA! KOYUZU'S GOT YOU!

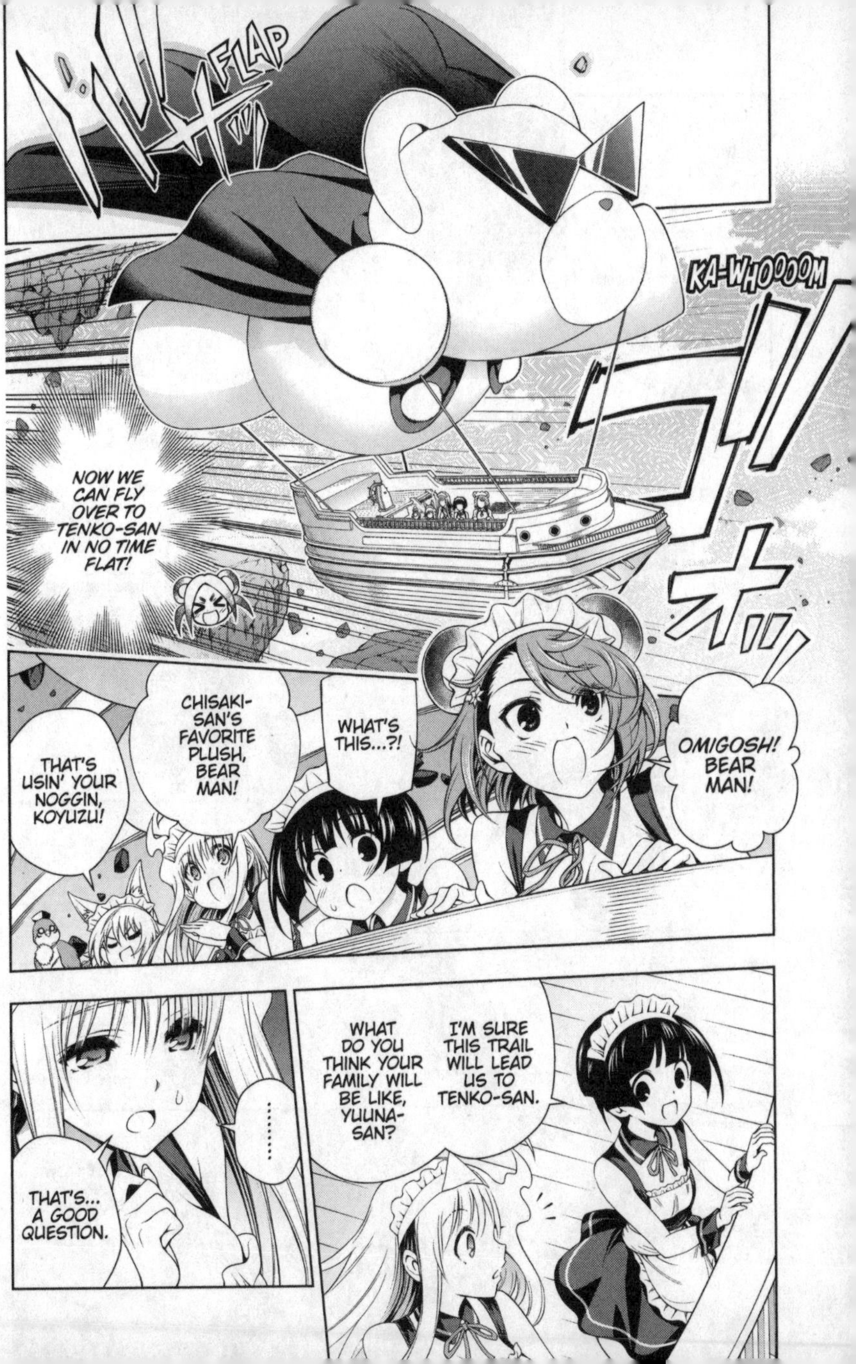
FLAP
KA-WHOOOOM
NOW WE CAN FLY OVER TO TENKO-SAN IN NO TIME FLAT!
OMIGOSH! BEAR MAN!
WHAT'S THIS...?!
CHISAKI-SAN'S FAVORITE PLUSH, BEAR MAN!
THAT'S USIN' YOUR NOGGIN, KOYUZU!
I'M SURE THIS TRAIL WILL LEAD US TO TENKO-SAN.
WHAT DO YOU THINK YOUR FAMILY WILL BE LIKE, YUUNA-SAN?
......
THAT'S... A GOOD QUESTION.

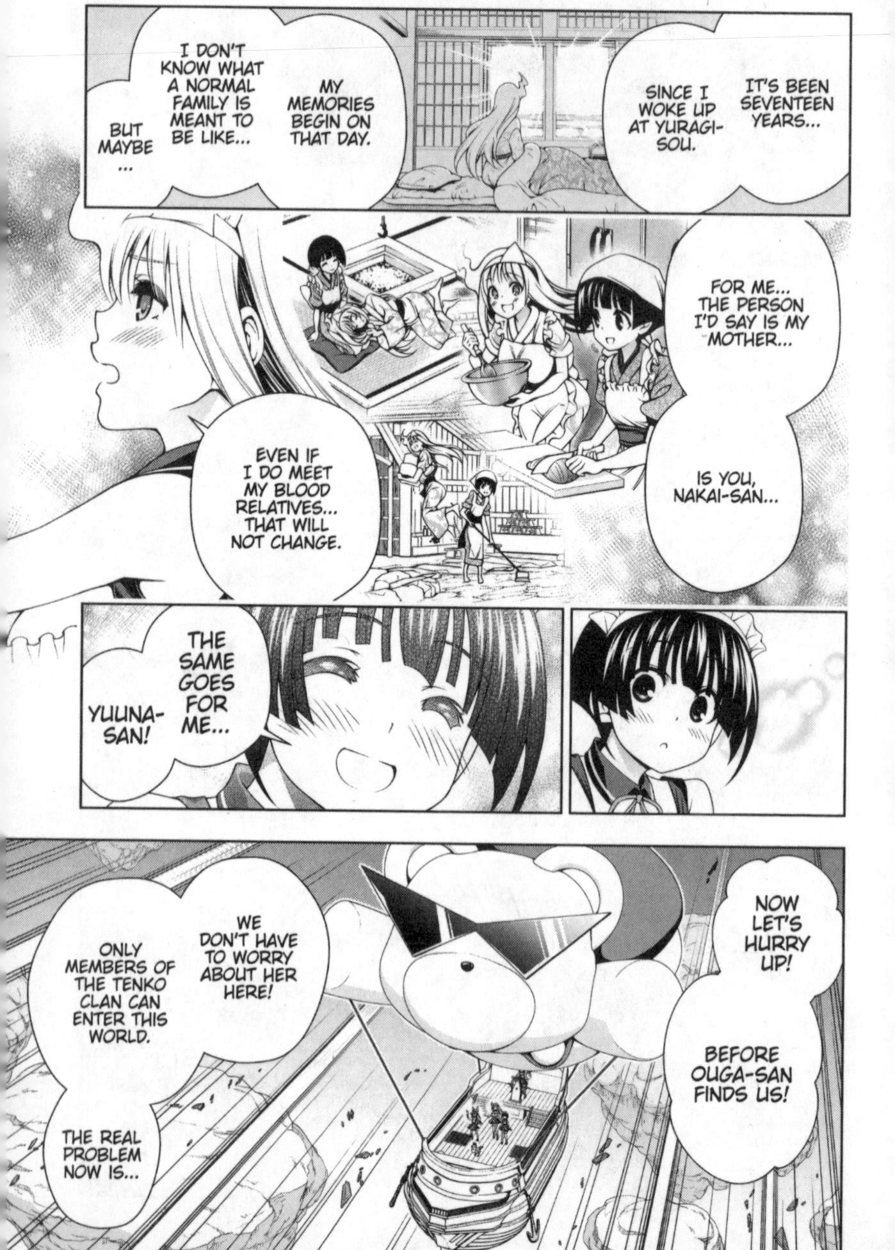
IT'S BEEN SEVENTEEN YEARS...
SINCE I WOKE UP AT YURAGI-SOU.
MY MEMORIES BEGIN ON THAT DAY.
I DON'T KNOW WHAT A NORMAL FAMILY IS MEANT TO BE LIKE...
BUT MAYBE ...
FOR ME... THE PERSON I'D SAY IS MY MOTHER...
IS YOU, NAKAI-SAN...
EVEN IF I DO MEET MY BLOOD RELATIVES... THAT WILL NOT CHANGE.
THE SAME GOES FOR ME...
YUUNA-SAN!
NOW LET'S HURRY UP!
BEFORE OUGA-SAN FINDS US!
WE DON'T HAVE TO WORRY ABOUT HER HERE!
ONLY MEMBERS OF THE TENKO CLAN CAN ENTER THIS WORLD.
THE REAL PROBLEM NOW IS...

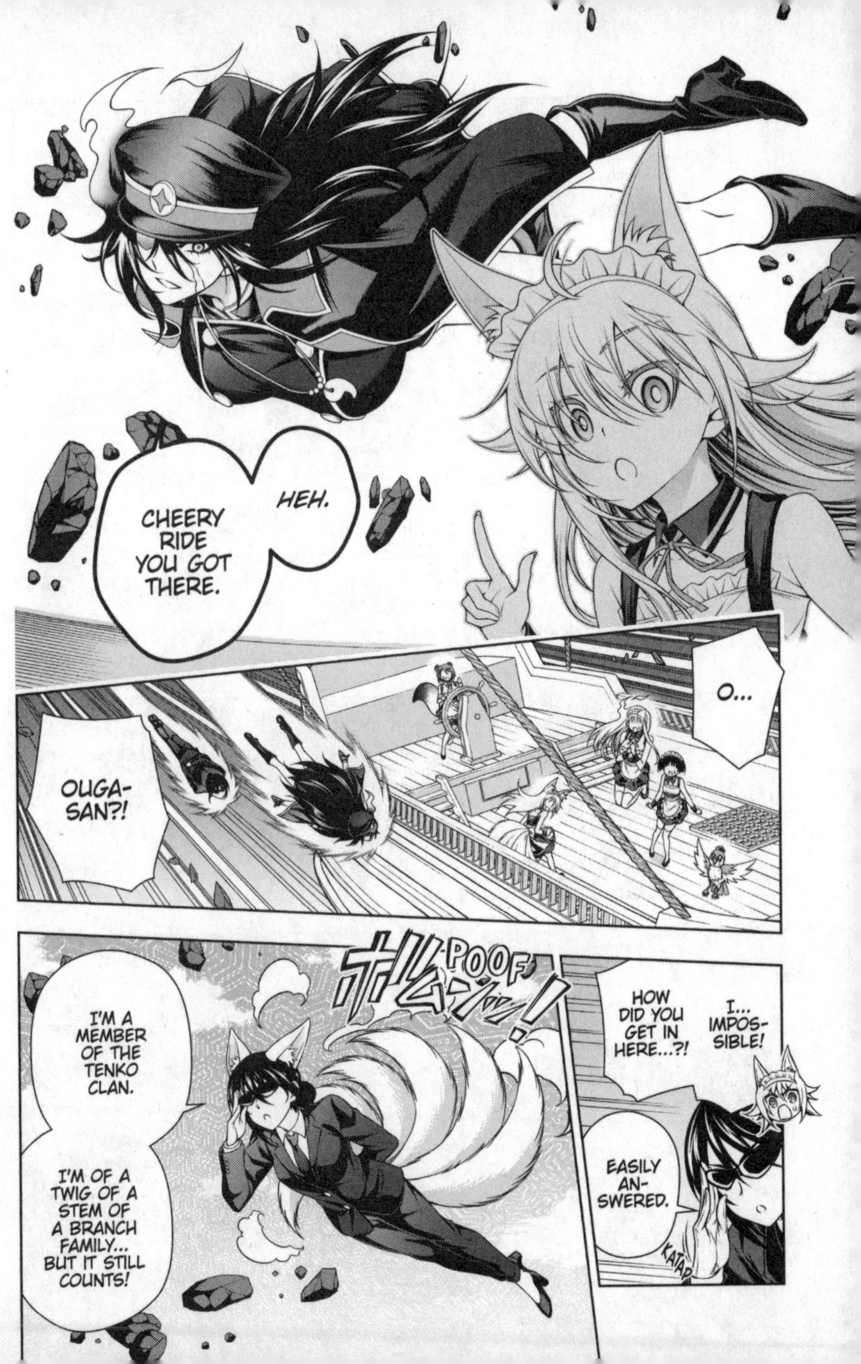
HEH.
CHEERY RIDE YOU GOT THERE.
O...
OUGA-SAN?!
I... IMPOSSIBLE!
HOW DID YOU GET IN HERE...?!
EASILY AN-SWERED.
KATAP
POOF
I'M A MEMBER OF THE TENKO CLAN.
I'M OF A TWIG OF A STEM OF A BRANCH FAMILY... BUT IT STILL COUNTS!

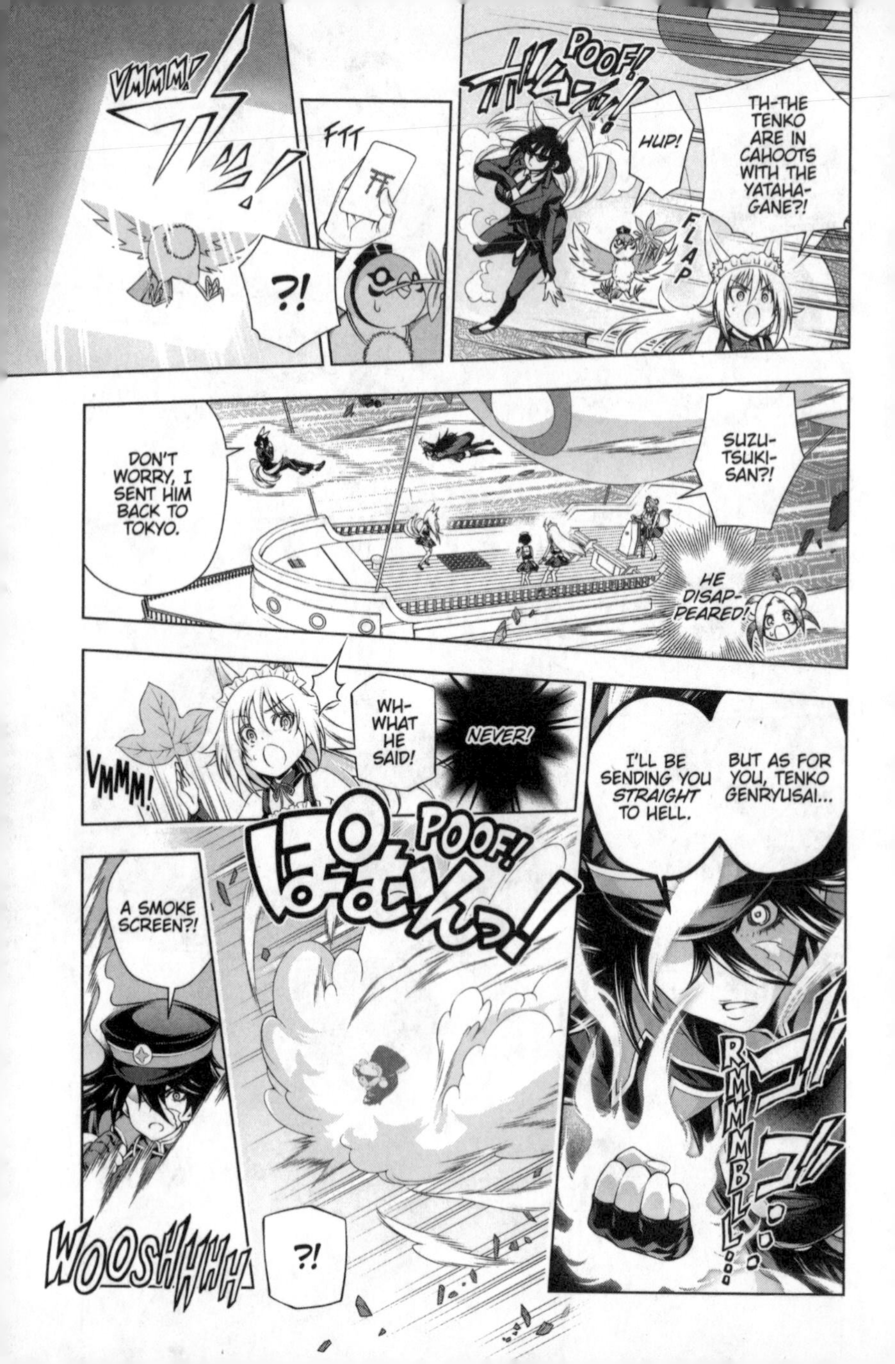
POOF!
TH-THE TENKO ARE IN CAHOOTS WITH THE YATAHA-GANE?!
HUP!
FLAP
?!
VMMM!
SUZU-TSUKI-SAN?!
HE DISAP-PEARED?!
DON'T WORRY, I SENT HIM BACK TO TOKYO.
BUT AS FOR YOU, TENKO GENRYUSAI...
I'LL BE SENDING YOU STRAIGHT TO HELL.
RMMMBL...
NEVER!
WH-WHAT HE SAID!
VMMM!
POOF!
?!
A SMOKE SCREEN?!
WOOSHHHH

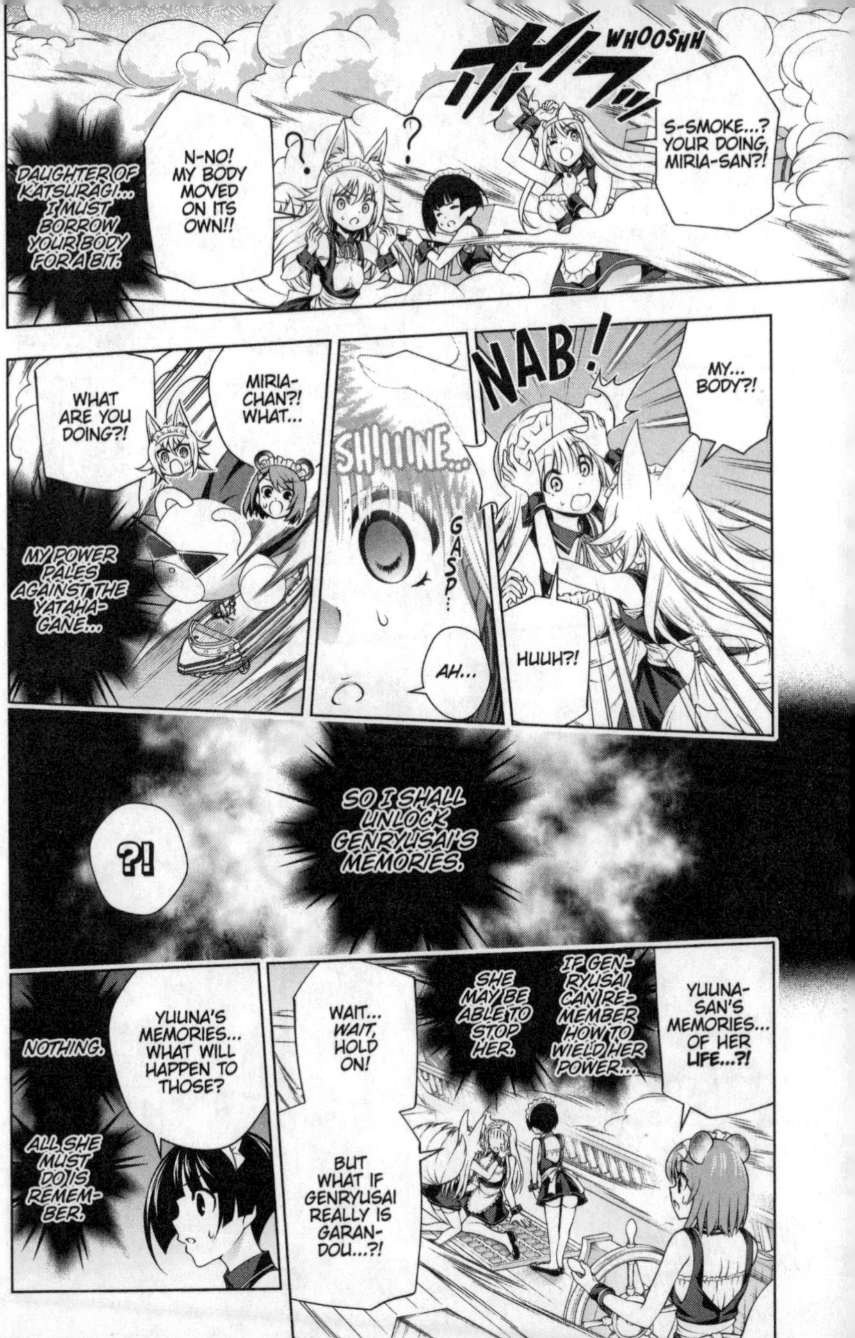
WHOOSHH
S-SMOKE...? YOUR DOING, MIRIA-SAN?!
N-NO! MY BODY MOVED ON ITS OWN!!
DAUGHTER OF KATSURAGI... I MUST BORROW YOUR BODY FOR A BIT.
MY... BODY?!
NAB!
HUUH?!
SHIIINE...
GASP...
AH...
MIRIA-CHAN?! WHAT...
WHAT ARE YOU DOING?!
MY POWER PALES AGAINST THE YATAHA-GANE...
SO I SHALL UNLOCK GENRYUSAI'S MEMORIES.
?!
YUUNA-SAN'S MEMORIES... OF HER LIFE...?!
IF GEN-RYUSAI CAN RE-MEMBER HOW TO WIELD HER POWER...
SHE MAY BE ABLE TO STOP HER.
WAIT... WAIT, HOLD ON!
BUT WHAT IF GENRYUSAI REALLY IS GARAN-DOU...?!
YUUNA'S MEMORIES... WHAT WILL HAPPEN TO THOSE?
NOTHING.
ALL SHE MUST DO IS REMEM-BER.

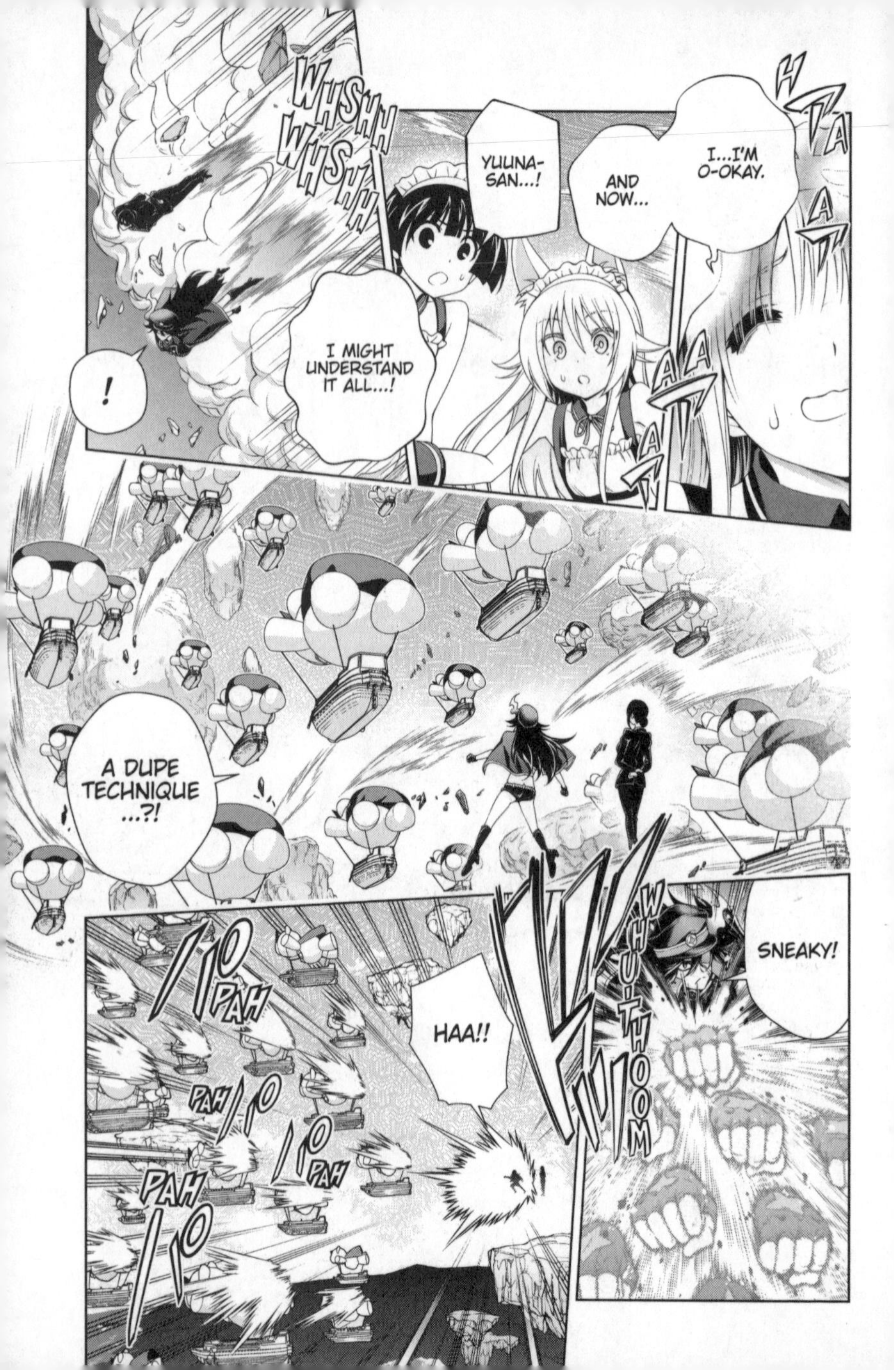
HAAA
I...I'M O-OKAY.
AND NOW...
YUUNA-SAN...!
I MIGHT UNDERSTAND IT ALL...!
AAAA
WHSHH WHSHH
!
A DUPE TECHNIQUE...?!
SNEAKY!
WHUTHOOM
HAA!!
PAH
PAH
PAH
PAH

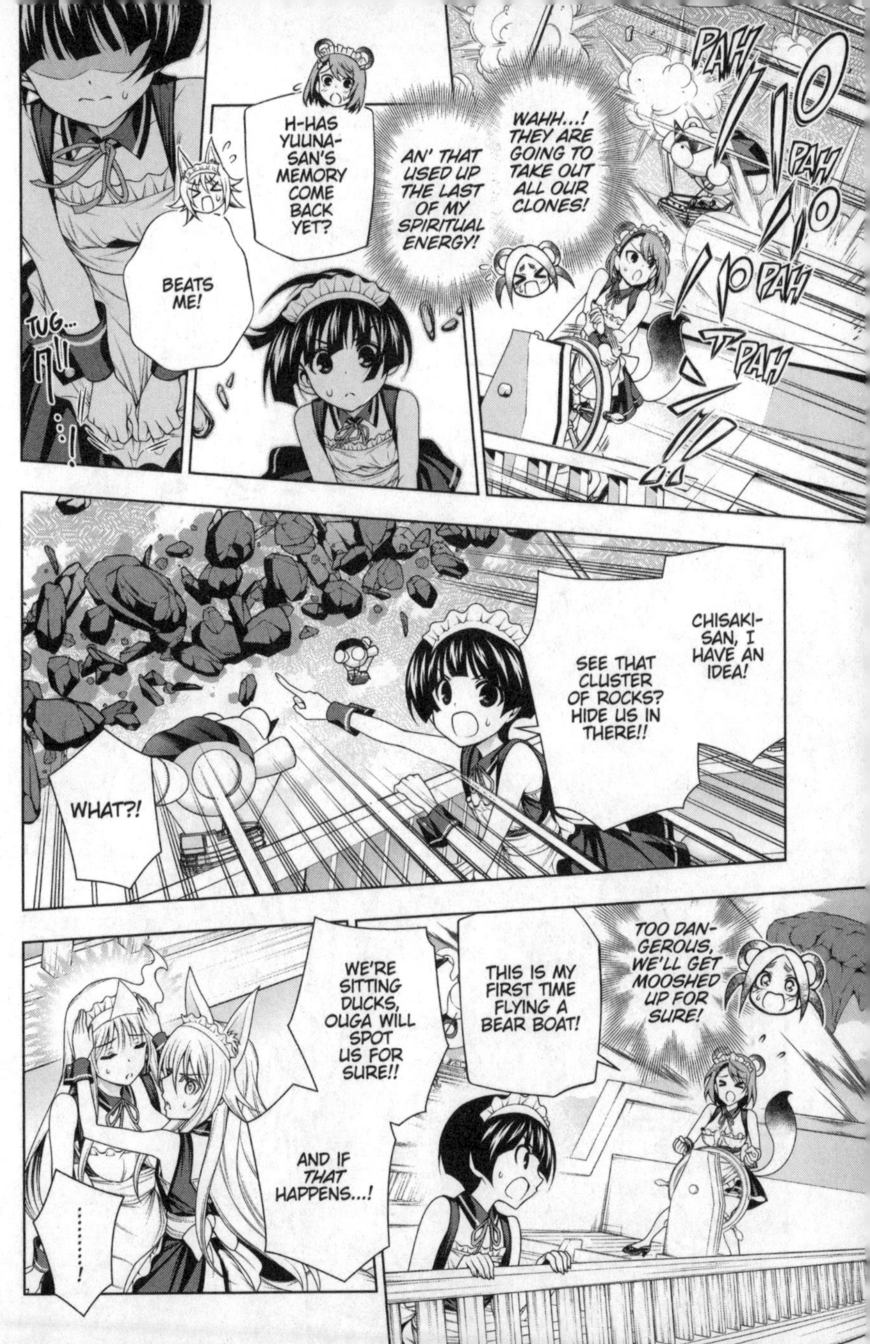
PAH
PAH
PAH
T-PAH
WAHH...! THEY ARE GOING TO TAKE OUT ALL OUR CLONES!
AN' THAT USED UP THE LAST OF MY SPIRITUAL ENERGY!
H-HAS YUUNA-SAN'S MEMORY COME BACK YET?
BEATS ME!
TUG...
CHISAKI-SAN, I HAVE AN IDEA!
SEE THAT CLUSTER OF ROCKS? HIDE US IN THERE!!
WHAT?!
TOO DAN-GEROUS, WE'LL GET MOOSHED UP FOR SURE!
THIS IS MY FIRST TIME FLYING A BEAR BOAT!
WE'RE SITTING DUCKS, OUGA WILL SPOT US FOR SURE!!
AND IF *THAT* HAPPENS...!
......!

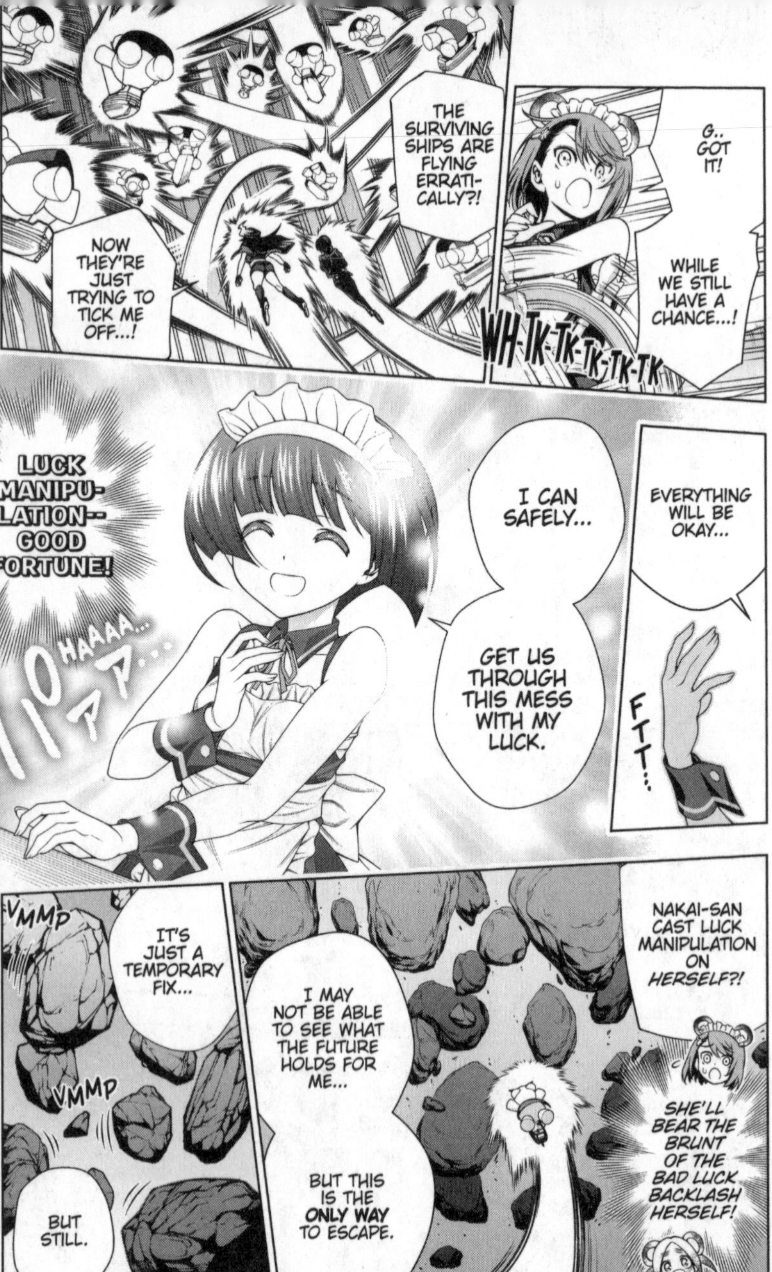
G.. GOT IT!
WHILE WE STILL HAVE A CHANCE...!
WH-TK-TK-TK-TK-TK
THE SURVIVING SHIPS ARE FLYING ERRATI-CALLY?!
NOW THEY'RE JUST TRYING TO TICK ME OFF...!
EVERYTHING WILL BE OKAY...
FTT...
I CAN SAFELY...
GET US THROUGH THIS MESS WITH MY LUCK.
LUCK MANIPU-LATION--GOOD FORTUNE!
HAAAA...
NAKAI-SAN CAST LUCK MANIPULATION ON *HERSELF*?!
SHE'LL BEAR THE BRUNT OF THE BAD LUCK BACKLASH HERSELF!
I MAY NOT BE ABLE TO SEE WHAT THE FUTURE HOLDS FOR ME...
BUT THIS IS THE **ONLY WAY** TO ESCAPE.
IT'S JUST A TEMPORARY FIX...
BUT STILL.
VMMP
VMMP

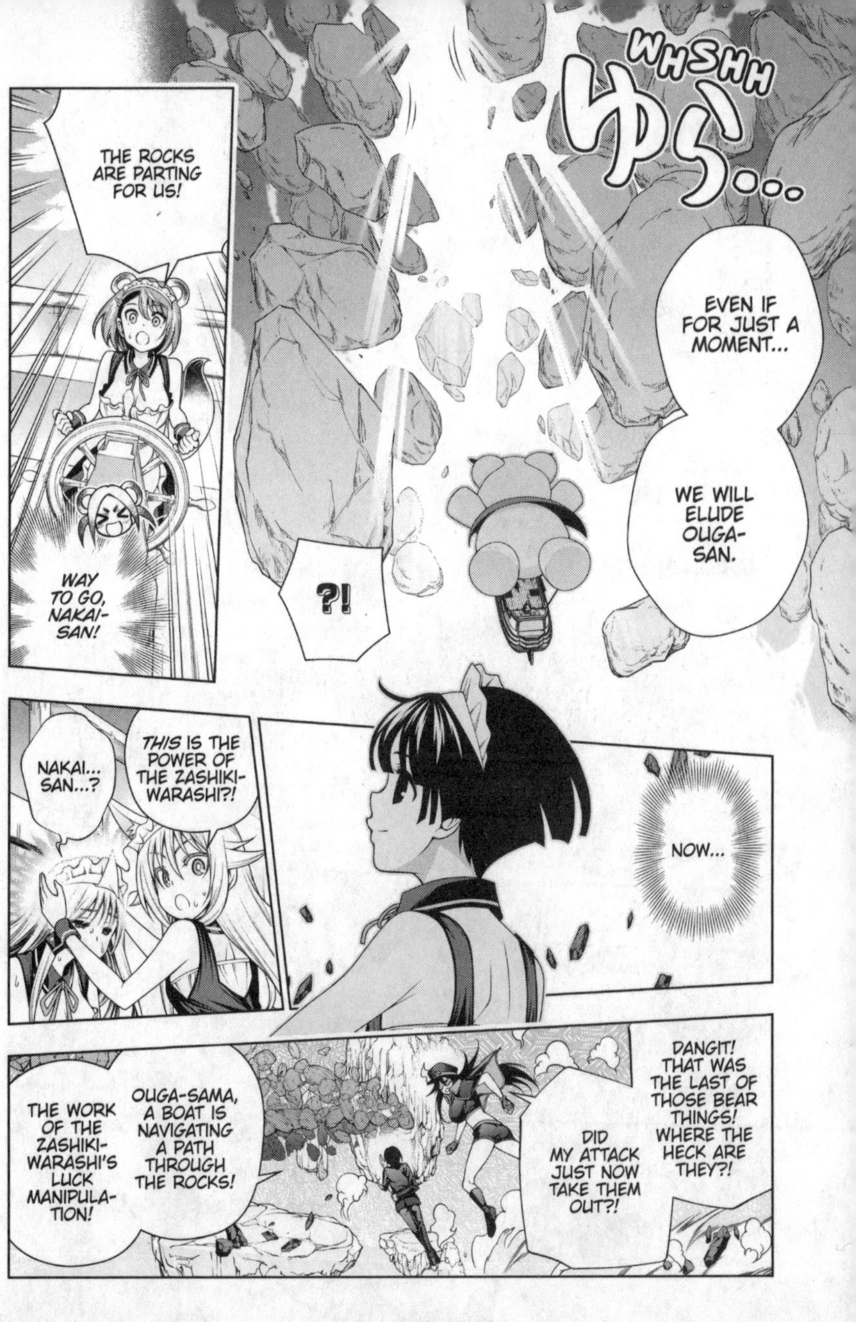
WHSHH
ゆら…
EVEN IF FOR JUST A MOMENT...
WE WILL ELUDE OUGA-SAN.
?!
THE ROCKS ARE PARTING FOR US!
WAY TO GO, NAKAI-SAN!
NOW...
THIS IS THE POWER OF THE ZASHIKI-WARASHI?!
NAKAI... SAN...?
DANGIT! THAT WAS THE LAST OF THOSE BEAR THINGS! WHERE THE HECK ARE THEY?!
DID MY ATTACK JUST NOW TAKE THEM OUT?!
OUGA-SAMA, A BOAT IS NAVIGATING A PATH THROUGH THE ROCKS!
THE WORK OF THE ZASHIKI-WARASHI'S LUCK MANIPULATION!

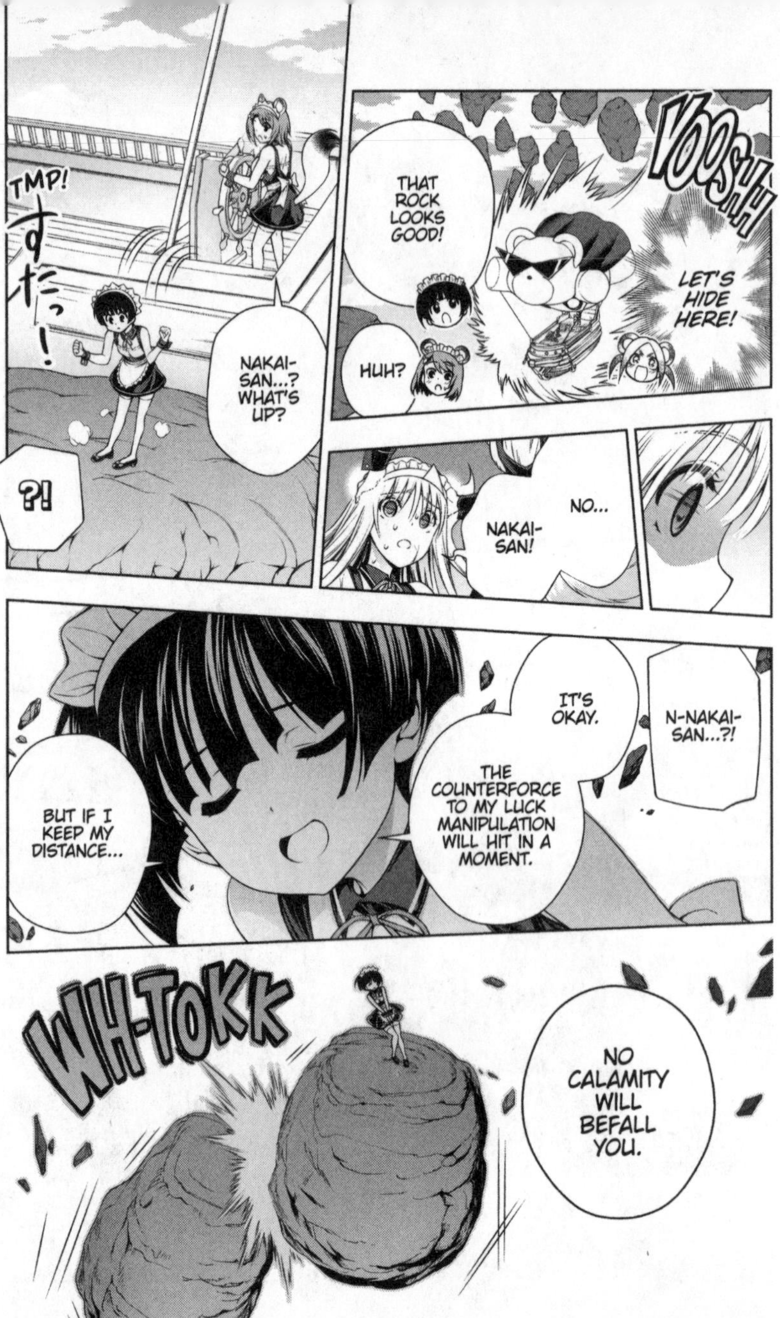
VOOSH
LET'S HIDE HERE!
THAT ROCK LOOKS GOOD!
HUH?
NO...
NAKAI-SAN!
TMP!
すたっ!
NAKAI-SAN...? WHAT'S UP?
?!
N-NAKAI-SAN...?!
IT'S OKAY.
THE COUNTERFORCE TO MY LUCK MANIPULATION WILL HIT IN A MOMENT.
BUT IF I KEEP MY DISTANCE...
NO CALAMITY WILL BEFALL YOU.
WH-TOKK

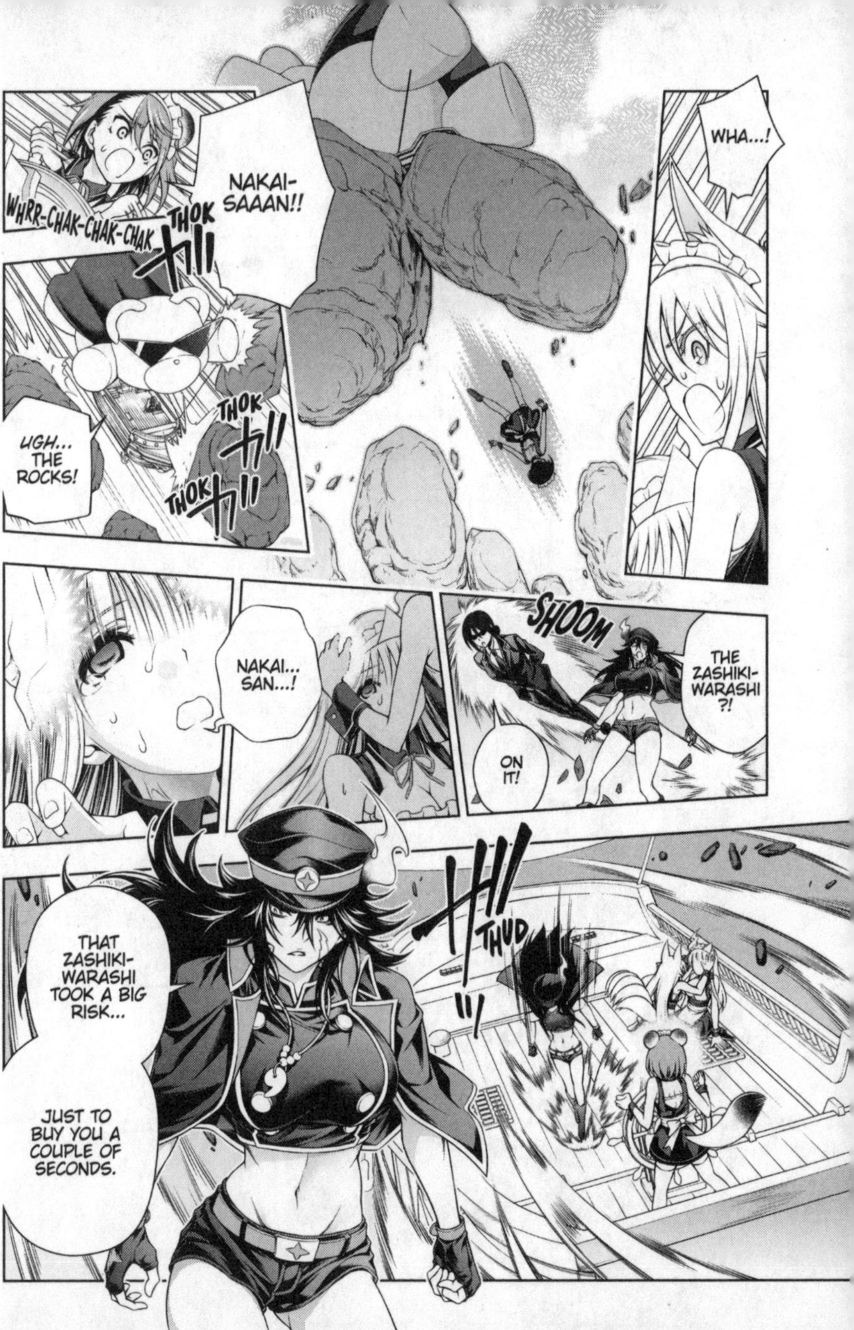
WHA...!
NAKAI-SAAAN!!
WHRR-CHAK-CHAK-CHAK
THOK
THOK
UGH... THE ROCKS!
THOK
THE ZASHIKI-WARASHI?!
SHOOM
ON IT!
NAKAI... SAN...!
THUD
THAT ZASHIKI-WARASHI TOOK A BIG RISK...
JUST TO BUY YOU A COUPLE OF SECONDS.

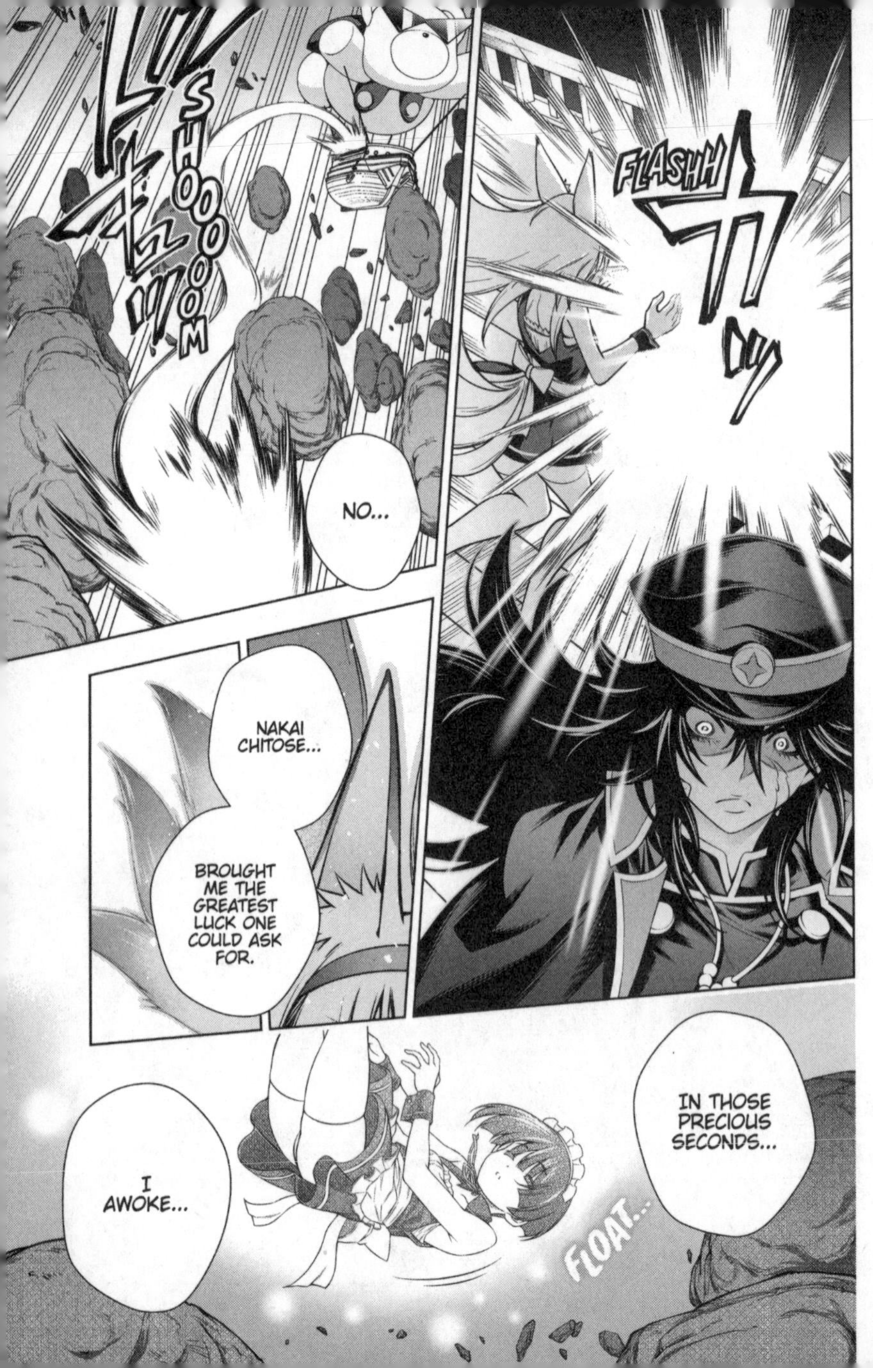
FLASHH
SHOOOOOOOM
NO...
NAKAI CHITOSE...
BROUGHT ME THE GREATEST LUCK ONE COULD ASK FOR.
IN THOSE PRECIOUS SECONDS...
FLOAT...
I AWOKE...

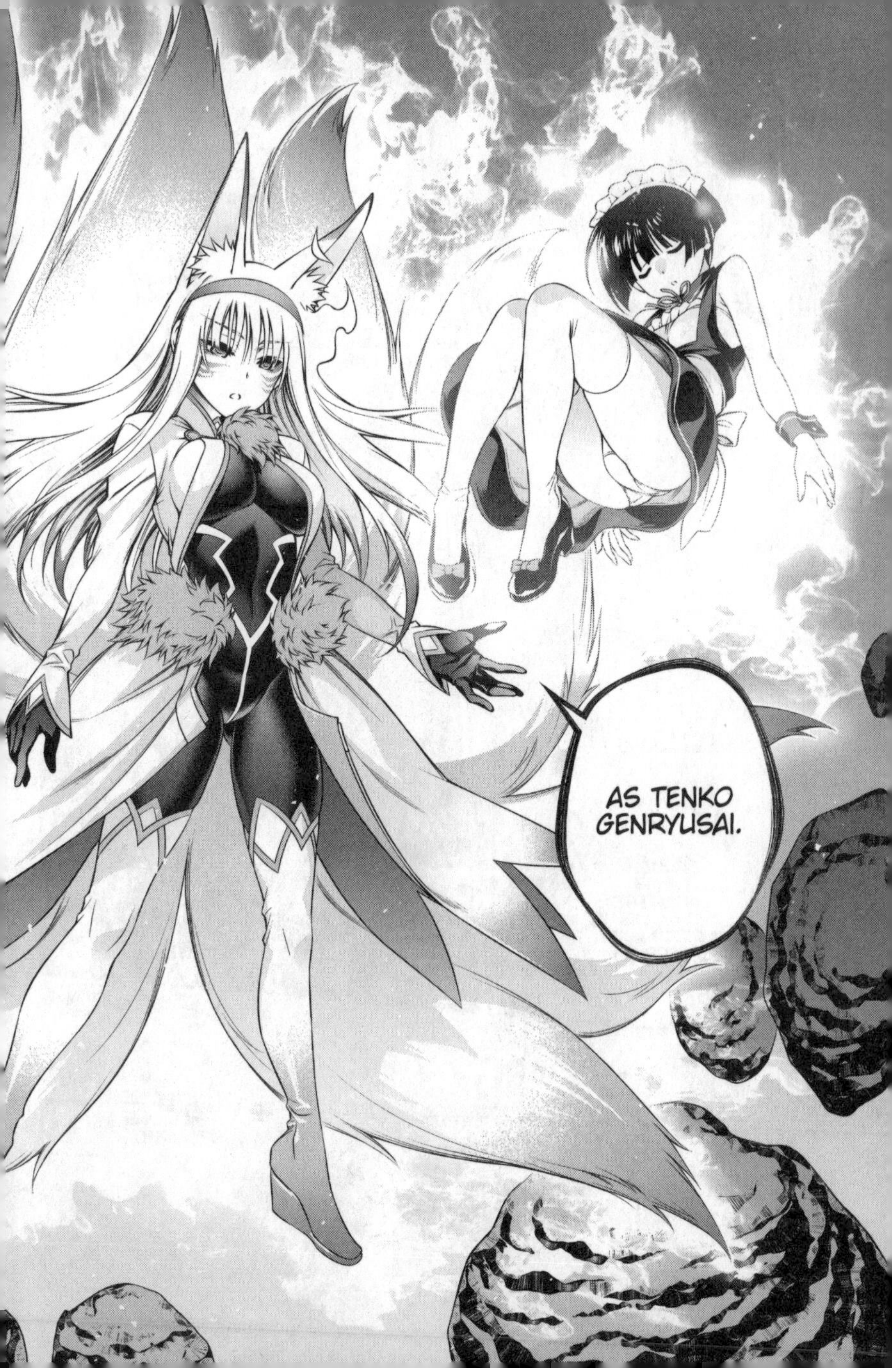
AS TENKO GENRYUSAI.

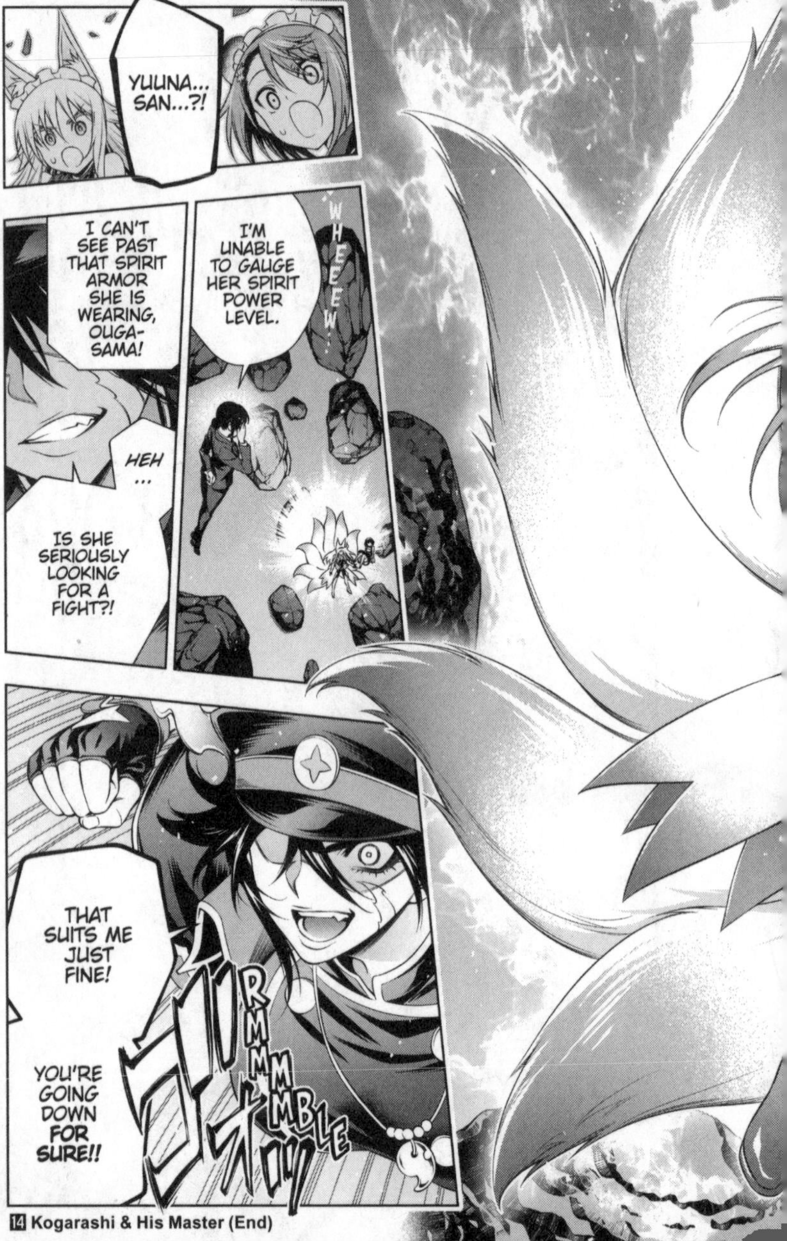
YUUNA... SAN...?!
I'M UNABLE TO GAUGE HER SPIRIT POWER LEVEL.
WHEEEW...
I CAN'T SEE PAST THAT SPIRIT ARMOR SHE IS WEARING, OUGA-SAMA!
HEH...
IS SHE SERIOUSLY LOOKING FOR A FIGHT?!
THAT SUITS ME JUST FINE!
RMMMMMBLE
YOU'RE GOING DOWN FOR SURE!!

14 Kogarashi & His Master (End)

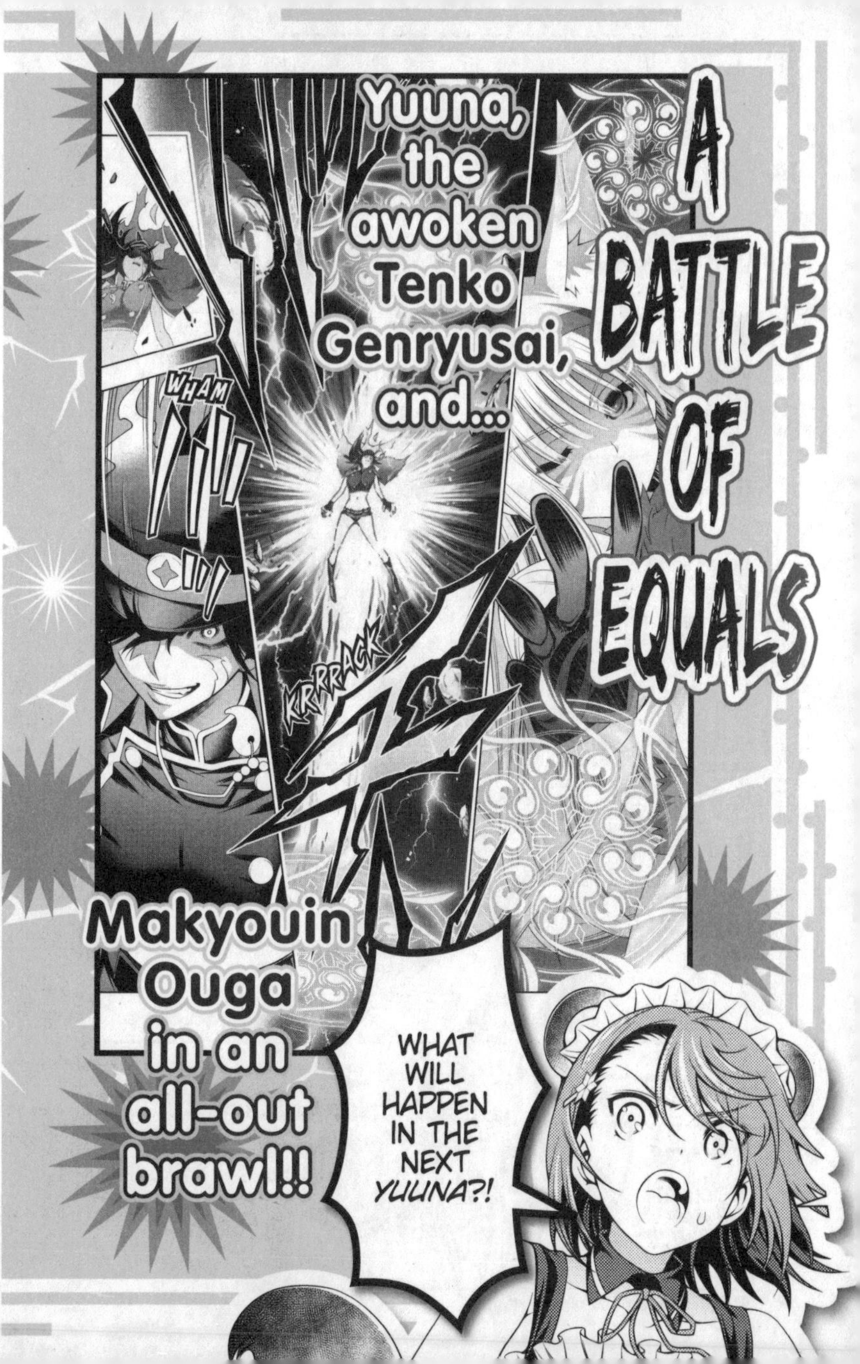
A BATTLE OF EQUALS
Yuuna, the awoken Tenko Genryusai, and...
KRRRACK
WHAM
Makyouin Ouga in an all-out brawl!!
WHAT WILL HAPPEN IN THE NEXT *YUUNA*?!

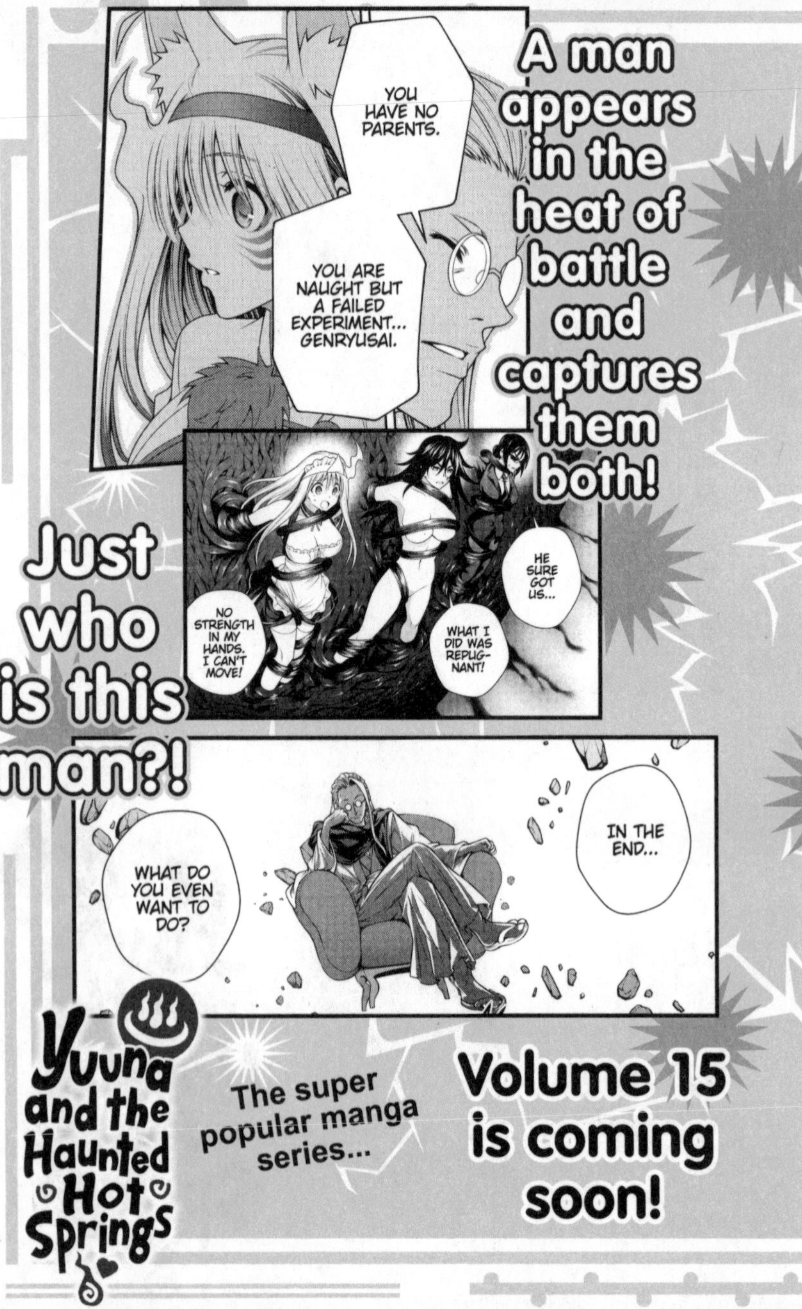
A man appears in the heat of battle and captures them both!
YOU HAVE NO PARENTS.
YOU ARE NAUGHT BUT A FAILED EXPERIMENT... GENRYUSAI.
HE SURE GOT US...
WHAT I DID WAS REPUG-NANT!
NO STRENGTH IN MY HANDS. I CAN'T MOVE!
Just who is this man?!
IN THE END...
WHAT DO YOU EVEN WANT TO DO?
Yuuna and the Haunted Hot Springs
The super popular manga series...
Volume 15 is coming soon!

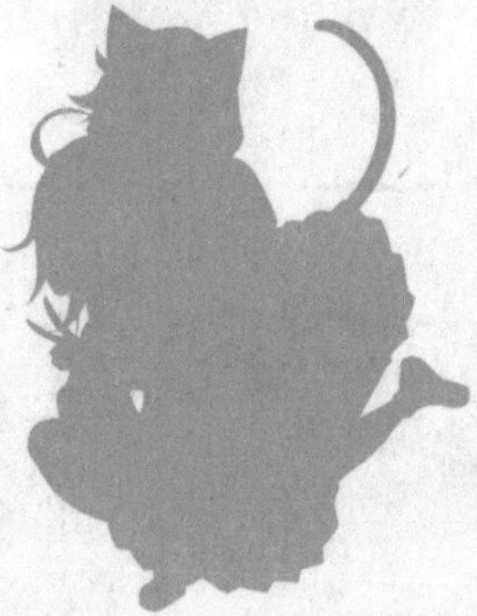

Yuuna and the Haunted Hot Springs